The
Historic Preservation
Movement
in
California
1940–1976

1992
374p.

by
Nadine Ishitani Hata

[California Office of Historic Preservation]

1992

California Department of Parks and Recreation/
Office of Historic Preservation
© Nadine Ishitani Hata
All rights reserved. Published 1992–OSP #82170
Printed in the United States of America
ISBN 0-941925-02-1

This publication has been financed in part with federal funds from the National Park
Service, Department of the Interior. However, the contents do not necessarily reflect
the views or policies of the Department of the Interior. Regulations of the Department
of the Interior strictly prohibit unlawful discrimination in departmental federally
assisted programs on the basis of race, color, national origin, age, or handicap. Any
person who believes he or she has been discriminated against in any program, activity
or facility operated by a recipient of federal assistance should write to the Director,
Equal Opportunity Program, National Park Service, Post Office Box 37127, Washington, D.C. 20013-7127.

Table of Contents

Preface

B y the eve of World War II, the historic preservation movement in California comprised nearly a century of efforts by a handful of history-minded individuals and groups, nativist organizations, the Catholic Church, and state and federal employees seeking to protect sites commemorating the European discovery and settlement of the Golden State. Driven by religious beliefs, filial piety, patriotism, a desire to educate residents and visitors by perpetuating the memory of people and events linked to a romantic history of the state, and the potential for profit, early preservationists pressed for the recognition and restoration of missions, adobes, gold rush sites, and architecturally significant buildings which were usually turned into historic house museums or landmark monuments. During the 1920s and 1930s, California conducted the nation's first statewide survey of scenic, recreational, and historic sites, and established a program of state registered landmarks and historic parks.

This study, which was initially a doctoral dissertation, emphasizes the evolution of preservation in California from the eve of America's entry into World War II until the celebration of this nation's Bicentennial of the American Revolution in 1976.[1] It is chronologically organized and begins with an overview of the decades before 1940 in Part One.[2] Part Two (1940-1966) examines twenty-five years of state-dominated preservation programs, local preservation activities, and the limited federal presence. Part Three (1966-1976) discusses the impact of new federal and state legislation on preservation in California and summarizes federal, state, and local efforts.

Because preservation projects at the state level in the post-World War II years were the responsibility of the Division of Beaches and Parks, and later the Department of Parks and Recreation, research focused on their respective files. The resulting perception of historic preservation in California reflects that emphasis. Interviews were conducted with state and federal officials who were active participants in the programs. Local preservationists were also contacted for their observations.

The term "preservation" has been used in its broadest generic sense to mean the act or process of saving a building or site either partially or entirely. "Restoration" refers to efforts to preserve and/or reconstruct properties to a specific historical period or architectural style.

A brief comment on resource repositories is in order because archival collections of preservation-related materials are at best uneven. The State Archives, for example, did not have a "preservation" category in its 1982 card catalog. State agencies have only recently developed "records disposition schedules" that allow various departments to review in-house files before they are automatically destroyed. Although this system still does not prevent the loss of valuable documents, it is a considerable improvement over the previous plan which regularly purged files after twenty years. Fortunately, some materials have been preserved in files and local archives. The V. Aubrey Neasham Collection at the Sacramento History Center, for example, contains the only extant set of correspondence from the 1950s for the History Section of the Division of Beaches and Parks. Other records remain in individual agency offices or with retired employees.

The archaeological dimension of California preservation is treated in two chapters. Historians have often excluded this aspect of preservation, claiming that archaeological preservation differs from historic preservation.[3] Although that may be both philosophically and methodologically accurate, preservation issues have had a direct impact on archaeology. Archaeology, in turn, has influenced preservation and has therefore been included in this study.

Acknowledgments

One of the joys of doing research on any topic is the opportunity to meet and work with new people and old friends. I was fortunate to have the invaluable assistance of many dedicated librarians, archivists, government personnel, and preservationists who gave generously of their time, materials and expertise.

The following librarians and archivists provided advice and suggestions: James de T. Abajian, Archivist, Archdiocese of San Francisco; Willa Baum, Director, Regional Oral History Office, Bancroft Library; Glenn Burchett, Chief, Archives Branch, Federal Archives and Records Center, San Bruno; Bruce Johnson, Director, California Historical Society Library; Gary Kurutz, Librarian, California State Library; Chuck Wilson, Archivist, California State Archives; and Richard Wilson, Central Records Supervisor, Department of Parks and Recreation. Mrs. Irene Simpson Neasham expedited access to the uncatalogued papers of V. Aubrey Neasham at the Sacramento History Center where Archivist Susan Searcy retrieved more than forty boxes from storage.

Federal personnel gave interviews and shared information. They included: Horace M. Albright, former Director, National Park Service (NPS); Patrick Andrus, Historian, National Register of Historic Places; Lawrence E. Aten, Chief, Interagency Resources Management Division, NPS; Gordon Chappell, Regional Historian, NPS; Robertson Collins, former Trustee, National Trust; John L. Frisbee III, Vice President, Office of Historic Properties, National Trust; Douglas L. Griffin, Assistant Regional Director for Cultural Resources, NPS; John A. Hussey, former Regional Historian, NPS; Thomas F. King, Director, Office of Cultural Resource Protection, Advisory Council on Historic Preservation; William J. Murtagh, former Keeper of the National Register of Historic Places; Thomas D. Mulhern, Chief, Park Historic Preservation, NPS; Sally G. Oldham, Acting Chief of Registration, National Register of Historic Places; Paul J.F. Schumacher, former Regional Archaeologist, NPS; Brit Allan Storey, Historian, Advisory Council on Historic Preservation; Hisashi B. Sugaya, former Regional

Director, National Trust; Joseph F. Towner, Historian, National Preservation Programs, NPS; Glennie Murray Wall, Chief, Legislative Compliance Division, NPS; and Louis S. Wall, Chief, Western Division of Project Review, Advisory Council on Historic Preservation.

Various state agency staff members provided access to in-house materials and files, and many shared personal observations of events and participants in the preservation movement. They included: Ann Barkley, Chief of Transportation and Planning, Caltrans; Dan Bell, Office of Historic Preservation (OHP); Karen Brattland-Shingle, OHP; Pete Dangermond, Director, Department of Parks and Recreation (DPR); Robin Datel, former student intern, OHP; Nicholas J. Del Cioppo, OHP; Eileen G. Dismuke, former Member, Historical Landmarks Advisory Committee; James M. Doyle, former Supervisor, History Preservation Section, DPR; Dwight Dutschke, Native American Coordinator, OHP; Sandra J. Elder, Assistant Executive Secretary, Historical Resources Commission; Joseph H. Engbeck, Jr., Information Office, author and Director of Publications for the State Park System, DPR; Connie J. Finster, OHP; Duane Frink, Office of Environmental Planning, Caltrans; Aaron Gallup, Historian, OHP; Alan P. Garfinkel, Caltrans; Adriana Gianturco, former Director, Caltrans; Raymond Girvigian, former Member, Historical Resources Commission; Kathryn Kaiser Gualtieri, former Chair, Historical Resources Commission; Earl P. Hanson, former Chief, Division of Beaches and Parks; Eugene Itogawa, Historian, OHP; Horace Jackson, Chief Deputy Director, DPR; Neil C. Johannsen, Deputy Director, DPR; John Knight, former Chief of Operations, DPR; Hans J. Kreutzberg, Historian, OHP; Clement Meighan, former Chair, Historical Resources Commission; Knox Mellon, State Historic Preservation Officer; John Michael, former Supervisor, History Section, DPR; Stephen D. Mikesell, Historian, OHP; Marion Mitchell-Wilson, Historian, OHP; Noel F. Moholy, former Member, Historical Landmarks Advisory Committee; Donald S. Napoli, Historian, OHP; Russell Porter, Associate Director, Statewide Planning and Assistance Programs, DPR; Francis A. Riddell, State Park Archaeologist, DPR; Michael F. Rondeau, Archaeologist, OHP; William Seidel, Archaeologist, OHP; and Allen Welts, former State Park Historian, DPR.

Preservationists at local, state, and national levels were very cooperative and helpful. They included: James Arbuckle, former Grand Noble Humbug, E Clampus Vitus; Margaret Bach, founder, Los Angeles Conservancy; Claire Bogaard, Pasadena Heritage; Paul Chace, archaeologist; Mary Louise Days, City of Santa Barbara; H. Grant Dehart, Executive Director,

Foundation for San Francisco's Architectural Heritage; Jane Ellison, City of Pasadena; David A. Frederickson, Professor of Anthropology, Sonoma State University; David Gebhard, Professor of Art History, University of California at Santa Barbara; Bruce D. Judd, architect; Peter D. King, Executive Director, National Conference of State Historic Preservation Officers; Ruthann Lehrer, Executive Director, Los Angeles Conservancy; Mrs. Leland S. Lewis, former Chair, Nevada County Historical Landmarks Commission; Nellie L. Longsworth, Executive Director, Preservation Action; John Merritt, OHP, National Trust staff, and co-founder, Californians for Preservation Action; Michael J. Moratto, archaeologist; David Nawi, Chief Counsel, Office of Legal Affairs, Air Resources Board; Charles Hall Page, Foundation for San Francisco's Architectural Heritage; Marian Parks, historian; Dan Peterson, historic preservation architect; Joseph Pitti, Professor of History, Sacramento State University; Mrs. G. Bland Platt, former President, San Francisco Landmarks Advisory Committee; Jean Bruce Poole, Senior Curator, El Pueblo de Los Angeles State Historic Park; Martin Ridge, former Member, Historical Landmarks Advisory Committee; Roger P. Scharmer, co-founder, Californians for Preservation Action; Albert Schumate, historian, former President, California Historical Society, former Member, San Francisco Landmarks Advisory Committee; Judy Tachibana, Project Coordinator, Gardena Historical Resources Survey; Ileana Welch, Coordinator, Los Angeles Cultural Heritage Board; Frederick C. Williamson, State Historic Preservation Officer of Rhode Island; Robert W. Winter, architectural historian and Member, Los Angeles Cultural Heritage Board; John C. Woodward, co-founder, Santa Barbara Heritage; and William Woollett, former Chair, Los Angeles Cultural Heritage Board.

The interviews with and assistance from the aforementioned individuals were in the roles noted after their names, and generally occurred between 1981 and 1983. Today, many of them hold different positions. The bibliography should be consulted for the dates of the formal interviews.

I am grateful to the administration and Board of Trustees of El Camino College who granted me an unprecedented three-year leave of absence (1980 to 1983) to complete my research and dissertation, and to my distinguished dissertation committee at the University of Southern California: Doyce B. Nunis, Jr., Professor of History and Committee Chair; Franklin D. Mitchell, Professor of History; and Rodger Swearingen, Professor of International Relations. I also wish to thank Charles B. Hosmer, Jr., Professor of History, Principia College and author of the definitive work on the evolution of historic preservation in the United States, for his advice and counsel during the early phases of my research; Joseph H. Engbeck, Jr., who read the manuscript several times and offered valuable suggestions; Gay Ann White and Carmelita Holleman for their careful editing; and senior graphic artist Audi Stanton for her book layout, cover design, and meticulous attention to detail during the final phase of publication.

This book is for three very special individuals whose steadfast encouragement and support made the project possible: Sandra J. Elder, Kathryn Kaiser Gualtieri, and Donald Teruo Hata, Jr.

PART I

The Early Years,
1875-1940

The movement to preserve California's historic places emerged more than a century ago. As early as 1850, the newly formed Society of California Pioneers voiced concern for the protection of documents and objects important to the state's heritage. Five years later, exploratory excavations were undertaken at the old Mission Church of San Carlos del Carmelo in an unsuccessful attempt to locate the grave of Father Junipero Serra.[1] It was not until after the Civil War, however, that long-term, serious efforts were made to preserve some of the new state's historic sites and structures.

Most of California's preservation-related activities between 1875 and 1940 centered on mission restoration; the preservation of adobes, gold rush sites, and architecturally significant buildings; the establishment of a statewide historic landmark program; and the creation of historic parks. A combination of historically minded organizations, nativist groups, the Catholic Church, and government officials comprised the membership of California's early historic preservation movement. Their motives were diverse: religious fervor, patriotism, education of both youth and newcomers, and profit. Together, they preserved monuments to God, promoted the perpetuation of a romanticized European dimension of California's discovery and settlement, and ignored the original California Indian population. In this process, most historic landmarks evolved into museums and tourist attractions removed from the daily lives of the state's residents.

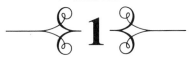

California's Pioneer Preservationists, 1875-1925

Private individuals and the Catholic Church dominated the historic preservation movement in California from 1875 to 1925. They directed their energies principally toward saving the rapidly deteriorating missions and surviving physical symbols of the state's pioneer heritage.

Preservation in the Late Nineteenth Century

Individual priests in the Catholic Church were the first to spearhead attempts to preserve California's Franciscan missions during the late nineteenth century.[1] Before the 1890s, their major concern was to restore the buildings as places of worship. Thus, when repairs were made, architectural and historical integrity had little priority. For example, the 1876 restoration of Mission San Luis Obispo de Tolosa by Father Apoll Rouselle consisted of boarding up adobe walls, shingling the roof, and adding a wooden belfry and a New England church steeple.[2] When restoration of Father Junipero Serra's chapel at Carmel's Mission San Carlos Borromeo was completed in 1888, the original arched tile had been replaced by a peaked shingle roof. A determined Father Angelo D. Casanova, who directed the project, had earlier located and identified Serra's grave under three feet of debris. On July 3, 1882, amidst the crumbling church walls, Serra's tomb was opened with great ceremony before 400 spectators who were visibly shocked by the neglected surroundings. Not only was it clear that Serra's church had to be saved, the event "awakened Californians generally" to the need for mission restoration. Casanova quickly raised $20,000, and a partially restored chapel was dedicated in 1884, the centennial of Serra's death.[3]

Popular interest in the preservation of California's missions was aroused for other reasons. Helen Hunt Jackson's bestseller, *Ramona* (1884), inadvertently drew attention to the state's Spanish heritage. Jackson hoped that her novel would help alleviate the oppression of California Indians. Instead, the resulting "Ramona Cult" brought tourists flocking to the state and sent writers scurrying to produce guidebooks and mission stories that romanticized California's mission history but also distorted the past.[4] In the 1880s, missions became favored subjects of artists, and Spanish fiestas celebrated a culture that many participants could still vividly recall. By the decade's end, architects in search of a "native" California style discovered the beauty and distinctiveness of the California mission, and in the 1890s, mission-style buildings began to appear.[5]

Before the end of the century, two groups formed to preserve the missions. In 1889, Tessa L. Kelso, Los Angeles city librarian, founded the Association for the Preservation of Missions. By organizing photographic exhibits and writing articles depicting the sorry condition of the missions, Kelso's members laid the foundation for their successor, the Landmarks Club of Southern California. Before its demise, the association contributed nearly $100 to the new club which was incorporated in 1895.[6]

The driving force behind the Landmarks Club was Charles F. Lummis, editor of the *Land of Sunshine*, a periodical that publicized his "preserve-the-missions" crusade as well as his other projects. Despite the club's erratic activities, which were largely due to Lummis' chronic shortage of funds and demands from his numerous interests, it contributed significantly to mission preservation. Most notable were repairs undertaken on Mission San Juan Capistrano, which came to more than $2,900, and Mission San Fernando Rey,which totaled approximately $6,000 by 1917.[7]

Lummis' home, El Alisal, was built between 1897 and 1910. It later became the headquarters of the Historical Society of Southern California, which was established in 1883. In his inaugural address, J.J. Warner, the society's founding president, observed that "in the midst of the inrushing flood of immigrants, old land marks are rapidly disappearing." What was common then, he predicted, would soon become rarities. The fledgling society's primary mission would be, he said, "to collect and preserve historical matter." This would include helping to rescue the crumbling missions.[8]

During the late nineteenth century, hereditary organizations arose to memorialize the legacy of California's pioneers. In 1886, the Native Sons of the Golden West proposed a monument to the memory of James W. Marshall whose discovery of gold in 1848 precipitated the gold rush. The statue of Marshall was paid for by state funds and dedicated in 1890 on land provided by the Placerville Parlor.[9] In 1888, the Grand Parlor, or state convention, adopted a resolution to preserve Sacramento's deteriorating Sutter's Fort. By 1891, the Native Sons had raised $20,000 to purchase the building; the California State Legislature matched the sum to acquire the surrounding property. The Sutter's Fort Commission established by the legislature supervised the restoration of the adobe and reconstruction of the fort, which were completed by 1894.[10] Popular attention was drawn to historical monuments two years later when the Associated Veterans of the Mexican War culminated their drive to commemorate Commodore John Drake Sloat's raising of the American flag on California soil with a gala parade and ceremony to mark the fiftieth anniversary of that occasion. The governor proclaimed July 7, 1896, a holiday, and the cornerstone for the Sloat monument was laid while several thousand interested people watched.[11]

The Native Sons greeted the twentieth century by campaigning for the preservation of the Monterey Custom House. They received control of the lease in September 1900, the fiftieth anniversary of California's admission to the Union. A year later, the Native Sons turned over the Custom House lease to the state, which in turn appointed trustees and appropriated $4,200 for much-needed repairs on the building. In 1903, some three years after the Native Sons began urging its preservation, state funds restored Monterey's Colton Hall, where California's first constitution was drafted.[12]

Preservation in the Twentieth Century:
The First Twenty-Five Years

Joseph Russell Knowland (1875-1966) was California's pre-eminent preservationist during the first half of the twentieth century. At one time the most powerful Republican in California, Knowland served as state legislator, congressman, publisher of the Oakland *Tribune*, and chairman of the State Park Commission. This partisan and often controversial politician and civic leader shared his passion for history preservation with several non-partisan organizations. It was a genuine interest "which gave meaning to his life so that whatever else he was doing that might wear him out, history and historic preservation work cheered him up and made him feel like he was doing something worthwhile." [13]

Knowland's direct involvement in preservation began in 1902 when the Native Sons, at his request, established a Historic Landmarks Committee "to ascertain the condition of the remaining buildings of the state, and endeavor to devise some practical method for their restoration and preservation." The unanimously approved resolution specified that the following buildings would become priorities: "the remains of old Fort Ross in Sonoma County, where the Russian settlement was first established in 1812; Colton Hall at Monterey, where California's first constitutional convention convened; and the old missions of California." The action was taken, said Knowland, so that the organization's original purpose "to perpetuate the memory of men and events intimately associated with the romantic history of California—might be carried out." Knowland, who joined the Native Sons in 1891, chaired the committee for several decades.[14]

In 1902, Laura Bride Powers convened a meeting in San Francisco of representatives from the Society of California Pioneers, Pioneer Women, Daughters of California Pioneers, Young Men's Institute, Women's Press Association, Native Sons of the Golden West, Native Daughters of the Golden West, San Francisco Teachers' Club, Sons of Exempt Firemen, and the California Club. These groups formed the California Historic Landmarks League whose founding president was none other than Knowland. The league's goals included the preservation and maintenance of structures, monuments, and sites of "historic interest, either from its associations with the early Spanish settlers or the American occupation of this State, or with the California pioneers." They would also erect monuments and plaques to commemorate historic places and events in order that "said monuments, sites and roads serve as object lessons to the students of California history." [15]

Membership dues in the league were a dollar a year, with the Native Sons providing an initial $1,100 to help the organization get off to a good start. Controversy about the group's name was confirmed by Powers, who denied any impropriety in the use of "landmark" in the official title. Unlike the Landmarks Club of Southern California, which focused on the area south of the Tehachapis, Powers stated that the California Historic Landmarks League proposed to serve "historic sites and buildings wherever they exist—barring, of course, the eminent domain of Southern California, which is already being well cared for by the older body." [16]

Although the league's activities declined after a decade, its members could point to three accomplishments. Their first project was Mission San Francisco Solano (Sonoma), the last built of the California missions. Led by Knowland, who convinced William Randolph Hearst to act as the group's treasurer and contribute $500, the league joined with the Native Sons and Daughters to raise $9,000 within two months. Together they purchased the mission in July 1903 for $5,000 and began restoration.[17] In September of that year, the league turned its attention to the Mission San Antonio de Padua in Monterey County. The mission's chapel was finally restored in 1907 after heavy rains during the winter of 1904-1905 and the 1906 earthquake forced two major rebuilding efforts. In the restoration process, nearly 7,000 adobe bricks were used and more than $7,000 was required for costs incurred.[18] The league raised sufficient funds in 1906 to acquire Fort Ross and present it to the state. When the California State Park Commission was created in 1927, it accepted responsibility for this coastal property.[19]

In the meantime, Knowland and the Native Sons continued their preservation activities. Between 1911 and 1913, for example, they contributed $2,500 of the $83,000 collected to restore Mission San Diego de Alcala.[20] Knowland's Historic Landmarks Committee provided $900 to the Mission Santa Ines bell tower fund after rains destroyed the tower in 1911. This was added to $50 from the Native Daughters and $6,725 furnished by the Church to make the much-needed repairs. When Mission Santa Clara de Asis was destroyed by fire in 1926, the Committee donated $250.[21] The Native Daughters later joined the Native Sons in other mission restoration projects. Between 1913 and 1917, a joint committee of both organizations restored the remaining adobe of Mission San Jose de Guadalupe in Alameda County for $5,346.[22]

The earlier mentioned work at Mission Santa Ines demonstrated the dedication of individual resident priests and the Church to the restoration of these historic buildings. Father Alexander Buckler, who arrived at Mission Santa Ines in 1904, raised $23,000 by 1924 and did most of the repair work himself. After the 1906 earthquake, Father Ricardo Valentin Closa at Mission San Juan Bautista started what has since become an annual fund-raising fiesta. At Mission San Juan Capistrano, Father St. John O'Sullivan spent his last twenty-five years on restoration work.[23]

The Landmarks Club of Southern California continued to support mission restoration projects with mixed results. In addition to San Juan Capistrano and San Fernando, the club assisted at Mission San Diego de Alcala. They contributed $100 in 1899, and in 1903 claimed to have spent some $5,000.[24] Re-roofing and other repairs were completed at the Asistencia of San Antonio de Pala in 1902 and 1903; additional funds were contributed in 1912.[25] In 1908, the club received title to La Purisima near Lompoc from the Union Oil Company on the condition that they spend $1,500 on its buildings. Unfortunately, little was accomplished because the club lost its main source of publicity and support when Lummis left the editorship of *Out West* in 1909. Only when a company representative recommended cancellation of the deed in 1916 did the club move to spend $110 for general cleanup in July of that same year.[26]

In 1914, the Landmarks Club of Southern California attempted to revitalize itself by expanding its regional focus to include the entire state. Little else happened until the club held a conference in June 1916 at the Mission Inn in Riverside. Forty participants gathered for three days to discuss preservation, form committees, pass resolutions, and dedicate a fountain to St. Francis at the base of Mt. Rubidoux. At the last recorded directors' meeting in August 1916, club officers reviewed the successful "Candle Day" fund-raising celebration at Mission San Fernando, which raised $3,500 to repair the mission roof.[27]

Missions were not the only structures salvaged and preserved during these years. For example, groups such as the Pio Pico Historical and Museum Society tried to save historic buildings in their community. The society convinced the City of Whittier to purchase the thirty-four-room adobe and lease it back to them for restoration. In 1909, they opened the museum to the public. In 1914, the city gave the mansion to the state in hopes of obtaining funds for complete restoration. Elsewhere, the Native Sons Parlor in Petaluma began work in 1911 on General Mariano Vallejo's Casa Grande Adobe.[28]

During these years, the marking of historic sites and roads or trails became a priority for several organizations. The California State Society of the Daughters of the American Revolution began their historic sites project in 1914.[29] Both the Native Sons and Daughters continued their plaque programs, which dated from 1890 and 1911, respectively. By 1925, the Native Sons had placed thirty-four markers or monuments, and the Native Daughters had erected five.[30]

Interest in historic travelways was not confined to the placement of suitable markers and monuments. Anna B. Pitcher drew up a plan to identify and restore El Camino Real, "The King's Road," which linked California's twenty-one missions. Her proposal to build a state route marked with milestones to record the road's historic importance received support from the General Federation of Women's Clubs and the Native Daughters in 1902. However, by the time the El Camino Real Association was formed in 1904, Pitcher had fallen ill and was replaced by Mrs. A.S.C. Forbes, who subsequently chaired the research committee and drew the design for the famous mission bell guideposts. For Forbes, the bells "would draw the wavering sentiment of this day of golden lust to an appreciation of the work accomplished by a band of noble pioneers." They would also serve to mark "the best and most direct route" from San Diego to San Francisco. The first of these bells was placed in front of the Plaza Church in Los Angeles in 1906. By 1926, there were 450 similar guideposts along El Camino Real, maintained in perpetuity by an agreement between the association, the Automobile Club of Southern California, and the California State Automobile Association.[31]

By 1925, a handful of pioneer historic preservationists had made significant progress toward saving the tangible remnants of early European discovery and settlement of California. Unlike these dedicated volunteers, the State of California had yet to develop a coherent preservation policy. Properties, such as the Monterey Custom House, which were deeded to the state were administered by trustees or commissions appointed by the governor. It was only in 1921 that individual groups and their historic monuments were made accountable to a single agency, the Department of Finance. This reorganization, however, did not provide the state with a mechanism to administer a preservation program. That would come later in the decade.

Despite the absence of an articulated policy, the state proved generally supportive of preservation. In addition to a modest appropriation of restoration funds, in 1915, the legislature established the California Historical Survey Commission at the University of California at Berkeley. It received yearly funding to evaluate and coordinate historic preservation proposals. Under the direction of historian Owen C. Coy, the commission also produced monographs on historic sites.[32] In 1923, the California State Historical Association, a coalition of historical societies, replaced the commission. Until World War II, the association focused its attention on research and publications on California history. The low priority given to historic landmarks was due partially to the fact that the association was administratively responsible to the State Board of Education.[33] During the second quarter of the twentieth century, the state's role in preservation would expand dramatically.

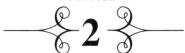

Extending the Frontiers of Historic Preservation: State, Federal, and Local Programs, 1925-1940

During the second quarter of the twentieth century, historic preservation in California expanded to include a state program that dominated preservation activities. Federal support put thousands to work on historic projects, and strenuous local and private efforts rescued properties important to their community's heritage.

The State Takes the Lead

Three pivotal events during 1927 and 1928 were the foundation for state participation and leadership: the creation of the State Park Commission, the completion of the nation's first state survey of landscape and historic sites, and the passage of a bond issue for the acquisition of historic sites. Thus strengthened, state-sponsored preservation programs overshadowed both federal and private projects during this period. Supporters of a coherent policy for the acquisition of state park properties placed highest priority on the conservation of natural resources in general and redwood groves in particular. Fortuitously for advocates of the preservation of the built environment, the conservation movement was sufficiently all-encompassing to embrace their concerns.

It was the Save-the-Redwoods League, founded in 1918, that launched the campaign to establish a state park system and commission. Prominent individuals, such as Madison Grant, chairman of the New York Zoological Society, and John C. Merriam, dean of faculties, University of California at Berkeley, feared for the survival of the coast redwoods in the face of rising postwar demands for lumber and congressional refusal to purchase private lands for parks. The league embarked on an extensive fund-raising and public relations effort by hiring Newton B. Drury, head of an already well-known advertising firm. Through persistence and persuasion, Drury and league members acquired enough private and state funds by 1921 to purchase several redwood groves in what is now Humboldt Redwoods State Park. Despite these and other successes, in 1925, the league realized that acquisition of the threatened coast redwoods would require more millions than could be obtained through private donations and piecemeal legislation. As a result, the California State Parks Committee was established in 1925, with Drury serving as secretary to both that group and the league. The committee supported two legislative bills introduced that year: one which would create a state park commission, and the other which would survey potential park sites. To their great disappointment, an unsympathetic Governor Friend William Richardson refused to sign both measures because of his unswerving commitment to reduce state spending.[1]

The 1926 election of Clement Calhoun Young to the governorship changed the league's fortunes. Young was a close friend and former business partner of Duncan McDuffie, realtor, civic leader, and chairman of the league's committee on state parks. In May 1927, Young signed three bills authorizing the creation of a State Park Commission to coordinate and administer the park system, a statewide survey of potential park sites, and the placement on the ballot of a $6 million bond issue for a 50-50 match of state and private dollars for land purchases. Young moved swiftly and in November, appointed five members to the Park Commission. A year later, in November 1928, with the Drury Company handling all publicity and administrative duties for the State Park Bond effort, Proposition 4 passed by a margin of nearly three to one.[2] Meanwhile, Frederick Law Olmsted had begun his survey of the state's scenic and recreational resources.[3]

The Olmsted survey was the first of its kind done anywhere in the United States.[4] Olmsted divided California into twelve districts with volunteer advisers from each area appointed by the Park Commission. In addition to these individuals, regional reporters and other selected advisers conducted on-site investigations and produced valuable reports. Two of Olmsted's historical advisers were Aubrey Drury and Joseph Knowland.[5] Furthermore, Olmsted had the benefit of Aubrey Drury's sixty-page "Survey of Historic Sites and Landmarks in California" compiled in August 1928 for the "Yes on No.4" campaign. The report, which was produced to assist Olmsted, was divided into three parts. It began with descriptions of the missions, followed by properties owned by public agencies, and concluded with historic sites in private hands. The diversity of historic places included in the report was enormous.[6]

By the time Olmsted completed his investigations in 1929, he had more than 330 proposals to review. He managed to narrow these down to 125 recommendations, of which only 10 were historic sites. When possible, he believed that the state should encourage private ownership and protection of places of historic interest. Olmsted felt that the state should take title and permanently assume the "burden" of caring for them only if they were of statewide significance and in danger of disintegration or vandalism. All of this would involve "considerable annual expense without much possibility of securing any corresponding revenue in any dignified and legitimate way."[7]

Olmsted's survey gave the town of Columbia the highest rating because it was "the most interesting, picturesque and historically valuable monument of the early mining days of California...."[8] Horace M. Albright, former director of the National Park Service, offered the following explanation of how Olmsted discovered Columbia:

> Mr. Olmsted asked me if I had any ideas on historic areas around Yosemite and I said that we did—Old Columbia. My grandfather went up there in the early 1850s. I knew Columbia well and Mr. Olmsted asked if I could take him over there and I said yes, I would. So I took Mr. Olmsted to Columbia. That would be about 1927-1928.[9]

The state park survey was more than a mere listing of park projects. It contained the warning that California's abundant natural resources were in imminent danger of being destroyed: "careless, hasty, shortsightedly selfish methods of exploiting the natural assets are rapidly killing the geese that lay the golden eggs." Olmsted urged the state to teach people how to enjoy scenic and recreational values and "*to curb and limit the activities of exploiters* who would destroy the birthright of their successors...."[10] Although these admonitions have oftentimes been ignored during the intervening years, nearly all of Olmsted's specific recommendations have been followed.[11]

By the end of the 1920s, the foundation for the expansion of the State Park System was laid. In 1928, the state had five historic monuments and twelve parks.[12] During the next decade, additional historic properties were acquired under the guidance of Newton Drury who served the Park Commission as acquisitions officer. By 1934, the number of state-owned historic monuments increased to eleven and parks to forty-nine. Although the Depression forced a subsequent curtailment of new additions, the State Park System was nevertheless significantly improved and developed during the remainder of the 1930s.[13]

The Park Commission's attempt to acquire the town of Columbia with bond monies underscored two common characteristics of the early preservation movement. Arguments in support of purchasing and restoring the town centered on its significance as a civics lesson for future generations. Like other historic buildings in California that had been restored, Columbia was destined to become a museum, although in this particular case, it would continue as a living town.[14]

Although no one could dispute the historic importance of Columbia, plans to preserve it could not be implemented until the 1940s. The primary obstacle to its preservation was the inability of local residents to raise their mandated half of the purchase cost. Furthermore, despite Drury's strenuous efforts, the delicate negotiations to keep property prices to a reasonable level collapsed by 1936. In 1937, acquisition plans were effectively sidelined when the commission began to channel Columbia's allocation into other projects. Shasta, and later Monterey's House of Gold, and Mission La Purisima Concepcion benefited from the impasse at Columbia.[15]

In contrast to Columbia, the move to preserve the town of San Juan Bautista as part of the State Park System proved to be an immediate success. San Juan Bautista, too, embodied an important phase of the state's past, and supporters of its preservation had been working since the 1920s to save it. The acquisition effort had the support of two State Park commissioners, cooperative local property owners, and the negotiation skills of Newton Drury. By October 1935, all obstacles had been overcome, and the state dedicated the plaza area.[16]

The 1928 bond issue also benefited two other local preservation projects. When the Park Commission allocated $9,000 for the purchase of the Vallejo Home in 1931, the General Vallejo Memorial Association began seeking matching funds. Despite donations from Sonoma County and the Native Sons, sufficient monies could not be raised because of the depressed economy. Vallejo's heirs were persuaded to donate a large portion of the land to the state, and in July 1933, Knowland received title to the property on behalf of the commission.[17]

The residents of Old Shasta demonstrated a similar preservation commitment. Although Olmsted's survey identified Shasta as one of ten recommended historic sites, the Park Commission was reluctant to allocate its dwindling bond dollars for its preservation. The town's supporters persisted, however, and in 1937, the state received the old courthouse and jail from the Native Sons. Later that same year, the commission took $1,500 from its Columbia allocation and assigned it to the restoration of Old Shasta.[18]

In October 1939, Newton Drury submitted a report on the status of the State Park Commission's acquisition program. The fifteen-page summary was a revealing account of what had been accomplished in a busy decade.[19] Drury highlighted several significant achievements. State investment in the parks increased from $1 million to $15 million during the decade. Equally impressive was the dramatic expansion in parks and monuments from fourteen to seventy and in acreage from 13,000 to 300,000. The new acquisitions, said Drury, reflected the commission's continued adherence to Olmsted's survey, both in principles and recommendations.[20]

The commission identified four principal areas of concern: natural scenery of unique beauty, rare natural objects, "objects of statewide historical interest," and recreational sites. In addition, the commission established three categories of parks: scenic reserves, recreational parks, and historic monuments which encompassed "sites or structures typifying important episodes in California's colorful past, including the influence of Spanish, Mexican, Russian and Early California regimes." By 1939, Drury reported that of the seventy parks in the system, twenty were park reserves, thirty-six were recreational, and fourteen were historic parks.[21] The historic units commemorated

> chief episodes in the state's romantic past. Typical of these are Fort Ross, Sonoma County, an outpost of the early Russian settlement; San Juan Bautista Plaza, San Benito County, with its century-old adobe buildings of the Mexican regime; the Custom House at Monterey, where Commodore Sloat took possession of California for the United States in 1846; and La Purisima Mission, Santa Barbara County, now being extensively restored under the National Park Service C.C.C., as a reminder of the last days of the padres.[22]

A brochure published by the Works Progress Administration (WPA) in 1940 identified the remainder as: Sonoma Mission, Vallejo Home, Solano, Marshall, Donner, Old Shasta, First Theater in Monterey, Junipero Serra Monument, Pio Pico Mansion, and San Pasqual Battlefield.[23]

On the eve of his departure to the National Park Service of which he served as director from 1940 to 1951, Drury could boast of the great diversity of lands acquired during his tenure as executive secretary and acquisitions officer to the State Park Commission. The bond act, he observed, had been generally beneficial. The matching requirement usually prevented pork-barreling, and, in most cases, the match was raised. Of the few exceptions, Drury included Columbia with

> its main street lined with brick buildings guarded by heavy iron shutters, quaintly reminiscent of the days of gold. It is hoped that contributors will be able to assist in holding intact this early community before modern 'improvements' have destroyed its atmosphere.[24]

After observing that the state's park program seemed "definitely set," Drury predicted that "future expansion of the system will take place, not so much through adding new parks, but more through rounding out existing parks and monuments so as to protect their surroundings and attain satisfactory administrative units." He was optimistic about increasing the acreage of existing redwood parks and saw the acquisition of much-needed recreational beaches in southern California as the only exception to his plans. Drury believed that these purchases would be made possible by anticipated oil royalties.[25] Unfortunately, these hopes did not fully materialize for over a decade. The park fund's share of state oil revenues did not meet expectations at first, and the state legislature and finance director later redirected monies to meet other more pressing needs. Furthermore, between June 1947 and September 1954, pending clarification of state and federal jurisdiction of submerged lands, the U.S. Supreme Court impounded oil royalty revenues.[26]

Drury's report did not remain in the dustbin. In 1966, the Department of Parks and Recreation resurrected and distributed it to all park unit supervisors. The accompanying memo read: "We thought this would be of interest to you and would enable you to familiarize yourself with the early history of the development of our state parks."[27]

Birth of the State Landmarks Program

By 1931, substantial public interest in historic landmarks was discernible. The California State Historical Association's "Quarterly Report" of March 1931 noted that

> Landmarks are now just uppermost in the minds of California citizens. This interest is reflected in the promotion work of the State Chamber of Commerce through regional and local committees, and is evident in newspaper and periodical emphasis on this phase of state history.[28]

This support prompted the passage of Assembly Bill 171 which was signed by Governor James Rolph, Jr., in April 1931.[29] Upon owner consent, the director of the Department of Natural Resources could designate both private and public properties as state landmarks.[30] The property would be listed on a register, and "a suitable numbered placard" would be placed in a prominent location.[31]

A second piece of legislation passed in 1931 required the State Highway Commission to erect and maintain all directional markers to guide motorists from state highways to registered landmarks. The Streets and Highway Code of 1935 extended jurisdiction for maintenance of markers on county highways to local boards of supervisors. When a monument or plaque was placed on a registered site, the State Highway Department erected a "small chocolate and white marker" at the site "along with directional markers starting from a point along the main highway and leading to the site from all routes in the vicinity. In some instances as many as 13 chocolate and white directive signs are used for one site." The California State Automobile Association or the Automobile Club of Southern California furnished the signs. The directional sign program was discontinued during World War II.[32]

To implement the landmark registration program, the director of the Department of Natural Resources asked the State Chamber of Commerce to establish a committee of historians to review landmark applications and to handle administrative tasks such as providing proper forms and acquiring sufficient information for the committee's deliberations. The first Official Approval Committee consisted of Orra E. Monette (chairman), Francis P. Farquhar, Carl I. Wheat, Aubrey Drury, Herbert Bolton, DeWitt V. Hutchings, Senator Leroy A. Wright, and Lawrence Hill.[33]

Registration procedures were handled in the beginning by the Highway Department of the State Chamber and in 1941, by the chamber's Travel and Recreation Committee because "it was more of a travel project than one of highways." [34] Applicants were asked to provide specific information regarding the proposed landmark's name, location, name of owner, and a brief history and description. At least two photographs were required along with a statement of property owner consent and documentation substantiating all claims. The completed form was then sent to committee members. If a majority recommended registration, the file was forwarded to the State Park Commission for dating and assignment of a registration number. Next, it was returned to the chamber, where a complete description was written and the landmark form was mimeographed for distribution to interested parties.[35]

Landmarks were numbered in the sequence in which they were processed. The first to be registered was the Custom House in Monterey on June 1, 1932. Nineteen other landmarks were registered with the same approval date; by the end of the year, the state had recognized a total of seventy-eight sites.[36] By 1935, official reports from the Department of Natural Resources, the State Park Commission, and the California State Chamber of Commerce, as well as the procedural guidelines handed out to applicants, carried the following disclaimer:

> In approving these historic sites as registered landmarks, it should be clearly understood that neither the Department of Natural Resources, the State Park Commission nor the Official Approval committee, subscribe to all of the statements or the dates contained in the history and description of each landmark. The above named agencies agree only that the historic site is of importance and should be registered by the State of California.[37]

By the eve of World War II, 376 landmarks were registered.[38] When the program came to an end in 1951, 499 landmarks had been approved and listed.[39]

It became apparent to those administering the program in the 1930s that registered sites needed permanent markers. In June 1938, Frank McKee, director of the chamber's Highway Department, reported to Joseph Knowland, chairman of the Park Commission, that he anticipated that some 500 points of historical importance would be registered. As of that date, 288 had been approved. McKee informed Knowland that 100 landmarks had permanent monuments or markers and that the other 400 would require appropriate recognition.[40] After Knowland approved his request to seek $18,000 from the state's emergency funds, McKee brought the matter to the attention of J.H. Covington, executive secretary to the commission, who forwarded the information to George D. Nordenholt, director of Natural Resources. Nordenholt did not receive McKee's proposition favorably because he did not view the need for 400 markers as an "emergency." [41]

McKee persisted in his efforts to obtain funds for permanent plaques from other sources. In a letter to Standard Oil of California, McKee insisted:

> It is perfectly clear that it is useless for the traveling public to be diverted to registered landmarks unless there is a plaque at the site giving a brief description of what tran-

spired at that particular place, and it is in this regard that
I feel that Standard Oil Company can render another very
useful service to the State by providing markers similar to
the ones shown in the attached photographs, to be erected
at all registered landmarks which do not at the present time
have plaques of a durable and lasting nature.

He suggested that a program could be worked out whereby Standard Oil
would be properly recognized for its support, thereby resulting "in a
tremendous volume of good will and publicity."[42]

Less than a month later, Standard Oil turned McKee down. Not only
did their projected cost estimates exceed McKee's anticipated $45 per
marker, they feared that their sponsorship of the program would be
misunderstood and seen as commercial exploitation.[43] In a counterpro-
posal, McKee observed that a decline in tourist travel in 1940 was predicted.
If the oil companies supported the program, they could revise their maps to
direct travelers to historical markers. In return, the State Chamber of
Commerce was prepared to begin a public relations program to stimulate
travel and bring attention to the plaque sponsors.[44] Nearly two months later,
McKee again wrote to Standard Oil's vice-president. He extended his
proposition to other members of the "oil group" and estimated that $40,000
would be needed for 450 markers. Again, he emphasized that the landmark
program served an educational purpose, promoted travel, and could even
ease traffic congestion.[45]

The Fair Practices Association, comprised of the major oil companies, cited "a diversity of opinion" regarding the perpetuation of "interesting
historical landmarks" and rejected McKee's proposal in July.[46] He pressed
again in August, insisting that the oil companies through their publication
and distribution of maps were the only group able to participate in a
statewide program to stimulate travel. Furthermore, they had a reputation
for advertising campaigns conducted with dignity.[47] Another rejection did
not deter McKee's successor, J.E. Carpenter, from trying again.

A year later, Carpenter wrote to Covington to inform him that he
intended to pursue the marker plan by obtaining wooden signs built by the
Civilian Conservation Corps (CCC). He also mentioned his desire to publish
a book of landmarks.[48] Neither project materialized. There were no funds in
the state park budget for such a book, and H.G. Prodger, director of the
Division of Work Projects for the National Youth Administration in California, could not comply with the request because "of the strong emphasis
being placed on preparation of youth for entrance into National Defense
industries...."[49]

The program to erect markers continued, however, under the auspices of nativist organizations such as the Native Sons and Daughters and the Daughters of the American Revolution. A July 1940 survey that was sent to county chambers of commerce under Carpenter's signature and a similar request made to the Native Sons and Daughters by Chamber Director Knowland identified 370 landmarks in the state. Of that total, 106 had not yet been marked.[50] In 1945, Carpenter reported that only eighty registered landmarks lacked plaques.[51]

The large number of registered landmarks approved in the 1930s, with the consent of the property owners, is one indication of the program's popularity. Carpenter's summary in his 1945 report of the virtues of the historical landmark program was typical of prevailing sentiments. Historic landmarks were supposed to foster a love and admiration for California's heritage among newcomers and residents alike and were invaluable to the tourist business. His remarks echoed earlier arguments that landmarks were valued for their educational and profit-making potential. Carpenter's prediction that preservation projects would provide jobs after the war was also prophetic. His conclusion that the program was near completion with the selection and registration of nearly 500 landmarks, however, underestimated what would transpire in the coming decades.[52] In November 1991, the number of sites in the State Historical Landmark Program reached 1,004.

The Park Commission did not approve landmark applications without careful consideration of their historic significance as demonstrated by policy guidelines drafted by Drury in 1937. It was "a cautious approach to restoration, reconstruction, the use of roads and plantings, and the granting of concessions...." The commission also agreed with Olmsted that state historic monuments should be self-supporting. By the eve of World War II, California seemed to have "the most highly developed and sophisticated state historic sites program" in the country.[53] On the other hand, the use of landmarks to highlight the state's history reveals another pervasive characteristic of preservation in California: the lessons taught by the markers glorified a heritage of European origins and too frequently ignored the diverse cultural and ethnic dimensions of California's past.

The Federal Government As Preservationist

The federal government contributed to the evolution of historic preservation in California during the 1930s in a variety of ways.

Make-work programs administered by the Civilian Conservation Corps put some 10,000 "man years" of labor into the State Park System. The Works Progress Administration (WPA) also sent the unemployed to research historic sites and record architecturally significant structures.[54]

One of the most ambitious CCC projects was the massive reconstruction effort at Mission La Purisima Concepcion in Santa Barbara County that began in 1934 with the construction of temporary housing for 175 workers. The 507-acre mission complex was finally dedicated after an investment of six years and more than $400,000 in labor and materials. By the time of the dedication ceremonies on December 7, 1941, the restoration included the rebuilt residence (1936); water system, fountains, and cistern (1938); church (1939); shops and quarters building (1940); and monument residences and other accomplishments such as the interior decoration of the church (1941). The State of California received "the most expensive, carefully researched, and well-planned restoration in the West."[55]

The La Purisima project brought together several enthusiastic groups. Owen C. Coy, director of the California State Historical Association, for example, advocated total reconstruction because he saw the mission as an educational tool.[56] On Knowland's recommendation, the Park Commission provided funds from the bond issue.[57] County officials donated half of the purchase price toward needed additional lands. The Advisory Committee which Drury organized from the neighboring Santa Barbara community shared the excitement of federal officials over the restoration of the entire complex.[58]

Because of restrictions on the CCC budget, reconstruction plans were made for only six months at a time. The successful rebuilding of the residence created so much enthusiasm, however, that the project could not be halted. There were, of course, disagreements during these years. One of these revolved around the question of how much of the original community should be reproduced. Should it be totally reconstructed or should only the existing remains be preserved? By 1937, the debate had been resolved because it was too late to argue preservation or reconstruction. Foundations, for example, were deteriorating rapidly, and entire structures were in danger of collapse. Preservation supporters agreed. "The only alternative in 1937 was a National Park Service pledge to make La Purisima the most authentic project of its type in the country." La Purisima would become the only comprehensive reconstruction project in a preservation movement that emphasized the restoration and protection of historic sites.[59]

By the time the mission was finally dedicated in December 1941, the

New Deal's historic sites program had forever altered preservation. "The Park Service had an Advisory Board and a restoration policy. The National Survey of Historic Sites and Buildings had started. The Department of the Interior had moved from an era of relatively unplanned expansion to a period of emphasis on scholarship in the restoration process."[60]

The landmark registration program, which produced its first designated sites in 1932, became the basis for an even more ambitious effort in the mid-thirties. With funding from the WPA, the State Department of Natural Resources and its Division of Parks began to research and publish detailed studies of California's registered landmarks in 1936.

Newton Drury administered the project for the Division of Parks; V. Aubrey Neasham, a former student of Herbert E. Bolton, supervised it at the Bancroft Library.[61] By July 1, 1937, Neasham reported completion of 105 studies for a total of 3,069 pages; yet to be done were 48 reports. Should additional funding be obtained, he planned to complete 91 studies within a year.[62]

Although Neasham left in November 1938 to accept the post of Southwest Regional Historian for the National Park Service, the project continued into 1941, when the last of the studies was published.[63] When the program ended, its prolific publications included 144 studies on historic landmarks and 34 reports on state parks. In addition, each of California's four capitals had been researched.[64]

In the midst of the Depression, President Franklin Delano Roosevelt signed the Historic Sites Act (1935). He hoped to "'lay a broad legal foundation for, and to develop and carry on, a national program for the preservation and interpretation of physical and cultural remains of our country.'"[65] The legislation gave new authority to the National Park Service which was empowered "to make surveys, secure data, and investigate archeological and historical sites anywhere in this country" to determine what was of nationwide significance and to obtain the assistance of federal, state, or private agencies.[66] One result of the 1935 act was the creation of the Historic American Buildings Survey (HABS).

Like other WPA projects, HABS provided work for the jobless. Funding began in 1933 under the Civil Works Administration, and the project proved so successful in its use of unemployed architects and draftsmen that it was continued with the assistance of Emergency Relief and Public Works monies (1934-1935) and the WPA (1936-1941).

The HABS project represented an official agreement between the

National Park Service, the American Institute of Architects (A.I.A.), and the Library of Congress to create "a permanent graphic record of the existing architectural remains of early dwellers in this country."[67] When WPA funds ran out in March 1941, 2,693 structures had been measured and drawn, with an additional 3,000 on index cards ready to be studied. Seventy-one A.I.A. chapters divided the country and its territories among themselves and prepared card files on selected structures, which then were arranged by significance and possibility of destruction and finally drawn or photographed. A cover sheet briefly summarizing the structure's identity, location, and date accompanied each set of drawings. An additional data sheet gave the owner's name, condition of the structure, name of builder, and date of construction when known.[68]

The 1941 HABS report listed 191 structures in California that had been recorded with at least one photograph.[69] The HABS listing, however, did not prevent the destruction of many historic properties. The collection itself has become a valuable historic record of structures that have since disappeared,

> such as the Montgomery Block in San Francisco. Built in 1853, on a foundation of redwood logs, the 'Monkey Block' became a thriving commercial center and bohemian haven for American writers including Samuel Clemens, Bret Harte and Jack London. It was torn down in 1959. Nothing remains of the building except the records made by the Historic American Building Survey.[70]

There were only four California entries in the 1959 supplement to the 1941 catalog, which updated the work done after HABS resumed operations in 1957. One of these was the Montgomery Block.[71]

Local Preservation Projects

Local preservationists continued their efforts to save historic sites in their communities. One notable example was in Santa Barbara, where the 1925 earthquake leveled much of the State Street business district and part of the Santa Barbara Mission. That the disaster had a silver lining was due to the Community Arts Association and individuals such as Bernard Hoffman.[72]

During the five years preceding that fateful June morning, the association had unsuccessfully sought to mandate Spanish-style architecture in new construction and to preserve the city's rapidly deteriorating adobes.[73] The destruction caused by the earthquake provided an unexpected opportunity for the Community Arts Association to gain acceptance for its desire to identify civic heritage with Spanish-style architecture. Three groups came into being with the purpose of ensuring that a unifying architectural theme was visible in the rebuilt downtown area. The newly formed Board of Public Safety and Reconstruction established the Architectural Advisory Committee to coordinate the city's architects, Planning Commission, and representatives of businesses and property owners. Chaired by Hoffman, and with the assistance of a forty-two member advisory board, the committee convinced State Street property owners to adopt a Spanish-style facade when they rebuilt their businesses. Also, in July 1925, the city council appointed an Architectural Board of Review to evaluate design plans for a building's exterior before a building permit was issued. Although it survived for only eight months, the board's regulatory impact was such that Spanish-style architecture thereafter dominated both commercial and civic structures. Finally, to ensure that architectural plans would agree with the requirements of both the Architectural Advisory Committee and the Review Board, a privately supported Community Drafting Room was organized to provide free plans and advice.[74]

In the meantime, work on the damaged mission continued. Dedication ceremonies were held in August 1927 as part of that year's fiesta activities. The Santa Barbara Relief Fund, in a statewide campaign, collected contributions for restoration costs, which eventually exceeded $400,000.[75]

At the same time restoration was in progress in Santa Barbara, preservationists in the Greater Los Angeles area continued to restore individual structures and adobes.[76] Their successes, however, paled beside the publicity garnered by Christine Sterling, the Oakland-born "Mother of Olvera Street."[77] Olvera Street adjoins the historic Plaza in Los Angeles. In the winter of 1926, Sterling was visiting the area when she noticed a condemnation sign in front of the Avila Adobe. Her initial efforts to save the structure resulted in supportive articles in the Los Angeles *Times*, but few donations. In desperation, she placed a large sign in front of the adobe in 1928 and called the press. Few could resist her argument that "this old adobe belongs to the history of Los Angeles. It is not ours to destroy, but an entrusted heritage left to us to preserve and pass on to future generations."[78]

There was more to her vision. Sterling wanted the Plaza converted into a romanticized "Spanish-American social and commercial center, a spot of beauty as a gesture of appreciation to Mexico and Spain for our historical past." With the help of Harry Chandler and others, she raised $25,000.

Despite some protests, the street was closed and work began in November 1929. The chief of police provided twenty-five prisoners as project laborers. After considerable delay, the street reopened as a colorful Mexican market place on Easter Day, 1930.[79]

Olvera Street became a commercial success and attracted thousands to the Old Plaza and surrounding area, which became El Pueblo de Los Angeles State Historical Monument in 1953. Sterling's pivotal role in the preservation of the area is indisputable; however, her exclusion of Chinese contributions, as well as those of Euro-Americans such as the French and Italians, has been the subject of critical discussion in recent years.[80] Although this does not diminish her place in the Plaza's evolution, it does emphasize the need for future research and interpretation of the Plaza's multi-cultural and multi-ethnic history.

There is evidence that Chandler's involvement with Olvera Street piqued his interest in the preservation of other historic structures. Upon the request of Newton Drury, for example, he recommended to his Tejon Ranch Company that they deed the crumbling buildings and five acres of land to the state. On December 29, 1939, the state assumed ownership.[81]

In the Monterey area, newcomers joined with established families and neighbors from Carmel and Pebble Beach to create a formidable base of wealthy, articulate supporters of a strong local movement to preserve historic buildings. The efforts of nativist groups, such as the Native Sons who had earlier encouraged the restoration of the Custom House and Colton Hall, were strengthened by the appearance of the Monterey History and Art Association, Ltd., in 1931. Its creator was Laura Bride Powers, then custodian of the Monterey Custom House and founder of the California Historic Landmarks League. Most of the original forty members of the association were long-time residents who feared for the survival of the city's many adobes. Their goals were "'to promote interest in the history of Monterey county; to protect its historic sites, landmarks, and buildings,'" and finally "'to cultivate and promote a widespread interest in the development of art in Monterey county.'" The latter objective reflected the organization's appeal to the area's large artist colony.[82]

The association was put to its first real test in 1937 when the U.S. Treasury Department informed the state that the Custom House could be purchased. Joseph Knowland, who had become chairman of the Park Commission, informed the Treasury Secretary that California would purchase the property if the people of Monterey could match the funds. Drury, the commission's acquisition officer, also believed that state ownership was beneficial. He was fearful that the city would build a road near the building, thereby destroying the historic character of the entire harbor area.[83]

With Drury's intervention, both the Treasury Department and the state agreed that the people of Monterey and the state would each contribute $10,000.[84] By mid-February 1938, the money was collected. In the meantime, landscape architect Emerson Knight began to study the properties near the waterfront and the Custom House and submitted a master plan to the city council in May 1939. The council adopted his recommended zoning ordinance in September 1940.[85]

Monterey's preservationists undertook other projects. The Robert Louis Stevenson House, for example, was presented to the Park Commission in 1941. These energetic and historically minded individuals rescued the Old Adobe Theater, the Thomas Larkin House, the House of Gold, and other structures which later became part of the Monterey State Historic Park.[86]

Although Spanish-Colonial Revival architecture was popular from 1920 to 1930, the number of mission restoration projects was small in comparison to earlier years. There were only three major public undertakings during the 1920s. One was a 1920 benefit ball for the Mission San Carlos Borromeo organized by Father Ramon Mestres. The $35,000 which was realized from donations was used for a sarcophagus for Father Serra. The other two projects raised funds for the earthquake-damaged Mission Santa Barbara and for the Mission Santa Clara church, which had been destroyed by fire in 1926.[87]

During the 1930s, mission restoration continued under the direction of the State Park Commission in cooperation with the Catholic Church. By this time, concern for historical accuracy began to supersede romantic notions of the past or attempts to "modernize" exteriors. It was cabinetmaker Harry Downie who dominated mission restoration work, beginning with the 1936 removal of Mission San Carlos Borromeo's peaked roof. Downie claimed personal involvement in the restoration of ten of California's twenty-one missions.[88]

Before World War II, funds to restore the missions came from tourist donations and diocesan monies. In 1947, the William Randolph Hearst Foundation gave $500,000 to the Catholic Church in California for mission restoration. It was the largest private donation received to that date and was distributed among the archdioceses of San Francisco and Los Angeles, and the dioceses of Monterey and San Diego. Downie himself supervised work on missions San Luis Obispo, San Antonio, and San Juan Bautista. The only mission to remain untouched by the foundation's generosity was Mission Nuestra Senora de la Soledad. The Native Daughters stepped in and collected $25,000 for the reconstruction of the chapel. The project, which was guided by Downie on Knowland's recommendation, was finally completed in 1954.[89]

By the eve of World War II, historic preservationists in California could point to several significant accomplishments. Under the auspices of the state, California's scenic and recreational resources were surveyed, historic properties were acquired and developed under a bond program, and historic landmarks were registered. The federal government reconstructed Mission La Purisima, underwrote studies of historic sites, and recorded architecturally significant structures. The preservation constituency now embraced new converts whose determination at the local level was matched by the commitment of individuals such as V. Aubrey Neasham and Newton Drury at the state level. These men began working for the National Park Service before war broke out and did not return to California until the early 1950s. Others like Joseph Knowland continued their efforts, albeit hampered by wartime demands. When peace returned to the nation and to California, preservationists were prepared to push forward with renewed vigor.

PART II

Reawakening of a Preservation Consciousness, 1940-1966

Wartime demands overwhelmed preservation and restoration concerns in California as well as in the rest of the nation. The groundwork, however, was slowly being laid for a resurgence of activity even before the war ended in 1945.

Governor Earl Warren's appointment of his political mentor, Joseph R. Knowland, to the State Park Commission in 1943 after his ouster in 1939 by Governor Culbert Olson, helped to revitalize that body. Other appointments such as those of entertainer and native Californian Leo Carillo, newspaper publishers George Waldner of Ferndale and Alfred Harrell of Bakersfield, and conservationist Charles Kasch brought vigorous support for wilderness and historic preservation in the face of increasing demands for commercial development.[1]

When planning for the Gold Discovery and Gold Rush centennials focused the public's attention on the state's heritage, historic preservation in California received a new lease on life. The return of professionals such as Newton B. Drury and Aubrey Neasham to state service further implanted preservation in the public's consciousness.

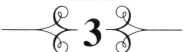

The Gold Discovery and Gold Rush Centennials, 1940-1950

The twin celebrations of the discovery of gold and the subsequent gold rush which directed the state's attention to California's mining heritage had a beneficial impact on historic preservation. Planning for the centennial celebrations began nearly a decade before the actual festivities occurred.

Laying the Groundwork for the Centennials

On December 6, 1940, the Board of Directors of the State Chamber of Commerce approved the concept of celebrating both the Gold Discovery and Gold Rush centennials because of their statewide and international significance. In January 1941, the Chamber's Sacramento Regional Council agreed to forward to the entire board a resolution that suggested the appointment of a special subcommittee of the Travel Committee "to bring to the attention of the proper authorities the feasibility and advisability of a Gold Rush Centennial Celebration of World's Fair proportions" to be held at the Sacramento fairgrounds. The committee did little about the proposal, and when war broke out, the chamber's priorities shifted elsewhere.[1]

Soon after his appointment to the State Park Commission, Joseph R. Knowland, who was quickly selected commission chairman, began to explore possible projects for the approaching Gold Discovery Centennial. Discussions began in the summer of 1943 and resulted in a request to study restoration costs for twenty historic sites, including Sutter's Mill. In the fall of 1944, the Native Sons and Daughters were asked for their opinions regarding new additions to the park system. By this time, the State Chamber of Commerce had agreed to continue its support of the state landmark registration program.[2]

As World War II drew to a close, California began planning for the future. In keeping with his support for new recreational facilities and the acquisition of beaches, Governor Earl Warren vigorously campaigned for the

Omnibus Park Acquisition Bill of 1945 which provided $10 million for beaches and $5 million for inland parks. The acquisition of beaches was of intense public interest, particularly in southern California during the prewar years,and was reflected in the renaming of the Division of Parks in 1941 to the Division of Beaches and Parks. In addition to the Omnibus Park Acquisition Bill, the governor signed legislation that funded plans for a statewide system of riding and hiking trails, encouraged an independent Park Commission, and established a recreation agency with a newly created Recreation Commission that was separate from the Division of Beaches and Parks.[3] There were also other developments that had a direct impact on preservation.

In May 1945, the State Assembly amended and passed Senate Concurrent Resolution No. 39 which officially designated 1948 as the Gold Discovery Centennial Year and 1949 as the Gold Rush Centennial Year. The resolution not only recognized the significance of these two events to the state and nation, but also anticipated that the celebrations would "add materially to the interest" and the attraction of a projected boom in postwar tourism. The legislators also concurred that the events would serve as a useful educational tool to instill pride among California's more than one million new citizens.[4]

The resolution's emphasis on the significance of these two events, to generate profit and stimulate patriotism, illustrates the continued public perception of historic events and sites as important primarily for economic and educational purposes. Architectural values, which later would rival historic importance as a criterion to determine a structure's significance, were not priority concerns during this period.

Marking Landmarks

The passage of Senate Concurrent Resolution No. 39 unleashed a flurry of activity. In May 1945, the State Chamber of Commerce ordered that

> the complete plan for historic landmark identification signs, and the specific recommendation of landmark loca-tions for the erection of informational signs and turn-out spaces be placed before the State Highway Department immediately so that this work can be included in their postwar work programs.[5]

The chamber's plans to modernize the landmark signs included the erection of two different markers. One would contain a brief description of the site and would be placed at the nearest major crossroads, with parking provided for motorists to stop and read the inscription. The other would consist of a warning sign: "Historic Landmark—1000 feet."[6] The plans, however, met an immediate roadblock. In September 1945, J.E. Carpenter, director of the chamber's Travel and Recreation Department, wrote to Knowland to seek his intervention with the governor. It seems that the state engineer and others had rejected the proposal on the grounds that, although worthwhile, "they did not feel that they could take the motorists' money and use it for this purpose."[7]

By spring 1947, Carpenter had overcome all opposition to the chamber's plans. In January, he reported to Knowland that "the State Department of Highways is anxious to go ahead with this project." In March, he informed the San Benito County Board of Supervisors that the State Highway Department had finally agreed to erect a permanent stone or concrete monument of approximately six feet in height, with an attached bronze plaque, at the intersection of the nearest road leading to the forty-four sites. The plaque itself would contain some forty words describing the landmark and would be placed at an appropriate turnout space where motorists could stop safely. The specially designed plaque would include a "Grizzly Bear and two stars at the top. The background color would be light tan or stucco with chocolate letters and border."[8] Advance signs stating "Historical Landmark Marker - 500 Ft. Ahead" were also ordered that same year.[9]

The marker program ran into problems by 1949. Carpenter wrote to A.E. Henning, chief of the Division of Beaches and Parks, that the stone monuments were no longer being constructed "due to a ruling...that the expenditure of highway funds for this purpose was not kosher. The erection of monuments since that time has been done by historic groups or communities, the plaques for most of them being furnished by the Centennials Commission."[10] Although some difficulties arose as a result of the construction of the stone bases, the Centennials Commission continued its plaque program, and in April 1950, it reported that sixty-three historical landmark plaques either had been placed or were in various stages of preparation.[11]

Other Legacies of the Centennials Celebration

In addition to a permanent marking program for registered historic sites, the chamber organized a 1948-1949 Gold Celebrations Committee to coordinate statewide activities. By August 1945, the committee, led by Park

Commission Chairman Knowland, had developed an outline of regional and county committees to assist in the planning. The working team was to include county supervisors, various historical societies and patriotic groups, travel and tourist interests, county fair representatives, chambers of commerce, and state automobile associations.[12]

Two months later, letters carrying Knowland's signature reached the chairs of county committees which had been appointed by their supervisors. These committees included representatives from area historical societies and were assisted by local chambers. Knowland's letter specified five activities: Historic Landmarks, Fairs-Fiestas, Special Events, Athletic Events, and Winter Sports. The chamber proposed that regional committees adopt four objectives for their History and Landmarks Program: a study of each county and region's gold rush history to assist in developing local fairs, celebrations, and historic tours; the registration of historical landmarks with accompanying literature and permanent markers; the compilation of a comprehensive bibliography of books and monographs by local experts; and the collection and publication of data on public and private historic museums and their holdings.[13]

The California Centennials Commission, appointed by Governor Warren, adopted many of the chamber's proposals. The chairman of the commission was none other than the indomitable Knowland, chair of both the Park Commission and the chamber's Gold Celebrations Committee. These positions not only linked the three organizations, they acknowledged and underscored Knowland's pivotal role in the state's preservation movement during the first half of the twentieth century.

The preparations for the celebrations, which formally began in January 1948 at Marshall Gold Discovery Park with 75,000 persons in attendance, had other lasting effects on the evolution of preservation in California. One of these was the restoration of the town of Columbia.

Public interest in the Mother Lode Country reinvigorated the efforts of those who had supported the restoration of Columbia during the 1930s. In June 1945, they successfully obtained new funding through a measure that appropriated $50,000 on a matching basis. When Governor Warren arrived at Columbia to sign the bill in July, he was greeted by an enthusiastic citizenry dressed in historical garb.

The restoration project moved quickly. Frederick Law Olmsted was hired in December 1945 to survey the proposed historic park. His August 1946 report stated that Columbia's significance was due to "the concentration here within a comparatively limited area of *so many* buildings and other features strikingly representative of the early mining days" and the fact that so few modern changes had intruded upon the town.[14]

Although sufficient matching funds had been raised to enable the Park Commission to begin purchasing property by the time Olmsted submitted his report, it was also clear that Columbia's restoration would require substantial commitments of additional funding. In September 1946, the Park Commission asked the legislature for $100,000 for preservation and $50,000, to be matched by private monies, for land acquisition; in January 1947, the legislature added an additional $50,000 for more land purchases. To facilitate fund raising and planning, the State Park Commission approved the preparation of detailed restoration plans and hired Aubrey Neasham in 1947 to produce them. Neasham's 1948 recommendations for the preservation and reconstruction of Columbia incorporated Olmsted's suggestions and envisioned a great historic park of 170 acres. "Through the establishment of Columbia Historic State Park, and the intelligent creation and execution of a master plan," Neasham stated, "it is hoped that it will be possible to recreate some of the atmosphere of the past." He recommended that "all buildings, yards, walks, and streets should be carefully studied, and returned where possible to a condition where their major structural features approximate their appearance prior to the decline of the town in the 1860's." Neasham concluded that "no other town of the Mother Lode country offers a better opportunity" to re-create the past. "Likewise, no other area offers a greater challenge in the field of historical preservation." Many agreed with Olmsted and Neasham, and by October 1949, some $113,000 had been expended on Columbia.[15]

In December 1945, the State Park Commission engaged Olmsted to examine the feasibility of constructing scenic parkways along the Sacramento and San Joaquin rivers and to suggest "how best to round out the park system."[16] Olmsted completed his second and final survey for the state in 1950 and recommended ways to utilize the $15 million that the Omnibus Park Acquisition Bill of 1945 had allocated for beaches and parks.[17]

Olmsted's report was written during a time when two increasingly vocal and organized interest groups were emerging: those who wanted to expand the park system, and others who wished to curtail its growth. There were additional concerns. The matching fund requirement meant that parks were acquired where funds were available, "rather than entirely where the Commission desired parks." Faced with demands for more parks in the interior than along the coast, the legislature, in 1950, froze all acquisition funds until new inland parks were added. "One of the main reasons for the second Olmsted report was to examine the problem of expansion of the system in the interior."[18]

Olmsted's second survey restated much of what he had said earlier. There were, he stated, two important reasons for establishing parks. They must preserve and protect features of

> widespread (as distinguished from narrowly local) public interest and recreational value because of special *scenic, historic, scientific* or other characteristics that are *mentally* or *spiritually* significant...,

and they must promote the public's enjoyment of these features while preserving them for future generations.[19] Although preservation of historic values could justify the creation of a state park, Olmsted insisted that a park also should provide suitable facilities for outdoor recreation. Widespread need and inadequate facilities were two more reasons for a new state park. He cautioned his readers that his second study would emphasize recreational uses instead of the preservation of areas of scenic value which he emphasized in his 1929 survey.[20]

After admitting his personal unfamiliarity with California history and archaeology, Olmsted made several observations regarding "sites of historic, archaeological, and other specialized scientific interest." He specifically called for "correlation" between historic parks or monuments in the State Park System, officially recognized historic sites, and those sites not recognized by the state. Olmsted hoped that the work of the recently created Historical Landmarks Advisory Committee would at least adjust "the relationship of sites to the park system, with the Commission or its staff carrying on from there."[21]

The response to Olmsted's survey was especially negative among southern Californians who wanted more parks in their area. Some of this negativism dissipated later when the legislature released the frozen acquisition monies. The study not only "successfully served to release the impounded funds," it also "served as a base for acquiring projects recommended in" Olmsted's four reports. By 1965, thirteen of the nineteen areas listed in Olmsted's survey had been completely or partially acquired.[22]

The preservation, protection, and acquisition of areas of recreational and scenic values remained primary concerns of supporters of the State Park System for many years. At the same time, pressures to expand the state's historic preservation program began to increase. The park system, however, would prove capable of meeting the new challenge.

More Preparations for a New Era in Preservation

In 1949, Governor Warren signed S.B. 1280, which authorized the appointment of an Historical Landmarks Advisory Committee to advise the State Park Commission on matters relating to historic sites. This piece of legislation would not be significantly altered for two decades.

Under the new law, the seven gubernatorial appointees were to:

- enumerate all existing landmarks registered by the Department of Natural Resources, by private groups such as the Native Sons and Daughters and historical societies, and by other public agencies;

- continue to survey historic sites which would be sent to the Park Commission for final approval and registration;

- review applications for designation and registration prior to forwarding to the Park Commission;

- recommend criteria for registration 'which shall include but are not limited to military, political, agricultural, educational, economic and cultural events and locations within the State;'

- recommend the type of plaque and descriptive wording prior to marking; and

- recommend historical buildings and landmarks which should be marked.

All recommendations were to be forwarded to the Park Commission. Upon the approval of both the commission and the director of Natural Resources, the historical buildings or landmarks would be entered into a register with an appropriate number and description attached. The law defined landmarks as "historical buildings, sites and places deemed important in the economic, social, political, military and cultural annals of California."[23]

The new legislation also authorized the State Park Commission to obtain markers and directional signs for landmarks upon committee recommendation. The commission was responsible for the repair of all markers and monuments on which plaques were erected.[24]

The governor did not complete his appointments to the new committee until February 1952. By that time, a familiar face reappeared in the

Division of Beaches and Parks. Newton Drury, who retired in 1951 from his post as director of the National Park Service, returned to California. An undergraduate at the University of California at Berkeley with Warren, and intimately acquainted with the State Park System and influential men such as Knowland, Drury was the logical person to be appointed the new division chief.

Drury's reappearance and the long overdue selection of the Historical Landmarks Advisory Committee ended the participation of the State Chamber of Commerce in the landmark registration program. On March 3, 1952, J.E. Carpenter, who was still in charge of the chamber's Historic Landmarks Approval Committee, told James Mussatti, the chamber's general manager, that they had a decision to make. Carpenter was convinced that if the chamber wanted to "remain in the picture," Drury would allow them to participate. In his opinion, the program did "not mean a lot...although it has given the State Chamber a lot of prestige in certain places where we are looked to as being the fountain head for matters historical." He also admitted that the work was time-consuming. Carpenter suggested that if the chamber were to relinquish the program

> we should make up a swell story on what should be done (our only place in the picture so far has been to send out application blanks, pass them along when completed and up to the final registration). However, we have gone far beyond that and have given advice here and there, taken the initiative in listing all of the 50 or so landmarks in Sacramento for instance, when but one has been registered.[25]

In response to Carpenter's final question, "should we step out or piddle along," Mussatti scribbled, "Let's give this activity up!"[26] Carpenter's short note to Drury a few weeks later confirmed that decision.[27]

The creation of the Historical Landmarks Advisory Committee has been attributed to the centennial celebrations. In the Department of Natural Resources' booklet on *Organization and Functions*, published in July 1960, the committee was described as having been "created to take over activities of the California Centennials Commission of 1948-1951 with respect to registering state historical landmarks."[28]

As for other legacies of the centennial celebrations, Carpenter concluded, "I can't say that with the $2,250,000 spent on the Centennials that the State of California has too much to be proud of." [29] His assessment may have been too bleak. Although all preservation-related projects may not have been completed, public interest in the state's heritage had been aroused. The next catalyst would be the return of pathfinders such as Newton Drury and Aubrey Neasham. In the coming decade, they would strive for master planning and professionalism in state preservation, thereby setting the foundation for a new era in historic preservation.

4

Master Planning and Professionalism in State Preservation, 1951-1960

Newton B. Drury's return to California after an absence of more than a decade augured well for historic preservation. Although his primary concern as chief of the Division of Beaches and Parks remained the conservation of natural resources, his determination to acquire as much land as possible for the State Park System benefited historic preservation as well. On his arrival in 1951, there were 104 parks comprising 1,113,269 acres in the park system. When Drury retired in 1959, the system had grown to 160 parks and 1,179,838 acres.[1]

Creation of the History Section

One of Drury's first actions was to reacquaint himself with the division's preservation projects. By the end of October 1951, he received a detailed status report on the registered landmark and plaque program.[2] Before the year was over, he was able to inform the State Park Commission that the State Finance Department had approved two new positions in the 1952-1953 fiscal budget: chief historian and stenographer. These appointments laid the groundwork for the creation of a history section in the division. Drury predicted that "the State will benefit greatly in having technical supervision and co-ordination of this important phase of our State park program."[3]

Drury had broached the idea of a history section to Aubrey Neasham earlier that year. In response to Drury's concern about "preservation and use in the historical areas owned and administered by the State," Neasham agreed that

> the key to the present situation, as you mentioned, would
> be the establishment of a History Section within the Divi-
> sion of Beaches and Parks. Such a unit, headed by a

qualified historian, would function to advise the Chief in acquisition, protection, administration, development, and interpretation among other matters.

Neasham suggested that Drury appoint an acting historian until the appropriate civil service mechanism was established. There was, he felt, a sense of urgency:

> The needs of preservation and use demand immediate attention and action on a statewide scale. The task of acquisition of the most important historical areas in California has been largely completed. It is now timely to disseminate more fully the story of each of these areas through appropriate exhibits, publications, guided tours, talks, and other interpretive devices.

As Neasham envisioned it, the program possibilities of the new section would be virtually unlimited, for "it would function primarily on a staff and planning basis and not an administrative unit."[4]

The History Section began operations with the arrival of Neasham in January 1953. Neasham had been serving as regional historian for the National Park Service in Santa Fe, New Mexico until war broke out. When he returned in 1946, he was assigned to Region IV, which included California. It was from the Park Service's San Francisco office that Drury enticed Neasham to join the California park system.[5]

News of the new post in the State Park System began to reach various segments of the historical community by mid-1952. Arthur Woodward of the Los Angeles County Museum of Natural History wrote to Neasham inquiring about the rumor that he had heard through the "grapevine that a new position was coming in the State set-up, relative to historic sites and monuments." Woodward wanted to apply for it, but had "a suspicion that it is one that had been set up with someone else in mind...." He voiced reluctance "to trespass on anyone's toes" and asked Neasham for more information.[6] Neasham encouraged him and others to apply and take the examination because "it would provide for proper future expansion of the historical work of the State to have as many as possible qualify."[7]

Neasham himself clearly intended to take the required examination which was finally held on September 20, 1952. In late November, he was informed that he had placed first on the eligibility list and was formally offered the position at $481 a month.[8] In a welcoming note to Neasham, Drury wrote: "We are surely happy in the circumstances that have made it possible for the Division of Beaches and Parks to have your guidance and help in building up a sound historical program."[9]

As it evolved under Neasham, the History Section served as staff advisers to Drury on matters relating to the preservation and interpretation of historical values and of park units. Their major responsibility was to formulate "an effective program...for the preservation, development, interpretation, and public use and appreciation of California's outstanding spots."[10] As supervisor of the section, the park historian was the division chief's adviser "in all matters connected with human history" in the park system. Thus, claimed Neasham, the historian was to be "the 'spark plug' for the history program...vitally concerned with all phases" of a project. The historian was also to serve as "the 'watchdog' of the State in matters of preservation of historic sites and buildings...."[11]

Toward the end of the 1950s, Neasham began to see another role for his section. Three memos proposing a drastic reorganization of the entire division appeared in the fall of 1958.[12] Neasham suggested to Drury that the division be renamed to reflect the three basic units into which the park system was divided: the Division of Parks, Historic Sites, and Recreation. His justification was that by 1988, the park system would have 300 park units to administer along with a corresponding increase in demand for specialized personnel to handle new responsibilities. The three bureaus would be divided into 100 scenic, 50 historic, and 150 recreational units; each would be supervised by a deputy chief. The division would establish twelve district offices: four for scenic parks, two for historic sites, and six for recreational areas. Each district would consist of twenty-five parks. Six key cities would contain all the district offices: Eureka, Redding, San Francisco, Fresno, Los Angeles, and San Bernardino. In addition, there would be regional offices where the services of administrators and staff could be pooled to cover more than one district.[13]

Drury was clearly unenthusiastic about the proposal, which he apparently viewed as not politically viable. In October, he wrote to Neasham simply promising to discuss it "soon."[14] Others were equally ambivalent. L.S. Hollinger, chief administrative officer for Los Angeles County, told Neasham that because the scheme was too expensive and duplicative, he was "throwing cold water on it."[15] A few individuals, however, were more receptive. Robert Power wrote that the plan "made good reading and good sense."[16]

Those in positions of influence did not share Neasham's ideas. When the Resources Agency was reorganized in 1961, the Department of Natural Resources became the Department of Parks and Recreation. The Division of Beaches and Parks was not renamed, and it became one of three divisions reporting to the department director. Despite Neasham's efforts, historic sites remained of secondary importance.

Master Plans and Acquisition Programs

During the 1950s, considerable interest was generated in the State Park System primarily because off-shore oil royalty funds became available in 1954. Impounded since 1947, the total amount designated for the Division of Beaches and Parks exceeded $31 million.[17] The legislature issued several reports during the 1950s, and the division conducted its own studies for the acquisition of new properties. Historic preservation projects became the direct beneficiaries of the royalty funds. Although recreational areas remained the division's highest priority, new historic parks were added and existing monuments were enlarged. Drury did not neglect the historical component of the State Park System.

The acquisition and development of new parks did not, unfortunately, result in a corresponding expansion of interpretive services such as museums, small exhibits, and technical support staff. In 1952, matters improved when Hubert O. Jenkins was hired to make recommendations for the expansion of the park system's interpretive program.[18] Although he was not asked to comment on historical monuments in the park system, Jenkins managed to briefly mention the fact that "some historical monuments also have natural history features and many natural parks have a wealth of human history as interesting to the visitor as the natural history." While he "was not suggesting that there is now any attempt to separate the interests of the historical monuments and parks," he felt it "necessary to look ahead and constantly build an integrated service of such a nature that any future pressure by special interests to separate these interests can have little effect.[19] Jenkins made a variety of useful recommendations, but in the final analysis, the interpretation of history continued to be lightly regarded, and his report "scarcely made a ripple in the program of the Division or its effect on the interest of the Department of Finance and other budgetary control people toward emphasis on this program."[20]

The fear of special interest pressure that Jenkins referred to was a very real one among park service personnel. During the 1930s, for example, an incoming governor replaced several well-respected state park administrators. Later, in 1957, a Senate concurrent resolution directed the Park Commission to allow grazing in two state parks despite commission opposition.[21]

The Jenkins report emphasized the need for long-range planning, an activity which Drury supported. One such master plan was the five-year program for the California State Park System that the Park Commission approved in December 1952 and which included specific reference to historic preservation projects. Out of an annual average budget of $2,270,000 for development purposes, Drury proposed that $400,000 be allocated for the restoration of historic buildings. In five years, that would total $2 million for restoration and more than $11 million for all development efforts. The justification for restoration of historic structures was clearly enunciated:

> The historic buildings owned by the State of California are priceless remains of the outstanding economic, political, and social activities of our past. Properly preserved and restored and interpreted, they will be a source of inspiration, education, and enjoyment to all who visit them.[22]

Columbia headed the list of projects that Drury presented to the Park Commission. The report also recommended museums in selected parks and interpretive exhibit centers "at key historical areas throughout the State to tell the story of our past." These would include "the Gold Discovery site at Coloma, Monterey, La Purisima Mission, Donner, Columbia, Shasta, Los Angeles Plaza, Will Rogers, Sutter's Fort, Fort Ross, Sonoma, Fort Tejon, and the State Indian Museum" in Sacramento.[23]

From the very beginning of his tenure, Drury demonstrated his concern for the park system's historical units. By the time he told Park Commission Chairman Knowland of his hopes that the History Section would provide a "comprehensive analysis of the historic areas of our System," he had already ordered an analysis of the categories and geographical locations of all historic properties.[24] Carroll Hall, curator at Sutter's Fort, provided Drury with an itemized list of thirty-two monuments that were classified into the following eras:

- Early Exploration (1540-1602): no monuments
- Spanish Colonization (1769-1822): 2 monuments
- Russian Colonization (1812-1840): 1 monument
- Mexican Period (1822-1848): 13 monuments/parks
- Westward Migration (1844-): 1 park
- Gold Rush (1848-1855): 7 monuments/parks
- Early Statehood (1849-1855): 1 monument
- Miscellaneous: 7 monuments/parks[25]

Drury told Hall that he "liked very much your breakdown of the categories of our State Historical areas" and that "you have given convincing reasons for your classification of each." He added that the analysis as to the geographical distribution and the distribution by historical periods is very interesting and shows at once some of the gaps in our 'system' that ought ultimately to be filled. A review of the historic site markers would help in this regard, as would also a comprehensive survey of the State, both by investigation and by correspondence.[26]

These comments to Hall became the goals that Drury's successors would strive to achieve.

Thus, by the time Neasham assumed his responsibilities as the division's first historian, the foundation had been laid for the compilation and acceptance of what emerged in November 1953 as the division's "Master Program of Acquisition" for historical areas. A year later, the Park Commission, which was showing "an especial interest in historical projects" under Knowland's leadership, approved the plan in principle.[27] Although a mere five typewritten pages, Neasham's recommendations had a significant impact on the park system's program.

Neasham's master plan presented six thematic periods: Aboriginal, Spanish, Mexican, English, Russian, and American. For each period, he discussed the merits of what was already in the park system and what should be acquired. For example, he urged a complete inventory of Native American sites in the park system and recommended the addition of Cabrillo's landing at Ballast Point in San Diego Harbor, and his burial place at Cuyler's Harbor on San Miguel Island to holdings representing the Spanish period. Neasham believed the acquisition of the Monterey Presidio was of special importance because it was the Spanish capital of California for more than half a century. He did not see a need to acquire more ranchos and believed that the system's emphasis should be on the interpretation of existing properties. Because the Mexican period was particularly well represented, he urged caution "in any expansion of the acquisition program into this period, with the exception of such outstanding historical centers as Monterey, Sonoma, Santa Barbara, and San Diego, where sites and buildings of this period can be considered as parts of key units or zones of preservation."

The Russian period was well covered by Fort Ross, unlike the English era which had no representative example. Although the site of Drake's landing was one possibility, Neasham believed that a suitable memorial could not be erected until the exact place of his disembarkation was determined. He concluded that historic sites of the American period were thematically well distributed and that future additions should consider greater geographic diversity and filling thematic gaps.[28]

Neasham's thematic divisions were validated in 1955 when the Senate Interim Committee on Recreation, State Beaches and Parks published the results of its investigation into matters impacting the park system and the state's recreational activities. This study was one of the responses to Governor Goodwin Knight's veto of the Omnibus Beach and Park Bill in 1955. In a brief discussion of historical monuments, the report reiterated Neasham's six thematic periods and recommended the acquisition of properties that showed historical turning points which could become major tourist attractions. The committee suggested that "places which approach the character of pilgrimage shrines, are the types which should be sought," and cautioned the state against trying to acquire "all adobes, all old buildings, and all historic sites."[29]

Another effect of Governor Knight's actions, which included vetoing several beach and park acquisition bills passed by a legislature eager to dispense accumulated oil royalty monies, was to enable Drury and the Division of Beaches and Parks to avoid the legislature's grab-bag approach to park land acquisition matters. In addition, because the governor's veto message emphasized the need for a comprehensive state park master plan that delineated acquisition priorities, policies, and needs, Drury was able to quickly update the plan that the Park Commission had approved in 1954 and present it once again to the legislature in 1956.[30] The response was shocking. Not only did the governor propose a $35 million budget for state parks which amounted to nearly one-half the master plan's five year estimates, the Assembly also added $9 million, and the Senate increased the figure still further. The grand total was an astonishing $44,852,762.[31]

Drury was ecstatic. He anticipated "a new era" in California's historic preservation and interpretive programs. Neasham predicted:

> As outlined in our Five Year Program, and confirmed by Legislative action, history in California will come into its own. Ours is a program primarily of improving the outstanding historical buildings and sites already within the system. In addition to expansion of boundaries, the improvement of interpretation, including exhibits, will be a major challenge. [32]

It was in this context that Neasham provided Drury with a supplemental list of twenty-eight new projects because "of increased pressures for the establishment of additional buildings and sites in the State Park

System." Neasham believed that this long-range program could be justified if it was "recognized that the historical themes of California—Indian, Spanish, English, Russian, Mexican, and American—shall continue as the basis upon which to build our future preservation program. Properly blended as to quality and quantity, each in its own way adds lustre to the colorful pattern of California's story." Drury agreed with Neasham and approved the new list the next day.[33] Later, these themes would form an integral part of the state's official history plan.

By 1956, Neasham could point to considerable progress toward acquiring historical properties for the park system. Historic adobes in Monterey were added, along with the Weaverville Joss House and Fort Humboldt. The town of Bodie had been saved, and boundary extensions were being contemplated in many areas. Two years later, Neasham still saw his list as "a guide for any future expansion of the historical units of the State Park System." By 1965, eight of the twenty-six sites that Neasham had recommended in 1953 had been acquired, and five properties on his 1956 list of twenty-eight had been added to the park system.[34]

The Park Commission, which used the recommendations as guide-lines for future acquisitions, received the Neasham program favorably. After all, his memos provided the commission with a history program at a time when some commissioners and outside groups expressed concern "that history was comprising a major part of the park system but that areas were being acquired on the basis of expediency and pressures rather than consideration of historical values." Not everyone, it seems, agreed with Neasham's proposals. Some were critical of his organization of historic sites into chronological periods because he failed to provide documented reasons to support his selections. Others "claimed that the selection was based primarily upon political and other pressures rather than historic values."[35]

The pressures that Neasham's detractors were referring to included threats from Los Angeles County officials and special interest groups who demanded more parks in their areas. Many insisted that northern sites, such as the redwoods, were overemphasized in the state park plans which did not objectively analyze statewide recreation needs. The controversy resulting from the disagreement over sites created serious problems for Drury and others who were trying to limit the number of park projects so that they could realistically accomplish their mandated responsibilities with limited funds. In response to these requests for increased spending and more parks in southern California, and to allow time for the preparation of a comprehensive state recreation program, the legislature funded a three-year comprehensive study of the state's recreation needs in 1957. The long-range study was to inventory "existing areas, facilities, and services;" analyze "future needs of the people for recreation and preservation of history and scenery;" determine deficiencies; and recommend which levels of government were responsible for overcoming the deficiencies.[36] The result was the California Public Outdoor Recreation Plan of 1960.[37]

The Outdoor Recreation Plan contained a separate report on "California's History, Routes, and Sites" which emphasized the importance of the preservation of historic sites for their educational and commercial value and as "an index to the pride of California citizens in the achievements of their state." It incorporated the same general chronological and thematic divisions that Neasham had adopted to determine which areas needed immediate attention. Of twenty-eight especially critical sites, ten were Native American properties and nine dated from the Spanish era. Responsibility for the preservation of certain categories of historic sites was assigned to federal and state governments and to local communities. Furthermore, the study recommended that jurisdictional questions should be decided by experts in history, anthropology, and archaeology who "should not be subject to local political influences. Perhaps the members of the board should be appointed by the governor, although this sounds like somewhat of a contradiction." What was to be avoided, if at all possible, was a situation "in which individuals of a community bring pressure upon the legislature to appropriate money to preserve a site which has only local interest. A board of experts with enough authority to get its recommendations seriously considered might save the state from a good deal of misplaced expense." The report also observed: "If preservation of historical sites is considered as a service to the public, the expanding population of California will require a greatly enlarged historical preservation program."[38]

Historian Lawrence Kinnaird and five colleagues from the University of California shared the opinion held by critics that "in recent years the primary basis of approving projects has been to a considerable extent based upon political and emotional pressures, some of which did not consider the historical values of the state." The historians emphasized the need for a "positive" historical sites program and were particularly critical of the state's registered historical landmarks program which they believed did little more than review "landmarks and projects that were recommended to the Commission." They estimated that 25 percent of the landmarks should not have been approved.[39]

It became increasingly clear that it was time for a re-evaluation of the entire historical sites program within the Park System and that it should include

> a definition of the periods of history; location geographically of the impact areas of each period; a classification of evidences that remain for each period; a development of standards for preservation; an inventory of sites; and a firm delineation of the state park responsibilities in relation to agencies of Federal and local government.[40]

The Historical Landmarks Advisory Committee

In February 1952, Governor Earl Warren finally appointed seven citizens to the Historical Landmarks Advisory Committee: Park Commission chair, Joseph R. Knowland; professor of History at Occidental College, Robert Glass Cleland; archivist and historian of the Western Provincial Order of Franciscan Fathers, Rev. Maynard Geiger, O.F.M.; Oakland city librarian, Peter T. Conmy; attorney, Carl Irving Wheat; former grand president of the Native Daughters, Henrietta Toothaker; and administrative secretary of the Save-the-Redwoods League, Aubrey Drury. [41] In preparation for the committee's first meeting in March, J.E. Carpenter, director of the State Chamber of Commerce's Travel and Recreation Department, wrote to Newton Drury to express his support and delight that the chamber would be relieved of its landmark responsibilities: "The Chamber desires to get out of this field of operation and is very happy that the State is ready to function. You know," he continued, "that we shall be happy to cooperate when we can be helpful."[42]

At their first meeting, held in San Francisco at the chamber offices, Drury was elected temporary chairman. He reminded committee members that their purpose

> was to perpetuate the memory of historical spots within the State, for the benefit of all, and especially for the newcomers, whose patriotism it was hoped to stir; and that not only should worthy sites be marked, but they should also be made readily accessible, and facts concerning them be made easily available.[43]

Only three members appeared at the second meeting in June. They appointed Knowland to head a committee to review landmark applications for statewide significance and to place them in the appropriate category by type. Approvals of landmarks would require a majority vote of members in attendance before they were forwarded to the Park Commission. A booklet of registered landmarks was recommended if funding could be found. The first edition of *California Historical Landmarks* was published nearly a decade later and contained 722 landmarks.[44] A request to register the discovery of Francis Drake's Plate of Brass was refused when "Mr. Wheat stated that he was not satisfied that the site desired for registration is authentic." The issue would be discussed at subsequent meetings without resolution.[45]

In January 1953, the committee held its third session in San Francisco. During this two-hour meeting, members approved their first landmark: the Eastern Terminus of the Clay Street Hill Railroad, the world's first cable rail system. Also during this session, they met Aubrey Neasham who served as their professional support staff until his departure from state service in 1960. Neasham reported on all landmark applications and responded to committee requests for additional information and follow-up. When a landmark received committee approval, he reviewed the wording, location, and size of each plaque.[46]

Throughout the 1950s, the meetings of the advisory committee were informal and lasted an average of two hours. A frequent topic of discussion was the need for criteria and standards to evaluate applications. Members agreed that high standards had to be maintained, that complete consideration had to be given each application, and that all landmarks had to "be considered in relation to their cultural and historical value on a statewide basis."[47] Their request for criteria was reiterated in 1958 when members again asked Neasham for more guidelines.[48]

The meeting place and the manner in which the committee conducted its business underscored the informality of the meetings. Often, the committee met during the noon hour at a restaurant, and members voted on landmarks by mail. Despite Neasham's opinion in 1960 that all polls had to be confirmed at a formal meeting before applications were forwarded to the Park Commission and director of Natural Resources, both the commission and the director continued to act on applications as soon as the mail vote was tallied.[49]

Early in its existence, the committee asked that all state-owned historical monuments be registered as historical landmarks and be given an appropriate number.[50] Since that time, although not all designated monuments have been registered, an attempt has been made to comply with the committee's request.

The committee seemed reluctant to become involved in matters outside its direct purview. For example, in December 1953, Neasham presented them with "a written draft of the Master Program of Acquisition of State Historical Areas" which he had submitted to Drury the previous month. The committee took no formal action on his proposal. Neasham also distributed a written outline of a proposed California Trust for Historical Preservation. Division Chief Drury, who was present to discuss the proposal, called "attention to the advantages of such a Trust...[which] he felt...would be of great help in the preservation of historical structures in California." Again, the minutes record that no action was taken.[51]

Passing of an Era

The inauguration of Edmund G. Brown in January 1959 marked the beginning of the end of an era. In that same year, Newton Drury reached the mandatory retirement age of seventy. He did not disappear from the scene completely, however. When his brother Aubrey died in October 1959, Newton replaced him as secretary to the Save-the-Redwoods League until his own death in 1978.

The new state administration changed the membership of the Historical Landmarks Advisory Committee. A completely new group replaced Drury, Knowland, Conmy, and the others. The venerable Knowland declined another four-year term on the State Park Commission, and in March 1960, Will Rogers, Jr., was appointed chairman in his place.

When Aubrey Neasham left in September to become president of Western Heritage Incorporated, still another pioneer preservationist disappeared from state service. Neasham expressed high hopes for his new venture:

> We will be working on a national scale, hoping to help such projects as Old Sacramento. Our theme will be 'Preservation for Use,' which indicates a major step forward in historical preservation. In other words, private effort will cooperate with public effort to assure the preservation of history. Of course, there will have to be a sound economic basis, if private funds are to involved, which means the establishment of period hotels, restaurants, stores, shops, offices, and other compatible activities....[52]

"Western Heritage Incorporated," claimed Neasham, "is the first of its kind in the West."[53]

Neasham had introduced the concept of "preservation for use" earlier. In his commentary on what was happening at El Pueblo de Los Angeles State Historical Monument in 1958, he noted:

> The adjustment of historic structures to modern use is a well-established practice in the United States. There is little need or desirability to return all historic structures to the status of house museums. Their use in the living community as places in which to live or where economic activities can be carried out is well-recognized.[54]

Neasham would apply this adaptive re-use commitment to projects in Old Sacramento.

During the 1950s, both Neasham and Drury grappled with the question of "just how far to go in the matter of antiquing modern reconstruction works." Drury called it a "puzzler" that raised the very important question of objectives in the preservation and interpretation of historic monuments:

> Granted that original workmanship should not be re-touched with modern paints, we do have another problem in the case of modern reconstructions. If part of our job is to give the visitor an experience of being returned to another age, with historic structures as they were during that era, we can go much further in such things as painting than we could if the building is original, with original workmanship, including painting, still in existence.

In the end, Drury conceded that the architect and historian would have to resolve the dilemma: "to return it as it would be had it continued its existence, going through all the phases of aging, which implies antiquing, or to return it as the original occupants had it at the time of their occupancy."[55] Succeeding directors and historians would debate this same issue.

In summarizing a decade's progress in 1960, the Division of Beaches and Parks could proudly report that as of December 1959, there were thirty-five state historic parks and monuments in the system. They were defined as "units established to preserve structures, objects or locations of historical interest from representative eras in California history." Development efforts would focus on "restoration and reconstruction where necessary, research and archeological trenching, and interpretation by signs, aids, booklets and occasionally museums." Interestingly, the report also noted that "being largely the work of man, historic sites may permit certain agricultural, mercantile, or other commercial activity usually prohibited in scenic parks provided those activities are properly regulated, are a part of the history of the individual area and enhance the historic scene."[56]

The History Section's accomplishments were also briefly chronicled. Neasham had investigated Old Sacramento, the Mother Lode, Sutter's Fort, Fort Humboldt and Fort Point, a possible Drake landing site, the Hugo Reid Adobe, the Anza-Borrego Desert State Park, Fremont's Gabilan Camp, Fort Bidwell, the Santa Barbara Presidio, William B. Ide Adobe, and the Petaluma Adobe. Preparations had been made for museum exhibits at Marshall Gold Discovery Park, the Donner and Morro Bay museums, and the Pacific Building in Monterey. By December 1959, the state's registered historical landmarks had risen from Number 500 in 1953 to Number 719.[57]

The legacy left by Knowland, Drury, and Neasham would be felt in the decade ahead. The division would acquire more trained specialists and experts to administer, develop, and interpret the state's historic properties. Long-range acquisition and development plans had been adopted, and an official advisory body was in place to review applications for historic landmark designation. These accomplishments were only the beginning of greater changes to come during the 1960s in California's park system and in the preservation movement.

History Preservation Programs in the State, 1960-1966

The early sixties witnessed the emergence of what President Lyndon B. Johnson described as "the new conservation movement." Aimed at halting the rapid deterioration of America's environment because of urban blight, uncontrolled waste production, and unplanned development, this new consciousness fostered an alliance between conservationists and environmentalists seeking to protect and salvage what remained of the nation's diminishing resources.[1] An unanticipated beneficiary of this new thrust was the movement to preserve the nation's historic resources.

In California, the return of the Democratic Party to power in 1959, with the election of Governor Edmund G. "Pat" Brown and a majority in the State Legislature, had a direct impact on the state's preservation programs. The Democrats introduced changes that affected both the Division of Beaches and Parks and the Park Commission, which Joseph R. Knowland, father of unsuccessful gubernatorial candidate, U.S. Senator William F. Knowland, still chaired. The commission's responsibilities were reduced to establishing policy for the director of Natural Resources and the division chief. No longer did the Landmarks Advisory Committee report to the commission but was instead advisory to the Department of Natural Resources.[2] And in 1961, the department was replaced by the Resources Agency which now included the Department of Parks and Recreation "so that the agencies concerned with recreation would be separated from those concerned with conservation and the material use of natural resources." The Division of Beaches and Parks, whose chief reported to the director of the Department of Parks and Recreation, was charged with the acquisition, development, and operation of parks, scenic reserves, beaches, recreation, and historic areas of statewide significance.[3]

The new governor demonstrated his interest in the state's recreational facilities early in his administration. Brown was an avid backpacker and very familiar with the State Park System. When he requested "a bold, dynamic and detailed program to meet California's recreational needs on a State level" in 1960, the division produced a report a year later that was a thinly disguised argument for a major park bond issue.[4] The subsequent $150 million State Park and Recreation Bond Act was defeated in June 1962 by less than 175,000 votes.[5]

The near passage of the bond act encouraged its supporters to try again. The Park Commission spearheaded plans for another attempt in November 1964. In July 1963, the governor approved the Cameron-Unruh Beach, Park, Recreational and Historical Facilities Bond Act of 1964 which authorized the ballot measure for the following general election.[6] While bond act advocates began a massive education and public relations campaign, legislators submitted to the department requests for feasibility studies of potential park sites. Only a handful of the 100 proposals that sought a share of the anticipated $150 million windfall were for historic projects: Old Sacramento, Old Town San Diego, Nevada City, sites in Los Angeles County such as the El Pueblo de Los Angeles State Historical Monument, and the Santa Barbara Presidio.[7]

The successful passage of the bond issue by more than 1.5 million votes created pressures to speed up the unwieldy and tortuously slow park acquisition process. The resulting replacement in the Department of Parks and Recreation of the "gentle and likable" Charles DeTurk with the "ambitious" and "decisive" Fred L. Jones in March 1965, as well as other shifts down the chain of command, did not significantly improve matters.[8] In November of the same year, Director Jones reported that the legislature had approved ten projects. Of five new park units, none were historic areas.[9]

In February 1966, Jones informed the legislature that all requested feasibility studies for park acquisitions or expansion under the bond act were completed. Only seven of the fifty sites in the report were historically significant: Malakoff Diggins, Murphy Ranch, Nevada City, Pena Adobe, Santa Barbara Presidio, Walker Pass and Parkway, and Watts Towers. Of the thirty that received positive recommendations, two were historic areas: expansion of the Malakoff Diggins State Historic Park at approximately $780,000, because it was feasible; and the reconstruction-restoration of the Santa Barbara Presidio at an estimated $7 million. The presidio project was approved because the park system lacked a comparable site, it was feasible, and "the interpretation of this phase of California's history is the responsibility of the State." Unfortunately, stated Jones in his letter of transmittal, although many of the proposals were "worthy of inclusion in the State Park

System, they did not place high enough in the rating system and were not recommended for acquisition under the provisions of the State Park Bond Act."[10] As 1966 drew to a close, half of the 1964 bond monies designated for state park acquisitions had been expended on only 10 of the 100 projects originally proposed by the legislature.[11]

A History Program For the Division of Beaches and Parks

In March 1961, the California Legislature approved Assembly Concurrent Resolution No. 25 to study the state's historical resources and formulate a long-range plan to preserve, restore, and interpret the state's historical values and resources. Assemblyman Paul J. Lunardi's resolution observed that the appearance of more than 100 local and regional historical societies during the 1950s had not stemmed the rapid disappearance of the state's rich heritage in the face of highway, dam, and subdivision construction. His arguments supporting the proposal to rebuild, restore, and mark significant and representative sites echoed those of earlier preservationists: such an effort would be invaluable to the education of both youth and newcomer, and would swell the state's economy by enticing thousands of tourists to California.[12]

The resolution's mandates were specific. The Division of Beaches and Parks was to work with groups such as the Conference of California Historical Societies to produce an inventory of marked and unmarked historical resources. The long-range, statewide plan was to include a program for the coordinated preservation of sites that represented California's geographic regions and historical periods, and proposals to encourage public and private acquisition, development, and protection of "authentic historical examples." The plan was to emphasize ways in which historic sites could be put "to uses other than as museums through their use as coffeeshops, restaurants, gift shops, playhouses, headquarters for community nonprofit organizations, and other such uses which would attract visitors, provide revenue to the State and not be incompatible with the historical significance of such buildings."[13] The latter goal of seeking adaptive re-use alternatives underscored a shift in emphasis that was beginning to take hold among California's preservation practitioners.

With $7,500 from the legislature, thirteen people met in Sacramento in January 1962 to begin work on a proposal for a historical resources study under the direction of H.L. Heinze, historical study coordinator for the Division of Beaches and Parks. The Conference of California Historical

Societies sent six representatives, including President Clarence McIntosh. Harold F. Taggart of the Historical Landmarks Advisory Committee and six division personnel also attended. Three recommendations emerged and were subsequently adopted: a Historical Interim Study Advisory Committee of volunteers was appointed to advise the division and produce the proposal, a Historical Information Resource File was established to identify and locate repositories of significant historical material, and pilot studies were undertaken in three counties to determine how best to undertake the survey.[14]

During the six months the advisory committee worked on the proposal, it field-tested a simple inventory form and criteria to determine what was historic. There were eight parts to the list of criteria used to decide if a site or structure was of outstanding significance. Geographical importance would be based on the site being "the first, last, only, largest, smallest site of a type in an area." It also had to exemplify the "broad aspects" of "cultural, political, economic, military, or social history of the local area, state, or nation." The site could be associated with an important person or event, or represent a distinguished architectural style, construction, or master builder, designer, or architect. Archaeological sites would be accepted if they either produced important scientific information or could be "reasonably expected" to do so in the future. Integrity of material, location, workmanship, and association was crucial. The Historical Resources Advisory Committee, which would be appointed by the governor to produce the long-range plan, would have the authority to determine the cutoff dates for historical events.[15]

The proposal that was finally submitted in June 1962 also provided the methodology by which the inventory could be accomplished. The emphasis was on "grass roots assistance" which the interim committee believed would "be the keystone of the success of this entire program."[16] For a projected cost of $180,725, and within a span of twenty-seven months, a master plan for "the preservation, restoration and interpretation of the historical resources and values of California" could be produced that would include: recommendations of outstanding sites and structures representing the six periods mentioned by the resolution (Indian, Spanish, English, Russian, Mexican, and American); specific suggestions when additional research and studies were deemed necessary; a plan for the preservation of local properties of importance; a policy whereby historical and/or archaeological investigations would be mandated prior to new park development; and, finally, a prioritized listing of outstanding physical remains for preservation, restoration, or reconstruction, and "by whom."[17]

The letter of transmittal that accompanied the proposal summarized the division's hopes for the project. Signed by both Department Director DeTurk and Division Chief Edward Dolder, it pointed out to Assembly Speaker Jesse Unruh that while the division lacked funds to implement the proposal, the recommendations "should be vigorously pursued. It is hoped that appropriate legislative action will be forthcoming so that a program for the preservation, restoration, and interpretation of California's historical resources will become a reality."[18]

Although the proposal for a historical resources study never materialized because of lack of funding, it had a direct impact on the division's history program. In 1966, DeTurk, who had returned to his earlier post as division chief, observed that despite all attempts to obtain support for the study, "the result of the recommendation was negative." We cannot, he said, "'squeeze blood out of a turnip.'" The advisory committee's effort, however, had not been in vain. In the same letter, DeTurk noted that "we were therefore required to make our own inventory and recommendations for the acquisition, restoration, interpretation of buildings considered needed to implement current and proposed park units."[19] In later years, portions of the proposed criteria for significance would be incorporated into the registered landmark criteria, and the emphasis on volunteer support for statewide inventories would become standard procedure. Equally important was the fact that the study's procedures, methods, criteria, and policies were comparable to those in the 1966 federal preservation law. The result was to enable "California to assess problems relating to the national and statewide inventory in advance and to embark upon the National Register program with a minimum of delay."[20]

The inventory and recommendations that DeTurk referred to were the result of plans laid in 1964. In March, Hugo Fisher, head of the Resources Agency, asked then Department Director DeTurk to begin exploring future plans for historic preservation by the state. It was Fisher's opinion that "the major subject areas of historical preservation interest in the State of California should be identified, and a coherent program outlined for consolidating and meeting these interests." He identified several locations that he thought appropriate for certain themes: Los Angeles and San Diego for the Mexican era, San Francisco for the transportation era, Columbia for the gold rush period, and Sacramento for the state's political history. He also suggested the establishment of a "general military museum" and recommended that the state work "with the Federal government to examine all of our historic spots in the various major fields to assure that jointly we are covering all we should of the various elements of California history."[21]

By this time, Allen Welts had succeeded Jack Dyson as division historian.[22] Coming to the department in 1957 from a career in commercial advertising and museum design and display, Welts produced the report in 1965 that outlined the division's history program and "plans for future preservation and interpretation of California's historic heritage."[23]

Welts used Aubrey Neasham's historic eras to categorize the park system's historic units in numerically descending order according to their major and secondary emphases in all or some of the following periods: Indian, English, Spanish, Russian, Mexican, and American. He also prioritized their individual needs according to acquisition, development, restoration-reconstruction, and interpretation requirements. Of those programs already in existence, Columbia headed his statewide list. El Pueblo de Los Angeles and Fort Ross were second and third in importance; La Purisima Mission was number eleven; and the Santa Barbara Presidio was nineteen. Of thirty-five recommended projects, the most pressing was a new site for the State Indian Museum; the development of Old Sacramento was second. The Historical Interim Study Advisory Committee had suggested such a priority list earlier.[24]

Although Welts did not clarify the basis for his prioritizations, correspondence from DeTurk sheds some light on the criteria used for the proposed history program. In explaining the division's inventory procedures, DeTurk identified factors affecting recommendations for the acquisition, restoration, and interpretation of buildings necessary for the implementation of current and proposed park units. The availability of fiscal support was a critical consideration, as were standards that ensured that the site was of statewide importance and on a scale worthy of inclusion, had unified and logical boundaries, and enhanced what remained of the state's heritage. The division chief lamented that

> a Historical Resources Study and legislative support might well have disclosed other areas which we could have embarked on. Unfortunately authorization for study of these has not been forthcoming; and we have had to list our recommendations for historical preservation, restoration, and interpretation of those sites felt to most represent need.[25]

A month after Welts submitted his report, Hugo Fisher requested the establishment of a Long Range Planning Task Force, which was created in July 1965. As division historian, Welts' part-time assignment was to analyze the need for historic preservation, inventory areas meeting the need, appraise deficiencies in the park system, and recommend priorities for acquisition and development. The study came to an abrupt end in October, some 20 percent short of completion. Welts expressed his regret and hope "that re-evaluation of need may yet disclose the wisdom of continuing the program to the material benefit of the State."[26]

Others in the division apparently shared this concern, and Welts' 1965 study was revised in April 1966. In September of that year, the division produced a twenty-year historical acquisition and restoration program for the park system.[27] The intent of both reports was identical: to outline "a program for preservation and interpretation of California's historic heritage" and to "serve as a guideline for all functions of the Department requiring such information in future studies."[28] There were, however, several differences between the reports. The twenty-year proposal did not contain prioritized lists "because such ratings change when detailed study of the State Park program shows imbalances."[29] Instead, Director Fred L. Jones proposed to chair a History Program Advisory Committee "to evaluate and schedule the historic units for action."[30] The proposal also included projected costs for salaried personnel, property acquisition, and development and research for each of the historic parks. Like Welts, the proposal adopted Neasham's historic periods. Itemized estimates were also provided for each park unit. Based on five-year increments, the grand total for the project was $81,958,880.[31]

At only eight sites listed in the proposal were costs for acquisition greater than estimated development costs: William B. Ide Adobe State Historical Monument, Casa Grande in Sonoma State Historic Park, Sutter's Fort, Fort Funston, Junipero Serra Landing Place in the Monterey State Historical Monuments, Carpenteria State Beach, Los Encinos State Historical Monument, and the Santa Barbara Presidio. Development monies would be used for the interpretation and restoration of existing buildings, as well as for the construction of museums and concessions. Included in this latter category were parking and zoning needs, landscaping, and archaeological studies where required. Angel Island State Park's exhibits required an estimated $1 million. In contrast, exhibits at Columbia and Old Sacramento were to be allocated $500,000; others were budgeted for considerably less. The concept of using these historical units as house museums dominated most of the development objectives. If existing structures were not appropriate, construction of new sites was usually recommended.[32]

The division's twenty-year program identified eighty-one park units as having historical values. In 1966, historic parks and monuments were defined as

> examples of cultural advance characteristic of human life and behavior. These examples expand our knowledge of architecture, religion, government, recreation, agriculture, exploration, industry, education, war and other elements of the past significant to California's heritage.[33]

It was a broader perception than that offered in the Park Commission's 1964 policy statement: "historical units should consist of areas established primarily to preserve objects of historical interest, and places commemorating important persons or historic events."[34]

Fred L. Jones, who anticipated chairing the advisory committee despite Governor Brown's defeat by Ronald Reagan, planned to send the proposal to the legislature for approval.[35] Unfortunately for Jones and Welts, the newly elected Reagan administration established its own history program, and the twenty-year plan did not materialize.

Other Preservation and Restoration Activities in the Division of Beaches and Parks

A growing interest in the preservation and protection of existing historical resources within the division's jurisdiction accompanied attempts to formulate a coherent history program for the Division of Beaches and Parks. In January 1964, the division's Interpretive Services Section produced a specific list of "Interpretive Guidelines for Historical Restoration" for the state's forty-one historical monuments and parks. Apparently, this was the first compilation of its kind and was necessitated by the "increase in number of these monuments and the scope of their activity in projecting the history of California to the public...."[36] The guidelines also were a response to Herbert Heinze's 1962 historical resources study which underscored "the urgent need for guidelines required in doing historical restoration." The guidelines were described as "a tool for those engaged in planning, preservation, development, operation and acquisition of historic sites in California."[37]

This new report, written by historian Welts and Interpretive Services Supervisor John H. Michael, once again used Neasham's thematic divisions of California history. It observed that the public, educational institutions, and even legislators were aware of the irrecoverable destruction of the state's cultural resources "by time, the mercenary, the vandal and waste." At the same time, the division had grown more cognizant of the importance of its own history program: "Where a choice of early parks was once predicated on public camp use and recreation, a broader viewpoint is now being taken, and the historical monument and archeological site has begun to assume its rightful place in the activity scale. We are especially thankful for this."[38]

This optimism was due in part to Interpretive Service's belief that "officers of the Division of Beaches and Parks are behind our efforts to preserve, protect, and develop examples of California's historical heritage." It was encouraged further by the creation of Historian I, II, and III classifications which, while unfilled as of January 1964, would in the future provide the park system with needed specialists. The anticipated effect on the history program was "a rise in efficiency."[39]

A month after these guidelines were issued, the division's Task Force on Reorganization submitted its findings and recommendations to Deputy Chief Earl P. Hanson. This analysis of existing staff and programs recognized the low priority given to the park system's interpretive programs in the past and stated that in the opinion of the task force, "Interpretive Services must be given an important role in our organization." The report observed that only one of the 110 staffed and state-operated units in the park system had a permanently assigned historian on board. The Monterey monuments had the only field historian in the system; Robert Reese is still on station. Of a permanent field staff of twenty-seven state historical guides, seventeen were at Hearst San Simeon State Historical Monument. The twenty-three state historical monuments and parks were served by only four curators, one of whom was Jack Dyson. Recommendations for regional historians, reclassification of positions, reassignments, training programs, and additional positions were not approved.[40]

The actual restoration of historic structures under its jurisdiction was another source of concern for the Division of Beaches and Parks. For example, Deputy Chief Hanson pointed out to the Office of Architecture and Construction the need to provide adequate research before the actual development and restoration of a structure. In a letter to DeTurk, he observed that the division's limited staffing precluded the necessary architectural, historical, and archaeological background work before they requested funds and submitted construction proposals. The problem was worsened by the shortage of experts in the Office of Architecture and Construction "to do this research, and as a result, many projects proceed on a hit or miss basis." Hanson concurred with Orvel Johnson of the Office of Architecture and Construction that his division needed additional personnel to conduct the necessary preliminary studies. "Once an inaccurate restoration has been made," Hanson explained, "it is difficult if not impossible to repair the error." He believed that "in restoration work, reliance should not be placed on data compiled by untrained or inexperienced persons nor should architectural, historical or archeological research be assigned to nonprofessional people. We should," he said, "be in a position where we can prove the authenticity of our work. In many instances this has not been true of our program to date."[41]

Later that same year, the division's senior architect, Robert F. Uhte, developed guidelines for the preservation of historic buildings upon the request of Elmer Aldrich, the division's preservation planner. In his transmittal memo, Uhte stated that the report was the product of "the techniques and principles established by the National Trust for Historic Preservation, the National Park Service Policies and Procedures for Historic Restoration, and the best thinking of this unit."[42]

Uhte's report noted that as part of its responsibility to acquire, administer, protect, and develop historic sites, the Department of Parks and Recreation could continue to use or adapt to new uses outstanding examples of architectural styles, including structures lacking historic association. Uhte stated:

> Varying architectural styles which contribute to the beauty and character of an area with historic monuments could be collectively protected as an old historic district; economic feasibility, quality of architectural styles and associated historic dates should be weighed collectively against the sum of individual buildings.

He urged the department to "conserve the cultural or historical environmental setting" in its acquisition and preservation programs and recommended that potential acquisitions be evaluated on archaeological, aesthetic, educational, and social values. "General understanding rather than scholarship," he said, "should guide administrative personnel in communicating to the public areas of major historic heritage." Uhte also suggested several general considerations: scale, cost, suitability for restoration or reconstruction, accessibility to the public, and definable property boundaries. Finally, he provided an "Outline of California Architecture" which began with five historic periods that did not correspond to those advocated by the division's historians:

> The Mission Period, 1800-1840
> The Hacienda Period, 1840-1850
> The Gold Rush Period, 1850-1860
> The Transition Period, 1860-1900
> The Contemporary Period, 1900-

Each contained architectural styles that depicted "the various building features native to California and expressive of its history."[43]

Ten months later, Uhte submitted revised guidelines which omitted his outlines of historic and architectural characteristics and which focused instead on summarizing division considerations for the acquisition, preservation, and restoration of historic structures. This section was an almost verbatim reproduction of a letter that he had written nearly a year earlier to a Sacramento resident.[44]

Uhte emphasized two widely accepted dicta within the division:

- 'It is better to preserve than to repair, better to repair than to restore, better to restore than to reconstruct'; and

- 'It may be better to retain genuine old work of several periods rather than to arbitrarily restore the whole by new work to a single period.'

To be preserved, historic buildings also should be the best examples of an historical type, significant because of their associations with an event or person, or "part of an important historical scene." In the interests of a balanced park system, said Uhte, the division makes every effort to include historic sites and monuments, carry on its preservation and restoration activities, and develop facilities for camping, boating, and picnicking for the public's enjoyment.[45]

Thus, on the eve of the 1966 general elections that influenced the direction of historic preservation in the next decade, the division had articulated its policies, objectives, and hopes for the future. Acting Chief Hanson described other significant changes that had occurred in the division. When the legislature first authorized the Division of Beaches and Parks in 1927, it had nine park units. By September 1966, the number increased to more than 183 state parks, historic parks and monuments, reserves, and recreation areas; 31 of these were historic parks and monuments. Of the division's more than $23 million fiscal 1966-1967 budget, 30 percent was budgeted for historical projects. Hanson's headquarters staff now included two historians, and there were 813 registered California Historical Landmarks.[46]

The Historical Landmarks Advisory Committee

Responsibility for the registered landmarks program meant that the Division of Beaches and Parks had to provide staff support to the Historical Landmarks Advisory Committee which reviewed all applications before forwarding them to the director of the Department of Parks and Recreation. Although the committee was an advisory body whose members served at the governor's pleasure, it managed to influence the division's historic preservation efforts.

The minutes of the Historical Landmarks Advisory Committee show an increase in activity after Governor Brown appointed an entirely new body. The committee met only once in 1959, but thereafter generally gathered at least four times a year.[47] Until the inauguration of Ronald Reagan in 1967, attorney and Native Sons President Richard F. McCarthy chaired the committee.

The committee took several actions that determined the future direction of historic preservation. For example, criteria for the registration of historical landmarks were approved in September 1961 when the committee agreed to the draft suggested by member Martin B. Ridge and staff historian, Jack R. Dyson. The criteria were discussed, edited, and formally adopted at the committee's December meeting and were subsequently approved by the State Park Commission. Although the standards were modified in later years, what was adopted in 1961 remains essentially unchanged: Historic sites must be of lasting statewide significance, such as "the first, last, only, largest, smallest site of a type in an *area*." Should a site be important because of an individual, the emphasis shall be on achievements of a statewide and lasting significance rather than the site of birth or death. Finally, the site must be readily accessible to the public and be maintained as a historical landmark.[48]

The "Statement of Policy for State Historical Landmark Registration" also included an evaluation procedure. Each request would be reviewed "in informal discussion at meetings of the Committee." Applicants were responsible for background investigations and submitting recommendations for the committee's consideration. The committee would then make its recommendations to the Park Commission which, in turn, would forward approved applications to the director of the Department of Parks and Recreation. The policy statement warned that the committee would "apply the policy strictly and consistently in order that the registration of state historical landmarks will not become meaningless."[49] There were, however, several exceptions to this policy.

According to the records kept by Sandra J. Elder, who served the committee as recording secretary, the director approved seven landmark applications during these years without the committee's approval: No. 761, Mission Inn in April 1961; No. 765, Temple Israel Cemetery in August 1961; No. 769, Birthplace of Archie Stevenot in December 1961; No. 773, Old Harmony Borax Works in August 1962; No. 774, Searles Lake Borax Discovery in August 1962; No. 785, Santa Catarina in March 1963; and No. 801, Reuel Colt Gridley Monument in January 1965. Of these, Director DeTurk signed five. Elder recalled,

> of the seven, the committee agreed with No. 773, Old Harmony; No. 774, Searles Lake; and No. 785, Santa Catarina. The reason these three were registered by the director was because there was some rush in getting a plaque dedication going and they would not have been able to meet their dedication date if they had waited for the applications to be heard by the committee...so the director approved them ahead of time. They were reconfirmed by the committee because they would have met the criteria. The other four would not have met the criteria and were not recommended by the committee."[50]

The most controversial of the landmark applications was the Reuel Colt Gridley Monument.

The Reuel Colt Gridley Monument application, like the request for Temple Israel Cemetery, was tabled in July 1961 until "a criteria is [sic] established whereby these and other applications may be evaluated." The committee unanimously denied the Reuel Colt Gridley proposal again in September 1961 because "it did not comply with the criteria established for official registration."[51] As DeTurk explained to the Governor's Office: "It was felt that the episode described in the request for registration was not of statewide significance...." Although DeTurk was not hopeful that the committee would reverse its decision, he added that should a sponsoring group reapply for registration, the committee would "be pleased to take it under study for the third time."[52]

The Stockton Rural Cemetery Association, the original applicant, was determined to get its plaque. At its request, San Joaquin County Senator

Alan Short introduced a resolution in April 1964. Short wrote to the association and suggested that they reapply. He promised to "do all possible to get this matter straightened out."[53] The association followed Short's recommendation in December with the observation that "in the register of numbered landmarks, graves of lesser importance historically, and much further removed from the criteria, have been numbered since our applications." DeTurk was informed that Short's resolution had been approved in April and that he was expected to "please handle" the matter.[54]

DeTurk then wrote to Hugo Fisher, administrator of resources, that the committee found the application did "not comply with the total criteria established for registration of State Historical Landmarks, which has been adhered to for the last three to four years since the date of the establishment of the criteria." He informed his superior that he had spoken to Senator Short about the matter and "since the final determination concerning this matter must be made by the Director, I intend to recommend to [the committee] that this matter be reconsidered."[55] A month later, DeTurk told the association's secretary that the committee would not recommend the monument. "However," he added, "I am exercising my prerogative as Director...by approving your application for registration...." DeTurk was clearly mindful of Senator Short's personal interest in the matter and sent him a copy of the letter in which he expressed hope that his approval of the application would "straighten out any misunderstanding."[56]

John Michael, supervisor of the Interpretive Services Section, informed the committee of DeTurk's decision at their March 1965 meeting.[57] The folder in the Office of Historic Preservation, where the landmark documents are currently filed, bears a red-bordered label which reads:

> This application was not subject to Committee action but was registered by the Director of the Department under the authority granted by Section 5020 of the Public Resources Code.[58]

The label carries the initials of John Michael.

Other issues of concern to the committee were the number of plaques approved and the wording on each plaque. Approval of a landmark application did not automatically include the granting of a bronze plaque. Applicants, however, usually requested a plaque when they submitted their forms, and "in most cases these are parallel actions completed simultaneously." The sponsors of the application provided the base for the state-furnished plaque.[59]

When Michael suggested to the committee in December 1960 that too many plaques were being approved, the committee agreed to be "stricter" in the future.[60] The matter was raised again a year later when Gertrude Harriman, chair of the Park Commission's Policy Committee, informed the committee of the commission's fear that the importance of the landmark program was being diminished because too many plaques were being allocated. The committee responded by asking the division staff to provide criteria for granting plaques and procedures for having the plaque design copyrighted. [61] Michael's March 1962 report noted the staff's consensus that it was "impracticable to have a criteria for the allocation of plaques" which "should be a prerogative of the Committee." Instead of trying to copyright the plaque, he suggested changing the Public Resources Code to make unauthorized use of official plaques a misdemeanor.[62]

For several years, the application process and plaque wording did not reflect the 1959 shift in the committee's accountability from the Park Commission to the director. Finally, in 1965, Michael requested eliminating outdated procedures as well as a new credit line on the plaque because the commission "no longer has any responsibility in this matter."[63] Although there is no official response to Michael's memo in the records, the plaques soon began to carry the name of the Department of Parks and Recreation, not the State Park Commission, as the cooperating agency representing the state.

The strict application of the landmark criteria and the desire to keep plaque allocations to a reasonable number prompted the committee to seek other ways to recognize local historical sites and to placate unhappy applicants. The matter was discussed several times and was raised again in September 1964 when the committee again expressed its belief than an appropriate sign might be erected to direct the public to a local point of historical interest. The division would keep all records of such signs, and the staff was directed to send copies of the minutes of the meeting to specified legislators and organizations to encourage them to take action.[64]

In addition to these discussions, committee member Ridge had already personally contacted Assemblyman James R. Mills, chairman of the Committee on Rules, in April 1964. A year later, Mills told Ridge that he was aware of the division's acceptance of Ridge's recommendation for "two categories of historical significance, the marker and the point of interest." Mills, who came from San Diego as did Ridge, agreed that the committee should raise the marker and that the Highway Department should place appropriate signs to designate points of historical interest. He promised to sponsor legislation "for a standard 'Hallmark' highway sign for historic sites which will implement your request."[65]

A month later, Ridge informed Michael that Mills had introduced A.B. 2166, and asked that Committee Chairman Richard McCarthy or Michael testify at the hearings. An optimistic Ridge wrote: "since we have wanted this and since I gather that Mills and Governor Brown are again on working terms, I hope the measure will pass."[66] The bill proposed to amend the Public Resources Code to allow the committee to review applications for points of historical interest and to recommend sites that "qualified for a sign indicating 'Point of Historical Interest' and appropriate directional signs." The signs would be erected and maintained by the Department of Public Works on state highways or by local authorities on streets under their jurisdiction. Local groups were permitted to erect their own markers at a registered point of interest.[67] The bill was approved in June 1965. The Historical Landmarks Advisory Committee now had responsibility for two programs: the registered historical landmarks and the points of historical interest.

Implementation of its new mandate was next on the committee's agenda. In December 1965, Michael submitted a progress report which proposed that each county board of supervisors be asked to appoint a local historical landmarks advisory group to identify points of interest in their areas. These selections would then be presented to the supervisors for their review. Approved sites would be forwarded to the committee for consideration and numbering. Selection criteria would be developed by the division staff. The committee endorsed Michael's suggestions and sent them to the director for his approval. The division staff also was asked to negotiate with the Division of Highways for an appropriate sign.[68]

By mid-January 1966, a letter to county supervisors had been drafted for the director's signature. It contained the program criteria which the committee had agreed to in December: Sites should be significant to the area's social, cultural, economic, political, religious, or military history. Individuals should be honored for their achievements in one of the aforementioned fields of history. All applications must be accompanied by appropriate documentation.[69] In January, Michael reported to the committee that the Division of Highways was beginning to develop "a unique and individualistic sign and color scheme" for the program.[70]

At the committee's March 1966 meeting, Michael formally reported that the letters to the county supervisors had been distributed and that the highway division had designed an enamel sign with tan lettering on a background of dark brown.[71] In April, the committee confirmed, in writing, its acceptance of the design.[72]

In addition to soothing local constituents, the Point of Historical Interest program had another objective. As Committee Chairman McCarthy explained to Ileana Welch, then executive secretary to the Cultural Heritage Board of Los Angeles: The Point program was the best way to obtain a comprehensive historic survey to implement the historical resources study recommended in 1962. McCarthy seemed hopeful that, although it would take years to complete the county investigations, the final survey would become the basis "from which preservation plans may be formulated." He anticipated that when the survey was concluded, "evaluation of those sites participating for funds under provisions of the National Historic Preservation Act can be made."[73]

Unfortunately, the program failed to generate the anticipated enthusiasm or material for the historic survey. "The response has been something less than overwhelming," wrote Michael in 1968 to the chairs of boards of supervisors to request that they appoint a county Historical Landmarks Advisory Committee of competent historians to assist supervisors in determining local sites of historical importance. The Point program was clearly not a local priority, for Michael received only twenty-three responses.[74] The anticipated statewide survey of historic sites would have to be undertaken through a different mechanism.

The committee's activities did not go unappreciated. In the fall of 1965, Deputy Chief Hanson informed Fred L. Jones, the new department director, that the Commission on California State Government Organization described the Historical Landmarks Advisory Committee as "'an example of the effective use of appointive bodies in state government....Its recommendations are based on information it hears and evaluates as a body of citizens appointed on the basis of their special qualifications.'"[75]

By 1966, California's historical landmark programs were firmly in place. During the next decade, the committee's mandate would be expanded and its status would be upgraded. Unfortunately, although its overall influence increased, the committee's official role remained strictly advisory to the parks director and the state preservation officer.

Other State Agencies Involved in History Preservation

In addition to the Department of Parks and Recreation, the Department of Education and the State Archives have sometimes been identified as being involved in history preservation.[76] Their concept of preservation, however, does not include the actual protection of historic properties and sites, but focuses instead on the teaching of California history, curriculum matters, and the preservation of documents.

In this context, the role of the Department of Education was very limited. The 1973 State Archaeological, Historical, and Paleontological Task Force report observed that "there has never been a program for a compilation, analysis, and evaluation of all historical information available about California." Furthermore, California history was taught only at the fourth grade level in the state's schools, although the Education Code permitted it to be offered at all grade levels. The task force noted that prospective teachers were not required to take courses in California history and government to obtain a teaching credential even though "it is required that California teachers give instruction in California history." Therefore, concluded the task force:

> it would seem that the institutions that train California's teachers should be obligated to provide those teachers with the knowledge needed to carry out their legally mandated responsibilities and to inspire interest in history in their students.[77]

The California Heritage Preservation Commission, which was originally formed in 1963 to prepare "a plan for the restoration, preservation and display in the State Capitol of the historic documents of the State of California on deposit with the Secretary of State," promoted the interests of the State Archives. In 1965, its duties were expanded "to provide that plans should be made for the exhibit of archival documents 'elsewhere in the State of California,' as well as in the State Capitol."[78]

Unfortunately, although all three agencies cooperate with each other "in history, research, and to a degree in preservation," coordination among them has proven unwieldy and difficult "since they are administratively separate entities." [79] The absence of a comprehensive statewide policy for preservation compounded this problem. This dilemma also confronted those seeking to protect the state's archaeological resources.

Preservation of the State's Archaeological Resources: A Small Beginning

Before 1966, the movement to preserve California's cultural heritage did not encompass a similar effort to protect the state's archaeological resources. The rich and diverse Native American cultures dating back 10,000 years were virtually ignored by preservationists who saw little of value in the remains of abandoned villages, ceremonial places, burial grounds, and Indian art.[1] Other contributing factors included the lack of large and extensive varieties of ceramic ware, and the absence of highly visible architectural traditions of stone, adobe, and earth found elsewhere in the United States.[2]

These opinions were shared by archaeologist Clement W. Meighan who compared the status of archaeology in California with the rest of the nation in a report submitted to the Division of Beaches and Parks in 1960. California, he wrote, differed in two important respects:

> First, California shows a general simplicity of archaeological sites due to the fact that the California Indians did not construct stone buildings, large mounds, and similar remains found in other regions. It is relatively rare for California sites to have visible surface remains likely to be of interest to casual visitors. A second factor of note is the small size of most archaeological remains within the state. Often they occupy only a small fraction of an area; except for some locations in the desert, the largest archaeological site is not much more than eight or ten acres in extent.[3]

The result was widespread despoilment of the state's archaeological resources. Meighan observed that "the rapid population growth in California, with its attendant construction activities of roads, reservoirs, and advancing suburbs, has led to a rapid destruction of areas of historical and archaeological interest." He estimated that two sites were being lost per day.[4] Part of Meighan's concern came from his belief that only a fraction of the 10,000 known Native American sites had been studied. Of those recorded, there was little information beyond their locations.[5]

The disinterest and disregard for the preservation of California's prehistoric resources was but one example of how Americans have long viewed their past. History texts often began with the arrival of Europeans to the New World, and the protection of America's heritage focused on those sites and structures identified with Europeans. The exclusion of Native American cultures, as well as the contributions of other minorities, from the preservation mainstream further perpetuated this distorted perception of the past.[6] This attitude notwithstanding, a foundation was slowly being laid for the protection of what remained of California's rapidly diminishing archaeological resources.

The Federal Program

Until the beginning of large-scale dam and highway construction in the mid-twentieth century, concern for archaeological resources at the federal level was minimal. It is true that the nation's first preservation law, the Antiquities Act of 1906, allowed the president to declare a site or structure a national monument and gave the secretaries of Agriculture, Interior, and War authority to issue rules and regulations regarding historic or prehistoric sites and objects of antiquity on federal property. It is a fact, however, that many of the provisions "have become standard practice only since about 1970."[7]

Another pre-World War II law that had a direct impact on archaeology was the Historic Sites Act of 1935. It set the scene for the emergence of the Interagency Archeological Salvage Program after the end of the war. Through its direct involvement in the program, the National Park Service moved into archaeological research outside the national parks.[8]

When World War II ended and a massive dam construction program began anew, a group of archaeologists who feared the destruction of nonrecoverable resources formed the Committee for the Recovery of Archaeological Remains. They served as liaisons among the National Park Service, the U.S. Army Corps of Engineers, and the Bureau of Reclamation. What emerged was the Interagency Archeological Salvage Program in 1945, with the National Park Service acting as the primary coordinating federal agency.[9]

The Interagency Archeological Salvage Program was responsible for two projects during the late 1940s and 1950s. In the first, the Smithsonian Institution, with funds from the National Park Service, initiated the River

Basin Surveys to "carry out archeological explorations and excavations in sites threatened with inundation behind the numerous large dams" being constructed in the Missouri River basin by the Corps of Engineers and the Bureau of Reclamation. The concept of salvage archaeology was further validated in 1960 with the passage of the Reservoir Salvage Act. This law authorized the Secretary of the Interior to provide for the recovery and preservation of data of "exceptional historical or archaeological significance" in proposed dam or reservoir construction sites.[10]

These early river basin salvage programs left another legacy in addition to legitimizing salvage archaeology as the primary means to preserve archaeological resources. Unlike the mandate of the Historic Sites Act of 1935, which "stresses permanent, physical preservation of historic things because of their intrinsic importance," the river basin salvage approach "accepts the premise that historic properties must be sacrificed to progress and attempts to obtain and preserve information about these resources before they are destroyed." This difference in approach has created sharp tensions among preservationists.[11]

The second interagency project allowed the Smithsonian to respond to problems caused by dam construction outside the Missouri River basin. In California, for example, funds from the river basin surveys were funneled into the agency's Pacific Coast Division. One of the results was a modest five-page report in May 1949 by then graduate student David A. Frederickson entitled "Appraisal of the Archeological Resources of New Melones Reservoir, Calaveras and Tuolumne Counties, California." Frederickson's conclusion that "nothing of paleontological interest was discovered in the surveyed tract" and his recommendation "that no further archeological activities be carried out in the New Melones Reservoir area as the results of the survey do not warrant it" would be cited numerous times in a later decade when the project would become the object of a major controversy.[12]

Another federal agency that had a direct impact on California's archaeological resources was the Federal Highway Administration. The Federal Aid Highway Act of 1956, subsequent modifications by agency memoranda, and the Department of Transportation Act of 1966 provided federal assistance for archaeological salvage programs. The 1966 legislation was particularly significant because it contained "one of the strongest historic preservation provisions of any law." Section 4(f) stated that

> the Secretary [of Transportation] shall not approve any program or project which requires the use of any land from

a...historic site unless (1) there is no feasible and prudent alternative to the use of such land, and (2) such program includes all possible planning to minimize harm to such...historic site resulting from such use.[13]

In general, aside from the activities of the National Park Service, little was done at the federal level to protect archaeological resources in California or elsewhere. The explanation for this was clear: "Prior to 1966 the primary responsibility for actions pertaining to cultural resources associated with federal programs was delegated by legislation to the Secretary of the Interior and through him to the National Park Service."[14] Those agencies concerned with federal properties had few, if any, archaeologists on their staffs before 1966. The Bureau of Land Management, for example, which administers one-fifth of the nation's land had one archaeologist in 1966. The U.S. Forest Service, too, had only one archaeologist in 1966, and the Corps of Engineers added its first professional in 1970.[15]

All this changed dramatically after 1966 and the passage of legislation such as the National Historic Preservation Act (1966) and the National Environmental Policy Act (1969), the signing of Executive Order 11593 (1971), and the enactment of the Archaeological and Historic Preservation Act (1974). Responsibility for resource protection would be shifted to agencies having actual control over the resources.[16] Archaeologists would become an integral part of the planning process and recommend alternatives for protection other than salvage.[17]

Efforts at the State Level

In California, several steps were taken to protect the state's archaeological resources. These included legislative action, programs developed by the State Division of Highways and the Division of Beaches and Parks, and investigations conducted by the state's academic institutions.

The State Archaeological, Historical, and Paleontological Task Force briefly summarized existing legislation concerning archaeology. This legislation included additions to the State Public Resources Code and the California Administrative Code.[18]

In 1965, a section on "Archaeological, Paleontological, and Historical Sites" was added to the Public Resources Code. Its major achievement was to provide some protection of sites on public lands from willful disturbance or destruction by making such actions a misdemeanor. In addition, state agencies could now submit construction plans to the

Department of Parks and Recreation "prior to the commencement of construction of any major public works project on any state lands."[19] Once the plans were received, the department "may conduct an archaeological site survey" to determine if the area contained archaeological, paleontological, or historic features.[20] The department's recommendations were to be forwarded to the appropriate agency which then "may undertake such surveys, excavations or other operations...as it deems necessary to preserve or record" whatever features may exist on the land.[21] Unfortunately, the law's effectiveness was seriously impaired by the permissive wording of the statutes and by the provision which prohibited any delay of state construction projects: "No archaeological program conducted by the Department of Parks and Recreation shall impair, impede, or delay any state construction project."[22]

Other attempts were made to prevent the destruction of the state's archaeological resources. For example, the California Administrative Code stated that "no person shall remove, injure, disfigure, deface, or destroy any object of paleontological, archaeological, or historical interest or value."[23]

Interestingly, another section permitted the director of the Department of Parks and Recreation to "remove, treat, disturb, or destroy plants or animals or geological, historical, archaeological or paleontological materials" in the best interests of the park system by granting the appropriate permits.[24] Earlier, in 1939, the Penal Code made it a misdemeanor to willfully injure, disfigure, deface, or destroy objects of historical or archaeological significance, whether on public or private property.[25]

The state legislature also expressed concern for California's archaeological resources, and in 1963 asked all state agencies to

> co-operate in current efforts by state and private agencies by reporting all archaeological discoveries of Indian culture in this State to the Division of Beaches and Parks of the Department of Parks and Recreation, and, when feasible and consistent with the reasonable exercise of powers of such state agencies, to preserve such findings.[26]

With the exception of the proviso in the 1939 Penal Code, the aforementioned directives were not only permissive, they did not apply to private lands and private property owners who could legally destroy sites and remains on their property. There were, of course, other factors leading to the demolition of archaeological resources: public ignorance of existing prohibitions, inadequate enforcement personnel, and the "lack of a systematic state-sponsored heritage management program."[27]

Despite these shortcomings in existing legislation, the State Division of Highways and the Division of Beaches and Parks sought to implement their respective mandates and fulfill their responsibilities to the best of their capabilities.

During these decades, there was little controversy surrounding the archaeological salvage program developed by the State Division of Highways, known today as Caltrans. Their program emerged after the passage of the 1956 Federal Aid Highway Act which, with other legislation, allowed the U.S. Department of Transportation to use "its own funds for the purpose of salvaging or protecting archeological resources."[28]

One of the first in the nation to develop a highway salvage program, Caltrans began its effort on March 6, 1957, when the State Highway Engineer sent a letter of understanding to the chief of the Division of Beaches and Parks. Caltrans agreed to provide proposed highway construction information to Beaches and Parks. If it was determined that archaeological remains would be disturbed by a project, Beaches and Parks would survey the proposed route, identify the sites, and provide estimates for salvage operations. The results would be reported to and reviewed by Caltrans and the Archaeological Salvage Committee. If approved, Caltrans would pay excavation and salvage costs and provide project designs and maps. Beaches and Parks would then contract out the project to a qualified academic institution, archaeological society, or occasionally to an in-house crew.[29]

There were, however, several problems with the funding process for salvage archaeology. For example, monies were available only for the actual excavation and salvage within the construction area. Nothing could be allocated for preliminary site surveys which were needed to determine costs. Thus, because of a shortage of personnel, the Division of Beaches and Parks had to depend on volunteers to conduct these surveys. The volunteers frequently came from the state's universities and colleges and from archaeological societies nearest to the proposed project. The response of these volunteer investigators ranged from "gratifying" to "poor," according to state archaeologist Francis Riddell, who said the best came from the Northern California Archaeological Society at Redding and from the Archaeological Survey at the University of California, Los Angeles. These two groups, who were among the first participants, quickly became part of an informal network of twelve regional offices.[30]

Another difficulty was the lack of funds for "the removal, cleaning, repairing, cataloging, and study of specimens" after removal "from the right-of-way of the project area," and for the preparation and publication of a report.[31]

These restrictions did not preclude Caltrans from funding salvage archaeology. Between 1959 and 1963, for only $6,000 to $13,000 a year, thirteen significant sites were investigated.[32] After 1963, funding rose dramatically. For example, in 1964, the agency contracted for four projects totaling $51,500. That figure increased in 1965 to $78,660 for six projects, and in 1966 to $100,850 for four projects. The most expensive project was Old Sacramento in 1966 at a cost of $43,000.[33]

It should be emphasized that the reports that resulted from the above contracts were neither "directly funded by Caltrans, particularly those investigations conducted before 1975," nor was any report required of the contractors. Many studies were produced by archaeologists who were not monetarily compensated. Some were able to use their research to meet dissertation and thesis requirements; others were able to fulfill "publish or perish" mandates. Although they were still few in number, "these studies did contribute significant information, especially regarding local and regional chronology and cultural sequence building."[34]

Until the Division of Beaches and Parks appointed its first in-house archaeologist in 1960, archaeological research in the State Park System, although often partially funded by the division, was usually conducted by academicians and graduate students from the University of Southern California, San Francisco State College, and the University of California at Berkeley, Los Angeles, and Santa Barbara. Those sites that were excavated and researched were primarily restoration and reconstruction projects.[35]

The division sponsored excavation projects at several missions during the early years, including those at San Luis Rey, La Purisima, and Sonoma. Historic adobes were carefully studied so the structures could be restored properly.[36] Anglo-American sites were not neglected. In 1946, for example, as the state prepared for its centennial celebrations, Richard K. Beardsley, then a graduate student who would later gain fame as an expert on Japan, reported that he had determined the location of the flag pole at the Monterey Custom House where Commodore Sloat had raised the first American flag on California soil. A similar find was made in 1959 at Fort Humboldt.[37] Support also was given to Adan Treganza's research at Fort Ross in 1953, and later at Sutter's Fort where reconstruction errors were exposed by the Anthropology Department at California State University, Sacramento.[38]

Many of the significant excavations in California between 1945 and 1960 "were initiated not at the suggestion of anthropological archaeologists, but rather by Aubrey Neasham...urging them into activity." Even before he became the division's historian, Neasham had already "helped to establish historical archaeology" in the American Northwest where he had served as regional historian for the National Park Service since the end of World War II.[39]

That there was still much to be done was emphasized by Neasham in 1954:

> we have barely scratched the surface in the field of historic archaeology in California. Many of our State- owned areas, including Sutter's Fort, Columbia, San Juan Bautista, Fort Tejon, Los Angeles Pueblo and Pio Pico Mansion, among others, have not been investigated archaeologically. Such sites as Cabrillo's burial on San Miguel Island, early mission sites, military posts, etc., some of which are in private ownership, have not been touched. So, you see, there is much to be done, as elsewhere in the United States.

Neasham was hopeful that "in California we can carry on a program of documentary and archaeological investigation for all State-owned historical areas prior to development and interpretation." He realized, however, that this would require funding. Neasham felt that this would be forthcoming because "fortunately, the public is becoming conscious of the value of such work, which, we hope, will be reflected in the Legislature."[40] Although such support did not materialize, the division did finally establish a position for a state archaeologist.

In 1960, Francis Riddell, an anthropology student who had worked for the archaeological survey at the University of California, Berkeley, was officially named State Park Archeologist. Riddell had begun his career in the State Park System in 1956 and was working as monument supervisor for the State Indian Museum in Sacramento prior to his appointment.[41] During the sixties, under Riddell's supervision, the division supported more than fifteen projects at Native American, Hispanic, and Anglo-American sites. Although some of the contracts were awarded to local archaeologists, Riddell gave the majority to the Central California Archaeological Foundation which provided graduate students with much needed part-time work and experience.[42]

From 1961 through 1967, Riddell also administered the archaeological program for Caltrans and the Department of Water Resources. Through an interagency agreement, the Department of Water Resources began a joint program of survey and salvage excavation with the Division of Beaches and Parks in 1960. In that year, the legislature expanded the department's mandate in recognition of "the vast damage their overall program in this state would do to the archeological resources."[43] For example, both agencies cooperated on the planning and construction of the California Water Project. Between 1960 and 1967, Riddell's section conducted investigations that were funded by the Department of Water Resources in amounts ranging from $25,000 to $60,000 a year. After 1967, funds were awarded on an individual project basis.[44]

Despite these efforts, many sites were lost. At Oroville, for example, of the 250 sites discovered and recorded, only 9 were tested and only 3 were extensively studied and excavated. By 1973, 149 prehistoric sites in the area had been flooded. There were, however, some successes. For $150,000, the Pioneer Cemetery at Oroville was relocated, and 110 acres were purchased for $65,000 to preserve archaeological values at Perris Reservoir. Between 1967 and 1973, the Department of Parks and Recreation received $114,000 from the Department of Water Resources for individual projects "to the extent requested by the archaeologists making the investigations."[45]

Riddell viewed the Water Resources programs as much more acceptable than those of Caltrans because the department was able to fund "nearly all phases of archeological activities" beginning with the initial exploratory surveys. There was also money for test excavations, laboratory work, and limited publication and administrative costs.[46]

Director Fred Jones, who observed that since the bill was "entirely permissive...the initiative process rests with us," expeditiously handled implementation of the 1965 statutes allowing state agencies to submit construction plans to the Department of Parks and Recreation. It was his understanding that review of the plans would not be automatic but that "submission of plans to the Department of Parks and Recreation would be a matter that would be initiated by us for construction projects in areas we knew or felt to be of Archaeological or Paleontological significance."[47] By the end of October 1965, Jones was able to forward a memo to the Office of Architecture and Construction in the Department of General Services that summarized his department's interpretation of its new responsibilities.[48]

The department viewed the intent of the legislation to be the recording, preservation, and/or salvaging of prehistoric and historic values endangered by state construction projects. State agencies which previously expressed "a willingness to participate in a preservation and salvage program if legislative permission was granted" were now provided that opportunity. Jones anticipated that the modest programs of Caltrans and the Department of Water Resources to "realistically record, sample and preserve aspects of California's past history" prior to destruction could be adopted by the Reclamation Board, Forestry, Fish and Game, and other agencies. Jones emphasized, however, that

> any programs should be so organized and operated that they would not interfere with the construction programs. Also, it must be stressed that recovery is limited to a fraction of the total values located. We feel, therefore, that a healthy program can be established which will be of maximum benefit to the people of California: one of construction and preservation.[49]

Although the permissive nature of the law allowed the Department of Parks and Recreation some flexibility in responding to proposed projects, when it was added to the directive prohibiting construction delays, it severely limited the department's ability to prevent destruction of archaeological resources. A more immediate obstacle was the absence of funding for necessary studies. Meetings between the Division of Beaches and Parks and the Office of Architecture and Construction showed that both agencies were willing to cooperate. What proved unresolvable was a "source of funds for checking out construction sites and to provide sampling from areas established as archaeological, paleontological, and historical sites." [50] These factors precluded the implementation of the law on a statewide basis, and archaeological resources continued to be vulnerable to the vicissitudes of humans and nature.

Archaeological Surveys and Site Records

Anthropologists at the state's public and private universities and colleges frequently provided the expertise needed by state agencies involved in archaeological projects. At first, there was little coordination among the various educational institutions. Instructors planned and conducted their excavations independently of each other and on their own time with the assistance of student volunteers. There was usually little time to construct a proper research design because excavations had to be started and completed shortly before the site was demolished. When there was cooperation, it rarely involved more than two institutions.[51]

The first effective statewide organization was the pioneering effort by the University of California's Archaeological Survey at Berkeley. Begun in

1948, it was directed by Robert F. Heizer.[52] A few years later, a survey office was established on the campus of the University of California at Los Angeles. Riddell reported in 1972 that these two had long been

> the focal point for California archaeology. Their programs were tied closely to student training and development, thus not staffed or oriented to give a wider service in depth to other governmental agencies. Theirs was an acknowledged specialized function which was of immense help to the problems facing California archaeology, but with the limited staff and budget the two survey offices could not meet the demands of the times.

These two centers housed extensive collections of archaeological field notes and manuscripts. Together, they "also produced a greater number of publications dealing with the State's archaeology than any other agency."[53]

Archaeologists have long wrestled with the problem of where to store their records and documents. Before 1957, site records were handled by the survey office at Berkeley. In 1954, records for the area south of the Tehachapis were given to the Los Angeles survey office to update. Meanwhile, the Division of Beaches and Parks developed its own limited set of site records, and when Caltrans began its salvage program in 1957, the division sent copies of its records to approximately eight universities to facilitate the volunteer surveys. At that time, "record keeping was not legally authorized or given funding by the Department of Parks and Recreation."[54] In a 1960 review of the preservation of archaeological remains in California, Clement W. Meighan of the Department of Anthropology at the University of California at Los Angeles noted that together the Berkeley and Los Angeles centers held information on some 10,000 sites. He observed that "the Los Angeles office, while maintaining a somewhat smaller file of site records, contains several hundred records not in the Berkeley files." Furthermore, "many of the individual site records are very fragmentary and include little information beyond the location of archaeological remains."[55]

The other pressing question of who would pay for the analyses and preparation of reports resulting from these archaeological studies remained unanswered during these years. As far as Caltrans and the Federal Highway Administration were concerned, these costs had to be borne by groups doing the archaeological survey and salvage. They required no records and confined all subsidized excavation activities to the highway right-of-way. The federal agency believed "that the recovery of archaeological materials was enough of a burden upon public funds and that research, analysis and report preparation were the responsibility of the scientific community."[56]

That these problems remained unresolved was the point of archaeologist Ernestine S. Elster's suggestions to the newly constituted State
Heritage Task Force in January 1983. Then a member of the California State
Historical Resources Commission, Elster requested the establishment of an
Office of State Archaeology to coordinate archaeological activities and serve
as a clearinghouse, completion of comprehensive excavation reports at the
end of each project, and funds to publish these reports.[57]

Salvage archaeology dominated the archaeological component of
preservation, both in California and across the nation. Unlike historic
preservationists who had a mandate through the National Park Service to
identify, protect, and preserve cultural properties *in situ*, archaeologists had
merely gained the right to extract data from sites on the verge of destruction.
As Thomas King pointed out, these are two very different approaches:

> One stresses permanent, physical preservation of things
> because of their living, intrinsic importance; the other
> accepts the premise that cultural resources must inevita-
> bly be sacrificed to onrushing progress and attempts to get
> and preserve information about those resources before
> they go under.[58]

While advocates of historic preservation sought new strategies beyond the
salvage approach of the Historic American Buildings Survey, archaeologists
continued to practice salvage archaeology throughout the mid-seventies. As
archaeologist King observed: "however much we may declare that we would
really like to preserve everything, deep in our guts most archeologists really
like to dig sites, and salvage, for all its unpleasantness, provides the
opportunity."[59]

7

Private Sector and Local Preservation: New Faces, New Methods

Growing public interest and involvement in preservation activities between 1940 and 1966 were also reflected in the appearance of new faces and new approaches in the public sector and in various local communities. Existing preservation-oriented organizations were joined by other groups being formed to preserve various dimensions of the state's heritage. Elsewhere, cities and counties passed ordinances that created historic districts and landmark commissions to preserve what remained of their historic and architectural environments.

Statewide Groups Preserve the Past

Many of the established statewide organizations that had actively supported preservation in the decades before World War II began to reduce their involvement in the post-war years. This was particularly evident in the decreasing visibility of the Native Sons and Native Daughters by the mid-sixties.

The disengagement of the Native Sons and Daughters was not immediately evident. Encouraged by Joseph Knowland's vigorous leadership, both groups continued to exercise a strong presence until the mid-sixties. For example, the minutes of the Historical Landmarks Advisory Committee demonstrate both groups' continued concern for the destruction of historic sites, the restoration of historic structures, and the registered landmark and plaque program. The presidents of both organizations were appointed regularly to the committee.[1]

It was Knowland's departure from state service that signaled the end of the Native Sons' dominance over private citizens' efforts in preservation projects. Local historian and Native Sons member Albert Shumate acknowledged the pivotal role that Knowland and his contemporaries played: "...the Native Sons of the Golden West, while they mention history a good deal,...are not oriented to history like they were fifty years ago when Joe Knowland and Louis Byington and so many others were prominent in the society." The organization's landmark and history boards began to meet only once or twice a year, and its historical plaque program dwindled. Instead, historical societies and the State of California emerged as the most frequent sponsors of plaques. Shumate observed: "Fifty or sixty years ago there were no really active historical societies, and the Native Sons of the Golden West was sort of the historical society of the state. Now that is not true, and their connection with history to a certain extent is sort of in the past."[2]

Another factor was the decline of the Native Sons as a significant political force. In earlier decades, their membership included most of the leading politicians and citizens of the time. This was no longer true, said Shumate, because "the caliber or type of person is a little bit different, often from the lower middle class. They're a conservation group politically and in their thinking, but they do not have the prominent members that they had at one time." The politicians in the organization were only "nominal members" who attended few if any meetings on a regular basis.[3]

The California Historical Society's interest in landmarks can also be largely attributed to Knowland, who was president (1952-1957) and later chairman of the board (1958-1963). Shumate, who served as trustee from 1958 to 1978, and president in 1962 and 1963, did not disagree that Knowland's interest in landmarks resulted in "a great many plaques and things...being put up...." As to whether or not the society "was a kind of marching and chowder society for a bit,..." Shumate retorted, "at least we were financially sound at that point. There were plaques being put up." He also noted that Knowland's power was displayed during the spectacularly successful centennial celebrations of 1948, 1949, and 1950 when

> he was able to get through the legislature a goodly sum of money, all of which did not happen in 1969 when we had our bicentennial, with our beginnings in San Diego and the discovery of San Francisco Bay. Then the legislature gave very little, if anything. It was very much of a fiasco when compared to the '48, '49, and '50. I think that all is due to Joe Knowland, because Knowland had the power and the interest, which no one had in the '69 bicentennial.[4]

For the most part, the society's preservation activities appear to have been confined to plaque programs and endorsing the preservation of threatened historic structures and sites when these matters were brought to the board's attention. Knowland's departure and the society's shift in fiscal priorities from a balanced budget to deficit financing in the early 1970s contributed to the organization's minimal involvement in preservation-related efforts.[5]

Shumate mentioned another factor that contributed to the society's low profile. He recalled that there were those among the society's leadership such as George Harding who "believed that we should keep out of...preservation in general. As a consequence, the California Heritage Council was really organized by the California Historical Society."[6] Self-designated as "the oldest state-wide historic preservation organization in California...[having] been active in the conservation of significant buildings and sites since 1959," the organization's origins were closely linked to the California Historical Society.[7]

The San Francisco-based California Heritage Council began as a small group under Augustin C. Keane with offices in the society's headquarters on Jackson Street. It experienced several widely publicized setbacks such as the loss of the Allyne House on Gough Street. In recent years, the council has begun to "avoid some of the very controversial things," noted Shumate who was still a board member in 1980. "They go on historic trips once or twice a year. They are not a fighting organization...like the San Francisco Architectural Heritage might be, or the National Trust for Historic Preservation." Shumate attributed the council's declining impact to the formation of the San Francisco Landmarks Preservation Advisory Board and the Foundation for San Francisco's Architectural Heritage. Although the council is not the statewide organization it claims to be, it remains influential in parts of northern California such as the Mother Lode.[8] Like the California Historical Society, the council's real impact is in the power and motivation of its individual members who are frequently preservation activists on other fronts.

Another organization promoting history and historic preservation is the Society of California Pioneers, which was founded in 1850. An exclusive and select group, its members are carefully chosen from those who can document the arrival of their ancestors before January 1, 1850. Once actively supportive of historical matters in the 1940s, the society had shrunk to a small, northern-based group without "an intense interest in history" by the 1960s. Because members qualified by accident of birth, and because their interests were "really in social affairs," honorary member Shumate concluded that historical concerns were only "a minor part of their organization."[9]

In contrast to the other organizations, E Clampus Vitus was born in West Virginia in the mid-nineteenth century. Its members, popularly known as "Clampers," moved to California with the forty-niners. The society was resurrected in 1931 by historian Carl I. Wheat, who expanded its original purpose of providing aid and protection to widows and orphans to include the recognition of historic sites in California and Nevada with markers and monuments. Interestingly, Wheat and many other Clamper stalwarts were and still are members of the California Historical Society.[10] The men cloak their rituals in secrecy and guard the meaning of their order's name. When asked what E Clampus Vitus means, former Noble Grand Humbug James Arbuckle said: "I don't know. And we give our new recruits the same answer."[11]

By 1966, there were twenty-one Clamper chapters; together they had placed 141 plaques. The first of these was not the work of Wheat's Yerba Buena Capitulus Redivivus No. 1, chartered in 1931, but the Platrix Chapter No. 2, which in 1934 marked the site where gold was discovered in the San Gabriel Canyon.[12] Since 1962, the Division of Beaches and Parks has maintained a record of Clamper plaques in its files. H.L. Heinze, then coordinator of the historical study mandated by Assembly Concurrent Resolution No. 25, agreed with Archie Stevenot's suggestion that all Clamper plaques be listed with the division. He recommended that all chapters use the form that was being utilized for the state's site and structure inventories.[13] The forms were subsequently simplified to provide information regarding plaque wording and location as well as some historical data on the site. Stevenot reported to Heinze that the Grand Council voted unanimously "to accept the offer of the California Division of Beaches and Park[s] [sic] to record the plaques dedicated by the Ancient and Honorable Order of E Clampus Vitus."[14]

Aside from their plaque program, however, the Clampers as an organization have had minimal impact on preservation. Shumate, the oldest living Ex-Sublime Noble Grand Humbug, agreed that "they joke and say there's always been a debate whether it was a drinking historical society or a historical drinking society." It is a debate that reflects their stated purpose of "stimulating interest in history and having fun in the process."[15]

In addition to these long-established groups, several new statewide organizations with preservation-related interests began to appear. One of the first was the Conference of California Historical Societies which was originally formed to coordinate a fragmented local historical society movement in the state.[16]

This coalition of historical societies was created in 1954 to serve as a clearinghouse for information and research. Although some viewed the conference as only partially successful because of inadequate funding, the lack of legal authority, and the great diversity of local interests, others such as Shumate perceived it as having been "especially influential...in the smaller county and city historical societies...." In the beginning, there were 50 or 60 members, and by the late 1970s, total membership increased to some 200. The association provided brochures on how to start a society. Symposiums encouraged local amateur historians to exchange ideas and information. These local historians have proven to be the conference's greatest source of strength, for it has continued to survive as a grassroots confederation whose officers are generally not academicians.[17]

Unlike the previous organizations which were concerned with a diverse spectrum of projects and issues, the Committee for El Camino Real, formed in January 1959, was organized for a single purpose. Like its predecessor, the committee sought to ensure that the road known as El Camino Real was properly marked and retained its identification as the Trail of Missions.

Eileen Dismuke, grand president of the Native Daughters of the Golden West from June 1958 to June 1959, learned in 1958 that El Camino Real had been renamed Cabrillo Highway during the 1957 legislative session. When she contacted her local legislator, Senator John J. Hollister, Jr., of Santa Barbara County, she was informed that

> the renaming of the highway was a fluke of the legislature, since the intention had been to name Highway 1, from Las Cruces to San Francisco, Cabrillo Highway, and through a mixup in securing the highway designations [from the Division of Highways] Highway 101 had been renamed from the Mexican Border to San Francisco.[18]

By November 1958, Senator Hollister had prepared draft legislation to "limit the use of the name 'Cabrillo Highway' to those portions of State Sign Route 1 south of San Francisco which do not coincide with U.S. Highway 101."[19] Hollister also told Dismuke that "he would need a strong back-up organization" to help him see the bill through the legislative process. Dismuke then contacted such influential individuals as "the Publisher of our Santa Barbara *News-Press*, who was a native Californian, and a good friend of then Governor Edmund G. Brown."[20] Another supporter was the California Mission Trails Association whose manager, Ralph Buffon, wrote to Senator A.A. Erhart in mid-November to transmit his association's request that he amend his resolution to allow for the elimination of Cabrillo Highway signs from Highway 101.[21] When he wrote to Dismuke a month later, Buffon proposed the creation of a committee to monitor the status of Hollister's proposed draft.[22]

In January 1959, representatives from the Native Sons and Daughters, Daughters of the American Revolution, the California Historical Society, Franciscan orders, county supervisors, and local businesses gathered at Santa Barbara's Carrillo Hotel. In her letter to publisher Thomas M. Storke of the *News-Press*, Dismuke summed up the intentions of the group. Not only were they seeking to remove the designation of Highway 101 as the Cabrillo Highway, they would endeavor to have Highway 101 designated El Camino Real with appropriate signs. Their goal included the placement of mission bells "which once were very evident on Highway 101 before the advent of freeways at strategic ingress and egress points in the location of Old Missions along 'El Camino Real.'"[23] The committee, which was first chaired by Edwin L. Carty, Ventura County supervisor, followed Hollister's bill until it was finally signed by the governor in April 1959.

As for the mission bells, Dismuke recalled that the same legislature that approved the redesignation of Highway 101 also passed San Diego Assemblyman Jack Schrade's bill to return the mission bells to the highway. It was agreed that the state would pay for the standards and would erect the bells, but private sources would have to fund the bells. The Committee for El Camino Real raised money for fifteen years for this specific purpose.[24] When the funds began to diminish in the early 1970s, Dismuke asked Assemblyman Don MacGillivray to write legislation to turn the program over to the state. Assembly Concurrent Resolution 101 was passed in 1974.[25]

Local Zoning Ordinances and Landmark Commissions

During the 1960s, local communities began to express concern for the preservation of their architecturally and historically significant neighborhoods. Through zoning and landmark commission ordinances and surveys of local resources, citizens and government officials in various urban and suburban areas helped to foster a preservation awareness that would later reach beyond their immediate environs.

In California as elsewhere in the United States, city and county governments found an easy and effective preservation tool in zoning, which provides the authority to regulate land under their jurisdiction. It does not require purchase of the property, nor does it demand "the consent of property owners to control uses of historic buildings or sites."[26]

The state legislature gave cities and counties the right to establish historic districts in 1959. The statutes permitted the establishment of historic districts through local ordinances.[27] In general, the historic district ordinances adopted by cities and counties sought to:

- establish special zoning regulations controlling the use and development of a specific area with a high concentration of architecturally or historically significant buildings....

- [create] a volunteer public body to administer the regulations of the historic district....

- prohibit the construction, demolition or modification of any building within the district without approval of the review board....

- require that proposed new buildings be 'compatible' with the architecture characterizing the district....[28]

State Park Historian Allen Welts confirmed the increasingly common use of zoning ordinances to establish architectural control of historic districts in 1966. As he described it, this process created a new area within which a special board could approve or reject plans for construction, repairs, alterations, or demolition, "thereby assuring development in character with neighboring buildings and with the general spirit of the entire historical district." He cited several examples of cities that were using historical zoning. They included Santa Barbara and Los Angeles.[29]

In the mid-fifties, a few vigilant citizens in California kept a close watch on the efforts of other states to enact and implement historic zoning ordinances. Among them were Santa Barbara preservationist Pearl Chase and City Attorney Harry W. Brelsford.

In November 1953, Brelsford wrote to the city's Architectural Board of Review to inform them that there was "a distinct possibility that an ordinance requiring a specified architecture within a specified area may be legally enforced." He was referring to a Louisiana Supreme Court decision upholding a New Orleans architectural control ordinance that "sought to preserve the quaint, distinctive and historical character of the Vieux Carre section" of the city.[30]

Because of this ruling, Brelsford believed that an ordinance might now "be legally valid in Santa Barbara that determines that a section of the city is now characterized by Spanish Colonial architecture and limits all future construction, repairs and repainting to architectural standards of this type."[31] To further document his position, he cited a 1948 opinion of the

Santa Monica City Attorney that both "Santa Barbara and Monterey have sufficiently distinctive and historical types of architectures so that architectural control ordinances would be valid to protect these community assets." Brelsford recommended that the board propose an architectural control ordinance to the city council that exempted single family dwellings and duplexes. The board, he added, should also survey the city to determine the boundaries of this proposed district, describe its historical and architectural characteristics, and "thus fortified, should set up general standards that would require such architecture in the future." He warned that immediate action was imperative, for "if the area mentioned continues to be diluted with obviously different types of architecture, it will soon lose its distinctive nature and there will be no legal basis for an enforceable ordinance."[32]

It was not until the state legislature authorized local governments to establish zoning regulations to protect historic structures in 1959 that the Santa Barbara city council adopted their "El Pueblo Viejo" ordinance. Passed in March 1960, it contained much of the same wording as the state law. The ordinance, which forbade the demolition of any adobe or building "of special historic or aesthetic interest or value" in that area, determined the boundaries of what would become known as "El Pueblo Viejo." All future buildings or alterations would have to be constructed in three architectural styles: California Adobe, Monterey, or Spanish Colonial. Only the Architectural Board of Review could issue permits for demolition or removal of existing structures, and such action was possible only if the structure was declared unsafe. The board also examined and approved all proposed construction or alteration plans.[33]

To carry out the necessary inventory of historic sites and structures and to determine which public and private buildings were of architectural and aesthetic significance, the city created the Santa Barbara Advisory Landmark Committee in May 1960. Consisting of nine mayoral appointees, the committee would also recommend the marking of historic places, advise city officials on the preservation and interpretation of these properties and those within the boundaries of El Pueblo Viejo, and cooperate with other groups to give proper recognition and protection to all of the city's historical landmarks.[34]

The El Pueblo Viejo ordinance had another impact on the evolution of a viable preservation movement in California during the early 1960s. W. Edwin Gledhill, museum director for the Santa Barbara Historical Society, stated in 1961 that the ordinance had demonstrated that many historic structures "that were permanently preserved could be taxed out of their ownership by the high value of the surrounding property." Thus, the historical society, with the assistance of the Conference of California Historical Societies, sponsored Senate Constitutional Amendment No. 12 for placement on the ballot in November 1962.[35] If Proposition 11 had passed, it would have enabled "an Assessor to assess for *particular use* historical buildings which are permanently preserved."[36] Although this attempt to enact "present-use assessment" failed to receive the necessary two-thirds majority vote in 1962, a decade later "a contract form of present-use assessment for historic property" was adopted by the state legislature with the passage of the Mills Act.[37]

Another city that responded to the 1959 addition to the California Government Code was Los Angeles. In 1962, the city passed Ordinance No. 121,971 creating and granting powers to a Cultural Heritage Board "to assist and advise the Municipal Arts Commission of the City of Los Angeles in the preservation of certain historical and cultural monuments."[38]

Architect William Woollett, who called a meeting of concerned citizens in May 1958, laid the groundwork for the ordinance. Woollett had been appointed by the American Institute of Architects (A.I.A.) to chair the Southern California chapter's Committee for the Preservation of Historic Buildings.[39] The national organization authorized him to assist private and public agencies and individuals concerned with historic buildings. To accomplish this in Los Angeles, the A.I.A.'s Southern California chapter formed the committee "to arouse the citizens to the importance of saving her [Los Angeles] past as the redevelopment of residential areas, new roads and new highways increase, and as private dwellings and buildings are torn down in their wake."[40]

In April 1961, a second meeting was convened. Those present included representatives from the Board of Education, Recreation and Parks Department, city council, City Attorney's Office, Planning Commission, Art Commission, Title Insurance and Trust Company, and Building and Safety Department, as well as architects. A draft ordinance prepared by Deputy City Attorney Marcus Crahan, Jr., was discussed at length.[41] In November 1961, Woollett was sent a final draft whose only significant change from previous drafts was "the inclusion of the term 'major alteration,' as it was felt the alteration of an historic building could be as disastrous as demolition." Kenneth Ross, director of the city's Department of Municipal Art, promised to expedite the matter "to make effective the important work which you

[Woollett], Mr. [Raymond] Girvigian and other members of the American Institute of Architects have labored on so unselfishly."[42]

When Mayor Sam Yorty introduced the ordinance a few weeks later, he told the city council:

> The City of Los Angeles has a long and proud tradition. As citizens of this community we should be in a position to share in that tradition through an awareness and an appreciation of the historic sites and examples of earlier architecture which are unique to this area and which, when lost, are irreplaceable.[43]

Woollett, who spoke on behalf of the ordinance in January 1962, reminded city council members that the state legislature had already demonstrated its support for historic preservation through passage of A.C.R. 25 and placement of Proposition 11 on the forthcoming ballot. Like other cities, development projects were destroying Los Angeles' "buildings which date back to the days of the Dons,....her great trees and her many historic sites...." The city, he said, lacked a central office concerned with establishing preservation criteria and recording historic structures "which need to either remain where they are or moved to proper locations." Woollett anticipated that the proposed board would also become a clearinghouse for information on historic landmarks which could prevent their destruction.[44]

On the same day that Woollett testified on behalf of the ordinance, the city council approved it for final drafting. It was formally introduced on April 23, 1962, and passed a week later.

Woollett had great hopes for the new mandate. Although some 50 buildings in the greater Los Angeles area had already been recorded for the Historic American Buildings Survey and an additional 100 were awaiting final approval, hundreds of others had already been demolished. Still more buildings would be replaced by shopping centers, parking lots, and housing developments. Woollett envisioned that the five-member Cultural Heritage Board would halt this "massacre" through the appointment of committees and with the cooperation of the departments of Building and Safety, Planning, and Recreation and Parks. After all, he reasoned, the board could decide what was historically significant, disseminate information on the city's cultural heritage, compile and publish a listing of designated monuments, and temporarily prevent their demolition or alteration by encouraging public or private purchase or preservation. A private fund to acquire or restore threatened structures could be established as well. "This means," Woollett explained, "that by law no building, historic site, or monumental tree, so designated as being 'historic' (by criteria set up in the ordinance) can be so demolished or remodeled without consent of the city prior to public notice, city inspection, and approval."[45]

For nearly two decades, the ordinance remained essentially unchanged. The Municipal Arts Commission, with the approval of the city council, appointed the five-member board. During these early years, the board was able to successfully implement the provision that allowed it to delay the issuance of required permits for demolition or alterations.

The Cultural Heritage Board was required to notify property owners whenever their building or property was named a cultural monument. Although owners could appeal the action, they could not demolish or remove the structure without first notifying the board. To ensure compliance, the board informed the Department of Building and Safety of all their decisions.[46] When told that a proposed project would directly impact a listed property, the board had 15 days within which to object. The issuance of the required permit could then be stopped for up to 360 days, during which time the board had to find alternative solutions.[47]

From 1962 to 1977, the board considered eighteen requests for permits that would have significantly altered designated monuments or sites. In only one instance did it agree to demolition, and this was for the Hyde Park Congregational Church on the grounds that a new church was the only way to satisfy the need for an improved facility on the same land. The Board filed objections to all of the other seventeen applications, asking for time extensions for sixteen. All but one of their requests were granted. The board developed satisfactory plans to preserve sixteen of the seventeen endangered sites. The most frequently mentioned of these was Historic-Cultural Monument No. 1: The Leonis Adobe in Calabasas, which was fully restored and opened to the public in May 1966. It was the city council that denied the board's requests for extensions of time. The Arts Commission never refused the board; nor did it ever overturn a board objection to the issuance of a permit.[48]

By March 1977, the Cultural Heritage Board identified 172 landmarks that met its criteria. During the 1960s, "the board declared an average of 7.8 landmarks per year." From 1971 through June 1977, it "declared an average of 16.6 per year."[49] Although these statistics testified to the achievements of the board, its role could have been stronger if the ordinance had declared that its intent was to improve the city's general and economic welfare. As written in 1962, it stated only that the board would "assist and advise the Municipal Arts Commission of the City of Los Angeles in the preservation of certain historical and cultural monuments."[50]

According to Ileana Welch, the board's coordinator and staff from its inception, the reason for the vague language was twofold. "I'm sure it was written by Marcus Crahan [Jr., deputy city attorney]," she said, "in a vague way because there weren't many precedents to go by....In order to avoid having the City of Los Angeles dealing with lawsuit after lawsuit, they decided to make it vague so it would be a matter of interpretation."[51]

Woollett intended that board actions would promote the city's economic well-being; he had testified to this before the council in January 1962.[52] He also hoped the board would play a major educational role through the distribution of information about the city's heritage to students, citizens, newcomers, and tourists.[53] Unfortunately, budgetary constraints precluded the realization of his hopes.

Historic preservation was never a priority item for the Los Angeles City Council. The underbudgeted Cultural Heritage Board was allocated a staff of two, including a secretary. By 1977, the absence of meaningful city funding along with the board's failure to actively seek outside grant support had resulted in the lack of an architectural and historical survey which could have validated the board's decisions and assisted in its preservation efforts.[54] Budgetary limitations also severely curtailed the board's ability to produce quantities of educational materials, thus restricting "its literature dissemination to those that initiate an inquiry." There was no money to print and mail updated material to the board's 5,000 person mailing list. Furthermore, as of 1977, there was still no "Board participation in Planning Department activities," in part because its involvement was neither required nor requested.[55]

The Los Angeles ordinance illustrates the restraints placed on most city landmark commissions.[56] The Cultural Heritage Board, for example, cannot act to preserve a landmark without prior approval of the city council. It also cannot acquire property, nor can it accumulate or spend public funds without prior approval. Finally, it lacks significant legislative or administrative powers, and acts strictly in an advisory capacity.[57]

In the 1960s, the Los Angeles ordinance was described as a model for others to follow. The Division of Beaches and Parks called the Cultural Heritage Board "a 'blueprint' which all counties and major cities would be wise to consider...." The Los Angeles example was described as "a significant precedent," and counties and large cities were "urged to investigate the possibilities of incorporating similar boards into their governmental bodies."[58] A few years later, division historian Allen Welts recommended the ordinance as a model for those seeking to create a historic zoning ordinance "within which a special board approves or rejects plans for building, repairing, altering or demolishing any structure."[59] Both Ileana Welch and Woollett recall sending copies of the ordinance to many cities, including New York, Chicago, and San Francisco. Welch stated that they were able to "make theirs better than ours" because

> we were able to point out things they should know about what we had already experienced. For instance, we suggested that they might consider some protection for trees which we didn't have here.[60]

During most of the 1960s, the board was "more or less dealing with Motherhood and apple pie," Welch observed. And it was, "there, there, everything is going to be all right. We'll preserve that old building for you." Most of the time, she recalled, "I was dealing with the little old lady who was interested in preserving this adobe structure." But for Los Angeles and other cities, things began to change toward the end of the decade. The passage of the federal preservation legislation in 1966 and the increased popularity of the National Trust for Historic Preservation were two factors that Welch perceived as having the greatest impact on a rise in national awareness of preservation which "brought it out of a closed circle of interests." Her more frequent involvement after 1966 with major developers and law firms in Los Angeles was a portent of future trends for all preservationists.[61] In fact, the board's powers, such as they were, were sharply curtailed in July 1980 when an amendment to the Los Angeles Administrative Code required city council confirmation by a majority vote before a property could be listed as an historical or cultural monument.[62] Welch noted: "In the early years, the board had unilateral approval. It just said 'this is a historical/cultural monument,' and that was it...."[63]

Los Angeles did not authorize special zoning to protect and enhance historic neighborhoods which are "unique and irreplaceable assets to the City" until May 1979, when an ordinance provided for Historic Preservation Overlay Zones and neighborhood historic preservation associations to evaluate all changes, projects, and architectural/historical surveys within the preservation zone, and to make recommendations to the planning commission, Cultural Heritage Board, and city council.[64] It was not until 1983 that the city council and mayor approved Angelino Heights as the city's first such historic preservation zone. In 1985, when a dispute arose over the granting of a permit to stucco a building's wooden exterior and replace windows with new aluminum ones, a newspaper account of the controversy indicated that preservationists had yet to convince the general public of the merits of such an ordinance:

> Special zoning has long been used to protect such historic neighborhoods as Georgetown in Washington and the French Quarter in New Orleans. But, in the go-go real estate atmosphere of Los Angeles, a so-called Historic Preservation Overlay Zone (HPOZ) still seems radical.[65]

In Sacramento, other than the Sutter's Fort restoration project and isolated cries of dismay when an old mansion or commercial structure was demolished, there was no significant preservation movement until the 1950s. Among the many reasons for the indifference were the lack of a tourist industry based on the city's heritage, a dearth of outstanding structures at a time when preservationists were interested primarily in the best examples of the past, the location of older buildings in the poorer sections of town, and, most important, the conspicuous absence of an active preservation constituency. Few were concerned in these early years because "the loss of old buildings was piecemeal and unalarming, and change was slow enough to be comfortable." However, when urban renewal and freeway construction programs threatened dramatic changes in the cityscape, preservation-minded individuals moved "to save pieces of Sacramento's past."[66]

When the West End of Sacramento's Old City was designated a prime redevelopment project, Councilman Edgar Sayre convinced the city council to create the nine-member Sacramento Historical Landmarks Commission. According to the 1953 ordinance, the commission could promote preservation by acquiring historic sites and landmarks as gifts or through direct purchase. It could also accept contributions to mark designated landmarks on behalf of the city. Together with the Sacramento *Bee*, the commission sought to preserve the historic structures in Old Sacramento. Jointly, they redefined and expanded the meaning of preservation in Sacramento to include not only specific buildings but entire streetscapes, to mean commercial as well as museum usages, and thus to become profit-generating and therefore economically viable.[67]

The growing interest in Old Sacramento engendered by redevelopment plans was evident in a 1957 legislative study to identify preservable historic sites and structures. The study, made by the Division of Beaches and Parks, revealed "a concentration of principal and secondary sites and buildings of historical interest in the area bounded by Front, 3rd, I and Capitol Avenue."[68] Of the city's thirty-one registered landmarks, seventeen fell within this area. The study also identified other architecturally significant structures which, if properly restored and utilized, could "add interest and charm as well as profit and cultural values" to the project. The division recommended the creation of "an historical zone of preservation" with strict architectural and traffic controls. Total restoration and reconstruction costs were estimated in excess of $2.6 million.[69]

In 1958, the city's landmarks commission suggested several strategies to implement the division's recommendations. By that time, however, an intense debate had arisen over the proposed construction of Interstate 5 through the part of town containing the area's oldest remaining commercial structures. The commission stood firmly in opposition to a freeway in "the waterfront area bounded by the river, Capitol Avenue, 3rd and I Streets."[70]

The city council established a historic district in Old Sacramento in May 1960. Like district ordinances elsewhere, the Sacramento version prohibited the alteration or demolition of exteriors without prior approval of the planning commission and its advisers, the landmarks commission.[71] The result was similar to what had happened at Sutter's Fort: both were frozen in time.[72]

During the early sixties, a variety of entrepreneurs led by the *Bee*, public-spirited citizens, and several local, state, and federal agencies became involved in Old Sacramento. In 1962, the Sacramento Redevelopment Agency was appointed the project coordinator. The agency began its planning activities after consultation with the National Park Service, the Federal Bureau of Public Roads, the State Division of Highways, the Division of Beaches and Parks, the city landmark commission, and the National Trust.[73]

Consultants were hired in 1963 "to prepare a plan...which would reflect the atmosphere, character, architecture, enterprise and color of the early gold mining period." The objective was "to provide for the development of a self-sustaining community achieved through a maximum of private investment."[74] These objectives were repeated a year later in a report by the Division of Beaches and Parks on the feasibility of creating a State Historic Park at Old Sacramento. Although the division agreed with the consultants' objective, it sharply disagreed with their recommendation that the state's responsibility "be limited to the development of scattered museums." Instead, the division proposed to develop and administer house museums and to "lease structures to concessionaires for activities that would be compatible to the historic scene."[75] Thus, the division wanted to assume responsibility for nine acres or 20 percent of the total project area in Old Sacramento, and the reconstruction of fourteen buildings to reflect the 1849 era. Of these fourteen, 60 percent would be reconstructed at state expense and leased to concessionaires. Other reconstructed or restored properties would serve as museums, exhibit halls, or would provide space for appropriate activities. Included in the park would be eight to twelve state-reconstructed buildings representing the period from 1850 to 1870.[76]

The division's report concurred with the January 1965 recommendation of the State Park Commission that the state acquire Old Sacramento under provisions of the Bond Act of 1964. It also suggested conducting archaeological investigations on properties being demolished for the construction of Interstate 5 and on state lands prior to any reconstruction of the 1849 era.[77] The division's 1966-1967 budget included the first substantial funding for Old Sacramento State Historic Park: $1.2 million.[78]

By the mid-sixties, Old Sacramento began to receive both statewide and national recognition. Numerous newspaper articles were written about the project, and on January 12, 1965, the Old Sacramento Historic District was declared eligible for Registered National Historic Landmark status in accordance with the Historic Sites Act of 1935 and a positive evaluation from the Advisory Board on National Parks, Historic Sites, Buildings and Monuments.[79] At the state level, it became California Historical Landmark No. 812. Old Sacramento was fast becoming what Aubrey Neasham had predicted and hoped for:

> As a model and guide in historical restoration, interpretation, and use, its influence will be exerted throughout the land, thus enabling us to better understand a part of that which made America great.[80]

The Old Sacramento project became a milestone of sorts. William Seline, Executive Director of the Sacramento Housing and Redevelopment Agency, claimed that "Sacramento was the first city in the nation to use tax increment financing." And when the first urban renewal restoration project began in December 1968, a HUD representative could claim that "'the Morse Building renovation is the first historic restoration project in the West to be given funds under the urban renewal program.'"[81]

The state park's component of Old Sacramento did not differ from its other historic parks. The Division of Beaches and Parks treated this new acquisition much like its other park units, freezing structures in time and using them as museums or leasing them for commercial activities. This "velvet rope" and commercial use approach had proven successful elsewhere, and there was no reason to anticipate that the results would be any different in Old Sacramento.[82]

The Sacramento Historical Landmarks Commission concentrated its energies on revitalizing skid row. Although the landmarks commission ignored the remainder of the city's historic residential areas during these years, the City Planning Commission managed to survey many of Sacramento's older homes in 1963. The resulting report, "Old Residential Buildings of Architectural and Historical Significance—Old City," merely listed 254 structures. By 1972, one-third of these properties were no longer standing.[83]

Sacramentans would have to wait until the early 1970s for the emergence of a broadly based and effective preservation movement that recognized that other areas of the city also had historic and architectural merit. It would take a convergence of factors, including city council willingness to modify regulations for historic structures, a growing constituency energized by publications and common cause projects, and finally, in 1975, an ordinance that established a preservation program for the entire city.[84]

Other Local Faces

The early 1960s also witnessed the growing involvement of organizations and individuals not usually associated with preservation in the previous decades. In addition to nativist societies that sought to preserve their past, the activism generated by civil rights and other concerns encouraged service groups to seek new causes. One of these organizations was the Junior League of San Francisco.

In 1962, a handful of San Francisco women began discussions with various local and national organizations to determine what course of action was most appropriate to forestall continued destruction of historic structures in San Francisco, San Mateo, and Marin counties. They were aware that other cities had passed historic district ordinances and established commissions to protect their buildings. The San Francisco league concluded that they had to survey these three counties to determine which structures were most worthy of preservation. The Historic Sites Project and Committee was formed in 1963 to identify architecturally and historically significant buildings constructed before 1920.[85]

To accomplish its mission, the committee sought the assistance of the A.I.A., the California Historical Society, the National Park Service, the Society of Architectural Historians, various city agencies, and local historical societies. It called on some 200 members, who were trained through a series of lectures on research techniques, architectural and local history, and preservation. Each volunteer received a reading list and an information kit. Some members interviewed knowledgeable local residents, while others participated in a visual survey of the three counties. The on-site inspections helped to confirm the existence and actual condition of all buildings identified by research, uncover structures that had been overlooked, and produce file photographs and detailed descriptions of construction materials and architectural styles. The criteria for significance were based on those advocated by the National Trust for Historic Preservation: age, a good example of a particular style, the work of a noteworthy architect or builder, the site of an important event, or association with a famous person. Each structure was then graded by community consultants whose input was included in either the text or appendix of the publication issued by the committee.[86]

In the Preface to the publication, the committee expressed its hope that the survey would "create a new basis for awareness of the West Bay's vast architectural heritage and a desire to retain the best of that architectural past."[87] In fact, the Junior League's effort was so impressive that the San Francisco Landmarks Preservation Advisory Board passed a resolution in September 1969 which stated that "the Board 'does hereby endorse and accept said survey and work of the Junior League as if it had been its own, and for its purposes.'"[88]

In addition to the publicity that the publication received, the Junior League of San Francisco was influential in obtaining the passage of an ordinance that created the Landmarks Preservation Advisory Board in 1967. The board's first president, Albert Shumate, however, recalled a somewhat different beginning. Although the league is convinced that they were the primary force behind the board's creation he said, "there were others that were interested. Certainly, Gus Keane and the California Heritage Council had something to do with its establishment as well as the California Historical Society."[89]

Elsewhere in the state, other organizations and historical societies have marked local landmarks and supported efforts to preserve threatened sites and structures. Despite local successes, their activities have had little visible impact on a statewide level. One such group is the Landmarks

Council of California, also known as the San Francisco Landmarks Council. Formed in 1938 by a handful of women, the Landmarks Council was first led by Mary Duncan Altman, a native of Belfast, Ireland. The organization's first objective was to preserve the city's Yacht Harbor, and they met monthly in different restaurants to discuss their projects. They continued their activities after World War II and joined those supporting the preservation of the Palace of Fine Arts and the Sutro Library. The council also dedicated markers in Union Square in 1958 and at the Saratoga winery of Paul Masson in 1960.[90]

By the time the federal government renewed its role as an active preservation advocate in 1966, local jurisdictions and private groups in California had already begun to dedicate more of their resources and energies to protect what remained in their communities. This was still, however, primarily an era of limited constituencies whose concerns were for house museums and individual landmarks. It would not be until the end of the sixties that the number of local commissions and organizations would increase dramatically. The ranks of the state's preservationists would also swell with new converts who were better equipped than their predecessors and motivated by the strongest incentive of all—profit.

The Federal Presence in California: An Era of Limited Concerns

In 1966, the Special Committee on Historic Preservation of the United States Conference of Mayors published the results of a year-long study which had been funded by the Ford Foundation. *With Heritage So Rich* found that "governmental concern for historic preservation in the United States has been limited at all levels, with some notable exceptions."[1] This conclusion applied to the federal presence in California as well.

The National Park Service

The National Park Service had the greatest share of federal responsibility for preservation. In addition to implementing the Historic American Buildings Survey and the Interagency Archeological Program, the Park Service also conducted the National Survey of Historic Sites and Buildings. The latter, which was also authorized under the provisions of the Historic Sites Act of 1935, was discontinued when World War II broke out.[2]

In 1958, the National Survey was reactivated to fulfill its 1935 mandate to survey "historic and archaeologic sites, buildings, and objects for the purpose of determining which possess exceptional value as commemorating or illustrating the history of the United States."[3] It became part of the park service's MISSION 66 program, a ten-year conservation effort aimed at developing and staffing the park system "to permit their wisest possible use, maximum enjoyment for those who use them, and maximum preservation of the scenic, scientific, and historic resources which give them distinction." MISSION 66 was to be completed by 1966, the fiftieth anniversary of the founding of the National Park Service.[4] It was from the National Survey that the Registered National Historic Landmark program emerged to recognize sites, buildings, and objects of national significance.

To accomplish its objective, the park service created the Advisory Board on National Parks, Historic Sites, Buildings, and Monuments. An eight-person Consulting Committee with expertise in history, architecture, and archaeology assisted the board by evaluating and recommending sites suggested by other agencies and professionals. Themes or historic periods were selected to ensure that only exceptional sites were chosen. These

> cover all major periods of aboriginal history from the earliest known culture to the American Indian of today, and from the periods of exploration and settlement, through the colonial period, the major wars, westward expansion, to the development of America as a world power.[5]

Criteria were also established. Structures or sites had to be outstanding examples of "the broad cultural, political, economic, military or social history of the Nation" or associated with pre-eminent persons. Buildings that represented exceptional architectural types or construction could be included. Archaeological sites had to have produced or be reasonably expected to produce significant data. All nominations had to possess integrity; in other words, "there should be no doubt as to whether it is the original site or structure, and in the case of a structure, that it represents original materials and workmanship." The "intangible elements of feeling and association" could also be factors for consideration. "As a rule," events, sites, and structures less than fifty years old would not be recommended.[6]

In 1965, California had thirty-five sites that met the criteria. Of these, only seven had not been recognized as State Registered Historical Landmarks.[7] The state also had its share of National Monuments and National Historic Sites. In 1979, for example, there were ninety-two National Monuments in the country, of which eight were in California and had been created before World War II. Of fifty-nine National Historic Sites in 1979, the state could boast two: John Muir (1964) and Fort Point National Historic sites (1970).[8]

Despite what might appear to be an impressive list of achievements during these years, the park service's contributions were limited. Former park service historian John A. Hussey observed that the State Division of Beaches and Parks under Aubrey Neasham's guidance actually "took the initiative in preservation matters in the state, though the Park Service assisted whenever requested to do so." As Hussey explained:

> We operated primarily in the areas where our duties were assigned by law, such as preparing studies and recommen-dations for the transfer of federal surplus properties for historical purposes (Angel Island was the principal one in California that I remember), the enforcement of the Antiq-

uities Act, the survey of archaeological and historical values in reservoir sites, and—later—the review of properties recommended for the National Register.[9]

This should not imply that the National Park Service failed in its responsibilities. Indeed, in addition to maintaining parks and other properties, the park service continued to produce useful guidelines and studies on how to categorize and preserve structures.[10] The service's priorities reflected its belief that historic sites exist to promote patriotism, "reminding us of famous persons and events that have made our American way of life possible. In a time of deep crisis, the survival of our Nation may depend on our knowledge and appreciation of the hardships, sacrifices, and ideals of our forefathers."[11]

One explanation for the minimal federal interest in California was that few preservationists could believe that there was something of value to preserve in the West. When asked about this attitude, former park service director Horace M. Albright responded that because of the West's late start, beginning in the mid-nineteenth century, "we just haven't anything like the amount of history that they have in the eastern states."[12]

The National Trust for Historic Preservation

Although it is not a federal agency in the strict sense of the definition, the National Trust for Historic Preservation serves as the federal government's preservation liaison. It is the only national, nonprofit, congressionally chartered organization with a preservation mandate.[13]

In 1949, Congress created the National Trust to stimulate private involvement in the preservation of sites, buildings, and objects of national significance. As a federally subsidized, charitable, and educational corporation, the Trust was the culmination of years of planning by preservationists who feared that the post-World War II era would inaugurate a confrontation between themselves and the proponents of "progress."

The postwar milieu in which the Trust began to function was a period of unprecedented explosions in birth rates, construction, and transportation projects. "New lifestyles grew from suburban development, new consumer needs and more leisure time." As massive changes began to occur in the appearance of both rural and urban America, the National Trust found fertile ground in which to grow. Through the 1960s and even into the early 1970s, the organization's objectives reflected the views of its first executive director, Frederick L. Rath, Jr., who believed that

> The National Trust first serves as a clearing house for information about buildings of architectural and historic importance and about preservation methods. Secondly, it seeks to assist in the preservation of such sites and buildings by offering advice. Thirdly, it stands ready to intervene, that is, to put the prestige and influence of a national organization behind movements to save local treasures. And finally, it has the power to accept and administer sites and buildings when no other solution to the preservation problem can be found.[14]

Despite its eastern seaboard orientation, the National Trust had some impact on California during these early years. Four Californians, for example, were charter members of the organization: Aubrey and Newton Drury, Aubrey Neasham, and Mrs. Nion Tucker. As early as 1947, the California Historical Society and the Monterey Foundation had joined with other national, regional, state, and local groups to encourage efforts to organize the Trust.[15]

The Trust's influence was evident in more substantive ways. For example, Neasham quoted directly from the report of the Trust's Committee on Standards and Surveys when he proposed criteria to evaluate California's historic sites and buildings.[16]

The first property to be acquired by the Trust was Casa Amesti, the adobe house in Monterey, California. Presented to the Trust in 1953 by Frances Adler Elkins, the gift carried no maintenance endowment. Its use as the Old Capital Club, a men's club that opened the house to the public at specified times, has proven mutually beneficial and serves as an example of a property that survives without direct financial assistance from the Trust.[17]

Aside from its Casa Amesti venture, the Trust exercised a presence in such preservation causes as the attempt to save the San Francisco Mint in the mid-1950s. These efforts, however, were minuscule when compared to its activities outside the state. It was not until July 1, 1971, that the National Trust would open its first regional office to serve areas west of the Rockies. Initially, the headquarters of the California Historical Society in San Francisco housed the office, which moved to permanent quarters a year later.

With Heritage So Rich: The Impetus for a New Beginning

In the conclusion of its findings, the Special Committee on Historic Preservation observed that not only were urbanization and the dangers to the nation's environmental heritage accelerating, Americans were also experiencing a sense of "rootlessness combined with a longing for those landmarks of the past" to provide a sense of stability and of belonging. The committee warned:

> If the preservation movement is to be successful, it must go beyond saving bricks and mortar. It must go beyond saving occasional historic houses and opening museums. It must be more than a cult of antiquarians. It must do more than revere a few precious national shrines. It must attempt to give a sense of orientation to our society, using structures and objects of the past to establish values of time and place.[18]

The committee recommended that preservationists recognize "the importance of architecture, design and esthetics as well as historic and cultural values." This "new preservation" should not restrict itself to individual buildings and landmarks but must also be concerned "with the historic and architecturally valued areas and districts which contain a special meaning for the community." Finally, the committee insisted that preservation could only succeed if "intensive thought and study...[are] given to economic conditions and tax policies which will affect our efforts to preserve such areas as living parts of the community."[9]

The members of the committee included members of Congress, state and local officials, and academicians; ex-officio members included cabinet officials. Their credentials, together with those of various consultants, were sufficiently impressive that their recommendations, coupled with pressure from preservationists, proved to be "a major contributing factor in the passage of the National Historic Preservation Act of 1966."[20]

The committee's recommendations for a national historic preservation plan included:

- a comprehensive national policy statement to guide all federal agencies;
- 'the establishment of an Advisory Council on Historic Preservation to provide leadership and guidance' and serve as liaison between state and local governments and public and private groups;
- an expanded National Register program to inventory properties and a federal assistance program for local efforts;
- more authority and funds for federal acquisition of threatened properties of national significance;

- federal loans and grants to aid and expand state and local preservation programs;
- 'federal financial aid to and through the National Trust' to assist private preservation activities and for educational purposes.[21]

These recommendations would be realized in the coming decade through additional legislation at federal, state, and local levels; through amendments to the Internal Revenue Code; and through an assortment of funding and training programs subsidized by private and public grants.

A new day was about to dawn for preservationists across the country. Californians, too, would benefit from increased federal involvement and largesse.

PART III

New Strategies and Renewed Commitments, 1966-1976

During the decade following the passage of the National Historic Preservation Act of 1966, California's historic preservation movement entered a new era. No longer was preservation to be dominated by the state. With the introduction of federal programs and with the granting of funds predicated on the implementation of an approved state preservation program, the impetus for preservation shifted away from Sacramento to Washington.

In California, the Division of Beaches and Parks (later reconstituted as the Department of Parks and Recreation) was given responsibility for the new federal mandates. The mechanisms necessary for the implementation of the new federal programs were established through internal reorganizations, the introduction of various preservation-oriented programs, the upgrading of the existing citizens advisory body, and the successful campaign for park bond monies. The election of a new governor resulted in the appointment of landscape architect William Penn Mott, Jr., as director of the department. Mott's role would be a crucial one, for he would shape the state's preservation programs at a time when federal regulations were new and flexible enough to be liberally interpreted.

The state legislature joined the growing environmentalist bandwagon and approved laws that tried to improve California's quality of life. Together with federal requirements, state laws forced governmental agencies at all levels to be more cognizant of preservation issues. Meanwhile, preservation advocates, who earlier felt isolated, now found their ranks swelled with converts reflecting an ever-widening proliferation of interests.

By the time Californians celebrated the Bicentennial of the American Revolution, the state's preservation program was well established. Armed with new strategies and strengthened by renewed commitments and energies, California's preservationists faced the future with confidence.

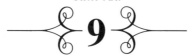

Legislative Foundations: Cornerstones for a New Era

The passage of the Historic Preservation Act on October 15, 1966,decisively altered the direction of the historic preservation movement in the United States. Within a decade, other laws implementing the recommendations of *With Heritage So Rich* were enacted.[1] In California, the state legislature responded to the new federal mandates and to public pressures to preserve and protect what remained of the state's natural and built environment.

Summary of Federal Legislation

Generally speaking, federal preservation law seeks "to support historic preservation programs at the federal and state levels and to protect historic properties when federal activities are involved." The federal government's role in preservation has not been to the exclusion of state participation but has, instead, frequently required state and local involvement.[2] Beginning in 1966, the federal government entered into an era of vigorous preservation leadership and extensive cooperation with public and private agencies and organizations.

The National Historic Preservation Act of 1966 stated that existing governmental and nongovernmental programs were unable to prevent the encroachments "of urban centers, highways, and residential, commercial, and industrial developments" on what remained of the nation's historical and cultural heritage. Congress therefore deemed it

> necessary and appropriate for the Federal Government to accelerate its historic preservation programs and activities, to give maximum encouragement to agencies and individuals undertaking preservation by private means, and to assist State and local governments and the National Trust for Historic Preservation in the United States to expand and accelerate their historic preservation programs and activities.[3]

To accomplish these objectives, provisions were made for the establishment of a National Register "of districts, sites, buildings, structures, and objects significant in American history, architecture, archeology, and culture." A grants program was started for the preparation of comprehensive statewide historic surveys and preservation plans, to match state monies for preservation projects, and for "a program of matching grant-in-aid to the National Trust" to carry out its responsibilities.[4] The Advisory Council on Historic Preservation was created as an impartial body to "assess the public interest in protecting a site."[5] Section 106 of the law that allowed the Advisory Council "a reasonable opportunity to comment" on the effect of a proposed federal undertaking on a National Register property offered designated historic sites some protection[6]

Thus, the new act strengthened and expanded the scope of the nation's preservation programs. Properties no longer had to be of national significance to be included in the survey mandated by the Historic Sites Act of 1935. The National Register program would now include structures, sites, and objects of local, statewide, and national significance. Categories of significance were expanded from history and archaeology to include architecture and culture. A comprehensive financial aid program was created for state participants. And through the Advisory Council on Historic Preservation, which advised the president and Congress on preservation matters, a mechanism for the protection of significant cultural resources was established.[7]

To implement the new law, the National Park Service created the Office of Archeology and Historic Preservation. Directed by Ernest A. Connally, this new unit housed the National Register Program. The influence of the National Trust was evident. Architectural historian William J. Murtagh left his post as director of the Trust's Department of Programs to become the first keeper of the National Register. The first executive secretary of the Advisory Council was Robert R. Garvey, Jr., who resigned as the Trust's executive secretary to assume the position.[8]

Through its program of highway salvage archaeology, the Federal Highway Administration and its predecessor, the Bureau of Public Roads, has been involved in preservation since the mid-1950s. The passage of the Department of Transportation Act of 1966, which "contained one of the strongest historic preservation provisions of any law" in Section 4(f), expanded the agency's limited mandates.[9] According to that provision:

> After August 23, 1968, the Secretary [of Transportation]
> shall not approve any program or project which requires the
> use of any publicly owned land...from an historic site of
> national, State, or local significance...unless (1) there is no
> feasible and prudent alternative to the use of such land,
> and (2) such program includes all possible planning to
> minimize harm to such...historic site resulting from such
> use. [10]

The provision was strengthened in 1971 when the U.S. Supreme Court ruled that "protected lands 'were not to be lost unless there were truly unusual factors present in a particular case or the cost of community disruption from alternative routes reached extraordinary magnitudes.'" Furthermore, when feasible and prudent alternatives were evaluated, the need for preservation was not to be overshadowed by factors such as cost and community disruption.[11]

Growing public concern over the deterioration of the environment prompted passage of the National Environmental Policy Act (NEPA) of 1969 which recognized the federal government's responsibility "to use all practicable means...to improve and coordinate Federal plans, functions, programs, and resources" for the purpose of preserving the "important historic, cultural, and natural aspects of our national heritage, and maintain[ing] wherever possible, an environment which supports diversity and variety of individual choice."[12] The protection of cultural resources was now included in an all-encompassing national policy to "encourage productive and enjoyable harmony between man and his environment" and "to promote efforts which will prevent or eliminate damage to the environment and biosphere and stimulate the health and welfare of man."[13]

The legislation's greatest potential and weakness lie in Section 102(c) which mandates a detailed environmental impact statement (EIS) for legislative proposals and "major Federal actions significantly affecting the quality of the human environment." Although the EIS must include both anticipated adverse effects and mitigation measures, it is required only if the federally assisted project can be defined as "a 'major federal action' with a 'significant' environmental impact."[14]

In response to widespread fears that significant properties were being lost before they could be placed under National Register protection, President Richard M. Nixon signed Executive Order 11593 on May 13, 1971, for the "protection and enhancement of the cultural environment." Accordingly, federal agencies had to establish policies and procedures to preserve and protect federally owned or controlled properties of "historical, architectural or archaeological significance." They were required to inventory and nominate all eligible properties under their jurisdiction to the National Register. The Advisory Council was also given an opportunity to comment on any proposed alterations of property considered likely to meet National Register criteria. In consultation with the Advisory Council, federal agencies were directed to "institute procedures to assure that Federal plans and programs contribute to the preservation and enhancement of non-federally owned" historic and cultural resources.[15] The latter provision gave the Advisory Council a means by which to issue "regulations protecting historic properties which might otherwise fall into the cracks between other statutes." E.O. 11593 has proven to be enforceable in the courts and therefore has emerged as "a crucial authority in preservation litigation."[16]

Strongly supported by the archaeological community, the Archeological and Historic Preservation Act of 1974 amended the Reservoir Salvage Act of 1960 "to include all Federal or federally assisted or licensed construction projects rather than only dam and reservoir projects." Equally significant was the provision that allowed up to 1 percent of the project budget for "archeological and historical data recovery, protection, and preservation." Agencies could contract out the data recovery program or do it themselves. The third option, however, "to do nothing at all, is not authorized by the Act."[17] The Secretary of the Interior was permitted to authorize a survey of private lands impacted by the project when federal grants or loans were involved, and take steps "to recover and preserve the archeological resources." Should any losses be incurred as a result of the salvage process, compensation could be paid to private parties.[18]

Although the law proved to be a reliable source of funding for archaeological projects, there was a major drawback built into it. By emphasizing salvage archaeology, it encouraged "removing archaeological resources rather than preserving them at their original site."[19] By 1979, the federal agency administering the preservation program recognized the need to change this policy. In describing how to approach the law, the Heritage Conservation and Recreation Service stated:

> Resource salvage is generally less preferable than preservation *in situ.* After identification of resources during the initial planning stages of a project, Federal agencies should give full consideration to courses of action that will not necessitate salvage.[20]

The passage of this legislation resulted in the replacement of the Interagency Archeological Investigations and Salvage Program by the Interagency Archeological Services Division (IAS). The new unit was placed in the Office of Archeology and Historic Preservation which was created in 1967 by the National Park Service to carry out the mandates of the 1966 legislation. The division claimed that its predecessor had "operated as a minor program of the National Park Service" through its regional offices or archaeological centers.[21] In contrast, the IAS had broad responsibilities as "the Federal coordinating program for recovery, protection and preservation of significant scientific, prehistoric, historic, or archaeological data."[22]

The division did not survive the decade. In 1978, IAS, along with the Office of Archeology and Historic Preservation, which had until then assumed the responsibility for all external preservation programs under the National Park Service, was transferred into the newly formed Heritage Conservation and Recreation Service (HCRS). The new agency, which was a reconstituted Bureau of Outdoor Recreation, was designed to be

> 'the focal point within the Federal government for planning, evaluating, and coordinating the protection and preserva- tion of the Nation's cultural and natural heritage, and for assuring adequate recreation opportunities for all its people.'

Unfortunately for historic preservationists, HCRS was "dominated by the outdoor recreation interests of its predecessor" and its director was per- ceived as "unresponsive and even hostile on occasion to his preservation constituency." Chris Delaporte's highly unpopular internal reform mea- sures, and the widely publicized departure of respected personnel such as Ernest Connally and William Murtagh contributed to intense public oppo- sition to the agency. In 1981, the arrival of a new presidential administration and a new secretary of the interior, James G. Watt, who was a former director of the Bureau of Outdoor Recreation, resulted in the abolition of HCRS whose responsibilities were returned to the National Park Service. Despite some differences, "integrating the in-park and extramural preservation activities of the National Park Service under a ranking official reporting to the director...resembled nothing so much as the original Office of Archeology and Historic Preservation."[23]

The spirit that encouraged preservation legislation in the late 1960s and early 1970s could be glimpsed in other laws that influenced the movement to preserve and protect America's historic and cultural resources. For example, a month after Congress passed the National Historic Preservation Act in 1966, it also approved the Model Cities Act which affirmed the "need for timely action to preserve and restore areas, sites, and structures of historic or architectural value in order that these remaining evidences of our past history and heritage shall not be lost or destroyed through the expansion and development of the Nation's urban areas." The preservation of historic and architectural values were validated as legitimate urban renewal costs and the Department of Housing and Urban Development could now provide "two-thirds of the cost of historic surveys in cities of 50,000 and more." The secretary of the department was instructed "to encourage cities to maintain historic sites and 'distinctive neighborhood features.'"[24]

Several years later, the Urban Mass Transportation Assistance Act of 1970 "declared [it] to be the national policy that special effort shall be made to preserve...important historical and cultural assets." Federal funds would not be approved unless the secretary found that there was "no feasible and prudent alternative" to an adverse environmental effect, and that "all reasonable steps have been taken to minimize such effect" on those assets.[25]

As amended in 1972, the Federal Property and Administrative Services Act of 1949 allowed the General Services Administration to transfer to state and local governments "without monetary consideration...any surplus real and related personal property which the Secretary of the Interior has determined is suitable and desirable for use as a historic monument, for the benefit of the public." The Housing and Community Development Act of 1974 consolidated and expanded previously authorized housing programs. "Grants for up to 66⅔% of the costs of the programs... [were] authorized for the relocation, restoration and/or acquisition of structures and sites of historic or architectural value by eligible cities, counties and towns." Under the 1974 law, block grant funding provisions gave local governments greater control over how monies were spent.[26]

In 1976, a decade after the passage of the National Historic Preservation Act, Congress approved two other laws that had a profound impact on preservation: the Land and Water Conservation Fund Act and the Tax Reform Act.

Title II, "National Historic Preservation Fund," of the Land and Water Conservation Fund Act amended the 1966 legislation to create important changes in the way matching grants were to be funded by the federal government. Not only was the amount of money increased, the equal match formula was changed from a 50-50 match to 70-30 for "statewide historic preservation plans and surveys and project plans." The 70 percent was from the federal government. Congress was clearly responding to a critical need for dollars to complete the national inventory of cultural resources.[27]

The Advisory Council was also directly affected by the Land and Water Conservation Fund Act. It became an independent agency of twenty-nine members who were accountable to the president and Congress. Section 106 of the 1966 legislation, which allowed the council to comment on federal undertakings, was now to include properties eligible for inclusion on the National Register, as well as those already approved. Finally, the new amendments allowed the Advisory Council "to promulgate such rules and regulations as it deems necessary to govern the implementation of section 106."[28]

By providing economic incentives for preservation, the Tax Reform Act of 1976 had a pivotal, long-term impact on the evolution of historic preservation. Until its passage, federal as well as state income taxes favored new construction over the rehabilitation of existing buildings. Owners who demolished historic structures could deduct the entire cost and "the remaining undepreciated basis of the original structure" as business expenses. They could also select from several "'accelerated depreciation' deductions." These alternatives for new construction did not apply to owners who maintained and rehabilitated historic buildings, nor were the owners permitted to deduct rehabilitation costs as a current business expense, or rapidly depreciate the structures or amortize them separately. Instead, historic property owners were forced to "add them to the basis of the building and depreciate them along with and at the same time as the rest of the structure." The legislation tilted the balance in favor of historic preservation by identifying incentives as well as disincentives for owners of "certified historic structures." Among the incentives was the deduction of all "certified rehabilitation" expenses over a five-year period. Furthermore, the same depreciation schedules that applied to owners of new buildings were allowed to owners of "substantially rehabilitated historic properties;" and charitable deductions were permitted "for contributions to eligible donees of remainder interests, leases, options to purchase or easements of at least 30 years' duration that are 'exclusively for conservation purposes.'" The disincentives included no deductions for losses or expenses if a certified structure was demolished. The act also denied "the accelerated depreciation benefits usually permitted on new structures if the new construction follows the demolition or alteration of historic buildings."[29]

Some of the confusing or counterproductive language of the 1976 Tax Reform Act relating to historic preservation incentives was clarified by the Revenue Act of 1978 whose efforts to stimulate the economy also benefited historic preservation. For preservationists, the act's most important feature was "its expansion of business investment categories which qualify for tax credits." In 1981, Congress passed the Economic Recovery Tax Act which "scrapped most of the incentives and disincentives originally enacted in 1976 and expanded the 1978 investment credit into the primary preservation tax mechanism." The legislation increased the rehabilitation investment tax credit and created a three-tier system to calculate the credit. In that same year, Congress also amended the 1966 National Historic Preservation Act to require owner consent before a property could be listed on the National Register.[30]

These federal tax incentives were only the first of several laws and regulations that helped to make preservation economically feasible, thereby widening its popularity and acceptance. Although the impact of these and subsequent legislative actions falls outside the purview of this study, several observations can be made. The need to comply with the new regulations has resulted, for example, in the emergence of preservation consultants and self-described experts in the private sector who are now able to earn a comfortable living assisting investors in search of tax benefits. The demand for trained professionals as well as skilled and unskilled workers has also improved the job market. In its 1981 report to the president and Congress, the Advisory Council on Historic Preservation spoke of successes since 1976:

> Since enactment, Federal incentives had stimulated more than $1.3 billion in private investment. The 2,500 projects certified had included historic hotels, office buildings, and factories, creating 13,700 new housing units, more than 6,300 of which have been for low- and moderate-income families.[31]

Understandably, persons displaced by inner city rehabilitation and neighborhood conservation projects and their advocates did not share the same perceptions. For example, the Sacramento *Bee*, in 1977, reported a "turnabout trend" as middle-class whites returned to rehabilitated inner-city neighborhoods, of which more than half "had been designated for 'historic preservation.'" In a study of forty-four cities, including San Francisco's Mission District and Pasadena, the National Urban Coalition concluded that low-income minorities and the elderly were dislocated in 73 percent of the cities surveyed. In 1979, urban revitalization was referred to as "devitalization" as the middle class continued to displace the poor and the elderly. A few areas, however, were able to maintain their ethnic diversity, "indicating that some black middle-class people are taking part in the renovation process." In 1983, an inner city dweller reported nostalgically that in many older urban neighborhoods, "the blacks and the Jews and the Irish have dispersed; we, the baby-boom kids, have taken their place." To the dislocated poor and elderly, he added the middle class, who have been driven out by the economic power of single individuals and childless couples, "making the cities the exclusive domain of the young and affluent." Displacement and gentrification are but two examples of the social impact of preservation that have yet to be adequately addressed.[32]

Summary of State Legislation

In California, the legislative foundations for preservation were laid before the passage of the National Historic Preservation Act of 1966. In the decade following that landmark act, however, several additional laws were passed that reflected a continued state commitment to preservation.

California's equivalent of NEPA was the California Environmental Quality Act (CEQA) of 1970. Henceforth, state and local agencies were required to prepare detailed analyses of the environmental impacts of proposed projects or to file "negative declaration" statements that described why their proposals would not significantly affect the environment, and why they need not prepare an environmental impact report (EIR). Should there be a potential effect on the environment, the agency was required "to indicate the manner in which such significant effects can be mitigated or avoided."[33]

In the first section on legislative intent, CEQA stated that the legislature finds it to be state policy to:

> take all action necessary to provide the people of this state
> with clean air and water, enjoyment of aesthetic, natural,
> scenic, and *historic environmental qualities*, and freedom
> from excessive noise. [Italics mine.][34]

When the section on "definitions" was added in 1972, "environment" was to include "the physical conditions which exist within the area which will be affected by a proposed project, including...objects of historic or aesthetic significance."[35]

The Mills Act of 1972 was California's attempt to introduce property tax reform beneficial to preservation based on "present use assessment." Such a system "would take historic properties as they are—assessing them at their present use—rather than...assuming that the most intensive and profitable use is necessarily the best." Under the "contract assessment" version which was enacted by the Mills Act, local authorities were authorized to contract with owners of qualified historic properties "to restrict the use of such property to retain its characteristics as property of historical significance." The owner was also required to preserve and, if necessary, restore the property and to provide reasonable public access. In return, the property would be assessed "on the basis of the best use which the owner can make of it."[36]

Implementing the law proved difficult. As written, there were several features that discouraged local governments from using it. There was, for example, no provision to reimburse them for lost revenues, and any cancellation fees collected would go to the general fund. There were also legal prohibitions, including the need to amend the constitution if the legislature wanted to change the basis for property tax assessment.[37]

To rectify the constitutional dilemma, Proposition 7 was placed before the voters in June 1976. Its passage added a second paragraph to Section 8 of Article XII of the State Constitution which provides the following:

> To promote the preservation of property of historical significance, the Legislature may define such property and shall provide that when it is enforceably restricted, in a manner specified by the Legislature, it shall be valued for property tax purposes only on a basis that is consistent with its restrictions and uses.[38]

The success of the Mills Act is unclear. The reluctance of local governments and property owners to use it has been attributed to the complicated standards and procedures involved, the restrictive twenty-year minimum term for a contract, a public access requirement that includes the building's interior, and the lack of state reimbursement to local jurisdictions for lost revenues, particularly after the passage of Proposition 13 in 1978. Thus, in California, property tax incentives have not yet proven to be a significant catalyst for preservation.[39]

By a plurality of 60 percent, California voters approved a new bond act in 1974, exactly a decade after agreeing to the sale of $150 million in park bonds.[40] Sometimes referred to as the Z'berg-Collier Park Bond Act, the State Beach, Park, Recreational, and Historical Facilities Bond Act of 1974 authorized the issuance of $250 million in bonds "to acquire areas for recreation, conservation and preservation" and to assist local governments in the development of these areas.[41]

The 1974 measure differed in several important respects from the earlier bond act. This time, the proposition before the voters clearly specified expenditures and contained an allocation for preservation. A total of $15 million was set aside "for development of historical resources for the state park system, including costs for planning and interpretation." An additional $90 million would go to cities and counties for acquisition and development of properties for park, recreational, beach, and historical purposes; a similar amount was allocated for state park acquisitions.[42] This time, state land acquisitions were to concentrate on open or natural lands, including "lands necessary for historic preservation."[43] The 1964 bond act had not mentioned preservation properties when it stated that all lands were to "consist predominantly of open or natural lands."[44]

Several other state measures had an impact on preservation in California.[45] State law requires that local governments "adopt a 'comprehensive, long-range general plan' providing guidelines for land use decisions" to ensure that zoning decisions are based on carefully considered,not ad hoc, plans. As passed in 1966 and later modified, the law mandated nine elements for every general plan: land use, circulation, housing, conservation, open space, seismic safety, noise, scenic highways, and safety. In addition, permissive elements such as recreation, community design, and transit were also suggested.[46]

In February 1974, the American Institute of Planners (A.I.P.) "adopted a national goal to include the Historic Preservation Element in the general plan."[47] In California, this objective was realized later that same year through Senator Peter Behr's S.B. 2309. This bill amended Section 65303 of the Government Code to allow local jurisdictions to voluntarily include a historic preservation element "for the identification, establishment, and protection of sites and structures of architectural, historical, archeological or cultural significance, including significant...plant materials" in their general plans. These guidelines were to be "developed by the Office of Planning and Research by February 1, 1976 in consultation with appropriate public and private organizations...."[48] The result was publication of *Historic Preservation Element Guidelines* in 1976. Now out of print, it remains the only state manual providing specific suggestions for why, what, and how to draft a historic preservation element.[49]

City planner Roger Scharmer, who helped draft the legislation, urged the Historical Landmarks Advisory Committee to support it because, unlike other planning elements, "historic preservation concerns are left operating on a crisis to crisis basis." The time had come, he insisted, to insert preservation into the comprehensive planning mechanism.[50] When he later recalled his activities on behalf of the measure, Scharmer said he realized that historic preservation was not mentioned in the State Planning Code. "Obviously,....planners didn't consider preservation as a planning tool—and much was lost as a result of bad 'preservation' planning." Preservation, he believed, had to be put "on the same level as other planning elements" if it was to be taken seriously.[51]

Also in 1976, the state legislature passed the Marks Historical Rehabilitation Act, which recognized that "properties and structures of historical or architectural significance are an essential public resource" and allowed local agencies "to make long-term, low-interest loans to finance the rehabilitation of properties of historic or architectural significance" by issuing bonds.[52] Four years after legislation was signed by the governor in September 1975, the State Historical Building Code was adopted in August 1979. Unlike other states, California "is unique in having enacted a separate State Historic Building Code which authorizes the adoption of alternative rules, regulations, and standards applicable to designated historic structures." The code's explanatory note observed that the uniqueness of the regulations was also due to their permissive rather than mandatory nature. Thus, most local agencies could implement the provisions without formally adopting the code. It is, however, applicable only to qualified historic buildings or structures. Above all, the code's intent is clearly

> to save California's architectural heritage by recognizing the unique construction problems inherent in historical buildings and offering an alternative code to deal with these problems.[53]

What was considered a positive feature in 1979 was viewed as a detriment in 1984. The California Heritage Task Force's report to the legislature concluded that one factor limiting wide-scale implementation of the code was its "discretionary" application: If local authorities "do not wish to apply the Code, they can refuse to approve any or all alternative means."[54] In September 1984, the governor signed S.B. 2321, which required "all local building authorities to administer and enforce" the provisions of the State Historical Building Code "and would thereby impose a state-mandated local program."[55]

In 1980, state agencies were told to conduct a general survey of their holdings and formulate historic preservation procedures in a timely fashion. Governor Edmund G. Brown, Jr., signed Executive Order B-64-80 in March and in September approved S.B. 1652, which required all state agencies to establish policies for the preservation and maintenance of all state-owned resources under their jurisdiction that could or did qualify for registration as a state landmark or for inclusion on the National Register of Historic Places. Holdings over fifty years of age were to be surveyed and an inventory of listed or potentially significant properties was to be presented to the state historic preservation officer by July 1, 1983. To mitigate possible adverse effects, the preservation officer was to be consulted before alterations to the properties could be made. It is still too early to tell how successful these directives have been, particularly because the legislation states that preservation polices were to be formulated "when prudent and feasible." If enforced, the directives could be used to save endangered resources because the state historic preservation officer is empowered to review a project that could have a potentially adverse effect on the resource. There is also a mediation procedure for the resolution of differences.[56]

Native American sites were another endangered resource which still remain inadequately protected. The legislature took a step to protect these sites in 1976, when the Native American Heritage Commission was created to identify sacred sites on public lands and review existing administrative and statutory protections. A.B. 4239 provided limited protection for sites of special religious significance by requiring agencies to forward copies of EIRs referring to these areas. If a proposed agency action could cause damage to the site, the commission could conduct its own investigations, hold hearings, and make recommendations. If these efforts failed to produce an acceptable solution, the commission could ask the attorney general to move for an injunction to stop the project. Unfortunately, the commission's powers are limited. As Dwight Dutschke, the Native American coordinator in the Office of Historic Preservation, observed: "The Commission's function is primarily advisory. It must achieve its goal by convincing those in authority of the importance of their concerns."[57]

10

California Implements the Historic Preservation Act of 1966: The Creation of a State Mechanism, 1966-1970

The mandates of the National Historic Preservation Act of 1966 necessitated the creation of a state mechanism to implement the new provisions. These included the preparation of a comprehensive state historic preservation plan and a statewide survey of historic sites; the nomination of properties to the National Register of Historic Places; and the administration of a matching grants-in-aid program for survey and planning activities, and for acquisition and development projects. These duties were at first performed by the State Liaison Officer, and after 1973, by the state historic preservation officer (SHPO). Both positions were filled by gubernatorial appointees.

In California, the Department of Parks and Recreation administratively housed the new federal program. The director served as State Liaison Officer and later as SHPO. His staff provided assistance, and the already functioning California Historical Landmarks Advisory Committee served as the official review board. The committee approved their first National Register nomination at their July 1970 meeting in Monterey. In September of that same year, the preliminary history plan, funded under the new law, was finally submitted to the National Park Service. Soon thereafter, the state applied for grants to acquire and develop units within the State Park System.

First Steps

California's participation in the Act of 1966 officially began on March 16, 1967, when Governor Ronald Reagan designated William Penn Mott, Jr., as State Liaison Officer. Earlier that year, the new governor had appointed Mott to head the Department of Parks and Recreation. Mott was a landscape architect with a master of science degree from the University of California at Berkeley. In order to complete ongoing projects, he had refused two offers from Reagan's predecessors to serve as director of the State Park System. Now, in 1967, Mott was both ready and willing to accept the governor's challenge.[1]

During Mott's first year as director, several important changes occurred. The Park Commission and the Recreation Commission were merged into a nine-member Park and Recreation Commission. The Division of Beaches and Parks and the Division of Recreation were combined into Parks and Recreation. The Division of Small Craft Harbors was removed from the department's jurisdiction; it later became the Department of Boating and Waterways. Internally, Mott centralized operations by regrouping staff and departmental functions into six divisions: operations, administrative services, concessions, information and interpretation, resource management and protection, and planning and development.[2]

In the midst of this reorganization, Mott was reminded of his responsibilities as State Liaison Officer "to represent the State in preparing surveys, plans and application assistance." Of these, the most urgent was preparation of the statewide historic preservation plan that the National Park Service had to approve before grants could be obtained. Earl P. Hanson, the last chief of the Division of Beaches and Parks, recommended to Mott that the division's program for "Historical Acquisition and Restoration, 1966-86" become the basis for the plan because it provided recommendations for preservation and interpretation within the park system. The mandated state survey could be produced, Hanson assured Mott, if the division's 1962 report, "A Proposal for a Historical Resource Survey," was updated and used as a guide. The report had been the division's response to Assembly Concurrent Resolution No. 25. He stressed that a committee of gubernatorial appointees had to review both survey and the plan.[3]

Work on the state plan began soon after Hanson wrote to Mott. Less than two months later, Mott stated that his department was preparing a statewide master plan for historical monuments and sites which would be completed by the end of the year. He also observed that no other state had begun work on their plan and that he anticipated California would have "no difficulty" obtaining a large grant from the available $10 million once a state plan was approved.[4]

Mott's eagerness to participate in the federal program was further emphasized a few months later when he wrote to Ernest Allen Connally, head of the Office of Archeology and Historic Preservation, to inform him that his department would request $50,000 in its 1968-1969 budget to serve as matching funds for the statewide survey. He also included a copy of the report that Hanson suggested become the basis of the state inventory and promised that when funds were granted, "we will carry out the survey in the manner outlined...[in] our 'Historical Resource Study.'"[5] Mott also enclosed a copy of the *Partial Inventory. Historic Sites and Buildings in California* that historian Allen Welts compiled in August.[6]

This partial inventory was one result of the $7,500 granted to the division by Assembly Concurrent Resolution No. 25. Produced with the assistance of local historical societies, it contained lists of significant sites in their respective areas.[7] Preparation of the inventory had not been without difficulties. As a representative of the Conference of California Historical Societies pointed out to Welts, many counties lacked funds and personnel to conduct local surveys, the inventory forms proved to be too complicated for many volunteers, and the state did not provide enough copies of the forms. Not only were completion deadlines unrealistic, many groups failed to see "the what, why, [and] where" of the process.[8] These criticisms were not lost on Welts, who noted in the inventory's Preface that these individual efforts sorely lacked "the strength and purpose of a statewide coordinated master plan." They did, however, "identify a need for a plan to weigh value against value."[9]

The hope that a state plan would be in place by early 1968 was not realized. In March of that year, the Department of Parks and Recreation hosted the Pacific Coast Regional Conference on the National Historic Preservation Act at Asilomar at the request of the National Park Service.[10] Departmental personnel later expressed concern over a lack of financial support from Congress for the program. The department, however, was urged to "make every possible effort to conform its historic preservation program with the National Historic Preservation Act regardless of Congressional allocations." Six specific recommendations were submitted to Mott: the National Park Service should recognize the Welts Survey as California's preliminary site inventory; the survey should be updated immediately to ensure its comprehensiveness; the governor should appoint the requisite advisory committee of experts; the State Park Master Plan's historic element should be broadened to qualify California for the grants-in-aid program; matching funds for both survey and master plan should be sought as soon as possible; and a permanent departmental task force should be established to coordinate all activities.[11]

Mott recognized the urgent need for an approved state plan.[12] In May 1968, it was agreed that the Grants Administration and Local Assistance branch headed by Russell W. Porter would assume primary responsibility for the new preservation program because it was essentially a national grants-in-aid program. Furthermore, the Welts inventory would be expanded to include local and regional sites and would become the responsibility of the Resource Management and Protection Division. Nomination of sites to the National Register of Historic Places could not begin until the site survey was completed and an official committee was appointed.[13]

If the state was moving slowly, so was the federal government. When Porter telephoned William J. Murtagh, keeper of the National Register, for clarification on several issues raised in May, he was informed that the National Park Service had yet to receive funds for the 1968-1969 fiscal year. The service had not yet approved or printed inventory forms which conceivably would have to be reproduced by the states themselves. Furthermore, the Welts inventory was unacceptable because it lacked photographs and precise boundaries. Murtagh suggested that California resolve these problems while waiting for the new forms, a process that would take some eight or more weeks.[14]

Funding was one of the problems confronting the National Park Service during these first years after the passage of the 1966 act. The law had authorized a total of $32 million for matching grants-in-aid for fiscal years 1967 to 1970 with the understanding that future funding would be requested for "matching grants-in-aid for acquisition, restoration, and preservation projects in accordance with the statewide surveys and plans." As of January 1969, only $400,000 had been appropriated because of budgetary constraints and because the National Park Service lacked specific data on projected costs for state surveys and plans.[15]

At the request of National Park Service Director George Hartzog, Mott submitted estimated costs for survey and planning activities and for preservation projects for fiscal years 1970 to 1974. The five-year total was more than $16 million. Survey and planning requests amounted to only $200,000 and were for only the first two years. The remaining $15.8 million equaled 12 percent of the park system's anticipated development budget, which would be used as the required state matching funds. No provisions were made for seeking local government monies or to fund non-state park projects. Mott also estimated that in the same five-year period, California would forward approximately a thousand nominations to the National Register.[16]

California received its first appropriation of $40,567 from the federal government under the provisions of the 1966 legislation in June 1969. That amount was applied to the planning and survey effort that produced the *Preliminary California History Plan* in 1970.[17]

Internal Reorganization: Sharing the Workload

By the fall of 1969, the question of who would be responsible for the statewide history plan and site survey became of concern to various division chiefs within the department. The number of inquiries from local jurisdictions had increased, and the department began to anticipate the implementation of the National Register process as soon as the Historical Landmarks Advisory Committee was reconstituted with the requisite experts.[18]

To expedite the state's program, James E. Warren, chief of the Planning and Development Division, forwarded Porter's suggested work assignments to Mott. Porter's Grants Administration and Local Assistance Branch would be responsible for obtaining funds for the site survey and history plan and would administer the grant program once funding was received. The Statewide Planning Branch, also under Warren, would coordinate the site survey and development of the history plan. The Resource Management and Protection Division's Historical Resources Section supervised by Allen Welts and the Archeological Resources Section led by Francis Riddell would develop the criteria to determine the eligibility of proposed properties and conduct the statewide survey. The resulting standards, site survey, and history plan would then be submitted to the Historical Landmarks Advisory Committee for approval and implementation. John Michael of the Interpretive Services Section in William C. Dillinger's Information and Interpretation Division would be responsible for registering all historic sites. This was logical because Michael already provided staff support to the Advisory Committee.[19] Although both Dillinger and then Acting Chief of Resource Management and Protection Frederick A. Meyer, did not disagree with Warren's recommendations, they individually stressed that they lacked "the capability of assuming any of this workload at the present time."[20]

Failing to receive a satisfactory response from Mott, Warren wrote again in mid-December 1969 to urge that the department act immediately to respond to "our most deficient planning area today." He stated:

> We need the California History Plan formulated to provide us with exactly what is needed to develop priorities and the Five Year Capital Outlay Program, and to direct other levels of government into performing their share of the total history preservation in California.

Warren reiterated his proposal to divide responsibilities between his division, which would develop the history plan for both the state and the park system, and the Resource Management and Protection Division, which would take charge of the National Register program. He also included a detailed work plan for the history plan and National Register procedures.[21] Warren was convinced that the Historical Landmarks Advisory Committee should be elevated to the director's office, and that under the guidance of a deputy director, it would become "a valuable policy guiding force for all of our historical matters, including the History Plan, the National Register, and the continuation of the Historical Landmarks Program." His dream that the committee would evolve into "the historical conscience" for the director and the department never materialized.[22]

Dillinger, whose division assisted the Historical Landmarks Advisory Committee, protested any change in its function or staffing. His staff kept in contact with nearly every historical society in the state through their work for the committee. Not only was this an important source of information, the network helped his division "locate historical objects we need for exhibits, and...resulted in many donations and opportunities to buy needed historical items." The program, Dillinger insisted, was primarily one of public contact, something his people were particularly skilled at. It also did not require extensive research by the staff inasmuch as the applicants were responsible for providing documentation. "In our experience," he concluded, "most of the staff time is devoted to working out procedural details with applicants and helping them to resolve internal differences."[23] Dillinger clearly did not share Warren's vision of the committee's future.

Most of Warren's suggestions, which were actually generated by Porter, were eventually adopted by Mott. In January 1970, Porter reinforced his continued concern over the lack of progress on the aforementioned recommendations. He informed Mott that "I am assuming that you are in agreement with this division of work" and that he would begin organizing accordingly. It was imperative that California move quickly to take full advantage of the federal allocation of $40,567; only three other states, he said, had received more. Furthermore, local projects were eligible for federal funds only if the state's National Register program was in place.[24]

Mott met with his division and section heads a week later to discuss departmental attempts to implement the federal legislation. In April 1970, he issued a memo to all division chiefs and supervisors calling for accelerated efforts to meet the federal requirements. The department was finally reorganized; an architect and an archaeologist were added to the Historical

Landmarks Advisory Committee; the state received $40,567 for the survey and history plan; and Mott was informed that more than $6 million in federal funds were available for fiscal 1970-1971.[25]

The Resource Management and Protection Division was assigned responsibility for the National Register program, including the development of criteria. It was also to complete the statewide survey in six months, and was therefore given the largest share of the first federal allocation to accomplish its tasks. The Planning and Development Division would develop and publish the state plan within six months, continue to seek funds for surveys and other plans, and eventually administer the grants program provided in the 1966 legislation. The division's Development Branch would serve as architectural consultants. John Michael later observed: "This all fell flat on its face. I was reassigned on June 1, 1972, for two years to develop and publish the History Plan."[26]

The Information and Interpretation Division would "devote its efforts to the interpretation of history and archeology," continue to implement the state landmarks program, staff the Advisory Committee, and act as liaison between the director and the committee. The responsibilities of the Historical Landmarks Advisory Committee were increased. The committee, which now reported directly to Mott, would serve as the review board for all National Register nominations, and approve the statewide plan and survey. Finally, the director established the In-House History Committee to coordinate all departmental activities. Chaired by Porter, it, too, reported directly to Mott.[27]

In August 1970, Porter reported that there were some twenty persons in eight departmental units at work on the federal program.[28] By that time, the statewide inventory was well underway and the preliminary history plan was nearing completion.

Preparations for the Statewide Inventory

The department's preparations for the statewide survey included an attempt to create a new historical chronology as part of the framework for the inventory of the state's historical, archaeological, and architectural resources.

Work on the revision of Aubrey Neasham's historical categories began in mid-1969 under the direction of historian Allen Welts and with the approval of Director Mott. In August, Mott sent a memo to all division chiefs in which he stated that:

The Resource Management and Protection Division has determined that the terminology used now in describing historical time spans, i.e.: Indian Period, Spanish Period, English Period, Russian Period,and American Period, may better be described by terminology which discloses these time spans as:

1. The Era of Aboriginal Life,
2. The Era of Early Exploration and Settlement,
3. The California Pastoral Era, and
4. The Era of Growth and Development.

The director said: "I am in favor of developing the era concept in lieu of that formerly used and hereby advise all Divisions that this change will take place immediately."[29]

The new chronology was intended to assist in the department's planning and interpretive efforts. It was to be "a compendium of California's historical resources against which [the department's] programs for historical preservation and interpretation" would be evaluated. Equally important was its anticipated use as the basis for the state's inventory of historic, archaeological, and architectural resources.[30]

In November 1969, Welts submitted three different chronologies to the section heads in his division for comment. He pointed out that the eras were based on specific and major events instead of "causes which may have originated decades before." He reminded everyone that "Mr. Mott has approved the use of the term 'Era' as applied to a span in time...." The three options had been reviewed and approved by National Park Regional Historian John Hussey and R. Coke Wood, professor of History and chairman of the Historical Landmarks Advisory Committee.[31]

The respondents endorsed the first list which duplicated Hussey's recommendations with few suggested changes. The most substantive came from John Michael who wrote that several eras needed to be re-examined. "Aboriginal Life," he said, would not be acceptable to Native Americans who "do not like to be referred to as aborigines." The proposed "Era of Early European Exploration" should be more properly entitled "Era of Exploration" and include Asian explorations of the New World. "European Settlement and Pastoral Life" was inaccurate because the missions that contributed to the pastoral scene were not strictly European. The last section, "Emergence to National Leadership" should end in 1945, said Michael, because the post-war period was a new and separate era. He added a provocative observation:

> Has California actually emerged to a position of national
> leadership or have we befouled our own nest? National
> leaders usually show progress and I submit that perhaps
> we're showing progress in reverse—i.e., smog, water pollu-
> tion, environmental exploitation, social degradation, etc.,
> etc., etc.

Finally, he made a strong case for maintaining both "era" and "period" in the
department's terminology. "Our understanding was the so-called eras were
to describe periods and allow us some flexibility for overlap between
periods." He cautioned:

> we must be very careful not to describe the six periods or
> eras of California history in such terms so that they are
> arbitrarily bound, but we must inject enough flexibility so
> that we can cross over boundaries. [32]

In early 1970, Welts discarded both the Neasham chronology and
the eras recommended by Mott and others. He claimed that neither proved
satisfactory, and he was therefore suggesting a topical chronology, "dividing
the early from the more recent by identifying one as *Revealing a New World
1542-1841*, and the other by *American Expansionism*—the latter with a
series of subheadings beginning in 1841 and continuing on to the present."[33]

In March 1970, Mott learned that Welts was well into his new
"California History. A Topical Chronology." Although still incomplete, it
incorporated the advice of the following experts:

> Dr. R. Coke Wood, University of the Pacific
> Dr. Clement Meighan, University of California at Los Angeles
> Dr. Merrill Mattis, National Park Service
> Dr. John Hussey, National Park Service
> Dr. W. Turrentine Jackson, University of California at Davis
> Dr. W.H. Hutchinson, Chico State College
> Dr. A.P. Nasatir, San Diego State College
> Dr. Joseph McGowan, Sacramento State College
> Dr. Doyce B. Nunis, Jr., University of Southern California

Welts also consulted the following departmental staff:

> John Michael, supervisor, Interpretive Services
> Robert F. Uhte, supervisor of Design
> Elmer C. Aldrich, manager, Statewide Planning Branch
> Francis A. Riddell, supervisor, Archaeological Resource
>   Section

The Welts draft incorporated National Register criteria and was to
chronologically identify "the events, causes, effects, and cultural manifestations which are significant in the story of human life in California." It was to

be flexible enough to respond to new data and to serve as a basis for the department's historic preservation and interpretive programs and as the framework for the historical, archaeological, and architectural resources inventory.[34]

This proposal, revised a month later with different subtopics such as "historical topics, archeological evidence, and archival evidence," was never included in the department's history plan. For reasons that are still unclear, "the concept was rejected and the former system of periods was perpetuated." The Welts proposal, "Man in California—A Topical Chronology," did not disappear, however. In 1973, it was forwarded again to Mott for review and comment because "from the standpoint of archeological and historical resources, the Welts chronology seems to highlight the 'flow of history,' and may be a springboard from which we can launch an effective implementation of the concept."[35]

What finally emerged in the preliminary history plan was a token modification of the categories that Neasham had proposed in the early 1950s: the Indian Era; the Hispanic Era (1540-1848) which encompassed contributions of the Spanish, English, Russians, French, and Mexicans; and the American Era (1848 to the present). To ensure a truly comprehensive state history program, each era would "be scrutinized from the standpoint of the following eight cultural aspects...: Architecture, Exploration and Settlement, Economic and Industrial, Military, Government, Recreation and Leisure, Social and Educational, [and] Religion." [36]

By January 1970, there were signs that staff members were still anxious about the state's lack of progress toward the development of a survey and plan. In a memo to Director Mott, Russell Porter, who coordinated the federal program, expressed his concern that the governor had yet to appoint the mandated experts to the Historical Landmarks Advisory Committee. The criteria for National Register nominations, the survey, and the plan had yet to be determined. Furthermore, local projects had to be nominated to the National Register to qualify for federal funds. Porter stressed that three other states had already completed their preliminary survey and plan. California had to act swiftly.[37]

Porter's memo and the knowledge that $6.1 million in federal funding was available for 1970-1971 prompted Mott to quickly mail letters to the chairmen of all fifty-eight county boards of supervisors requesting their assistance in the development of "a register of districts, sites, buildings, structures, and objects significant to California's history, architecture, archeology and culture." The inventory of sites of national, state, regional, and local significance would become "an authoritative guide by which federal, state and local governments and private groups and citizens may know what should be protected from destruction or impairment." The supervisors were urged to convene county committees of experts and Native American representatives to evaluate and recommend sites for inclusion on the inventory. Mott held out the incentive of financial aid for those properties that qualified for the National Register. The supervisors were warned, however, that the survey had to be completed within five months for California to be eligible for federal funds available in June.[38]

Despite these efforts, the county supervisors were slow to respond. In April, another mailing went to county clerks. By May 1, 1970, of the thirty-nine respondents, twenty-seven had appointed committees and ten counties had either turned the project over to a historical society or similar group.[39] By the end of June, 200 nomination forms had been mailed to thirty-two counties. Twenty-one counties had properties on the National Register; eight more had submitted nominations. Although these statistics appear impressive, they could not disguise the fact that by the end of June, only twenty-one counties had submitted even partial inventories. It was clear that all realistic plans for a complete statewide inventory and a fully representative county submission of National Register nominations could not be accomplished by September 1970. It was anticipated, however, that at least a priority listing could be obtained from all counties by September to form the foundation for an acceptable general survey. A comprehensive survey could then be completed by June 30, 1971.[40]

The difficulties that Welts encountered reflected the diversity of supervisorial responses to Mott's request. Some assigned the survey task to amateur historians and archaeologists, while others gave it to a historical society, a county parks and recreation department, or to no one at all.[41] The real problem, however, seemed to be the citizen volunteers who, despite their enthusiasm, proved to be "neither self-generating or continuously motivated." Furthermore, progress was slowed because of "sporadic or infrequent meeting schedules...illness, vacations or other absences of key individuals."[42]

In early August 1970, Porter received a preliminary historic site survey. Admittedly, it was only a partial inventory with a scope that was "token, pending preparation of a comprehensive History Plan which will offer a multi-year program for the advancement of State historic preservation." Entries were listed by county and represented properties in the State Park

System, various county listings, the Historic American Buildings Survey, the State Historical Landmarks and Points of Historical Interest programs, archaeological survey records, National Register programs, and properties being nominated to these programs. Aside from archaeological properties which were cited separately, no attempt was made to identify why a property was considered significant.[43]

Although it was anticipated that a final and acceptable inventory would be submitted by June 1971, it was not completed until 1973.[44] In the meantime, a one-page summary of sources for locating historic sites, structures, and artifacts for inclusion in the first plan was incorporated into the preliminary plan that was submitted in September 1970.[45]

When both Mott and Porter informed National Park Service representatives in June 1970 that California would be unable to complete its history plan to meet the federal timetable, they were permitted to forward instead a "draft 'plan for a plan'" as a way to meet the minimum qualifications for the National Register program. The Park Service's willingness to accept this alternative revealed their near desperate desire to implement their new mandate.[46] It is also clear that other states were having difficulty meeting the deadline. A memo from Ernest Allen Connally, chief of the Office of Archeology and Historic Preservation, to all state liaison officers less than a month after the San Francisco regional meeting urged states to submit their plans by the end of August. Cognizant "of the difficulties faced by each of you," Connally reinforced his hope that states that were unable to forward a fully developed plan would use "the provisional acceptance procedure...to prepare a brief, broad discussion of the major topics to be covered in their plan,...and to submit it as the first edition of their plan" by September 1.[47]

California's preliminary plan was submitted on schedule and in accordance with these revised and very lenient conditions.

California's Preliminary History Plan

By the summer of 1970, preparations for the state's first history plan were well underway. The Historical Landmarks Advisory Committee, reorganized in July 1969, finally included a historian, an architect, and an archaeologist. It now met federal requirements for the National Register review board. County data were being solicited for the inventory, and a table of contents, a preliminary work outline, and a schedule had been submitted to Director Mott for his approval.[48]

Mott's response to the table of contents, which was reproduced in the preliminary plan with only minor stylistic changes, was to show it to the keeper of the National Register, who approved it at the June 1970 regional meeting of state liaison officers. He cautioned his staff, however, that Murtagh stressed "the philosophy of interpretation and preservation of history...[and] would like for us to discuss our feelings concerning philosophy relative to historical preservation, restoration and interpretation."[49] The keeper also recommended inclusion of a section for projected funding needs for the next three to five years.[50]

In contrast to his reaction to the table of contents, the director challenged the need to identify and chart all historical classification systems for the history plan. He deemed such an effort unnecessary because it would only add "to the confusion and controversy," and asked: "Can't we just present what our classification system is going to be in connection with our program here in California?"[51] That is exactly what the preliminary plan did. California history was divided into three major eras—Indian, Hispanic, and American—with the explanation that this "adopted classification reduces to its most simple form the occupancy of the State by man."[52]

The purpose of the preliminary plan as set forth in its Introduction was to implement the state's historical philosophy:

- To assume the leadership in coordinating efforts, both public and private, to preserve the valuable examples of the State's colorful history, its sites, structures and artifacts

- To assume a prominent historical 'supplier role' in acquiring historical areas of State significance and protecting them as units of the State Park System

- To interpret California history, its themes, stories and significances to the general population, to educators and students, to history hobbyists, to professional historians and to special groups as required

- To provide new 'social utility' to the meaning of history to help in the struggle to solve present nationwide social problems by relating better our past to our present and future.[53]

The preliminary plan clearly favored the State Park System. Simply put, criteria for the preservation and interpretation of historical resources were twofold: the resource had to be of statewide significance and be accepted into the State Park System. The discussion of historical deficiencies dealt with park properties and acquisitions. The same was true for the first grant submissions which were for acquisition and development projects in the park units. The reasons were:

> first, there is money budgeted at the State level that can be used for matching purposes; second, it is necessary to complete the Comprehensive California History Plan in order to recommend projects for matching funds at the local levels or for private enterprise.[54]

Connally informed Mott on December 31, 1970, that the National Park Service had approved California's preliminary plan. The lengthy delay between submission and approval was due to Connally's request for additional proof of official state review and approval of the plan, including approval by the Historical Landmarks Advisory Committee whose individual signatures attesting to their positive recommendation were forwarded to Washington in mid-December. Connally stated to Mott that all states whose first plans had been accepted would be given a minimum of two years of eligibility "to expedite funding of projects and to respond to the exceptional efforts made by so many States to produce a comprehensive and functional plan." Thus, California's preliminary plan was approved for January 1, 1971, through December 31, 1972.[55]

It had been a productive year for the Department of Parks and Recreation. With the official acceptance of the preliminary history plan by the National Park Service, California was now eligible for acquisition and development monies. Earlier, in October 1970, the department received its second apportionment. Of a total $129,190, the department designated $63,954 to develop the state's comprehensive history plan. Planning for this work began before year's end, and the mandated plan would be produced several years later.[56]

Reconstitution of the
State Historical Landmarks Advisory Committee

The 1966 federal legislation increased the responsibilities and membership of the State Historical Landmarks Advisory Committee. Its reporting relationship had been altered, for the committee now advised the Director of the Department of Parks and Recreation instead of the Park and Recreation Commission. Administrative support, however, continued to be provided by John Michael's Interpretive Services Section.

The in-house debate over the implementation of the federal preservation program had an impact on the advisory committee in several ways. During 1968, there was considerable staff discussion regarding possible changes in support personnel for the committee because of its added National Register duties. John Michael, the committee's executive secretary, aggressively defied all attempts to remove responsibility for the committee from his purview. Michael believed that the committee's contacts with nearly all of the state's historical societies, combined with "the unofficial interplay between the Interpretive Services Section and the historical societies," were some of his "most important informational pipelines and...which, if stoppered, will prove a serious blow to the quality of our interpretations." This advantage did not detract from the committee's primary function of reviewing and marking historical landmarks. There was no need for additional staff for that task because the burden of proof rested on the applicant. Committee members included eminent historians; additional research had been requested of the Resource Management and Protection Division only once in more than twenty landmark applications. Furthermore, a clerical worker had already established an efficient tracking and filing system.[57]

Through his supervisor, Robert Bates, Michael vehemently rejected James Tryner's suggestion that the committee be renamed the California Historical Resource Advisory Committee and that his division historian, Allen Welts, become secretary to the committee on National Register matters.[58]

Bates reminded Mott that Michael's section was "doing an excellent job" as staff to the committee and stood ready to assume the added National Register responsibility with support from Tryner's division. As for the name change, Bates cautioned: "If the name of the Committee and subsequent duties of the Committee are changed so that they become the Historical Resource Advisory Committee, the landmark program could well be submerged and relegated to a secondary role in our program." Bates emphasized that both Tryner's staff and Deputy Director Ray Hunter had previously agreed that the committee would serve two functions:

> Primarily that of recommending to you historical landmark
> sites for registration...Its secondary responsibility would be
> to review and possibly recommend sites to be included in
> the National Register.

Bates urged that the committee remain "status quo in name and staff," and that an archaeologist and an architect be added as previously agreed. The addition of these two disciplines would be an interim solution and would enable the committee to consider both landmark and National Register requests. "As you know," said Bates, "work on the National Register has all but stopped, due to lack of appropriation, and the future looks somewhat bleak." Should federal funding become available later, a separate professional and technical committee could then be appointed to conduct the historical inventory that was called for in Assembly Concurrent Resolution No. 25.[59]

The debate ended when Mott decided to follow Bates' recommendations in January 1969. The committee was to remain "status quo in name and staff relationship" and to include an archaeologist and an architect.[60] The issue of a name change, however, did not disappear.

Director Mott informed the committee of their expanded role under recent federal law at their first meeting in 1970 in San Leandro. In addition to reviewing National Register nominations, they would also become "directly involved in the historic planning program" for the department's history plan. These new responsibilities, he said, justified a new name, which he recommended the committee consider. Legislation making that change could be introduced as early as 1971.[61]

Attending that meeting were two new gubernatorial appointees to the committee: Professor of Anthropology Clement W. Meighan, Ph.D., and architect Raymond Girvigian, A.I.A. The decision to add these two disciplines to the existing committee, instead of creating an entirely new board, reflected Russell Porter's reading of the political realities of the times. As he explained to Keeper Murtagh when he requested approval for these additions in 1968:

> I do not believe that the Governor will wish to appoint a separate and parallel body for the purposes of the Historic Preservation Act program when, by law, he must appoint the 'best qualified' people to this existing body.[62]

Porter's prediction was accurate. In July 1969, Governor Ronald Reagan signed A.B. 1213 which revised the Pubic Resources Code. The governor was now authorized to appoint a seven member committee "to include such professional persons in the field of history, architecture, archaeology, and such other disciplines as he may deem are best qualified to carry out the purpose of this article...." Appointments were now for four years instead of service at the governor's pleasure. The committee's mandates were expanded to include the maintenance of "a comprehensive record of all archaeological sites in California," and obtaining data from all appropriate sources.[63] A year later, the committee approved its first National Register nominations and forwarded fifty-nine recommendations to the keeper in Washington, D.C.[64]

As the committee began to examine National Register nominations, they found themselves wrestling with unclear criteria and guidelines. In August 1970, for example, Mott asked Murtagh "whether all eligible local, regional and state sites that meet the federal criteria should be placed on the National Register—or whether an attempt should be made to be more selective in our nominations." He relayed concern that unless the committee and staff could practice some selectivity, "the public records could be cluttered with conceivably thousands of historic sites." Furthermore, there would be "no long-term function for the advisory committee to fulfill unless the Committee is allowed to exercise its judgement on the quality and significance of each nomination proposal."[65]

The keeper insisted that the criteria had to be broad "to insure the greatest latitude of interpretation and to keep them applicable to optimum degree in such a diverse country as ours." This, he said, required the professional expertise of the review board. The nominations "should be considered an objective assessment" of California's "contribution to the collective patrimony of our Nation, irrespective of ownership." He also enclosed the section of *With Heritage So Rich* that contained the following challenge:

> if we wish to have a future with greater meaning, we must concern ourselves not only with the historic highlights, but we must be concerned with the total heritage of the nation and all that is worth preserving from our past as a living part of the present. [66]

The National Register program did not dominate the committee's agenda during these early years. Its focus continued to be the historical landmarks program, and in that regard, two concerns deserve special mention.

One issue was the continued pressure on the committee by state legislators to approve historic monuments in their respective districts. In 1967, for example, Michael reported to the committee that Senate Resolution No. 114 requested the placement of a historical monument on the site of San Diego's Carlsbad Well. The committee agreed to forward an application form to the city of Carlsbad.[67] A year later, the committee received House Resolution No. 387 seeking recognition for the grave site of Russell G. O'Brien, who was "credited with originating the custom of rising and standing when the National Anthem of the United States is being sung." The legislature was informed that the request did not meet the landmarks criteria and that, furthermore, the committee did not recommend birth sites and grave sites of historical figures. It was suggested that a patriotic group such as the Daughters of the American Revolution be contacted instead.[68]

Such requests prompted Director Mott to write to the state legislators regarding "some misunderstanding" concerning the landmarks program. Although his department wanted to be cooperative "in registering and marking appropriate and significant historical landmarks," he informed them that the committee's duly authorized responsibility was to process all requests in accordance with approved criteria. Mott told the legislators that all applications, whether requested by constituents or generated by other individuals, had to be reviewed by the committee. Mott therefore asked that they direct their constituents to his department for forms and staff assistance. The letter, however, fell on deaf ears, and the department continued to receive resolutions from various legislators on behalf of their constituents.[69] Although Mott, as department director, had final approval power over the landmarks, not once in his entire tenure did he overrule the committee. Nor did he ever approve a landmark without the committee's consent.

The reconstituted Historical Landmarks Advisory Committee had an immediate impact on the criteria for the landmarks program. Upon Michael's suggestion, the committee in mid-1970 quickly revised its policy statement and produced specific criteria to evaluate applications. Not only were sites to be of statewide importance, nine "historical influences" were identified as major categories for consideration: "anthropological (archeology and ethnic history), cultural (including social, education, and arts), military (significant military actions and activities of primary importance to California), political, architectural, economic, scientific and technical, religious, and experimental." At Girvigian's request, a new section on architectural landmarks was added. Hereafter, applicants were encouraged to seek the assistance of the American Institute of Architects because it was "the leading authority concerning background and technical information pertinent to historical architecture." A special architectural supplement was required of all architectural requests for registration.[70]

A statement regarding historic trail signs was another addition. The committee had earlier recommended to the director that a special marker be designed to identify historic trails such as the Emigrant, Portola, and Anza trails. The reasoning was that "one typical and representative site identifying an important trail should be registered in each county and that all other sites and camps be identified" by this marker. The committee feared that a proliferation of landmark plaques to mark the same trail would detract from its significance. Thus, they recommended that in each county, a representative campsite on a trail be selected and registered with a plaque; other campsites would either be acknowledged as Points of Historical Interest or marked with the new trail signs.[71] One number would apply "to all trail signs along a specific trail."[72]

The Point of Historical Interest program that had been established in 1965 did not live up to the expectations of the committee members who implemented the program. In August 1968, Michael wrote a second letter to all county boards of supervisors at the direction of the committee who saw that requests for point registration "were being presented to the Boards of Supervisors by others than the local advisory committee."[73] Michael's letter, which asked the supervisors to appoint a local Historical Landmarks Advisory Committee to recommend registration of county sites of significance, resulted from the committee's discussion of historian Allen Welts' protest over registration of the Lopez Adobe and Descanso Gardens as Points of Historical Interest. Welts, who now supervised the Historical Resources Section, viewed neither of the sites as "significant to the history of Los Angeles." He told the committee that he was recording his "objection to rubber-stamped approval of every deposition sworn to by misguided but well meaning history enthusiasts."[74]

In his response to Welts, committee chairman R. Coke Wood explained that the staff and committee did not wish to "intrude on a county's prerogative" to make recommendations to the program

> because it was felt that they are in a better position to recognize and evaluate Points of Historical Interest within their own sphere of influence, and it would be presumptuous of the State to try to tell local people what is or what is not historically important from their standpoint.

Wood agreed that the committee did "not wish to 'rubber stamp,'" but would continue to act "upon the previous advice of staff and accept...the recommendations of the Board of Supervisors." [75]

When the committee adopted criteria in 1970, they did not include requirements for a county advisory committee. The supervisors were simply to endorse and transmit those applications they considered suitable, along with adequate research and bibliographic evidence attesting to their significance to the "area's social, cultural, economical, political, religious, or military history." [76] Throughout the remainder of the 1970s, the committee did not change its practices and continued to approve supervisorial recommendations with little or no dissent.

CHAPTER

11

California's Historic Preservation Program: Completion of State Plans and Inventories, 1971-1975

The accomplishments of the Department of Parks and Recreation during the first half of the 1970s determined the direction of the state's preservation programs for the remainder of the decade. The department's external, or non-state park system, preservation programs were grouped under a new section, History Preservation, which produced California's comprehensive preservation plans, a statewide inventory of historic resources, and annual updates describing programmatic achievements and the status of the state's preservation grant projects.

Creation of the History Preservation Section

In the summer of 1972, Director William Penn Mott, Jr., again reorganized the Department of Parks and Recreation. The preservation-related responsibilities of the Interpretive Services Section were grouped into a new History Preservation Section supervised by John Michael which was relocated both physically and administratively. Placed in the Resources Building, Michael now reported to Russell Porter, manager of the Grants and Statewide Studies Branch.[1] Thus, from July 1, 1972, to October 20, 1975, when the section was dismantled and its functions assumed by the Office of Historic Preservation, the department's History Preservation Section coordinated California's preservation efforts.

The History Preservation Section united under a single supervisor the key components of the department's non-park system preservation programs: the National Register of Historic Places, California Historical Landmarks Program, Point of Historical Interest, statewide preservation planning activities, federal funding and grants-in-aid proposals. In addition to the state history plan and annual updates, the section was responsible for "reviewing Environmental Impact Statements to determine the effect of public works projects on historic sites, and for the protection and safeguarding of sites" either on or eligible for the National Register.[2]

From Director Mott's perspective, the section "was organized expressly to work with matters associated with the National History Preservation Act and to serve" the Historical Landmarks Advisory Committee. The section was established only because the department received federal planning and survey monies:

> We could not have hoped to establish this section as a General Fund supported activity....In light of the administration's attitude toward the funding of new, independent units of government, we could not have done otherwise.[3]

The unit's staff perceived the new organizational structure in a somewhat different light and claimed that the section was the first example of "a total commitment by the Department to statewide historical concerns and [by] knowledgeable staff to properly carry out the Director's duties as State Liaison Officer for the National Historical Preservation Act." In addition to the responsibilities mentioned earlier, the History Preservation Section was to assume the liaison officer's duties regarding reports and preservation coordination, including contacts with federal officials.[4]

Michael remained in charge until June 1974, assisted by three professionals and a secretary.[5] His primary responsibility, as former Chief of the Operations Division John H. Knight recalled and Michael later confirmed, "was to complete the federally mandated comprehensive history plan. Once that was finished, he was given another assignment."[6] Michael's replacement was James M. Doyle who remained in that position until the section was disbanded in 1975.[7]

Completion of the Comprehensive Plan for the Preservation of California's Resources

Intensive work on the three-volume comprehensive plan began in August 1971. Volume One would be the history plan, which was in part an expanded version of the preliminary plan; completion of this volume was scheduled for February 15, 1972. Volume Two would be a county inventory of all projects proposed for inclusion in the history plan. Volume Three was to be the annual action program and was to include a summary of deficiencies as well as potential projects. Volumes Two and Three were to be ready by February 20, 1972.[8] To expedite matters, Mott sent sixty letters to various county commissions and administrative units, museums, and historical societies requesting materials on local inventories and suggestions for projects. These agencies were to respond by December 15, 1971, if they wanted to be included in the state plan.[9]

The department revised its timetable in the spring of 1972 when the National Park Service extended California's eligibility under the preliminary plan to July 1, 1973, rather than December 31, 1972. What was non-negotiable was the submission by June 1, 1972, of a list of proposed expenditures for specific preservation projects that would constitute California's application for federal funds for 1972-1973. Volume Three, the *Annual History Preservation Program*, was completed on schedule.[10]

The revised deadlines were timely for several reasons. The first volume had to be rewritten to make it more readable and because it failed to adequately describe the state's historical and archaeological problems as well as the department's responsibilities and project selection criteria. There were two additional concerns: the unexpected retirement of Staff Historian Cliff Bisbee who was to write two chapters, and the anticipated creation of the History Preservation Section. Russell Porter, who supervised this section, believed that it was only "appropriate that John [Michael] participate in the final stages of the writing of the plan, since it will be his responsibility to later interpret the findings and recommendations and help implement the plan."[11]

Volume One: California's Comprehensive Preservation Program

California's *History Plan*, Volume One, was finally published in December 1973. Although it claimed to be a "comprehensive preservation program" for the purpose of developing "an organized system for preservation and interpretation of the state's historic resources,"[12] the plan was clearly designed to further the programs and projects of the Department of Parks and Recreation.

From the outset, departmental personnel who worked on the history plan knew exactly what Mott's objectives were. Mott intended to establish departmental criteria and priorities for the acquisition, development, and maintenance of historic sites of statewide significance. Properties that failed these tests were to be given to other agencies for maintenance and operation. Not only would contributions made by gold mining, missions, agriculture, railroading, and lumber be interpreted at appropriate sites, California's ethnic communities would also be represented: Japanese (Coloma), Chinese (Weaverville), Black (Allensworth), and Russian (Fort Ross). Mott further recommended that the history plan include a discussion of federal, state, county, and municipal preservation responsibilities and a list of preservation-related historic boards, commissions, and societies. The plan was to implement Mott's belief in the "living museum concept and use of history areas by the people."[13]

The history plan's focus on projects and programs most beneficial to the department did not go unnoticed. An in-house reviewer noted that "its overwhelming emphasis on this Department's own history, background, circumstances, and desires tend to make it little more than a plan for this Department's efforts in this field." Without objective criteria to judge proposals and in the absence of a complete inventory, "many of the projects recommended in this plan look like nothing more than someone's pet ideas and all the old chestnuts grandfathered in." Criticism was also leveled at the plan's lack of consideration for display and interpretive requirements of proposed acquisitions, its failure to mention anticipatable shortages of trained personnel, and the exclusion of other organizations and agencies.[14]

Director Mott's conviction that the history plan and the department were closely intertwined was evident in another part of the plan. In the section on "History Preservation Philosophy," the plan recommended implementation of the "flow of history" concept:

> Under this concept, the primary historic theme or value is emphasized, but it is enhanced and amplified by interpretation of secondary historic values both prior and subsequent to the interpretive period of the primary value.[15]

The "flow of history" concept had been introduced earlier in 1973 for incorporation into the department's *Resource Management Directives*[16] and later was approved by the Historical Landmarks Advisory Committee for inclusion into the plan.[17]

When completed, Volume One contained seven chapters, a short bibliography, and five appendices.[18] It was organized in accordance with suggestions made by S. Sydney Bradford, Grants Program administrator for the National Register. These suggestions included an expansion of the treatment of California history, removal of the summary of California's preservation efforts from the appendix to the main body of the plan, and development of chapters on preservation planning and preservation philosophy. In return, Bradford agreed to extend the deadline for submission of Volume One to January 1, 1974.[19]

Before final publication, various individuals and groups received copies of the draft plan for comment. With the exception of the first chapter, the draft generated little debate. As Mott explained to Norman B. Livermore, Jr., secretary for resources, the remainder of the report was not controversial because "it deals essentially with the eras of California history, project selection processes, preservation guidelines and a discussion of preservation and registry programs in California." [20] It was the portion on findings and recommendations that provoked discussion.

Chapter One contained thirty-two recommendations divided into six categories. The following segment of Recommendation No. 1 produced the most heated exchange:

> It is...recommended that steps be taken within the next five years to create an office of History to centralize all present and future state responsibilities relating to California history, including planning, technical assistance, financial assistance, coordination, research, and the care, treatment, and housing of artifacts and historical objects, and that this office be created in conformance with legislative acceptance of the recommendations of the task force established by Section 5097.91 of the Public Resources Code.[21]

Among the vocal opponents to the proposed Office of History was Secretary Livermore, who stated: "I could not support that part of your Recommendation...which makes reference to the creation of a separate Department of History."[22] Mott told Livermore that not only were both his staff and the Historical Landmarks Advisory Committee supportive of such an office, they also felt it should assume a greater statewide historical preservation role "to plan for and monitor a more broadly scoped program." Mott believed that his department should continue to expand and enhance its "history function." Should a need for a department be demonstrated in the future, it belonged under his jurisdiction as "a Division of History...to coordinate history activities, but leaving the operation of historical units within the State Park System."[23]

The Historical Landmarks Advisory Committee strenuously disagreed with Mott's position. In July 1973, committee chair Kathryn Kaiser wrote to Mott to endorse a separate agency and to suggest amending the recommendation to include "a good professional administrator...whose responsibility shall be limited to administering our state historic preservation program." She also criticized the plan's failure to provide a mechanism for implementing its recommendations, and asked "*how* are recommendations like #1 going to be put into effect?" Kaiser stated: "I would like to see California *be* a leader, and not settle for a minor role in the State's historic preservation plans."[24]

The committee discussed the plan at its July meeting, and Kaiser later reported to Mott that they had reaffirmed the need to insert a specific date for implementation of Recommendation No. 1.[25] In August, Kaiser informed the committee that Mott had agreed to put "within the next five years" into the recommendation. This was an acceptable compromise because it was "essentially the same as our suggested wording of 'by 1978.'"[26]

Another source of contention between Mott and the committee in was over a change in wording in Recommendation No. 1 from "Department of History" to "Division of History" and finally to "office of History." In January 1974, six members signed a letter of protest to Mott regarding the substitution of "Department of History" with "Division of History" without prior consultation or approval from the committee. The committee condemned Mott's "unilateral decision" which "jeopardized" its position as "ethically wrong."[27]

The director's response was quick and lengthy. Mott first expressed his disappointment that the committee did not discuss the matter with him when they had met earlier that same month. He informed them that Secretary Livermore frequently emphasized the governor's desire "to reduce the number of separate, uncoordinated departments, and to suppress proposals that call for the creation of new independent entities in state government." For these reasons, and because of plans to reorganize and consolidate existing departments, Mott decided to replace "Department of History" with "Office of History." This was, he explained, the only way to obtain approval for both the recommendation and the history plan. The substitution, he reassured the committee, in no way changed the intent of the recommendation. The selection of "office" was deliberate, because it was an organizational description that could be "interpreted to mean any of a wide range of governmental units." Mott also reminded Kaiser that they had earlier discussed and agreed to the substitution of "office" for "department." The director stressed his personal support for "a separate working body for history preservation," which he claimed was embodied in the year-and-a-half-old History Preservation Section.[28]

Two weeks later, Kaiser informed Mott that the committee would agree to the distribution of the plan "with the understanding and contingent upon the proviso that the Department will actually cooperate with us in the submission of legislation to the current session of the State Legislature for the creation of an independent Commission."[29] Because the legislative process was too time-consuming to permit the introduction of such a law before the April 15 deadline, Mott suggested to Kaiser that the committee consider other ways to broaden its responsibilities. The best course of action, he advised, would be to change the committee's title and increase its duties, while simultaneously building a constituency to support legislation for an Office of History.[30] The result of his advice was the creation of the State Historical Resources Commission in 1974 and the Office of Historic Preservation in 1975. They were not to be independent agencies, but would remain under the jurisdiction of the Department of Parks and Recreation, just as Mott wanted.

Another recommendation with long-lasting import was No. 11, which suggested the addition of a historic restoration provision to the Uniform Public Building Code which "should meet the intent of protecting public health and safety but should retain enough flexibility to allow restoration of a historic feature while maintaining its historic integrity."[31] The State Historical Building Code became a reality in 1979 when it was adopted as Section 8 of Title 24, the State Buildings Standards Code.

The history plan also contained two specific recommendations for the protection of the state's archaeological resources. Recommendation No. 4 requested a state-sponsored program "to identify and inventory archeological sites, areas, and regions," and that the information collected be computerized.[32] The second recommendation was that archaeological sites in the State Park System not be destroyed when other feasible alternatives existed, that professional archaeologists be allowed to investigate a site before its destruction, and that salvage archaeology be permitted only as a last resort. Livermore's objection that this recommendation differed from Mott's "previous verbal commitment that it is unnecessary to save *every* archaeological site if the time zone contained in a given site has been adequately covered by preservation of a previous site or sites" resulted in Mott's reassurance that "my staff has already corrected this error and it will be changed to read that 'significant' sites will be protected rather than 'every' site." [33] Interestingly, the final recommendation did not include the word "significant."

The inclusion of archaeology in the plan was largely the result of the National Park Service's warning to the states that as far as it was concerned, whenever "history" was used, "it should be considered to include archeology.[34] With this directive in mind, and supported by the committee's archaeologist, Clement W. Meighan, the final plan made an effort to protect the state's archaeological resources.[35]

Volume One of the plan elicited criticism from the keeper of the National Register, William J. Murtagh. Some objections were simply related to format. For example, the title was too general and incorrectly implied that the plan covered more than historic preservation issues. The cover and title page excluded the volume's edition number and mention of related state programs. Volume One also lacked a state map.[36] Although these shortcomings were easily rectifiable, others were of a much more serious nature.

The keeper was particularly critical of the plan's section on preservation problems and recommendations. He echoed a concern that others had voiced earlier:

> it is our opinion that too much emphasis has been placed on State acquisition of historic sites....The chapter as a whole appears, in fact, to be geared too much toward the California State parks system and its acquisition and protection functions. This focus is, from our point of view, misdirected since the preservation program of the Department of Parks and Recreation appears to take precedence over the National Register historic preservation program. A de-emphasis on the State's role as chief protector of historic resources and an increased emphasis on the role of the private sector and its involvement seem appropriate.[37]

Another of the plan's deficiencies was its brevity. The historical summary needed "more emphasis on social and cultural history" and "more detail...to make a better balanced and complete picture." The chapter on preservation philosophy was also too brief and needed to include "the 'what' of preservation, as well as the 'why.'"[38]

Murtagh's comments were designed to assist California in the planning and compilation of a revised edition of Volumes One and Two. The keeper saw the state plan as "first and foremost a planning tool subject to continuous review, refinement, and revision." He expected California to submit the comprehensively revised volumes by March 31, 1976, a not unreasonable expectation inasmuch as he had extended the deadline for nearly a year at the state's request.[39]

In the end, California never submitted its two-volume revision because late in 1975, the National Park Service suspended this requirement.

Although the revised history plan did not materialize, the Office of Historic Preservation decided to complete work on the statewide inventory.[40]

Volume Two: California's Statewide Inventory

California published inventories of historic sites and resources in 1973 and 1976. The August 1973 edition of Volume Two of the history plan, *Inventory of Historic Features*, contained approximately 3,000 entries. Confined to those properties submitted before September 1, 1972, and based in part on county surveys, this first survey provided limited information. Listed only by county, each entry was checked off by category: historic era, cultural significance, recognition in existing programs such as the National Register and California Historical Landmark listings, and private or public ownership status. The historic values within each site were not identified.[41]

The history plan's overall emphasis on the State Park System was apparent in this volume as well. The Introduction to the inventory concluded that the data demonstrated "that deficiencies within the State Park System parallel those in the statewide inventory...." Therefore:

> it is evident that priority must be given to the addition to the State Park System of historic features from the early and recent Indian suberas, both Hispanic suberas, and the late American subera. Plans are now underway to locate historic features that clearly typify significant characteristics of each of these suberas, and steps will be taken to acquire such features as soon as they can be identified.[42]

Although Volume Two is dated August 1973, State Historic Preservation Officer Mott did not send copies of the inventory to Murtagh until February 1974. In an accompanying letter, Mott certified that the Historical Landmarks Advisory Committee had approved the inventory and that the state had taken an active role in the compilation of the survey, despite the statement in Volume One that the inventory "was compiled from published source materials and was augmented by some input from county surveys and local registers."[43]

Mott felt compelled to clarify the state's role in the survey procedure because of questions raised by National Register officials. At issue was the statement in Volume One that the State Historical Landmarks Advisory Committee would

> monitor local participation in the survey and inventory, although the State Historic Preservation Officer will retain

overall responsibility for the program, and his staff will continue to act in an advisory capacity.[44]

Mott insisted that

> I, as the State Historic Preservation Officer, retain overall responsibility for the program; my staff serves the California Historical Landmarks Advisory Committee through organizing the survey, publishing and distributing all survey materials, setting up a computer program data bank, conducting workshops, day-to-day liaison with the local jurisdictions and historical organizations, evaluating and recording survey data and publishing the survey.[45]

Despite Mott's reassurances, Murtagh refused to believe that Mott understood his charge. Throughout Mott's tenure as state historic preservation officer, Murtagh remained firmly convinced that Mott did not realize that the statewide survey was his responsibility. Although local input was important, Murtagh warned Mott that it "should not totally make up the inventory but rather represent parts of the survey which must be comprehensively understood and collectively planned as a State responsibility on a statewide basis at the State level." The keeper charged:

> There is no clear indication that you as State Historic Preservation Officer through staff representatives are assuming responsibility for initiating that kind of comparative survey, supervising the comprehensive survey effort, and planning for its fulfillment.[46]

In May 1974, Murtagh continued "California's eligibility to receive grants under its preliminary plan" through June 30, 1975, but cautioned Mott that the statewide survey was to be incorporated into the next comprehensive edition of the plan. "We are gratified to learn," said Murtagh, "that during the 1974-75 program you will assume responsibility for conducting a comprehensive statewide survey of the historical resources of California."[47]

Murtagh's skepticism was apparent in a letter informing Mott's successor, Herbert Rhodes, that California would receive an extension of eligibility for preservation matching grants-in-aid until March 31, 1976. By that date, Murtagh expected to receive revised editions of both Volumes One and Two and a statement from Rhodes "regarding the State's acceptance of responsibility for the comprehensive statewide survey."[48]

The keeper provided the new state historic preservation officer with additional observations on the deficiencies in California's survey effort. One area of concern was "the lack of centralized control and responsibility at the

State level for the conduct of the statewide survey," an issue he had previously raised with Mott. The second was the need for more than a system of charts listing county sites, and Murtagh requested a thematic listing of sites with a brief description and statement of significance. Furthermore, instead of including "architecture" as part of the "domestic" theme which he found questionable, Murtagh recommended "arts" as a more applicable general theme for the inventory.[49] These suggestions were adopted in the revised version of Volume Two, which was published in 1976.

The goal of Phase II of the state's inventory was to identify an additional 50,000 historic features.[50] It fell to the newly created History Preservation Section to implement this county-by-county survey. Groundwork for the survey began in the fall of 1972 and by July 1973, the section's staff held its first pilot orientation meeting with volunteers from Placer, Nevada, and Sierra counties to discuss the statewide inventory and the creation of a county historical advisory committee or heritage commission. The trial session was successful. Beginning in August with the assistance of personal letters from Mott to local historical societies and other groups, the staff scheduled and completed similar workshops for every county in the state.[51]

Progress was swift, and by the end of October 1973, thirty counties had selected liaison persons to represent their respective areas in the inventory. These representatives were crucial in the process because all survey forms had to be submitted through them.[52] By the end of May 1974, all of the state's fifty-eight counties had coordinators appointed to work with the History Preservation Section to develop the statewide inventory, and six counties had submitted a total of seventy-two forms.[53] On the eve of the demise of the History Preservation Section and completion of the inventory for the revised Volume Two, thirty-six counties had sent in a total of 554 forms. As of March 1, 1975, there were 25,377 sites listed in the inventory.[54]

One interesting criticism of the inventory procedure came from Lowell Smith, chairman of the Northern California Regional Conservation Committee of the Sierra Club. Smith wrote to Mott to express his fear that involving county supervisors in the review procedure would open the entire process to political pressure and influence. After all, Smith observed, "it is no secret that many supervisors in California have rather close associations with real estate and development interests....Thus it would not be too surprising to see supervisors prejudicial against the historical importance, and authenticity of a site submitted for inventory." He suggested the review be done instead by "a competent historical society." Although Mott shared Smith's concerns, he stated that when the state tried to work with groups purporting to speak for the county but lacking official recognition and sanction, there was "complete turmoil." As for an official state historical society to coordinate the program, Mott said that in accordance with the recommendations in Volume One, "we will recommend that a special board or department be created which will coordinate all history programs throughout the state." At that time, however, no single society was equipped to review the anticipated 50,000 site recommendations.[55]

The revised inventory of 1976 reflected continued discussions between the California staff and the National Park Service through the summer of 1975 and incorporated many of the park service's suggestions. For example, the thematic organization of the 3,000 sites was redone, and a brief description now accompanied each listing. The appendix identified sites alphabetically and by county; a glossary and state map were added. Accountability for the survey was clearly attributed to "the State Historic Preservation Officer and the Office of Historic Preservation [who] have assumed full responsibility for this continuing project."[56]

In late November 1975, it was decided to proceed with plans to publish the revised edition. Historian Knox Mellon, historic preservation coordinator, informed Director Rhodes that, although Volumes One and Two were not required until new federal guidelines were developed, the Office of Historic Preservation planned to print 2500 copies of Volume Two because $14,000 had already been spent on the project, and to stop then would have saved a mere $500. Furthermore, the publication would assist the planning efforts of governmental and private groups, would fulfill outstanding promises to survey participants, and would provide a public statement of the state's preservation philosophy and goals.[57]

The elimination of the federal requirements prompted William E. Padgett, historic preservation specialist, to write to the National Register staff with a summary of California's experiences. His comments elucidated perceptions that federal mandates regarding the history plan and inventory were too detailed and "overly burdensome." Staff energies, said Padgett, would have been better spent if "geared to active and effective preservation work. Plans should guide historic preservation and not preclude it through diversion of staff time." The history plan in particular lacked a well-defined focus, serving as a "catchall" to address too many diverse audiences instead of providing leadership and useful information to preservationists. The inventory should be viewed as a planning tool and delete the requirement that sites be organized by themes with narrative summaries. Padgett insisted that because planners want to know only what and where sites exist, inventory requirements for thematic organization and narrative descriptions "divert literally hundreds of hours of staff time away from genuine preservation efforts."[58]

Although some staff members may have found the federal mandates "burdensome," it is obvious that many of their positions could not have existed without the yearly allocations of federal monies for plans and programs intended to promote preservation.

Volume Three: California's Annual Preservation Program

Volume Three of the state's comprehensive plan was California's annual preservation program. The first plan was dated June 1, 1972, and was a mere thirteen pages long. It marked the beginning of yearly plans that combined annual grant applications with updates on the status of preservation in the state.[59]

This brief document revealed the continuing state emphasis on preservation programs within the park system.[60] It included a list of priorities for the parks and historical units of the Department of Parks and Recreation which constituted the core of the plan's long-range preservation effort.[61] The plan anticipated that in the next two decades, the department would require some $73.7 million for "restoration, boundary protection, and...acquisitions." As for providing adequate historical facilities for the remainder of the state, the department declared that it did "not yet presume to know what portion of this huge undertaking" was its responsibility.[62] The plan's first paragraph succinctly stated the department's position:

> While the state offers this program as a demonstration of its intentions [to add significance and understanding to the preservation efforts of the public and private sectors by combining preservation into one program], it does not wish to dictate the direction of such local efforts but merely to provide leadership, to offer its guidance, and to cooperate with such local agencies, private organizations and individuals as may be requested.[63]

The bias toward state park projects continued throughout Mott's tenure as state historic preservation officer. In 1975, Keeper Murtagh again expressed his concern that California's preservation programs funded by federal grants were too heavily supportive of state park projects. He urged an increase in funding for local and private projects to involve larger numbers of participants:

> In order to make a truly meaningful historic preservation program for all the people of California, it is necessary to allocate a larger proportion of grant funds to local and private groups.[64]

The first annual program, completed before the creation of the History Preservation Section, was quickly reviewed by the keeper. Although he observed that it lacked a thematic summary and data regarding plans to update the first two volumes, he found no other serious objections.[65]

The second annual program was forwarded to Washington in July 1973. In September, the National Park Service approved the apportionment warrant in the plan and informed Michael "that an outstanding job had been done on the volume."[66] The well-designed forty-one page document updated the state's progress toward completion of its comprehensive plan and expanded the section on preservation philosophy. The goals of the 1970 plan were reiterated, and a policy for the acquisition and restoration of significant features was specified.[67] The program also introduced the "flow of history" as a preservation concept. Describing history as "a flow of human experiences highlighted by important events, each growing out of the accumulated human activity preceding it and each influencing all that follows," the State of California declared its intent to "fully present this 'flow of history'" through the preservation and interpretation of California history. Therefore, "all preservation and interpretive programs should be analyzed in terms of the 'flow of history' and should consider the period of the historic feature's greatest influence, its period of supporting influence, and its period of waning influence." California assured the park service that it considered the survey and inventory to be of "paramount importance" in the state's planning process.[68]

The 1974 submission differed from its predecessors in several ways. For the first time, the program included requests for funds for privately owned properties.[69] It also identified five recommendations from Volume One as priorities that the department would attempt to coordinate with activities sponsored by the National Trust for Historic Preservation.[70] A detailed explanation of the procedure used to select projects for acquisition and development under the 1974 park bond act was placed in an appendix.[71] Finally, two interpretive programs from the state's thirty-six historic park units were specifically mentioned: the Hyde Street Fair at the San Francisco

Maritime State Historic Park, "the largest living interpretive history program" in the nation; and the Environmental Living Program, which permitted overnight stays at historic parks and national monuments for students, parents, and teachers.[72] The inclusion of these two projects reflected Mott's criticism of the 1966 legislation which deleted interpretation from its mandates. As Mott had explained earlier:

> It seems to me to be almost fallacious to spend the funds and effort toward restoring historic sites and buildings with no money appropriated for the interpretation. It would seem to me that the most important aspect of this program is the interpreting of the historic sites to make them 'live.'[73]

Keeper Murtagh responded at length to the 1974 plan. Not only was he still critical of California's emphasis on its own state park system, he remained disturbed about what appeared to be the state's continued delegation of the federal program to the counties rather than assuming it directly through the preservation officer's staff. To illustrate his point, Murtagh cited reliance on county coordinators to implement the inventory and the solicitation of county volunteers to produce National Register applications. Although he commended California for increasing its National Register nominations from 40 in 1972 to 123 from January 1973 through March 1974, he expressed great disappointment that only 284 sites had been listed thus far: "For a State the size of California with such a rich historical heritage, we expect that your 'track record' should be much better."[74]

The annual plan submitted in June 1975 requested nearly $20 million more than the previous year. This sudden increase reflected a dramatic rise in public interest in preservation, as shown by the receipt of fifty-six letters expressing an intention to seek grants as of the January 1975 deadline. A year earlier, the History Preservation Section received only twenty-three letters.[75]

The 1975 plan differed from the previous annual plans in another way. The subtle change in title from the annual program for "The California History Plan" to the annual program for "The California Historic Preservation Plan" reflected a more substantive shift in policy, which was revealed in the description of California's long-range preservation planning effort. Instead of repeating what was said in Volume One, the new initiative was to be firmly tied to "the new preservation" which

> attempts to preserve the integrity of physical remains of historic development patterns and groups of structures,

such as agricultural settlements, industrial complexes, residential neighborhoods, and commercial districts. These historic resources—existing structures as well as interrelated archeological sites—present tangible remains of past ways of life rather than isolated references to a single individual or event.[76]

Careful, long-range planning was essential if significant sites and structures were to be identified before the bulldozers arrived. And early identification would generate

local community support for preservation through increasing awareness of resources, formulation of local ordinances for preservation, registration of sites that meet certain criteria, application for preservation grant funding in a variety of programs, conveyance of preservation easements or development rights, development of tax incentives, and study of alternative methods of use to recycle historic structures within the community.

This "new preservation" emphasis claimed to be a response to the state's cultural diversity and promised to acknowledge the contributions of all groups by protecting and preserving "representative sites and districts that tell how its various citizens earned their livings, conducted their businesses, spent their leisure time, and expressed their concerns with religion and the arts."[77]

This shift in the state's preservation policies was alluded to in May 1975, when the newly appointed director of the Department of Parks and Recreation, Herbert Rhodes, wrote to Murtagh to assure him that the forthcoming plan would "fully define the State's acceptance of responsibility for the survey."[78] Another indication of a policy change came a few months after the 1975 plan had been submitted. In September, the State Historical Resources Commission (formerly the Historical Landmarks Advisory Committee) approved "Local Project Criteria" for matching grants. The significance of this decision was the recommendation that 70 percent of federal funds be disbursed to local projects, a percentage recommended by both the National Register staff and the National Trust. Under Mott, 50 percent had been retained for state projects. Precedent for the even split between state and local governments was set by the disbursement of Land and Water Conservation funds as determined by the state legislature.[79] Mott believed that priority should be given to properties that were publicly owned and to projects "that are available for public use for which funds are available for continued maintenance, operation, and interpretation." Grant funds were given only to cities and counties and not "to the private sector for the preservation of private structures of historical significance...[because] the funds become state funds and may not be granted to private individuals."[80]

These new directions in preservation policy, however, cannot be attributed solely to the appearance of a new governor. Criteria for allocation of funds and changes in the disbursement ratios, for example, had been considered when Mott was department director. In June 1971, Mott suggested the creation of a task force to develop criteria. The task force, which met for the first time in September, recommended that individual projects be reviewed by a "committee of fairly high level staff people" instead of a citizens' body. Interestingly, John Michael "made clear his feelings that the lion's share of the funds for projects should go to local agencies. This would be in compliance with the promises which have been made by the Director." Although specific ratios were not selected, it was suggested that local allocations be increased to 75 percent, with the state's share reduced to 25 percent. The minutes of the Historical Resources Commission show that it was presented with grant selection criteria to review. The commission was also requested by Mott to hold hearings on how the funds should be allocated and to make recommendations on what percentage of the monies was to be given to non-state owned properties.[81]

Thus, the annual plan that was submitted to the keeper in June 1975 was a mixture of Mott's ideas and those of the new administration. It announced several ambitious objectives for the next decade: completing the statewide inventory, enacting legislation to preserve and restore properties, increasing public awareness and support for preservation, and encouraging both federal and local agencies to plan for preservation. For the first time, the state provided "local communities with matching grants-in-aid to conduct comprehensive professional surveys and inventories" in the hope that this would further the inventory and preservation.[82]

That California was able to contemplate these goals was the result of a decade of progress on other fronts. These included the involvement of the History Preservation Section and the Department of Parks and Recreation in preservation projects outside the State Park System.

12

Statewide Preservation Programs Administered by the History Preservation Section, 1972-1976

The History Preservation Section of the Department of Parks and Recreation had other preservation-related responsibilities in addition to compiling the comprehensive history plan and the inventory of historic resources. These included processing nominations for the National Register of Historic Places, reviewing applications for the California Historical Landmarks and Point of Historical Interest programs, commenting on Environmental Impact Reviews, and providing staff support to the State Historical Resources Commission.

The National Register of Historic Places

Unlike other states where applications are initiated by staff members, California's National Register program depends entirely on nominations generated by private individuals and organizations and other governmental agencies. Local participation became critical after the passage of Proposition 13 (1978) drastically reduced property taxes, causing budgetary and hiring constraints in the face of increasing workloads.[1]

The dependence on applications prepared by the general public created problems for the staff. Submissions were of uneven quality, and workshops had to be held to explain National Register guidelines and procedures. A variety of form letters was developed to handle the increasing workload. The reliance on the public meant, too, that the number of nominations processed each month varied greatly. As many as twenty-six applications, for example, were received in one month, while in other months as few as one nomination was sent to the office.[2]

These and other problems notwithstanding, the National Register program continued to flourish. As of March 1974, 284 sites had been placed on the Register, an increase of 78 over the previous year. Of the 284 sites, 58 were historic districts. By March 1, 1976, 410 sites were on the National Register in the following thematic categories:

Architecture/domestic 133
Economic/industrial 60
Exploration/settlement 102
Government 27
Military 15
Arts/leisure 11
Religion 17
Social/education 38
Aboriginal 8

The number of historic districts increased by 12. Of the state's fifty-eight counties, only four still lacked National Register properties: Alpine, Glenn, Sutter, and Tehama.[3]

Throughout these early years, two issues were of persistent concern to the staff and review board. One of these was the criteria for National Register nominations which William Penn Mott, Jr., director of the Department of Parks and Recreation, and the Historical Landmarks Advisory Committee believed were too general. Better guidelines, Mott told Keeper William J. Murtagh, had to be issued to ensure that the Register did not "become cluttered with a lot of secondary historical structures, thus discounting the important and significant historical structures and areas within a state."[4] Murtagh responded that he was "unsympathetic to any attempt to narrow the criteria" because it would undermine the clearly "environmental intent" of the 1966 federal legislation. "It, therefore, follows that any narrowly drawn criteria to selectively include only what may be considered landmarks, intellectually isolated from their environment, defeats the intent of the legislation and narrows the scope of applicability of the law." Murtagh also reminded Mott that although the criteria were "purposely broadly drawn" to maximize inclusion of a state's environmental resources, "the latitude of interpretation is the state's responsibility" and that "quality professional staff and value judgements are eminently important in making decisions."[5] Mott was not pleased with Murtagh's response, as revealed in a note to Russell Porter, chief of the Grants and Statewide Studies Division:

> It would appear that we cannot 'narrow the criteria.' Would this be your conclusion? If so, the States are told what to do by the Fed. for a pitance [sic] of funding.[6]

Mott continued to argue for narrow criteria. When asked for clarification about statements made during a 1974 presentation before the

Napa city council regarding the "lax" criteria and plans to introduce his own replacement standards, Mott replied that the existing criteria "dissipated" the significance of registered properties. His concern, he said, was exacerbated by a recent and disturbing trend:

> of late, there has been a great deal of activity on the part of some individuals in placing any building that appears in their minds to be of historic value simply to stop development rather than for the historic significance of the building, structure, or site. This is not the intent of the Historic Preservation Act.[7]

This tactic would become a familiar one in the late 1970s as preservationists sought to halt the bulldozing of whole districts in urban areas.

Another issue was property owner notification of and consent to proposed National Register nominations. By 1973, the Department of Parks and Recreation developed property owner notification procedures that included sending letters to individual owners. Although John Michael, supervisor of the History Preservation Section, agreed that it was sometimes a "cumbersome" process, the state had "an obligation to the public to furnish this information to the property owners because we, in our work in registering their property, can have an effect or place a cloud on the Title." Furthermore:

> Owners are alerted to the fact that there are sites on their property that deserve protection. As they also become possible recipients of matching grants-in-aid for restoration and preservation, they must be notified in a fair and equitable manner.

The notification procedure was clearly a courtesy to owners and not intended "to allow them to object for any other reason than historical authenticity."[8] By the time Mott departed in 1975, the department had developed additional procedures which he carefully explained to Assemblyman Barry Keene:

> The land owner, local government, city or county, and local historic groups must be informed of this proposal [to nominate a site] and provided the opportunity to furnish comments. When these comments are received, they are reviewed for additional information that they may provide and considered in the review process.

Mott reassured Keene that placement on the National Register had "absolutely no effect on the value of the property, the use of the property, potential uses of that property in any way unless Federal funding or Federal licensing procedures are involved."[9]

Discussions of property owner notification took on a different dimension when State Senator Clare Berryhill introduced legislation in 1976 that would require owner approval before the property was listed on the Register. Berryhill's bill came on the heels of unsuccessful attempts to nominate the communities of La Jolla and Volcano to the Register as historic districts.[10] By this time, the Office of Historic Preservation was already notifying property owners of a Register application three weeks before it was to be evaluated by the review board.[11] Knox Mellon, then head of the Office of Historic Preservation, conceded that the office still needed "to do a better job of talking with property owners and other interested citizens about the implications of National Register listing."[12]

Although the measure sponsored by Berryhill did not pass, the demand for property owner consent did not disappear. It surfaced again in September 1977 when the California League of Cities resolved to support legislation requiring city approval of Register applications before submission to the state review board.[13] The state legislature's response came in 1979 with the requirement that all nominations be forwarded to the appropriate city council or county supervisors for comment prior to a hearing by the state board.[14]

The debate over property owner consent was subsequently decided at the federal level. As a result of the 1980 amendments to the 1966 National Historic Preservation Act, owner consent is now required for a nomination to be listed on the National Register. If the owner objects, the property is determined "eligible" and is not listed until such time as approval is granted.[15]

The State Registered Historical Landmarks Program

During the first half of the 1970s, the number of registered historical landmarks did not significantly increase. In fiscal 1972-1973, for example, only 2 were approved, bringing the total to 858 sites. By March 1975, 879 had been registered; of these, 10 had been approved during the 1974 calendar year.[16] The landmark requests generated little controversy during these years, with two exceptions: the proposed plaque wording for Landmark No. 850, Manzanar Relocation Center, and the landing site of Sir Francis Drake.

The landmark application for Manzanar Relocation Center was approved by the Historical Landmarks Advisory Committee in January 1972 with little portent of what was to come. At first, Mott and his staff thought the problem over the plaque wording revolved solely around the desire of the Japanese American Citizens League (JACL) to include the phrase "concentration camp" on the plaque. His staff recommended using "relocation center" as the descriptive phrase for Manzanar. In an explanatory chronology submitted to Assembly Speaker Robert Moretti, the heated discussions were described as hinging at first "on the words 'concentration camp' and strong feelings on the part of the [Historical Landmarks Advisory] Committee that 'concentration camp' were improper words and just as strong feelings on the side of the JACL that 'concentration camp' were most proper words."[17]

After a series of discussions throughout 1972 with representatives from the JACL and the Manzanar Committee, including two very emotional sessions at the August and October meetings of the Landmarks Advisory Committee, Mott and his staff thought the matter had been resolved.[18] They believed that by agreeing to insert "concentration camps" into the wording, the JACL would be satisfied "because it was our assumption that this was the hangup. Apparently this was only one of the hangups because the wording was not approved."[19]

The staff's confusion over the nature of the "hangup" was understandable in light of the internal politics of the Manzanar Committee and the JACL. The Manzanar Committee was formed in January 1970 to educate the public about the World War II incarceration of Japanese Americans and to have Manzanar designated a registered state landmark. The landmark application was submitted to the state in November 1971 by Warren Furutani, then chair of the committee and also national JACL coordinator for community involvement. The application's sponsors were both the JACL and the Manzanar Committee, in cooperation with the Los Angeles Department of Water and Power as the property owner.[20]

There was a sense of urgency in getting the application before the Landmarks Advisory Committee because the Manzanar Committee wanted to announce the site's landmark status at its spring 1972 pilgrimage. To meet that timetable, Michael's staff had to rewrite the improperly completed application. When presented to the Landmarks Advisory Committee for consideration, the revised application no longer contained wording for the plaque. The form was signed on January 6, 1972, by Michio Suzuki who represented the applicant now identified as the JACL. Nowhere in the revised form was there any mention of the Manzanar Committee. Part of the difficulty lay in the fact that the original application had been unsigned when submitted. Michael contacted James Murakami, JACL vice president, who agreed with his suggestion that if a Sacramento JACL member signed the application, it could be put on the committee's agenda. Because Furutani was working for the JACL at that time, Michael saw no problems with the decision. Unfortunately, Furutani later left the JACL, and the Manzanar Committee lost its direct link to the state's correspondence regarding the application.[21]

When Michael tried to resolve the plaque wording dispute at a September 1972 meeting, Furutani, who had been invited, was not present. In attendance, however, were JACL representatives from both national and regional offices.[22] Thus, by January 1973, "the State took for granted that the Manzanar Committee was a sub-committee of JACL, which it never was." Manzanar Committee Co-Chair Sue Kunitomi Embrey's conclusion was corroborated by Michael who claimed, "we were led to believe that the Manzanar Committee was a function of JACL."[23]

Manzanar Committee members Embrey and Amy Ishii met with JACL Vice President Murakami, Michael, Landmarks Advisory Committee Chair Kathryn Kaiser, and Staff Historian David Tucker in February 1973 at the JACL's request because "the State wanted this matter 'off their backs.'"[24] The following draft plaque statement emerged:

> In the early days of World War II, 110,000 [persons] of Japanese ancestry were interned in relocation centers by Executive Order No. 9066, issued on February 19, 1942.
>
> Manzanar, bounded by barbed wire and guard towers, was the first camp confining 10,000 persons, the majority being American citizens.
>
> May the injustices and humiliation suffered in these concentration camps as a result of racism, hysteria, and greed never emerge again.[25]

Mott's vigorous objection to the inclusion of "racism" and "greed" in the plaque text resulted in yet another meeting, this time between Mott and Murakami. Mott reiterated his position that the two words were unacceptable and indicated his willingness to consider alternatives. He would not object if the sentence read: "May the injustices and humiliations suffered in this concentration camp as a result of hysteria never emerge again."[26]

Infuriated by Mott's insistence on "documentation to prove that racism and greed were involved in the evacuation," the Manzanar Committee appealed to the state legislature for assistance. On March 19, 1973, a meeting was arranged and chaired by Assemblyman Alex Garcia in Sacramento between JACL officers, Manzanar Committee members, Chair of Ethnic Studies George Kagiwada of the University of California at Davis, legislative aides to Speaker Moretti and senators Ralph Dills and Mervyn Dymally, Director Mott, and Deputy Director William Briner. What transpired behind those closed doors has not been transcribed for the official record. Embrey claimed that Mott accepted the revised wording because "he had no choice. The controversy would have gone to the State Legislature and embarrassed Mr. Mott."[27] Several months later, John Michael defended the state's decision in his response to an inquiry about the plaque: "the statement concerning racism and greed was questioned by various organizations, but the Japanese-American Citizens League and the Manzanar Committee presented substantial evidence that this did, in fact, occur."[28] Still later, Mott confirmed to another letter writer that "through research and after several hearings, it was determined that the wording as proposed was not inaccurate."[29]

Mott's explanation for the acceptance of "concentration camp" on the Manzanar plaque is important not only because of the public reaction and controversy it generated, but also because the issue would rise again in 1975 when a plaque was proposed for Tule Lake.[30] Mott stated:

> I well agree that originally the camps were set up as 'relocation centers.' However, it was pointed out to the Historical Landmarks Advisory Committee, and to several legislators conducting hearings on the subject that the dictionary definition of 'concentration camp' in almost every instance is a place in which 'political prisoners' were detained. I think you will agree, for the most part, internees were 'political prisoners;' therefore, the words 'concentration camp' were not thought to be improper.

Mott claimed that most of the opposition to the proposed wording came from his staff and the Landmarks Advisory Committee who "insisted that the statement on the plaque be proven."[31]

Just before the dedication of the plaque, the JACL informed the department that the Manzanar Committee should be listed as a co-sponsor on the landmark application "since they were initially left off the application through error, and since they have been the primary moving force in this effort."[32] On the plaque of California State Historical Landmark No. 850, which was dedicated on April 14, 1973, were the following words:

> In the early part of World War II, 110,000 persons of Japanese ancestry were interned in relocation centers by

Executive Order No. 9066, issued on February 19, 1942.

Manzanar, the first of ten such concentration camps, was bounded by barbed wire and guard towers, confining 10,000 persons, the majority being American citizens.

May the injustices and humiliation suffered here as a result of hysteria, racism and economic exploitation never emerge again.[33]

There was one other repercussion from this sequence of events that merits a final comment. Assemblyman Moretti's involvement in the controversy was partially due to his introduction of a resolution in June 1972 that asked the Department of Parks and Recreation to conduct a feasibility study for the acquisition and preservation of Manzanar as part of the State Park System. Moretti's resolution was approved in November but without appropriations for implementation.[34] To comply with the request, the department finally produced a feasibility study in 1974, which was forwarded to Oakland Vice-Mayor Frank Ogawa and Masamori Kojima, executive assistant to the mayor of Los Angeles. Both were cautioned by Mott not to divulge its contents to anyone who could release the material to the press prematurely.[35] At Russell Porter's suggestion, Mott sent the report to them because of their "influence in the Japanese [American] community." He was aware that they did not represent the views "of the rather radical young group that is pushing the Manzanar project...in a way that would exaggerate the actual conditions that existed there...." Mott's intent was "to present our recommendations on the basis of the general feeling of the Japanese community."[36]

The study had no direct impact on state park acquisitions because the lack of funding precluded any action on the proposal. The five-page, typewritten preliminary study was still gathering dust when Assemblyman Floyd Mori expressed his concern for Manzanar's protection and accessibility in 1978. Although appropriations have yet to be allocated to incorporate Manzanar into the State Park System, the National Park Service officially acknowledged Manzanar's historical significance by designating it a National Historic Landmark in 1985.[37]

No sooner was the dispute over the Manzanar plaque resolved than the Historical Landmarks Advisory Committee was again asked to recognize the landing site of Sir Francis Drake in California. The committee's April 1973 agenda included an application from Robert H. Power, requesting registration of a Drake Historical Site in Marin County. The Drake Navigators Guild, represented by President Raymond Aker and Director Edward P.

Von der Porten, rose in firm opposition to the application. After expressing a disinclination to identify a specific location, the committee agreed to table the request until its next scheduled northern California meeting when suggestions on how to commemorate the Drake expedition would be accepted.[38]

At their September meeting in San Rafael, the committee heard testimony for and against sites commemorating the Drake voyage and landfall. Unable to come to a firm determination, the committee agreed to postpone a decision until the anticipated 1979 quadricentennial celebration of Drake's arrival.[39]

In October 1978, a special three-day meeting of the Historical Resources Commission convened in the San Francisco Bay area to determine "once and for all" Drake's 1579 encampment and careening place. Submitted as the sites of Drake's "Nova Albion" were: Point Reyes Peninsula at Drake's Estero (Drake Navigators Guild), San Quentin Cove in San Francisco Bay (Robert H. Power), and Bolinas Lagoon at Bolinas Bay (V. Aubrey Neasham). After formal presentations by Power and the Drake Navigators Guild, a field trip to the Marin Headlands, an airplane flight over San Quentin Cove and Drake's Cove, a site visit to Rancho Olompali, an all-day sea voyage to inspect the ocean approaches to the proposed landing sites, and a final walking tour of Drake's Estero, the commission heard additional testimony from nineteen interested citizens and experts, including Neasham. Commissioner John H. Kemble, an eminent maritime historian, moved to deny the application to designate a specific landing site "for the present time" because "the evidence for any one landing site was not so overwhelming as to preclude the possibility of another location." With the exception of architect Robert Ferris who believed that "a probable site" should be designated, commission members voted in support of Kemble's motion.[40] Once again, the decision was left to the future.

The Point of Historical Interest Program

No significant changes occurred in the Point of Historical Interest program during the first half of the 1970s. Until 1975, yearly additions to the program remained fairly consistent. In 1972-1973, 34 historic features were added.[41] In 1973, 50 were registered to bring the total to 334.[42] In 1974, 54 points were approved, and by May 1, 1975, the program totaled 400 points of interest.[43] The staff of the History Preservation Section anticipated a sharp rise in the number of registered points as additional sites were identified in the statewide survey. This increase did not materialize until 1975-1976 when 98 sites were approved.[44]

The dramatic increase in the points of historical interest can be partially attributed to the use of the program to require environmental impact reviews and to qualify for bond act funds. Commissioner Kathryn Kaiser raised these concerns in 1976 when she questioned the continued existence of the program, the original intent of which was to generate local interest in historic sites. In her opinion, this intent was being circumvented. All three state-run programs, she stated, affect "the review process required by CEQA [California Environmental Quality Act] guidelines." If a property is listed on either the State Landmark, National Register, or Point program, "an Environmental Impact Review is being recommended as a requirement before any further action may be taken." Kaiser claimed that many counties used the Point program "as an interim method to get local properties registered by the State, thus halting local projects with a very limited amount of effort since the designation is relatively easy to obtain. After the approval of the County Board of Supervisors, there is little or no review by the state staff and the Commission." Listing in the program also qualified a property for bond act monies. The newly found importance of the program meant that the past practice of "rubber stamping" applications that lacked adequate documentation was inadequate. Kaiser recommended that Point designation not qualify a property for CEQA review and bond monies, that qualified points be required to complete National Register forms, and that the program be discontinued by May 1977.[45]

While the minutes of the May 1976 meeting state that no decision was made regarding Kaiser's proposal, the commission's "Statement of Policy for State Historical Landmark Registration and Point of Historical Interest Registration" noted that additional requirements such as a bibliography and photographs were added to the application process at that meeting.[46]

Kaiser's suggestion that the Point program be eliminated did not go unchallenged. Arthur L. Ogilvie, staff to the Santa Clara County Historical Heritage Commission, testified at the May meeting that local governments concerned with preservation used the program constructively and that it should be strengthened rather than dismantled. Harry Kelsey, chief curator of history at the Los Angeles County Natural History Museum, stressed that "sites of local interest deserve official recognition, and in addition their historical significance should be considered when plans are made that might threaten their significance."[47]

The fate of the Point program was raised again in January 1978 when, after a lengthy discussion, the commission asked that the program "be redesigned in such a way that responsibility and authority will reside with the County Board of Supervisors."[48] At the May meeting, Aaron Gallup, staff architectural historian, reported to the commission that problems had developed since the January decision to turn the program over to the county supervisors. Because of concerns over grant funding and building code considerations, the commission agreed to retain and continue administration of the Point program. There was, however, a stipulation: each application would have to be accompanied by a completed National Register form.[49] Local organizations strenuously objected to the new requirement, and it is still not enforced. A new form was introduced in 1991.[50]

Environmental Impact Reviews

The History Preservation Section was responsible for reviewing environmental impact studies and statements generated by Section 106 of the National Historic Preservation Act (1966), the National Environmental Policy Act of 1969 (NEPA), and the California Environmental Quality Act of 1970. During the first few months of its existence, the section did not enumerate studies reviewed by staff. Moreover, staff reports did not differentiate between state and federally mandated reviews. The workload soon increased, however, and it became clear to the staff that environmental reviews were destined to become "a major part of the History Preservation program."[51]

By fall 1972, the number of environmental impact reviews stabilized at ten per month. One of these was a Section 106 review of the Corps of Engineers' proposed flood control project in the Tahquitz Canyon archaeological district near Palm Springs, which was forwarded to the Advisory Council on Historic Preservation for further comment and evaluation in December. The Tahquitz Canyon project later gained fame as the first archaeological Section 106 dispute in California.[52]

Between November 1972 and February 1973, the History Preservation Section reviewed approximately 575 project impact reports, of which 120 required comments from the state historic preservation officer to mitigate possible adverse effects. The annual preservation plan for 1973-1974 estimated that the Advisory Council received three or four projects per month for further scrutiny. The report accurately predicted an increase in projects requiring state and federal action as National Register submissions increase.[53]

In 1973, the number of environmental statements and reports reviewed by the staff rose dramatically. For example, during April, 52 were processed, "a substantial increase above the number handled in previous months."[54] In May, a new procedure was instituted whereby reports were reviewed only if they involved National Register properties.[55] In July, 75 environmental impact statements and reports were reviewed; in August, the number rose to 90.[56] And in October, the total swelled to 195.[57] By year's end, the history section reported that it had examined more than 850 environmental impact reports for their effect on National Register properties.[58]

During the next year, the staff consistently reviewed more than 100 environmental impact reports and statements a month. Archaeological sites such as those involved in the construction of Warm Springs Dam consumed staff time as a result of Section 106 and Executive Order 11593 mandates. The destruction caused by freeway projects such as the extension of the Long Beach Freeway in South Pasadena also involved the staff in lengthy consultations.[59] The workload increased so alarmingly that in April the entire history section staff found themselves "involved in environmental reviews and Section 106 and Executive Order 11593 actions." A substantial number of the 135 reviews handled in April involved "direct requests to the State Historic Preservation Officer for comprehensive reviews of historical resources in compliance with 106 and 11593," and necessitated staff participation in numerous meetings, consultations, and field trips. Commenting on the historical resources component of the environmental planning program of Caltrans was another activity that required staff time.[60]

By summer 1974, it was obvious that the overworked staff of six full-time employees could not keep up with the mushrooming number of reviews pouring into the office. In June, seventy-five letters were written after 308 projects were examined.[61] A month later, 475 projects were reviewed and ninety-five letters or memoranda had been written.[62] By year's end, staff members began to actively seek ways to reduce the avalanche of paperwork. Federal agencies and consultants preparing impact statements on private development projects were advised to do their own research before seeking state assistance. There was also general staff agreement "to concentrate on federally sponsored projects coming through the State Clearinghouse, commenting on State projects only under special circumstances."[63] It seemed to be a reasonable approach to an increasingly burdensome task. At year's end, the history section had reviewed over 3,100 projects, most of which involved federal assistance or licensing that affected cultural resources. From January to December 1974, monthly environmental impact reviews had increased from 65 to 436; during the same period, the number of Executive Order 11593 and Section 106 actions rose from 36 to 72.[64]

The total number of project reviews completed in 1975 is not clear. In-house reports are lacking for half of the year, and the 1976 annual report stated that it was difficult to provide statistics because there were "countless short term cases, as well as actions such as Warms Springs Dam, which last for a prolonged period."[65] The 1977 preservation plan identified 2,600 environmental impact statement reviews and 130 Section 106 actions that consumed staff time between April 1976 and March 1977. The total number of review and compliance projects for that period was an astonishing 11,755.[66]

What few statistics exist show a very important trend that would continue throughout the latter half of the 1970s: the rise in direct inquiries to the state historic preservation officer requesting information and guidance in the preparation of environmental impact statements and reports. For example, in January 1975, of the 207 projects reviewed, more than 93 resulted from direct letters.[67] Although still understaffed, in 1976, the newly created Office of Historic Preservation recognized the importance of assisting agencies "at an early stage of planning in the preparation of environmental documents" and "helping federal agencies develop guidelines for complying with procedures." Early involvement was crucial because it allowed the preservation officer

> to direct planners in the preparation of environmental documents prior to the formulation of an irreversible course of action which may endanger cultural resources in the area of the project's potential environmental impact.

To do this, the office decided "to concentrate on urban areas where the greatest number of extant historic resources exists and where the greatest threat to those resources prevails." [68]

This new posture was a far cry from the situation in 1973, when John Michael described his section's involvement in the environmental impact review process as "merely input to a coordinator" who develops or furnishes information to others who produce the environmental impact statement or report.[69]

From Committee to Commission:
Emergence of the State Historical Resources Commission

The creation of the State Historical Resources Commission in 1974 was the direct result of Director Mott's response to Recommendation No. 1

in *The California History Plan*. Instead of establishing an Office of History, the director had long advocated a change in the committee's name to reflect its new responsibilities under federal mandates. He continued to emphasize this approach when he met with the committee in February 1974 and again suggested that the first step toward implementing the recommendation would be to:

> rename the Committee using a title more descriptive of their function and to suggest changes in sections of the Public Resources Code which authorizes the Committee and describes their duties.[70]

By that time, the committee had started to discuss possible alternatives, and in September 1973, Rev. Noel F. Moholy, O.F.M., was appointed to review suggested name changes.[71] Meanwhile, the director's staff also commented on the proposed reconstitution of the committee.[72]

The department's revised legislative draft of March 1974 recommended a seven-member State Historical Resources Commission with staggered four-year terms. The commission would receive and evaluate nominations for existing state and federal programs, "conduct and maintain a statewide inventory of historic resources," establish criteria to review and preserve historic and archaeological resources and to recommend deletions when necessary, "review and recommend statewide history plans and inventories," maintain comprehensive records of the above resources, conduct public hearings to review the history program, and submit to the director an annual report of activities, unattained goals, and recommendations for needed legislation. These recommendations were forwarded to Assemblyman Eugene A. Chappie who subsequently introduced A.B. 4139.[73]

In the meantime, Assemblyman Dixon Arnett introduced A.B. 4146 to create a commission administratively divorced from the Department of Parks and Recreation. It would assume all of the department's history preservation duties and would appoint its own executive director who would then serve as the state historic preservation officer.[74]

The department was adamantly opposed to the Arnett bill. Not only was there lack of funding for such an agency, but the bill would create an independent unit without clear ties to any other governmental agency. This, said the department, would make it "impossible for them to accomplish all of the duties and responsibilities given them with a limited staff."[75]

To resolve the differences between the two bills, Mott's staff suggested that the Chappie bill be amended after consultation with Arnett.[76] In late summer, a meeting was arranged with Arnett, Landmarks Advisory Committee members, and Mott; and with Arnett's consent, Chappie's bill was revised and subsequently passed. At its September meeting, the committee voted to ask the governor to sign A.B. 4139, which he did on September 23, 1974.[77]

In addition to the duties suggested by the department in March, the legislation also empowered the commission to recommend designs for landmark plaques and Point of Historical Interest signs, consult with and consider recommendations from others interested in historic preservation, review grant requests for federal funds and "establish a priority rating system for such projects," and recommend a budget to the director for the statewide preservation program.[78]

Archaeological resources were included in the Public Resources Code a year later when Assemblyman Arnett obtained passage of A.B. 1991 which required the commission

> to develop criteria and methods for determining the significance of archaeological sites, for selecting the most important archaeological sites, and for determining whether the most significant archaeological sites should be preserved intact or excavated and interpreted...

The commission was "to develop guidelines for the reasonable and feasible collection, storage, and display of archaeological specimens." These added responsibilities had been recommended by the legislative analyst in a 1975 report requested by the state legislature "to study the feasibility of consolidating the work of five state agencies" with jurisdictions relating to California's heritage. A year earlier, Secretary for Resources Livermore had observed:

> The Department of Parks and Recreation does not now have a well-defined direction from the Legislature to preserve and salvage the archaeological and paleontological resources of the State. Following review of the California History Plan, it would be appropriate to further define the Department's authority and responsibility to these areas.[79]

The Historical Landmarks Advisory Committee's active involvement in preservation-related legislation at the state level during the 1970s was largely due to the efforts of committee member Raymond Girvigian who, the minutes reveal, focused the group's attention on a variety of pending bills.

It was architect Girvigian, for example, who informed the committee of plans to build legislative office buildings that excluded provisions to restore the State Capitol. At their July 1973 meeting, the committee members reiterated their opposition to proposals to tear down the capitol, and unanimously approved a Girvigian-sponsored resolution urging the state legislature to preserve and restore the landmark.[80]

By the time the committee took this action, the structure had been declared unsafe by earthquake safety standards. Posted on the building's entrances were signs to warn those who entered that they did so at their own risk. Girvigian was later hired as the project's historical consultant, and after years of controversy, the capitol was finally restored at a cost of $67.7 million and opened to the public in January 1982.[81]

At that same July 1973 meeting, Girvigian also submitted another resolution asking the Resources Agency through Mott's office to include cultural and historic landmarks in the revised guidelines for implementation of CEQA.[82] When the committee approved a resolution to support the 1974 park bond act later that year, it was Girvigian who asked to add a paragraph urging local governments to use their share of the $90 million for historic preservation.[83]

Another of Girvigian's contributions came in March 1974, when the committee approved his resolution calling for the director to work with the state architect to explore with other agencies ways to amend the state's Building and Safety codes to develop "alternate standards where feasible that would permit the restoration of historic structures in a manner that would satisfy the intent of the codes, as well as preserve the historic integrity of the buildings."[84] Mott agreed with "the spirit of the resolution" and directed Michael to initiate a preliminary meeting with the state architect, members of the Landmarks Advisory Committee, the A.I.A., and his staff to produce an agenda for a May workshop with legislators, the state fire marshal, and individuals who enforced the building codes.[85]

Although the meeting was called on very short notice, sixty people attended. The Building Codes Restoration Steering Committee was formed with John Fisher of the California Council of the A.I.A. as chair. Girvigian became a committee member and chaired its Legislative Subcommittee. After meeting for nearly a year, Girvigian's subcommittee was authorized to take the necessary steps to ensure that the proposed code was enacted into law. As he explained it, the bill would "grant authority to the state agencies affected by this Code [to adopt standards for historic structures], with the advice and counsel of an Advisory Board of public and professional experts, but the bill itself would incorporate only the guidelines to implementation— not the entire technical code."[86]

Senator James Mills introduced S.B. 927 which authorized "alternative building regulations for the rehabilitation, preservation, restoration, or relocation of qualified historical buildings or structures." It also created a thirteen-member State Historical Buildings Code Advisory Board in the Office of Architecture and Construction to prepare, implement, and later interpret the regulations that went into effect in 1979.[87] Until the passage of S.B. 2321 in 1984, the law's provisions were permissive and not mandatory. Except for charter cities, local enforcement officials could apply the Historic Building Code without having to formally adopt it. The new Marks bill required "all local building authorities to administer and enforce its provisions and would thereby impose a state-mandated local program."[88] In 1976, the legislature adopted S.B. 1803, allowing handicapped access to historical buildings to be covered by the new code.[89]

In 1971, the Landmarks Advisory Committee began to plan for the celebration of the Bicentennial of the American Revolution. Both the Bicentennial Commission of California and the Landmarks Advisory Committee rejected Mott's proposal that California's contribution to the year's festivities focus on the Mother Lode. Agreeing with the Bicentennial Commission that the gold rush was too narrow in scope, committee chairman Glen Settle forwarded two suggestions to Mott. At regular intervals, the state's Bicentennial celebration would highlight regional activities featuring one of California's registered landmarks. The result, said Settle, would be "heightened awareness of our landmarks...as well as stimulating the public's interest in our State history and the need to preserve its cultural heritage." To commemorate the occasion, a special design for the bicentennial landmark plaques was also recommended.[90]

Mott replied that the lack of state and federal funding precluded implementation of the committee's "ambitious program." In his opinion, the best the committee could hope for was to make suitable references to the bicentennial during landmark dedications. He rejected the special plaque designs because they would be "confusing in future years."[91] The committee was not deterred, however, and a subcommittee was appointed with Raymond Girvigian and Clement Meighan doing much of the work. Nearly a year went by before they again pressed Mott for a special landmark plaque. This time they provided specific historical, archaeological, and architectural examples that would illuminate the three themes adopted by the national commission: Heritage '76, Festival USA, and Horizons '76. R. Coke Wood, who served on both the Landmarks Advisory Committee and the state Bicentennial Commission, heartily endorsed their concept of a special emblem for the plaques.[92]

What resulted was not a special plaque, but a revision of the department's best-selling *California Historical Landmarks* booklet which was published in 1975 bearing the official logos of the national commission.[93] Unfortunately, without the support of a statewide patron of history and preservation such as Joseph Knowland during the earlier gold rush centennial, the Landmarks Advisory Committee was unable to capitalize on the bicentennial festivities to promote California history and historic preservation.

Although its responsibilities were increased in 1974 and again in 1984, the reconstituted Historical Resources Commission remains essentially an advisory body.[94] Recommendations, criteria, and reports regarding state-related matters are forwarded to the department and those involving federal mandates are directed to the state historic preservation officer. Short of staff and without enforcement powers or meaningful access to the Director of the Department of Parks and Recreation, the commission had yet to emerge as "the conscience of the department."

Establishment of the Office of Historic Preservation

The election of Edmund G. Brown, Jr., in 1974 had a direct impact on the Department of Parks and Recreation. His selection of Herbert Rhodes as director was "a surprise to almost everyone" because Rhodes lacked experience in parks or recreation.[95] More importantly for preservation, it was not until May 1975 that Rhodes was finally appointed the state historic preservation officer.[96]

The failure of the governor to designate a state historic preservation officer until 1975 caused the History Preservation Section to refrain from initiating several restoration projects.[97] During the delay, a flurry arose over a pervasive philosophical issue.

In February 1975, former State Park Historian David A. Tucker wrote to the newly appointed Secretary for Resources Claire T. Dedrick, to suggest the selection of a preservation officer who was not concurrently director of the department. Tucker stated that if the same person wore both hats, he (or she) could be put "in the tenuous position of serving two masters at once." The director was responsible for a park program whose historical units amounted to 12 percent of the overall total. In addition to administering the 1966 federal legislation, the director had to ensure that National Register properties were "adequately safeguarded." Tucker told Dedrick: "In many cases, both the National Register sites and the historical parks are the same."[98]

Dedrick responded that most preservation officers had other management responsibilities and that "all managers have this dual problem of directing ongoing programs and yet retaining a review status over the program itself." Furthermore:

> The establishment of the Preservation Officer as a separate and distinct function of government is a move that requires extensive and thorough consideration of many factors, and this matter is one of the many things which the administration will be involved in in the coming months.[99]

Tucker's opinion was shared by Mrs. Leland S. Lewis who also wrote to the secretary in February. She, too, emphasized that the history plan merited a full-time, professional administrator and that the existing system made the program a mere "extension of the Department of Parks and Recreation." In her view, "this format and double duty assignment places an undue demand upon the Preservation Officer who is already charged with the directorship of one of the major and complex departments of state government."[100] Dedrick tersely informed Lewis that her suggestion would be taken under consideration.[101]

When queried about the appointment of the preservation officer at the May 1975 meeting of the Historical Resources Commission, Russell Porter, chief of the department's Grants and Statewide Studies Division, explained that the delay was due to "a possibility that the SHPO and the History Preservation Section will report to the Director of the Department of Parks and Recreation." Commission Chairman Meighan was asked to inform Rhodes of the commission's strong support for "the appointment of a separate individual to serve as History Preservation Officer" because it would be beneficial for that person to attend commission meetings and hear discussions of increasingly complex and controversial National Register applications. The commissioners also requested that an Office of History be established as recommended by the history plan.[102]

In response to a question about the need to separate the two functions, Mott stated that he saw only advantages in keeping both positions under the same individual: "I couldn't pass the buck. If I made a bad decision, I was it." In states that separated the two positions, "there was not," insisted Mott, "the opportunity to do the implementation as effectively as in California. As the director of parks in setting the bond issue, I could say we've got to have money for historic preservation in that bond issue in addition to other things."[103]

The appointment of Rhodes as state historic preservation officer was the prelude to organizational changes made later that same year. On July 6, 1975, Rhodes hired historian Knox Mellon to evaluate the History Preservation Section with respect to its

> failure to comply with certain guidelines required under the National Historic Preservation Act of 1966...[and] to develop close ties with the State Historical Resources Commission, to inquire of its membership as to their feelings regarding the function of said Commission, and to make recommendations from these contacts.

In October, Rhodes created the Office of Historic Preservation to serve as his staff to implement the federal preservation programs. Mellon, the spouse of the new governor's appointments assistant, was named both historic preservation coordinator and executive secretary to the commission.[104] With the exception of James Doyle, who became head of the department's Environmental Review Section, the remaining History Preservation Section staff members became part of the new office.

Although an independent History Office had not been created as recommended in the history plan, a separate unit responsible directly to the state historic preservation officer and the director of Parks and Recreation was now in place to implement the provisions of the federal legislation.

The tenuous status of the newly created Office of Historic Preservation was demonstrated in 1976 when a departmental reorganization proposal suggested moving the Office of Historic Preservation from the director's office into the Resource Preservation and Interpretation Division. The possible relocation raised fears that the office's "capability to function as an effective leader and partner in historic and cultural resource conservation in California will be forfeited."[105] The Foundation for San Francisco's Architectural Heritage apparently took its concerns to Senator Milton Marks who inquired about the proposed reorganization. Resources Secretary Dedrick responded that Rhodes had "no intention of weakening the Office of Historic Preservation. On the contrary, he has signified to the entire Department that one of the highest priorities for fiscal year 1976-1977 is in the area of preservation." The move, she said, was designed "to strengthen the State's role in the general area of cultural heritage," and to cope with fiscal constraints.[106]

Mellon, who replied at Rhodes' request to Robert Berner, Heritage's urban conservation officer, reiterated his "conviction that the current

Director is committed to historic preservation in its broadest context and to the continued upgrading of the Office of Historic Preservation." He assured Berner that Rhodes had promised "that in any proposed restructuring the Office of Historic Preservation will retain its direct contact with the State Historic Preservation Officer."[107]

Despite outward appearances, there were signs that all was not well between Mellon and Rhodes. In September 1976, for example, Mellon suggested a three-hour meeting to enable his staff to explain "in detail what it is they do and how the office functions." The reason for the session was "in keeping with your injunction to me that we communicate more closely."[108] At Rhodes' request, Mellon subsequently submitted a memo in July 1977 that summarized the functions of his office and "the progress it has made in the last two years."[109]

The appointment of Russell W. Cahill to replace Rhodes on September 2, 1977, had an immediate impact on Mellon's position. On September 7, Cahill requested that the governor designate Mellon as state historic preservation officer, which he did officially on September 21, 1977.[110] The positions of director and preservation officer were finally separated.

In reviewing the status of the Office of Historic Preservation, the California Heritage Task Force found that the office was not authorized by State law; nor was its relationship to the State Historical Resources Commission and the Department of Parks and Recreation legally defined. The task force recommended that the Public Resources Code be appropriately amended. Governor George Deukmejian signed S.B. 1252 in 1984 which finally codified the responsibilities of the state historic preservation officer and the Office of Historic Preservation.[111] Mellon resigned at the end of 1984, and in April 1985, the governor appointed former State Historical Commission Chair Kathryn Kaiser Gualtieri to the post.

13

A Decade of Expansion in Other State Preservation Programs

Preservation in California during the first decade after the passage of the 1966 federal legislation was not limited to the programs administered by the Department of Parks and Recreation through its History Preservation Section. Public agencies, including the department itself, either expanded or introduced preservation-related programs for areas under their jurisdiction.

The State Park System

Among the diverse responsibilities of the Department of Parks and Recreation is the management of a vast network of state parks. In January 1968, the State Park System consisted of 796,441 acres of land organized into 205 units, of which 32 were designated "historic."[1]

One of Director Mott's immediate objectives was to prepare a long-range master plan for the future development of the park system. The proposal he submitted in June 1968 to Governor Ronald Reagan contained a five-year plan for park development and acquisition, and guidelines for the next twenty years.[2]

Work on the five-year plan had begun in 1967. In October, the departing chief of the Division of Beaches and Parks, Earl P. Hanson, gave Mott a brief status report on the department's program for historical acquisitions and development, which would be included in the master plan being developed by Elmer Aldrich. Hanson stated that it would not only include recommendations for future acquisitions and development, but also identify "historical resources essential to a well balanced historical program" and recommend "transfer to local government certain historical units." When published, the five-year plan included sizable requests to develop historic areas although it concentrated on beach and water-related recreational areas in Southern California. These requests included: $450,000 for Columbia, $2 million for El Pueblo de Los Angeles, over $600,000 for the Monterey monuments, more than $1 million for Old Sacramento, and $790,000 for Old Town San Diego. The plan suggested that funds should be allocated to historic units in proportion to park attendance, which came to 12 percent of the development budget of nearly $60 million for the next five years. Acquisition requests totaled $30 million, with priority in historic units to be given to eliminating private inholdings and to consolidating historic properties.[3]

The department's three perceived functions were the preservation of history, the preservation of landscape, and recreation.[4] Its history preservation mission was to "preserve and interpret outstanding examples of California's colorful history for public interest, recreation, education, and inspiring patriotism." To accomplish this, the department would acquire and develop sites, structures, and artifacts representing the same cultural categories and six historical periods that emerged later in the comprehensive history plan of 1973. Criteria for prioritizing acquisition projects included integrity, urgency, cost, accessibility, and user potential.[5]

The long-range plan emphasized strengthening the department's public information and interpretation programs. This posture reflected Mott's belief that, in the past, the department had not given sufficient consideration to cultural and historical resources because it had "thought of resources as being natural resources." For Mott, interpretation of the park system's historic resources was "terribly important as a means of getting support from the general public because you are giving them information about the park, and they will transmit it to others. It makes them feel good." His insistence on sound professional interpretation resulted in the hiring of permanent park employees after 1967 to replace summer seasonal employees.[6]

Included in the 1968 plan was a departmental organizational chart that contained a Historical Parks and Monuments Office which would

> conduct a continuous review of these units from the standpoint of adequacy of staffing, quality of maintenance activities, and effectiveness of the interpretive program. The office will work with the districts and the units in improving the overall quality of the historical program. It will also keep the division chief informed on problems in connection with the program and steps that are being taken to solve them.

The rationale for this new unit was that historical parks and monuments had operational and maintenance problems "sufficiently different from those associated with other units of the State Park System."[7] According to former Chief of Operations John Knight to whom the staff was to report, the office never materialized. Knight recalled that this was an example of a "Mottism," one of the director's ubiquitous "inspirations." He decided against staffing the office because he felt that district supervisors should be responsible for every unit under their care; bypassing the chain of command directly into headquarters as Mott proposed would create "chaos." Knight said of his refusal to comply: "I still have the scars."[8]

The plan generated considerable comment from a number of other agencies. For example, Director of Finance Caspar Weinberger questioned the economic benefits of parks and recreation areas. In his defense of historic parks, Mott stated:

> Historic park areas provide an important educational func-
> tion for visits by school classes, places of historical re-
> search, and for preserving examples of California's six
> periods of history. Our society must draw upon the wise
> decisions and mistakes of the past. Because of general
> public and hobbyist interest in history, this program con-
> tributes substantially to the State's economy.[9]

The department saw the plan as one in which they were not taking sides either for or against preservationists or developers: "We are saying, in effect, that the general public needs both concepts and that we are going to meet the needs of the public not on the basis of majority needs, but on the basis of fair proportion to both needs."[10]

The department's historical units and programs were not neglected in other general plans and policy guidelines. For example, the *California Coastline Preservation and Recreation Plan* of 1971 contained fourteen pages on California history and the department's historic resources priorities. It relied heavily on the 1970 preliminary history plan and reinforced the department's position that the state should acquire only properties of statewide significance.[11]

The 1974 *Resource Management Directives* clearly defined the objectives and responsibilities for the park system's properties and historic resource programs. Included was Mott's "flow of history" concept which had a significant influence on the department's interpretive philosophy and which was still in place in 1979.[12] As he recalled, the "flow of history" resulted from his concern that the department "in its historic interpretation tended to chop out a chunk of history and say 'that's what we're going to talk about.'" The department, Mott observed, did "not think in terms of what happened before and what happened afterwards." His objective was to present the total picture in the historic parks instead of isolating a particular segment. "If we use the flow of history," Mott insisted, "we can then say that this is the primary time and the most significant period, but there was history prior to that and following that."[13]

During the Mott years, the department demonstrated an interest in ethnic minorities. In 1968, for example, John Michael's Interpretive Services Section requested a comprehensive and annotated bibliography of books and manuscripts about ethnic groups with an emphasis on "the Negro's role in California history." The section felt a "responsibility to identify and interpret" their story "because of increasing awareness and response to ethnic minority groups' role in California history."[14] In his qualified approval of the project, Chief James Tryner of the Resource Management and Protection Division warned that it should not "isolate any particular ethnic group from the sum total of all Americans." He stated:

> Our people are Americans first and members of ethnic minorities second; we must strive by whatever means are available to us to foster the latter concept and to avoid strengthening the isolation and 'nationalistic' tendencies which tend to arise among ethnic groups and which tend ultimately to cause such groups to forget that they are, in fact, Americans.[15]

Although little progress was made on the project during the early 1970s because of a manpower shortage and a sharp internal disagreement over work assignments, the arrival of Herbert Rhodes reinvigorated the department's efforts.[16] In 1976, Rhodes applied to the U.S. Department of Housing and Urban Development for a $140,000 grant to conduct an Ethnic Minority Sites Survey of Black, Spanish-surnamed, Japanese, Chinese, and Native American contributions. When the proposal was rejected, the department did its own inventory. The state budgeted $92,500 to match federal survey and planning funds, and the project was contracted out to private consultants in 1978. The survey has proven to be a milestone because, as State Historic Preservation Officer Knox Mellon noted: "I believe [it to be] the Nation's first survey of historic properties of significance to ethnic minority groups."[17]

Despite the existence of long-range plans and other policies for the acquisition and development of historic units, the department had yet to cope with the need to do archaeological, historical, and architectural research before beginning a preservation effort. Guidelines for the actual preservation and restoration of structures existed, but Division Architect Robert F. Uhte's memos reveal that his section was not given an opportunity to review departmental land use plans and other development proposals for historic areas early enough in the evaluation process to have any meaningful impact. Nor did he have the staff "to do the needed historical research before restoration" began.[18]

Restoration projects in the park system depended on either the State Office of Architecture for large-scale efforts or private architects and restorationists for a single project. In the latter case, it was the division architect who supervised the work that day laborers performed. Individual contractors were hired to install utilities and other services. It was impractical to carry out such a project by a general contract for the entire restoration, said Mott, "because of the nature of the work and the impossibility of determining in advance the actual problems that arise." Of necessity, the department's restoration team developed expertise through on-the-job experience, additional course work, and "a keen interest."[19]

The department's concern for historical structures was highlighted in 1969 by the publication of a report by the Historical Structures Task Force that Mott created six months earlier. Chaired by Herbert L. Heinze of the Operations Division, the four-member body examined thirty-three historic monuments and parks and recommended a two-year study of each unit. The study would include a master plan to accurately identify what elements each completed unit would have, "specific land acquisition requirements based on the master plan," detailed work plans to implement the master plan, and a complete operational plan for each unit.[20] Many of these suggestions were subsequently required of individual historic units in the park system.

During Mott's tenure, the park system was enriched by the addition of new historical units and the development and expansion of existing parks. In addition to monies received under the 1966 federal preservation legislation for planning, restoration, and reconstruction, funding came from such sources as the 1964 bond act and from citizen volunteers whom Mott actively cultivated. Acquisitions in 1968 included Indian Grinding Rock State Historic Park in Amador County and the Governor's Mansion in Sacramento; a new museum at Malakoff Diggins State Historic Park was completed that same year.[21]

The inclusion of Colonel Allensworth State Historic Park in Tulare County in 1974 filled a significant void in the State Park System. Efforts to preserve the only California town founded, financed, and governed by African Americans began in the aftermath of the tumultuous mid-1960s urban unrest. Governor Reagan was told: "The political climate and cultural awareness programs being initiated now indicate an urgent need for this project."[22]

The department became officially involved in 1968 when African American landscape architect Edward Pope brought the existence of the townsite which had been founded in 1908 by former slave and retired Army officer, Lt. Colonel Allen Allensworth, to Mott's attention. The director moved swiftly to seek the governor's support, arguing that it was the ideal way to correct a long-standing departmental deficiency "in our historical preservation and interpretive program in not having given attention to the contributions made by our Black citizens."[23]

In 1969, departmental staff toured Allensworth, and two months later, the governor's cabinet reviewed the proposed project and requested cost estimates. Legislative support came from then State Senator Mervyn Dymally who introduced S.C.R. No. 124, recommending the town's preservation. By year's end, the governor's office established the Allensworth Advisory Committee to assist the department and serve as liaison to local agencies and other interested individuals.[24] In 1970, Governor Reagan signed Dymally's bill requiring completion of a feasibility study for the acquisition and development of Allensworth as part of the State Park System. The study concluded that the town was of statewide significance and should be added to the State Park System. It also recommended a 240-acre purchase, the focal point of which would be "a 120-acre historical story zone." In addition, the reconstruction of such structures as Allensworth's home and the construction of an educational and cultural center were proposed along with an outdoor exhibit area and support facilities such as camp grounds. The unit was to be restored to reflect the period from the birth of the town in 1908 through 1918, the decade of its greatest growth.[25]

Although no one opposed the project, it was not easy to purchase and develop the land. Finally, in 1974, the legislature approved the final $300,000 of the required $500,000. In that same year, Allensworth was officially designated a state historic park. Two development plans presented to the Park and Recreation Commission in 1974 and 1975 were rejected because commissioners felt "the extensive recreation development proposed in the plan would detract from the historic integrity of Allensworth." By 1976, an additional $558,700 had been raised for the restoration and/or reconstruction of several structures and for the construction of parking lots, picnic areas, and exhibits. That the "flow of history" was still a viable policy was evident in the department's development and management plan for the park:

> The preservation, restoration, reconstruction, and inter-
> pretation of resources at Allensworth will be guided by the
> flow of history concept, as endorsed by the State Park
> Commission on September 14, 1973.[26]

Of all the historic units, Columbia State Historic Park remained the most important in the department's priorities. The state legislature continued to show concern for Columbia, and departmental staff spent considerable time and effort on the park's development and interpretive program.[27]

By the time of Mott's appointment, conflicting philosophies of management, development, and interpretation of Columbia began to surface. For example, historian Allen Welts perceived the park's 1964 "Declaration of Purpose," which called for "Columbia's development in a manner characteristic of 'an outstanding example of a living community *representative* of the early gold mining days,'" as a departure from the legislature's 1955 request for the preparation of a master plan to restore the park to "*those early days* (1850-1870)."[28]

Other problems were highlighted in an October 1986 study conducted for the legislature by the auditor general. In the past, restoration work performed at Columbia was "very expensive because the buildings have been restored to a condition equal to or better than the original construction." The report noted that Mott believed "too much time and money is being expended on restoration work" and that future work should "probably...be limited to stabilization and necessary reconstruction work" to ensure the public's safety and maintain historical accuracy. The auditor general concurred that future restoration efforts should emphasize stabilization, and suggested that the department "de-emphasize increasing the aesthetic value, which is the present thinking of department management." The report also highlighted contradictions in the department's 1968 general plan, which requested new acquisitions as well as additions to existing holdings to ensure adequate representation of cultural categories from each historical era. At the same time, the department was giving priority to "now-or-never" projects. Although Columbia was given first priority for property acquisition and listed as fifth in importance for development and interpretation projects, it was only budgeted $450,000 for both objectives; "lower priority projects have higher budgets." The report concluded: "It appears that the department's thinking in regard to the development of Columbia State Historic Park has shifted from a piece-meal, long-range development program to a more urgent short-term development program."[29]

By 1970, little had changed. Columbia's purpose was still interpretation: telling the story of the town between 1850 and 1870 and allowing visitors to experience "the living gold rush town" through concessions operated in the restored structures. Unfortunately, the conversion of the stores into "Coney Island" souvenir shops created a carnival-like atmosphere. The department's 1970 interpretive plan suggested the replacement of concessionaires by departmental employees who would assume the roles of historic merchants or craftsmen, demonstrating and selling their wares. "The profit motive," declared the plan, "should not be permitted to take precedence over historical integrity." [30]

The Columbia of 1970 had fewer taped-up signs and better costumed exhibits, but as Park Historian David A. Tucker observed: "plastic hanging from doors, Columbia 'T' shirts, and amplified steel guitar music are still very evident." He complained that the park was "rapidly heading towards a Knotts' Berry Farm effect. Knotts' Berry Farm is honestly hokum. Columbia is dishonestly original."[31] Five years later, little had changed. The goal of having concessions and businesses "built around the historic crafts, artisans, and merchandise" as in "Colonial Williamsburg, Old Sturbridge Village, Cooperstown, Plimoth Plantation [and] Shakerstown" was still a long way off.[32]

The California State Parks Foundation held its first meeting in the governor's Council Chambers in October 1969, less than a month after filing incorporation papers. The nonprofit foundation appealed to the governor and answered the department's need for more funds.[33] As Mott explained: "The foundation was organized by me...for the express purpose of receiving gifts and contributions to assist the Department of Parks and Recreation in the development of the California State Park System."[34]

The foundation had no difficulty soliciting and receiving gifts on behalf of the park system. For example, at its first meeting, Trustee Ken Murray donated to the foundation, in perpetuity, his film, "The Golden Years," which depicted William Randolph Hearst's hospitality at San Simeon during the 1920s and 1930s. Amidst pledges of $11,500 to keep the foundation's program and staff in operation, an executive director was quickly hired.[35] By the end of fiscal year 1970-1971, the foundation had received more than $1.7 million to purchase properties that would have been sold to developers and could not have been otherwise obtained because of the state's fiscal constraints. These properties included a 4,944-acre parcel and 90 acres containing oak trees estimated to be 700 years old. The foundation also supported additions to the Poppy Preserve in Apple Valley and the reconstruction of the chapel at Fort Ross.[36]

The organization reflected Mott's philosophy that with the cooperation and guidance of the department, citizen volunteers should play an active role in park projects. After six years, the foundation had generated $11 million for the park system, donated over 10,000 acres of park lands to the state, and completed or nearly completed eight major and twenty-four smaller projects. Although the state's natural resources benefited most, historic preservation projects had also been recipients of the foundation's generous support of the park system.[37]

The State Archaeological, Paleontological, and Historical Task Force

Governor Ronald Reagan signed S.B. 215 on October 1, 1971, thereby creating a task force "to preserve and salvage the archaeological, paleontological, and historical resources of the state" by developing a plan or recommending appropriate legislation.[38] In 1972, Secretary of Resources Norman Livermore, Jr., appointed fifteen members who represented various state agencies and institutions of higher education.

Groundwork for the task force was laid as early as 1970 when the Society for California Archaeology proposed a draft outline of an archaeological element for inclusion in the state's General Plan. This outline was the basis of legislation to establish state-level archaeological survey programs similar to programs in other states. Assembly Bill 1788 would have created the California Archaeology Survey to "replace the Department of Parks and Recreation as the agency primarily responsible for the preservation of archaeological and paleontological resources on State lands." Reagan vetoed the bill in 1971 on the grounds that it "contained unclear wording, had an undetermined fiscal impact and was redundant." It was redundant because he had approved its weaker companion measure, S.B. 215, which had also been proposed by the society as part of its "effort to improve the State Highway Salvage Program and develop a unified State archaeological program."[39]

Although S.B. 215 requested merely a study and recommendations,

it still contained two important provisions: "a moratorium on the disturbance of native California Indian burial sites abandoned less than 200 years
until such time as the Legislature acts upon" the task force report, and the
inclusion on the task force of California Indian representatives from
northern, central, and southern California.[40] Now, "for the first time in
California law, California Indians had a role in protecting resources which
comprise their heritage."[41] Unfortunately, the law provided no fiscal support.

That the task force created by S.B. 215 had an archaeological bias
would be a common criticism. The criticism was valid in part because of the
nature of the task force's origins and the mandated composition of its
membership, which included five archaeologists out of seventeen members.
Staff support was provided by Francis Riddell, archaeologist in the Department of Parks and Recreation.[42]

The task force's most controversial recommendation was that a new
state agency be created to promote and coordinate a comprehensive
statewide heritage preservation program. The suggestion first emerged in
September 1972 when archaeologist Michael Moratto submitted a proposal
entitled "Suggested Operational Parameters for a California Heritage Department."[43] Discussion continued at the October meeting when members
agreed that the name should be changed from "department" to "California
Heritage Agency" and reviewed the first sections on "Purposes and Powers."[44]

Director Mott's reaction was that the task force should not be
proposing a separate agency with jurisdiction over all of the state's cultural
resources, including park units. "It appears to me," he said, "that they are
taking part in activities that are not part of their...responsibility."[45] A few
weeks later, Mott told Secretary Livermore: "A new department is not
needed." Not only was the projected cost of $7 million impractical, he
believed that his department could adequately inventory and protect the
state's archaeological sites if given a few additional personnel. The problem,
however, was that:

> According to Riddell, the committee's objection to placing
> responsibility for the work in our Department is that it feels
> that the matter of protecting, investigating, inventorying
> and interpreting archeological sites throughout California
> would not be given the same attention as would be given
> such work within the State Park System.[46]

Mott's opposition did not deter the task force. In their interim report
to Livermore in September 1973 was a proposal for a Heritage Department to

take all necessary action to preserve, protect, study, and

> interpret the State's historical, archaeological, cultural, and paleontological resources and remains in a coordinated and organized manner in the interest of science and for the benefit of the public as a whole.

In the face of "an urgent need to generate statewide guidelines and strategies for the long-range management, preservation, and interpretation of California's cultural resources," the report concluded that "the state is the only entity capable of, or responsible for, such a restructuring of heritage operations."[47] Task force chair Robert J. Stoddard urged Livermore to move with all deliberate speed to introduce the requisite legislation, for "the members of the Task Force have clearly seen the adverse effect on our resources...which has resulted from a lack of central leadership and meaningful laws to protect them."[48]

In all of the task force's activities, there was a curious absence of participation by the History Preservation Section. Although there is evidence that each knew about the other's activities, no direct communication or cooperation existed between the task force and Michael's unit or the Historical Landmarks Advisory Committee.[49] This was also apparent to John L. Frisbee III, western field representative of the National Trust for Historic Preservation, who urged both groups to work together because the forthcoming state history plan was likely to propose "a new department to administer statewide historic preservation programs." In his opinion, "the tone of the legislation and the makeup of the Heritage Board are inadequate to fulfill the aspirations of a major part of the preservation community."[50]

Frisbee was also critical of the task force's partiality toward archaeology. He admonished Riddell:

> California's heritage connotes more than the archaeological and ethnic heritage of this state. It should include far reaching, comprehensive measures to protect and preserve the historic and architectural resources which are part of the living urban and rural environments.[51]

Not only did Mott share Frisbee's concerns, he also insisted that the task force's report "was taken almost verbatim from the California History Plan, and many of the concepts and ideas are the same as or are similar to those which will be expressed in the California History Plan." Landmarks Advisory Committee Chair Kathryn Kaiser also saw the same similarities.[52]

Mott was obviously concerned that the proposed agency would jeopardize what he had in mind for his own department. He informed Livermore that if the state history plan was approved, a "heritage agency" would be gradually phased in, first as part of his department, and later as a separate unit within the Resources Agency "as the needs become apparent and as progress occurs." Mott agreed that "a Division of History and Archeology or Heritage, or whatever title is appropriate" was needed, but insisted that it belonged in his department since it had the appropriate expertise. Moreover, because of the impossibility of funding the estimated $9 million cost, "the time is inappropriate to accept the recommendations of the Archeological Task Force at present."[53]

By spring 1974, it was clear that the proposed Heritage Department would never materialize. Livermore's letter of transmittal which accompanied the task force report reiterated Mott's concerns that the report was too narrowly focused on archaeology instead of all dimensions of the state's heritage, duplicated much of the material in the attached state history plan and therefore should be considered simultaneously with the plan, should consider ways to utilize existing university and college professors, and was unrealistic in its recommendation of an expensive heritage agency whose "separateness" contradicted the necessity to coordinate heritage activities. Livermore was unable to recommend full implementation and requested instead permission "to further study the best way to implement the proposal before you take action."[54] Task force member and archaeologist Robert F. Heizer agreed that it was an unrealistic proposal because of the large budgetary requirements. As an interim measure, he suggested the compilation of a comprehensive statewide archaeological site map file in Sacramento under the supervision of the Department of Parks and Recreation.[55]

From the legislative analyst's perspective, the proposal was unacceptable because the Heritage Department lacked clearly defined responsibilities suitable for a state-level agency and because many of its duties duplicated those of the Department of Parks and Recreation. Provisions for harsh "regulations of investigations, and destruction or removal of materials from archeological or paleontological sites on both public and private lands," and the protection of as many as 45,000 archaeological sites, "most of which are Indian sites," contributed to the criticism that "the concept of California's heritage needs to be tempered with realism and feasibility." It was unrealistic to try to protect as many sites as possible; instead, the objective should have been to identify and preserve the most important ones. Part of the difficulty was that the task force report "assumed rather than established the nature of the state's interest in archeology and paleontology." The legislative analyst suggested that the newly created State Historical Resources Commission "develop and recommend methods to select the best archeological sites for inclusion in the state park system."[56]

Mott and Frisbee's criticism of the task force's failure to adequately respond to historical, historic architectural, and architectural issues was well taken. As Mott pointed out, the archeological bias was further exacerbated by the task force's letterhead which proclaimed it to be the "Archaeological Task Force."[57]

In all fairness, this shortcoming had not gone unnoticed by the archaeological community and the task force. The minutes show genuine concern for the lack of involvement of the historical subcommittee headed by L. Thomas Frye, who attended few meetings. In March 1973, the task force agreed to ask an absent Frye to suggest a replacement to represent the California Historical Society if he was no longer interested in serving. Task force member Mary Hill of the Division of Mines and Geology volunteered to begin correspondence with various historical societies to inform them of the task force's activities.[58]

Unfortunately, little progress was made. Riddell expressed his amazement several months later that the historical community was not responding to this "opportunity to make substantial input to the Task Force." He warned that the task force report could go to the legislature "without an adequate historical input because of the seeming lack of concern in the aims of the Task Force by the historical community."[59] In June 1973, Riddell told Livermore that Frye had resigned. "This," he said, "has severely handicapped our efforts to finish the report...."[60]

These deficiencies notwithstanding, the report's conclusions provide a useful perspective on the status of preservation in the early 1970s, particularly with respect to archaeological resources. These include:

- absence of a systematic search for heritage remains;
- absence of a central repository for "the collection, coordination, and dissemination of information regarding California's cultural past";
- absence of a central agency to provide information and assistance to prepare heritage components of environmental impact studies;
- increasing destruction of the state's non-renewable cultural resources;
- employment by the state of only two archaeologists, six historians, and three archivists;

- employment by the federal government of only two archaeologists in California;

- ineffectiveness of existing legislation to protect the state's heritage due to public ignorance and inadequate enforcement;

- inadequate state interpretive facilities and a failure to integrate heritage resource programs into California's elementary and secondary schools;

- absence of an accreditation program for archaeologists;

- lack of coordination among existing state specialists involved in heritage protection.[61]

The task force held its last meeting in December 1973. The future of the group had been discussed in November, and members agreed to seek legislation for additional funding and support for another year.[62] There was some optimism that the task force would be re-established in the spring of 1974 when draft legislation was prepared.[63] It was still defunct a year later, and when a new administration appeared in Sacramento, its fate was sealed. To his credit, Moratto seized every opportunity to press the task force's recommendations. For example, he wrote to Herbert Rhodes, the newly appointed state historic preservation officer, in 1975 to urge him to review the task force's report and "to establish a properly-funded agency to oversee all of the historical and archaeological programs of the State." Rhodes' response presaged the creation of the Office of Historic Preservation. He informed Moratto that he was in the midst of a departmental reorganization and expected to give the history plan's recommendations for a History Office "very close scrutiny to see if I can implement it. Possibly, we will not be able to attain the ideal, but at least we can get a functional office working to which we can add increments each year."[64]

The task force officially disappeared on September 29, 1976, when Governor Edmund G. Brown, Jr., signed A.B. 4239 which created and funded the Native American Heritage Commission. The bill repealed those sections of the Public Resources Code that dealt with the task force and replaced them with new provisions to identify, catalog, and protect Native American historical, cultural, and sacred sites. Although the moratorium on the excavation of sites less than 200 years old was now removed, California Indians actually emerged with a stronger role in the protection and management of their resources.[65]

The California Department of Transportation (Caltrans)

In addition to salvage operations along highway corridors, Caltrans was forced to consider ways to mitigate damage to the built environment in the path of its construction projects.[66] After consultation with the History Preservation Section of the Department of Parks and Recreation, Caltrans issued a policy and procedure statement on paleontological, archaeological, and historical resources in July 1974. The department recognized that the "preservation and protection of these resources" were "a beneficial consequence of transportation planning" and promised to "exercise all practical means to minimize adverse effects of transportation programs upon these resources." To do this, Caltrans would identify resources early during a project's planning and development phase, evaluate the project's impact on the resources, develop measures to mitigate or avoid adverse impacts on the resources, discuss the impact in environmental clearance documents, salvage resources if other mitigation measures failed, and cooperate with responsible agencies and organizations.[67]

Although the focal point of the agency's involvement in preservation-related activities was with paleontological and archaeological resources, there were several notable exceptions involving perceived non-compliance with Section 106 of the 1966 Historic Preservation Act, Executive Order 11593, and the procedures of the Advisory Council on Historic Preservation.

As a recipient of federal funds for highway construction, Caltrans was directly involved in procedures requiring cooperation between the federal agency granting the funds and the state historic preservation officer to identify significant cultural resources within the proposed project's environmental impact area. National Register criteria would be applied to all significant properties so identified. The federal agency and the state historic preservation officer would attempt to reach an agreement on ways to avoid or mitigate adverse effects. Should consensus be reached, a memorandum of agreement would be signed by the federal agency, the state historic preservation officer, and the Advisory Council on Historic Preservation.[68]

Consultations were held in 1974 between the staff of the History Preservation Section, representatives of the Federal Highway Administration, and Caltrans regarding the South Pasadena extension of the Long Beach Freeway.[69] As late as January 1976, Staff Architectural Historian Aaron Gallup reported to Historic Preservation Coordinator Knox Mellon that "at least 54 properties within the freeway corridor" had "historical or architectural significance including a number of buildings actually listed in the National Register." Gallup cautioned that "evaluations of all these properties must be made in accordance with the National Register criteria to determine their eligibility and the effect of the project upon them." Furthermore, since alternate routes would affect these resources "in different combinations," a careful evaluation was needed to determine the minimum impact upon the properties.[70]

Another construction project which festered for years was the Eureka Freeway, which threatened the demolition of more than 300 houses over fifty years old in the freeway corridor.[71] A historic property inventory, completed for Caltrans in 1975, was deemed to be unsatisfactory by Mellon because it showed "little regard" for the "special environmental quality" of the northern California community of Eureka. Substantive research and evaluation of individual structures were lacking, as were evaluations of the route in terms of potential historic districts in the area and the properties outside the corridor that could be visually impacted by the freeway. Moreover, there had been little consultation with local individuals and organizations.[72]

To rectify the situation, meetings were held between all concerned parties, field inspections were conducted, and a supplemental volume was added to the four-volume inventory. In mid-April 1976, representatives from Caltrans, the Federal Highway Administration, Office of Historic Preservation, and survey consultant David Gebhardt met in Eureka "to resolve the issue of the adequacy of the inventory to identify all cultural resources to be submitted for the determination of eligibility." It was agreed that the residential buildings in the freeway corridor comprised "one large district expressing the continuity of architectural styles which gives Eureka a quality unique among California cities" and that the entire area "should be submitted for a determination of National Register eligibility with key buildings identified in the defined area of impact." An additional fourteen structures were added to Caltrans' list of significant buildings. Although additional historical research on individual structures was still needed, the state historic preservation officer concluded that "all available documentation which is readily accessible has been consulted to identify significant associations with historic persons or events within the proposed freeway study area." Therefore, "the identification of resources phase of the procedures for protection of cultural resources for the Eureka Freeway Executive Order 11593 Action" was officially resolved.[73] Work on the freeway continued during the latter half of the decade, resulting in consultations on other preservation issues.

The Legislative Analyst

The flurry of legislative activity in the early 1970s resulted in the passage of Assembly Concurrent Resolution No. 274 in 1974, which directed the legislative analyst to review the feasibility of consolidating five state agencies with responsibilities for the state's heritage: the State Archives, the California Heritage Preservation Commission, the Historical Landmarks Advisory Committee, the Cultural Resources Section of the Department of Parks and Recreation, and the proposed State Historical Resources Commission. The proposed agency was also to review the state's interest in archaeology, paleontology, and California history. The study, which did not use a penny of its $50,000 allocation, concluded that the Department of Parks and Recreation had the greatest responsibility for California's heritage, which it defined as "those aspects of California's history, culture, natural resources and development which are appropriate for assignment to state agencies." Therefore, "any consolidation or reorganization of state functions should center around the existing activities of the department and not duplicate its capabilities."[74]

The department's mandates relating to paleontology and archaeology included providing recommendations to state agencies for "the preservation, recording, or excavation" of archaeological, paleontological, historic or prehistoric features, or burial grounds on state lands. Unfortunately, stated the report, the "archeological excavation undertaken to date has been minimal and paleontological exploration at construction sites is virtually nil." The reason was obvious: there were only two permanent archaeologists on the staff and no paleontologist.[75]

The brief thirteen-page report contained five specific recommendations: The Public Resources Code should separate the staff duties of the Department of Parks and Recreation from the deliberative and public hearing functions of the State Historical Resources Commission. References in the Public Resources Code to paleontology as a state activity should be deleted except to allow the department to recommend paleontological excavations on construction sites. The State Historical Resources Commission should establish criteria to determine and select the most significant archaeological sites to preserve or excavate. Historical units in the park system should include archaeological sites. Finally, both the commission and the department should develop guidelines to collect, store, and display archaeological specimens.[76]

The report generated a sharp response from the State Historical Resources Commission, which found it not "particularly helpful in the problems of history preservation in California."[77] Commissioner Kathryn Kaiser was even more critical when she expressed her "displeasure" to Legislative Analyst A. Alan Post. Not only had Post's staff overlooked the legislation's intent, wrote Kaiser, but they had "put no effort into the findings." Kaiser contended that his office had given the study a low priority, refused to spend the allotted funds to produce what could have been a "first-rate analysis of problems in dealing with the state's historical resources," and interviewed "only those who had a bias against A.B. 4146."[78]

Assemblyman Dixon Arnett, author of the unsuccessful A.B. 4146 in 1974, shared with Kaiser his own "same sense of frustration" and explained that he had spoken with Post and Rhodes. Both were unsupportive of the legislation's proposal to consolidate agencies with preservation-related responsibilities under a separate and independent State Historical Resources Commission. Nor did they wish to see the commission chair serve as the state historic preservation officer. Arnett, who had watched his bill go down to defeat, told Kaiser: "My guess is that unless the organized citizen groups which are concerned with historic preservation themselves take an active role in structural changes in the law, we are legislatively dead, at least for the time being."[79]

There was one unexpected legacy from the study. A year later, Arnett obtained the passage of A.B. 1991 which amended the Public Resources Code to require that the commission develop criteria to determine the significance of archaeological sites; select the most important of these sites and to determine which should be preserved or excavated and interpreted; and develop guidelines to collect, store, and display archaeological specimens.[80]

The State's Educational Sector

In 1975, James M. Doyle, supervisor of the History Preservation Section of the Department of Parks and Recreation, noted that "at present, there are no programs underway in California on historic preservation. A few of the colleges and universities have extension classes in archeology and architectural types. These are very localized."[81]

The department was qualified to make such an observation because it was contacted throughout this period by universities and colleges seeking information and suggestions for courses, both in the regular curriculum and extension programs.

Some of the early discussion centered around the department's interest in assisting master's and doctoral candidates in the completion of their degrees in exchange for the performance of "a meaningful research service for the State." Allen W. Welts, supervisor of the Historical Resources Section in 1968, noted that when this possibility was raised at an archival symposium at the University of San Francisco, the universities and colleges were unsupportive because they felt "the State Park System should pay them for assigning students to research projects without our exercising so much as a modicum of control over the projects." Welts refused to accept this condition because he was "responsible for limited public funds whereby to pursue the best possible interests of" the department.[82]

A year later, Director Mott heard from Kenneth H. Cardwell, acting chairman of the College of Environmental Design in the Department of Architecture at the University of California at Berkeley, who expressed willingness to develop a historic preservation program. Mott encouraged the idea because "the utilization of graduate students in a program of basic historic architectural research, and the measuring, surveying and recording of historical structures and sites could be a valuable service to the State Park System."[83]

As for the other disciplines, the 1973 report of the State Archaeological, Historical, and Paleontological Task Force concluded that there was little coordination among schools engaged in any kind of heritage work and almost no funding for their projects. For example, the state universities employed archaeologists as anthropology instructors, thus forcing those who conducted excavations to do so on their own time with their own funds and with student volunteers. To complicate matters, much of the work was done at sites destined for immediate demolition and, thus, proper research design was virtually impossible.[84]

By the time Doyle wrote his memo in 1975, there were some signs that preservation education was shifting away from random courses and classes in diverse disciplines toward the creation of comprehensive programs in historic preservation and cultural resources management.[85]

In 1975, California State College, Sonoma, received a grant from the California State University and Colleges' Fund for Innovation to develop a

"Pilot Undergraduate Program in Historic Preservation." A publicity brochure promised that the program would go "beyond the traditional scope of preservation activities to a broader, more community-based orientation" with a balanced cultural and professional introduction to the philosophy and techniques of preservation.[86] In the meantime, the History Department at the University of California at Santa Barbara, completed preparations for a graduate program in Public Historical Studies. In the fall of 1976, the first students were enrolled in a program designed "to create a new kind of professional person: the *Public Historian*," or in other words, research historians to work in the community.[87]

As the 1970s drew to a close, public history and preservation programs began to proliferate at other institutions. In 1977, the University of San Diego announced the establishment of a Graduate Certificate Program for the Historic Site Archaeology Technician.[88] In 1979, the History Department at the University of California at Riverside, changed its Master of Arts program in Western American Studies to a Master's in Historic Resources Management.[89] In that same year, a cultural heritage minor was proposed at California State University, Fresno.[90] During the 1980s, several other campuses of the California State University system introduced preservation programs.[91]

The growth of programs at four-year institutions paralleled a similar expansion in preservation curricula. Archaeologist David A. Frederickson, professor of Anthropology at Sonoma State University, who has been involved in cultural resources education for nearly two decades, observed that "as the regulatory context associated with environmental protection and historic preservation matured, the educational context has expanded to include a much larger array of cultural resource interests" beyond prehistoric archaeology to "historic archaeology, history, ethnography, vernacular architecture, and Native American concerns." In addition to formal course work, he noted that educational programs now include internships, research-related activities, and public service projects. Frederickson explained that these diverse experiences help prepare his students to understand and respond responsibly to the ever-widening range of interest groups and values that may not all support the preservation of cultural resources. "The important question is not simply, 'What should be preserved?'" he insisted. "It is, rather, 'How best can preservation take place with the least violation of the values of any of the several interest groups?'" [92]

From historian Ronald Tobey's perspective, the preservation curriculum of the future must move beyond the traditional training in historical research, policy, and practical application of the 1970s to include material culture and ethics. In 1984, Tobey, the director of the Historical Resources Management Program at the University of California at Riverside,commented that not only were students lacking intuition and knowledge about material objects and conservation techniques, they also needed to be taught basic concepts of fairness and integrity which they could apply as preservation advocates and in future relationships with clients.[93] Tobey's remarks presaged a 1986 Carnegie Foundation report which included the recommendation that majors' programs should be prepared to integrate "the historical, ethical, social and technical dimensions of their discipline."[94]

Although preservation programs have emerged in four-year institutions, a similar trend has not occurred at other levels. In 1984, the Heritage Task Force noted that

> the California Department of Education has not incorporated any program, or elements of such [preservation curriculum] programs, into the history or social studies curriculum for grades K-12. The use of programs which introduce children and young adults to aspects of the historic built environment, folklife traditions, architectural history, or archeology is now left entirely to the discretion of the individual teacher.[95]

Only two community colleges appear to have complete preservation packages. In 1976, Cypress Community College in Orange County began offering "a two-year para-professional, vocational program for those who will work in historic homes, write environmental impact reports, and do similar work." Gavilan College in Gilroy developed a forty-two hour certificate program in preservation construction technology and rehabilitation.[96]

Academicians have only begun to gain acceptance and a measure of respect for cultural resources management, public history, and preservation studies programs, all of which have attracted advocates because of a diversity of employment opportunities. The survival of many of these programs will depend on the quality of instruction given to students, on maintaining and increasing student enrollment, and on how well graduates of these programs succeed in the real world.

14

Archaeological Preservation: New Policies and New Directions

By the mid-1970s, archaeological preservation, like historic preservation, had developed new policies, the beginnings of a cadre of preservation specialists to identify and evaluate archaeological resources, contracting organizations and institutions, along with federal, state, and local programs of varying degrees of effectiveness. Although salvage remained the priority focus, a concern for preservation and conservation archaeology began to emerge, especially among those seeking to retain representative archaeological sites. The concern for site preservation, which mobilized like-minded archaeologists who believed that the preservation of archaeological resources should be a matter of public policy, led to the passage of the Archaeological and Historic Preservation Act in 1974. Later that same year, archaeologists formed the American Society for Conservation Archaeology.

Impact of Federal and State Legislation

The passage of the 1974 law, along with earlier legislation such as the National Historic Preservation Act, the National Environmental Policy Act (NEPA), and Executive Order 11593, had a direct impact on archaeological preservation. Previously, archaeologists concerned themselves with the acquisition of information before the site was destroyed. They were, in fact, so busy doing salvage archaeology in reservoir construction areas during the 1960s that they were not part of the preservation thrust that resulted in the passage of the landmark 1966 legislation.[1]

These laws and policies enlarged the scope of archaeological preservation. Now archaeologists had a role in an agency's planning procedures and could "recommend rerouting, relocating, or redesigning projects to preserve archaeological sites" in place.[2] This was the preferred approach because it prolonged "the useful life of the properties and their data" and because it was less expensive than salvage archaeology.[3]

Consideration of a project's impact was extended to include not only those areas in its immediate path, but tangential and secondary effects as well.[4] This generated problems, in part because the Department of the Interior failed to clarify "the limits in which archeological salvage work should be considered." Some agencies limited archaeological data recovery to the project's primary impact area, whereas others "require[d] surveys and data recovery work in secondary effect areas, sometimes even when the secondary effects may never occur." In California, the Office of Historic Preservation requested grantees of the Environmental Protection Agency "to perform historic surveys of several California towns as part of cultural resource compliance for wastewater treatment projects." In 1976 and 1977, three grantees surveyed three small towns at the suggestion of the state historic preservation officer. When the archaeologist for the California State Water Resources Control Board reviewed the surveys, which consisted of architectural descriptions of all buildings over fifty years old and histories of important families and individuals, he found them to be too broad, for they covered the entire town and not the immediate project area. As a result, in 1977, the Office of Historic Preservation stopped requesting these surveys.[5]

With the expansion of their involvement, preservation archaeologists have found a common cause with like-minded experts from other disciplines who are interested in the same properties, albeit for different reasons. Although most of these specialists have clearly defined criteria to determine the significance of these properties, archaeologists still grapple with the problem. For many, "the significance of an archaeological site [still] clearly depends on the intellectual predilections of the viewer..."[6] In addition to the changes that influenced the evolution of preservation archaeology in the state, Californians felt the impact of the passage of the California Environmental Quality Act of 1970 (CEQA) and the *Friends of Mammoth v. Mono County* decision in 1972.

CEQA required that environmental impact reports (EIRs) similar to the federal environmental impact statements (EISs) under NEPA be prepared for all proposed projects undertaken by public agencies that had a potential impact on the environment. The *Friends of Mammoth* decision by the State Supreme Court expanded CEQA's EIR coverage to include private projects that were regulated by state or local governments or received funding from state or local governments. This ruling was important because, unlike NEPA, the court refused to limit CEQA applicability to National Register properties. Indeed, it "specifically stated that the very act of issuing a building permit constitutes state action."[7] The reaction to the *Mammoth* decision was swift:

> many cities and counties stopped issuing building permits, bulldozers sputtered to a halt on every hilltop, and 'environmental assessment' firms sprang up like mushrooms after a spring rain. Architects, engineers, biologists and gardeners proclaimed themselves environmental impact specialists and began collecting fancy fees for their services, while the counties and cities groped for guidance.[8]

CEQA and the court decision created a demand for archaeological consultants, as well as a need to identify qualified archaeologists. The latter became especially critical now that archaeologists could stop projects. To cope with the problem, the Society for California Archaeology produced a "Directory of Qualified Archaeological Consultants" in 1974. To be accepted, the applicant had to "meet minimum educational and experiential qualifications and must formally commit him or herself to professional ethics and communication with the profession as a whole."[9]

The problem of policing the profession to eliminate the unscrupulous and incompetent has yet to be fully addressed and resolved. The temptations are great, especially when one considers that large sums of money are frequently involved in contract work. For example, 1 percent of a project budget as allowed under the Archeological and Historic Preservation Act can amount to a sizable sum if the total budget runs into tens of thousands of dollars.

It should be noted that archaeological ordinances were enacted at the county level during these years. Among the earliest were those passed by Marin and Inyo counties in 1967. The Marin code was particularly stringent for several reasons. It forbade uncontrolled excavation or disturbance of archaeological sites on public or private lands by untrained persons. Those wishing to excavate such areas or who discovered such sites while doing construction work needed a county permit to proceed. Upon receipt of a permit application, the county notified an appropriate educational institution or archaeological society which then had five days to evaluate the site. If the site was determined to have significance, the owner or contractor could not excavate for sixty days. Violations were considered misdemeanors, subject to fines and jail terms. Furthermore, "in the event of a continuing violation, each day that the violation continues constitutes a separate and distinct offense."[10] As archaeologist Thomas King recalled, the Marin law was the first county ordinance in the nation that protected archaeological sites on private and public lands. Although it did not provide "a whole lot of protection,...it was something. By the time CEQA was passed, the ordinance was sort of an anachronism and got in the way. But at the time it was passed, it was the first."[11]

Federal Efforts in California

With few exceptions, federal agencies failed to demonstrate a strong archaeological preservation commitment during the decade after the passage of the 1966 legislation. It is a curious fact that, for the most part, "those agencies with no tradition of involvement in archaeology, such as the Forest Service, have generally been more responsive to the new laws and more innovative in their implementation than have agencies like the Department of Transportation with a long and often fossilized involvement in salvage archaeology."[12] Federal programs were most often reactive, especially since construction projects could be delayed or stopped because of inadequate consideration for archaeological resources. An example was the halting of the Tahquitz Canyon Dam project in 1973 by the Agua Caliente band of Mission Indians in Palm Springs. According to King, who was involved in the case on the side of the Native Americans, the case was important because it became "the first archaeological 106 case in California and virtually the first in the nation." Furthermore, it was the first to "stop the Corps of Engineers in their tracks. They gave up the project, abandoned it and ran away." Nationally, the Corps "saw that they had something to contend with here, and they began developing their whole program."[13]

Another project that involved the same federal agency was the Warm Springs Dam project in Northern California. Authorized in 1962, by 1975 construction had been delayed by litigation involving the Corps' violation of both the Historic Preservation Act of 1966 and Executive Order 11593. Of great concern to the 178 descendants of the Dry Creek band of Pomo Indians was the Dry Creek Archaeological District which was on the National Register and which would be flooded by the dam. Although the dam was not stopped, the Corps was forced "to do what is still probably the most massive data recovery project of its kind with prehistoric and historic archaeology and ethnography." King, who was a plaintiff in the case along with the Pomo, observed that although the case may not be a model because "it was probably more than they could have done in the real world,...it sure was the biggest."[14]

Another even more controversial project was New Melones Dam in Calaveras and Tuolumne counties. After a hiatus of more than two decades, construction finally began in 1966 amid the passage of the aforementioned federal laws and policies. Although the earlier legislation provided for identification of cultural resources on federal lands, it was not until 1974 that funding became available "for cultural resource mitigation efforts on specific types of Federal construction projects." By 1974, construction work on the 625 foot dam was 25 percent complete. In December of that year, the New Melones district was declared eligible for the National Register.[15]

Preservation of the area's archaeological and historical resources in the New Melones project area became an immediate focal point of controversy. This dispute largely reflected the limited scope of early cultural resource studies which forced the Corps of Engineers to begin "an archeological program which was totally out of phase with the construction program." By the time the Corps awarded the project's phase one cultural resource mitigation contract to Science Applications, Inc., in 1978 for $1 million, at least fourteen different reports had been produced at a total cost of $494,000. The real problem was the absence of mitigation guidelines and a comprehensive cultural resources management plan. With the completion of the fifteenth study in 1979, a total of $2.4 million had been spent out of a maximum $3.46 million based on the 1 percent limit specified by law. In the midst of this study, the "second highest earth-rock filled dam in the United States" was completed in 1978.[16]

The controversies surrounding the project have been numerous and diverse. They included the question of what precisely is "required in the form and extent of cultural resources mitigation and who should judge the adequacy of the process and its products." Heated discussions focused on saving a nine-mile section of white water rapids which would be lost when the dam was filled.[17] Another point of contention was over how much money was available to complete the mitigation program. All this contributed "to the uncertainty of how much is enough to satisfy Federal archeological requirements."[18]

According to archaeologist Michael Moratto, who produced three of the fourteen project reports and had also served as vice-chairman of the State Archaeological, Paleontological, and Historical Task Force, the real problem was that, after spending $3.4 million and testing some 100 sites, the amount of useful data that Science Applications "produced was minuscule. It is not unfair to say that it could have been gathered for ten percent of the cost or probably less."[19]

The uproar and concern generated by the New Melones project resulted in an inquiry by the General Accounting Office on "how well United States archeological resources are being protected by law."[20] The two reports that were subsequently issued reveal their conclusions in their titles:

> "Uncertainties Over Federal Requirements For Archaeological Preservation at New Melones Dam in California" (December 21, 1979); and

> "Are Agencies Doing Enough or Too Much for Archeological Preservation? Guidance Needed" (April 22, 1981).

The 1981 report was especially critical of the role of the Department of the Interior. It concluded that "because the Department has not provided strong guidance and leadership, historic preservation efforts have been characterized by disorder, confusion, and controversy."[21] It was a conclusion reached by others in the past about the way the National Park Service had implemented mandates of the Secretary of the Interior.

There were other federal agencies involved in archaeological preservation in the state. Many lacked trained archaeologists and clear guidelines. For example, Region 9 of the General Services Administration did not have a full-time preservation staff or an approved preservation program as of 1977 and had to contract for "all but the most rudimentary archaeological studies."[22]

When the Soil Conservation Service of the Department of Agriculture published its draft "Procedures for the Protection of Archeological and Historical Properties Encountered in SCS-Assisted Programs" in June 1976, State Historic Preservation Officer Herbert Rhodes commented that the proposed guidelines were inadequate and contradictory, and failed to offer a meaningful identification process for significant properties. He believed that the suggested procedures not only offered less protection than those provided by other agencies, they promoted confusion and would eventually destroy many archaeological sites. Interestingly, Rhodes stated that his criticisms applied to the agency's nationwide policy and did not reflect his office's relationship with the California bureau which he said has "shown remarkable sensitivity to the cultural resources" of the state.[23] Rhodes' compliment had some substance in fact. Although the federal geologist was still contracting all archaeological projects to outside consultants in 1977 because he had no professional on his staff, his bureau still managed to conduct some twenty archaeological surveys by that date.[24]

Unlike other agencies, the Forest Service demonstrated a very early commitment to preservation at both state and national levels. In 1966, it employed only one full-time professional archaeologist; by 1975, there were seventeen nationwide. A year later, the number rose to twenty-three. From 1966 to fiscal 1977, its budget soared from zero to $1.5 million for cultural resources surveys and $400,000 to manage and protect previously identified cultural resources.[25]

During the early 1970s, the Forest Service was the only federal agency besides the National Park Service that had an archaeological program in California. Its only archaeologist had responsibility for all of the state's national forests. The shortage of staff forced him to emphasize "prehistoric resources management and in-forest ranger training, rather than stabilization, research, or public interpretation activities."[26] By 1975, the Forest Service had produced several management manuals that included specific references to federal preservation legislation and the agency's responsibilities and objectives in California. Regional archaeologist Donald S. Miller reported that his agency's priority in Region 5 was to inventory and professionally evaluate the cultural properties within California's seventeen national forests.[27]

The Bureau of Land Management, the nation's largest federal land managing agency, was also mandated to include preservation concerns in its programs. It, too, had few cultural resource professionals in place; for example, in 1966, the bureau employed only 1 archaeologist. During the mid-1970s, however, their number rose dramatically across the country. In 1973, there were 4 archaeologists and 1 historian on the staff. By April 1978, there were 103 archaeologists, 3 historians, and 1 historic architect working for the bureau. This sharp increase was the result of the legislation mentioned earlier and the passage of the Federal Land Policy and Management Act of 1976 which declared that archaeological values, among other resources, would be protected on public lands.[28]

The Bureau of Land Management's California office reflected similar changes in policies and staffing. Although the bureau as a whole lacked an up-to-date cultural resource procedural manual, its statewide policy included "consideration of all cultural resources and mitigation for all resources, commensurates [sic] with the research potential of the site or area, to be effected." As of April 1977, the bureau had district-level cultural resource staff positions in five of its six district offices, in several area offices and on their Desert Planning Staff, and in the state office. The state director reported that his office employed twelve archaeologists and expected to spend $350,000 for cultural resources during fiscal 1977.[29]

By 1976, significant improvements had been made in the staffing of cultural resources personnel and the development of preservation program guidelines at the federal level. Their actual success would be determined by how well they could be integrated into each agency's overall policies and procedures.[30]

Emergence of the Society for California Archaeology

Throughout the 1960s, California archaeology could best be described as a "beggar's trade." Michael J. Moratto recalled that the phrase, which was coined by Thomas King, referred to the period before the passage of CEQA and the *Mammoth* decision. It was a time when archaeologists lacked "legal clout" and were "constantly scrambling after bulldozers and begging developers for a bit of time…a bit of funding." It was a time, noted Moratto, when archaeologists were dependent on volunteer assistance and a mere $300 to $400 budget for an entire field season. It was a time when archaeology was a labor of love with only a few practitioners participating for remunerative reasons, and when most of the professionals were academicians.[31]

By 1970, there were some forty institutions and fifteen avocational groups in California "elbowing each other around," having "a certain amount of difficulty just keeping on top of the gossip."[32] The absence of a statewide organization capable of assuming the role of a central coordinating or record-keeping agency compounded this state of "creative anarchy." That the resulting confusion was due to the non-existence of a master file of sites was clear to California archaeologists. They could do little, however, to resolve the problem because of the lack of legislative guidance and support, and because of the existence of agencies with similar revenue sources but without clearly defined areas of responsibility.[33]

In the meantime, archaeological sites continued to be destroyed. In its assessment of the state's archaeological resources, the Archaeological, Historical, and Paleontological Task Force reported in 1973 that half of California's 90,000 sites had already been lost. The task force stressed that its estimates were imprecise because there had never been a systematic search for prehistoric remains. The report also noted that its figures could not accurately depict the extent of the real damage because major sites "were located in prime areas for modern development….In this light, perhaps 80% of the large, deep, and ancient prehistoric sites in the state are gone entirely, and a significant percentage of those left is badly disturbed or faces imminent destruction."[34]

In addition to the aforementioned problems, archaeologists faced another, equally serious situation within their own ranks. There was an internal schism between university archaeologists and those in the state colleges and museums who found common cause with federal and state park archaeologists. Professional jealousies were further fueled by the disdain "card carrying" academic archaeologists shared for the "avocationalists, as though self-trained pre-historians were somehow members of a different species." The problem was compounded by the fact that archaeological site records were stored at two University of California campuses where faculty archaeologists could dictate who had access to them. As the demand by non-university-affiliated archaeologists for permission to use these records increased, so did the tensions.[35]

In 1965, a group of archaeologists attempted to improve communications through a letter campaign urging the formation of a unified, mutual cooperation society to work jointly on common goals: "to harness our...scattered energy for a better fight for resource preservation,...to provide political clout for protective legislation," and "to establish a code of ethics, which would enable avocationalists to understand and adopt a professional stance...."[36]

The nucleus of the new organization emerged in April 1966 when the Southwestern Anthropological Association Conference met at Davis.[37] A statewide Committee on Plans for Coordination of Archaeological Site Records was created "to study the feasibility of establishing through legislation a central agency or system of regional centers, for the compilation and maintenance of archaeological site records."[38] In November, the committee of eleven men, including King who represented avocational archaeologists, met at the University of California at Los Angeles to form the Society for California Archaeology (SCA) "to promote, coordinate and set standards for archaeology in California."[39]

By the time the society was formally incorporated in October 1968, the original committee had submitted a bill to the legislature to create an archaeological agency. Also, King and state archaeologist Francis Riddell began discussions on the division of California into regions in which a cooperating institution handled site records. A constitution and bylaws were approved in March 1967, and membership quickly rose to well over 200 scholars, non-academic practitioners, and graduate students.[40]

Another of the new organization's early activities was the review of Caltrans' ten-year-old archaeological program. By 1968, several problem areas had been identified. For example, the Department of Parks and Recreation was critical of the lack of funding for removal of field data and collections for analysis, the absence of a publications program for reports and findings, and the agency's dependence on unpaid volunteers. When SCA met with the State Highway Commission, similar concerns were voiced. In July 1969, SCA submitted a thirty-page report to the commission which included several suggestions for the improvement of the highway salvage program. Not only did it agree with all of the criticisms raised by the Department of Parks and Recreation, the report called for the reduction of the department's overhead charges, an end to free services volunteered by local institutions, and adequate funding for studies, analyses, and publications. The Department of Parks and Recreation explained that it was legally required to collect administrative costs; it could not subcontract directly with local institutions. The State Attorney General's ruling that state highway funds could not be used for survey, analysis, or report preparations in June 1970 strengthened the department's determination to terminate its participation in the Highway Salvage Program. Thus in July 1970, the Department of Parks and Recreation formally ended its involvement with Caltrans.[41]

The departure of the department from the Highway Salvage Program paved the way for new relationships between Caltrans, SCA, and the academic institutions. Caltrans accepted SCA's offer to serve as a clearinghouse for the receipt and dissemination of highway project data. The society arranged for the initial site surveys and preparation of cost estimates, coordinated contracts between Caltrans and the universities, and saw to the storage of archaeological materials on various campuses. The services of archaeologists from various academic institutions were acquired for each of the existing eleven Caltrans districts to serve as District Liaison Archaeologists who, after 1972, arranged for salvage contracts for their respective institutions. The first salvage contract was arranged by Michael Morrato and was between the Environmental Factors Unit of Caltrans District 04 and the Frederick Burk Foundation of San Francisco State University. In May 1973, the system of SCA district representatives was replaced by eleven district clearinghouses "to more effectively oversee and coordinate professional activities and standards within each district" in view of "the increased workload and modified funding situation resulting from the *Mammoth* decision and generally increased application" of federal and state laws.[42]

The SCA viewed the clearinghouses as interim operations to maintain, review and store data and to provide consultant referral services when needed. Not only did they emerge as "the best sources of archaeological information and expertise in a region of the State," the concept worked so well that the Cultural Heritage unit of the Department of Parks and Recreation signed a Memorandum of Agreement in 1975 with all eleven clearinghouse coordinators and four others to establish the fifteen regional offices that became the California Archaeological Sites Survey. Beginning in January 1976, annual contracts from the state historic preservation officer under the direction of the Cultural Heritage unit distributed a total of $22,000 in federal funds among the fifteen regional officers whose only assignments were to correct the files, assign new site numbers, and provide Sacramento with duplicate records. In January 1977, the Office of Historic Preservation assumed responsibility for the department's archaeological site documents and the regional offices. By 1980, the state's Archaeological Sites Survey had been transformed from a nonfunded volunteer organization with 23,000 site records to thirteen regional offices which were funded at $130,000 and had 47,000 site records.[43] Thus, David Frederickson could observe in 1980 that

> the basic problem of site records maintenance, which was a major factor in bringing the SCA into existence, has been solved. At least the apparatus for the solution exists and is working in different regions with varying degrees of effectiveness.[44]

Indeed, by 1980, the regional offices had "become the primary element in the State's effort toward planning, synthesizing and managing the archaeological data." However, as William Seidel, staff archaeologist in the Office of Historic Preservation, observed, they "have no legal coercive powers and are dependent solely on the powers of persuasion and cooperation."[45]

The society's success with the problem of site records maintenance did not compensate for its inability to attain its legislative objectives in the early 1970s. This had direct repercussions on the society's evolution. As members began to realize that their hopes for a statewide archaeological research and salvage coordinating agency were unattainable, they also became aware that their constituency's needs were changing and becoming more complex. The number and complexity of governmental requirements were increasing dramatically. Thus, by the mid-1970s, traditional practitioners of archaeology began to find themselves surrounded by "increasing numbers of archaeological bureaucrats, archaeological consultants, preservationists, and, ultimately, the descendants of those responsible for a very significant amount of the cultural remains being studied by archaeologists." Furthermore, SCA's enthusiastic advocacy of "'in-house archaeology'...the hiring of archaeologists and [the] establishment of archaeological administrative units within the larger existing agencies" began to decline as archaeological bureaucrats were perceived as being co-opted by the system for which they worked. In the face of increasing numbers of archaeological entrepreneurs, SCA, by mid-decade, became "a promoter of contract archaeologists...a business referral agency." Thus, what was supposed to have been an interim organization to coordinate archaeological site data and find opportunities for noncredentialed archaeologists to use those data was now seeking ways to establish itself as a "lasting 'alternative'" to "coordinate, facilitate and monitor the activities of governmental and non-governmental institutions alike in California."[46]

In 1975, SCA re-examined its constitution and bylaws. A year later, new bylaws were adopted which committed the newly designated "scientific and educational organization" to facilitate "coordination and cooperation among archaeologists in California and...between archaeologists and all citizens of California." In 1977, doctoral candidate Clyde Kuhn agreed "to develop a historic overview of the Society and to create a modelled approach for the future needs of the SCA as a community-related organization."[47] Although Kuhn's proposal was not disseminated to the general membership when it was submitted in 1978, the topic continued to be discussed as the society entered the decade of the eighties.[48]

State Activities and Programs

According to the State Archaeological, Historical, and Paleontological Task Force, the status of the state's heritage preservation programs was discouraging and grim:

> state agencies are barely scratching the surface in their efforts to preserve rather than destroy the cultural heritage....Almost every state agency that owns or has jurisdiction over lands in California has, either knowingly or unknowingly, encountered cultural or paleontological sites.

The problem, it seemed, was not so much a lack of interest or concern, but a shortage of funds.[49] Although that continues to be a perennial issue, those state agencies that have committed staff and monies on behalf of archaeological preservation have demonstrated considerable progress.

At Caltrans, for example, the first in-house archaeologist was hired in August 1972. After three months in the field, he was transferred to Sacramento, where he became the agency's chief archaeologist.[50] Caltrans' dependence on consulting archaeologists under contract for all archaeological projects ended in 1975. Thereafter, surveys, test excavations, and mitigative studies were performed by in-house professionals who were added to the staff. In that same year, federal highway funds became available for analysis and report preparation. Paid Native American consultants were also hired as beginning in 1973.[51]

Although Caltrans has been recognized as a leader in archaeological programs among state departments of transportation and highways, Louis S. Wall, chief of the Western Division of Project Review for the Advisory Council on Historic Preservation, cautioned that the agency did not get involved willingly:

> They were forced into it primarily through the efforts of the State's archeological and Native American communities. If these outside forces fail to continue the pressure they have applied through the 1970s, there will be back-sliding on the part of the agency.[52]

The Department of Parks and Recreation continued its archaeological studies and excavations in the State Park System under the supervision of the Cultural Heritage Section and state archaeologist Francis Riddell.[53] In 1979, the section produced a list of studies on the park system's archaeological sites that dated back to 1947. Although admittedly incomplete, the number of survey and excavation reports shows a marked increase after 1975. Those surveys conducted before 1975 discussed only prehistoric sites. In contrast, most of the post-1975 surveys addressed all cultural values, a clear indication of the widening horizons of preservation archaeology.[54]

Riddell and other department archaeologists had difficulty persuading other agency professionals to accept "the concept that archeological methodology has a serious part to play in the reconstruction and restoration of historic structures in the State Park System." He lamented that, "except in rare instances, buildings were in the past restored without benefit of professional archeological assistance." At Columbia and Coloma, few archaeological investigations were conducted before restoration activities were started. The resulting "loss to subsurface features and data was monumental." Even the restoration activities at Sutter's Fort, Fort Tejon, and Fort Ross were undertaken without benefit of archaeological studies. The problem was not only a limited budget, Riddell insisted, but the need to convince "old line park supervisors and planners" of the "clear and beneficial relationship between a carefully executed archeological project and the ultimate restoration of an historic structure."[55]

The state's archaeologists did not universally endorse the department's National Register program. One reason was a disagreement with the state's property notification procedure which required a complete list of all property owners. In 1974, Thomas King, western coordinator of the Committee on Public Archeology for the Society for American Archaeology, explained that these complex requirements were in conflict with federal policy and deterred people from nominating large parcels with multiple owners to the Register. The placement of districts on the Register was especially important for archaeological preservation because it was not feasible to put all known and potential sites on the Register individually. Because the properties were nominated solely for their historical and scientific merits, King reasoned that "the plans of landowners, while certainly pertinent to preservation, do not appear to me to be appropriate matters for consideration in deciding whether to accept a property to the Register."[56]

John Michael, the History Preservation Section's supervisor, wrote back to inform King that, although he agreed that the procedure was "cumbersome," it was a courtesy that the department believed was integral to its preservation efforts. Not only should owners be informed that their property contained significant sites that should be protected, Michael said, because "they also became possible recipients of matching grants-in-aid for restoration and preservation, they must be notified in a fair and equitable manner."[57] The correspondence between the men continued through the spring of 1974 but failed to resolve the disagreement.[58]

Meanwhile, the placement of large parcels on the National Register with boundaries extending far beyond known archaeological sites led commissioner and archaeologist Clement Meighan to ask what constituted an archaeological district. He informed the State Historical Resources Commission that he had heard from property owners who were willing to preserve known sites but were unwilling to see their entire parcel placed on the Register when the sites were located on only one portion of their property.[59] Meighan supported the continued use of archaeological districts to preserve these sites because of convenience and as a feasible way to protect groups of contiguous sites of different periods and functions. Each district nomination was required to provide "the exact location and reasonably precise indications" of each site in the district, draw boundaries around only the sites, and meet all Register criteria. As Meighan explained later, he was also concerned that the National Register had been used "to throw an improper bureaucratic roadblock against *any* use of extensive pieces of land even when most of it has no archaeological value whatsoever." Not only was credibility lost when this happened, he believed that "archaeologists are obliged to justify their claims with real sites that have been reasonably well-recorded, not imaginary sites that may someday be found." He warned: "we are going to win battles but lose the war if we allow slovenly documentation of archaeological sites to stand as the basis for creation of archaeological districts." In July 1975, the commission accepted his recommendations.[60]

Archaeologists remained reluctant to nominate sites to the National Register throughout the 1970s. Meighan tried to encourage nominations through the SCA *Newsletter*. He informed members that registration did not cloud title to the land but instead provided protection for archaeological sites "to the extent of requiring advance notice and planning before the sites can be altered or destroyed."[61] Another frequent concern was that once the site was listed, it could be easily vandalized by someone with access to the Register's records. Repeated assurances that precise locations were not revealed to the public did little to assuage these fears.[62] These and other explanations did not convince archaeologists that the time and energy needed to complete the nomination forms resulted in substantial and beneficial returns.[63]

The situation had not improved by 1982. Meighan observed that archaeologists remained not only indifferent, but "a considerable number are very hostile to the National Register because it is used primarily to prevent them from conducting their studies. Some have found by experience that it is not in their interest to get any public recognition of the more important sites." Meighan concluded, "we still have a long way to go in inventorying archeological resources and deciding what to do about them."[64]

One final dimension of the state's effort to preserve archaeological resources deserves a brief comment. The 1970s witnessed increasingly active involvement by California Indians to preserve their heritage. Until the early 1960s, there were few adversarial encounters between California

Indians and archaeologists, primarily because archaeologists excavated in areas where surviving Indian groups were few in number. This changed when archaeologists appeared in the Sierra Nevada foothills, the California desert, and on the northwest coast in the sixties.[65]

Tensions began to ease by the early 1970s as both sides slowly realized they could work together constructively on preservation-related issues.[66] By mid-decade, however, the pendulum had swung in the other direction. Some archaeologists on salvage projects "were perceived—probably quite correctly—as lackeys of the government" who paved the way for projects that damaged sites of cultural importance to Native Americans. Others who were employed by public agencies were accused of "whitewashing" agency actions when they affected sacred sites. "The growing market for archeological consultants created 'hired guns' whose ethics...were not above reproach." At the same time, California Indians emerged as a visible and vocal interest group whose demands could not be ignored. They asserted "their right to practice traditional religions," claimed their traditional lands and fishing rights, and became actively involved in protecting archaeological resources. The creation of the Native American Heritage Commission in 1976 was the direct result of California Indians' involvement in resource protection.[67]

During the decade after the passage of the landmark federal legislation of the mid-1960s, preservation archaeology, as it was practiced in California and elsewhere, focused on salvage efforts. That, after all, was where the funds were.

As the Bicentennial of the American Revolution approached, a clear shift in emphasis could be discerned. The state's archaeological community began moving toward the management of California's cultural resources and away from digging and dodging bulldozers. "More specifically," observed archaeologist William Seidel, "it has devoted the vast majority of its personnel, time and resources toward identification, evaluation, and preservation of archaeological sites."[68] This shift was encouraged by new legislation and policies, pressures from governmental agencies at all levels, and changing attitudes among those archaeologists who came of age in the years when conservation and environmental issues were widely debated and who now held positions in federal, state, and local agencies.

During the 1970s, archaeological preservation benefited directly from legislation that permitted archaeologists to gather scientific data and to obtain funding for their effort. As the decade drew to a close, however, it was archaeological preservation in particular that began to attract careful scrutiny and widening criticism. At the federal level, the General Accounting Office concluded that "the National Archeology Program, which costs about $100 million a year, is not working well."[69] And in California, the State Heritage Task Force, which was created by the state legislature in 1981, had archaeological resources deleted from its mandate to forward recommendations on the status and future of the state's heritage programs and policies.[70] How archaeologists cope with this crucial challenge will determine how well they survive in the future. It will also have an impact on how well preservationists in other fields survive in the face of a troubled national economy and an uncertain political future for all environmental causes.

15

Preservation-Related Efforts Elsewhere in California: A Rising Tide of Acceptance

Although federal and state programs dominated the preservation scene in the first decade after passage of the landmark 1966 federal legislation, new converts emerged to strengthen and change the practice and direction of preservation in California. Two unmistakable signs demonstrated historic preservation's impact on community awareness and acceptance by the mid-1970s: the proliferation of local ordinances and commissions, and of preservation organizations.

Local Ordinances and Commissions

Several cities and counties had incorporated historic preservation elements into their general plans before this optional component was authorized in 1974. Among the first to adopt preservation-related ordinances were Monterey County in 1968, and Grass Valley and Half Moon Bay in 1973. A year later, five more cities and counties adopted preservation elements and, in 1975, three more were added to the list. By 1980, twenty-eight local governments had adopted preservation elements.[1]

One of these early pioneers was the City of Santa Cruz, which added its historic preservation plan element in September 1974. The plan articulated a very pragmatic reason for preserving the town's unique townscape: tourism. "It makes both economic and environmental sense," the plan stated, "to protect and enhance this valuable, cultural resource." To preserve and protect their architecturally significant structures, the city council created a five-member Historic Preservation Commission in 1975 to recommend landmarks, designate historic districts, and review alteration, construction, relocation, or demolition permits. A year later, the commission recommended the establishment of a revolving preservation fund to purchase endangered structures, and "through renovation and other improvements increase the amount of loan that private lenders can make to purchase these buildings upon their resale by the revolving fund." [2]

Although historic preservation elements differ, most begin with a regional overview consisting of a historical summary and description of local resources, followed by supplementary drawings and photographs of common architectural styles, preservation policies and activities, and guidelines and methods for implementation. Like Santa Cruz, most jurisdictions with preservation elements established advisory committees or commissions to develop landmark and historic district criteria and maintain appropriate listings. Also incorporated into many ordinances were policies pertaining to design review, exterior alterations, new construction, and demolition in historic districts. [3]

The number of local landmark and historic district commissions in California reached a sizable figure by the mid-1970s. The National Trust for Historic Preservation's 1976 directory identified twenty-six city and four county commissions and review boards. [4] A year later, Sandra J. Elder, then recording secretary to the State Historical Resources Commission, listed thirty municipal bodies and eleven county agencies. [5]

Several commissions were relative newcomers. San Buenaventura's seven-member Historical Preservation Commission, for example, was established in June 1973 to advise and recommend landmarks and points of historical interest to the city council. [6] In that same year, Oakland's seven-member Landmarks Preservation Advisory Board began recommending landmarks and historic districts to the Planning Commission and advising on "new construction and exterior alterations to landmarks, including interiors of publicly owned structures." The board may also recommend delays of 120 days when landmarks are threatened with demolition or removal; decisions can be appealed to the city council. As of 1976, fifteen landmarks and two districts had been designated. [7]

Nearly a decade earlier, in addition to Los Angeles, other California cities such as San Diego established historical site boards. In 1965, San Diego's fifteen-member board was created "to advise the Mayor, City Council, City Planning Commission, Park and Recreation Board, and City Manager" regarding the identification and preservation of historic sites. The board was later authorized to recommend 180-day delays if landmarks were threatened with demolition, alteration, or removal. By 1976, it had identified 111 landmarks and was in the process of designating its first historic district, the thirty-eight-acre Gaslamp Quarter. [8] San Jose's Historic Landmarks Commission was established more than a decade earlier in 1949. Its responsibilities were increased by a 1975 ordinance which stated that the commission's purpose was:

> to promote the public peace, health, safety and welfare through the preservation of landmarks and thereby stabilize neighborhoods and areas of the City; enhance, preserve and increase property values; increase cultural, economic and aesthetic benefits to the City and its residents; preserve, continue and encourage the development of the City to reflect its historical, architectural, cultural and aesthetic value or tradition; and enrich the quality of life to serve intellectual, spiritual and material needs by fostering knowledge of the City's historical heritage.[9]

San Francisco's Landmarks Preservation Advisory Board first met in June 1967. Its nine voting members were required to be "'specially qualified by reason of training or experience in the historic and cultural traditions of the City, and interested in the preservation of its historic structures, sites, and areas.'" Like its counterparts, the San Francisco board's functions were limited to recommending landmarks and historic districts, and commenting on requests for new construction, removal, or demolition of landmarks. It could also maintain studies and surveys, consult with interested groups, conduct inspections and investigations, offer advice and information to property owners, and recommend a 180-day delay for threatened landmarks and 90 days for districts. Decisions made by the planning commission to which the board reported could be appealed to the elected board of supervisors. By 1976, eighty-three landmarks had been approved; these included a fountain, a street clock, and the Jackson Square Historic District of some eighty structures.[10]

On paper, local landmark commission and preservation boards carried little clout because they were advisory to the elective body who appointed them. Their recommendations could be and were ignored or overruled. Little could be done if the city council or board of supervisors was unsympathetic to preservation. However, one way for preservationists to exert influence was explained by Ralph A. Mead, secretary to the San Francisco Landmarks Preservation Advisory Board: "Even though the Board operates as an advisory body, in practice its opinions are given great weight because of the expertise of its members and their exclusive concentration in this one field of public activity."[11]

Whether completely successful or not, the efforts of local landmark commissions and boards continue to encourage and reinvigorate the preservation movement at the grassroots level.

Proliferation of Preservation Organizations

When John L. Frisbee of the National Trust observed in 1972 that "in California, there are a multitude of private preservation groups," he was accurately describing the local scene in the decade after the passage of the 1966 federal legislation.[12] Most of these groups were galvanized by an endangered local landmark.

The Santa Barbara Trust for Historic Preservation, for example, was established in 1963 to restore the deteriorating Santa Barbara Presidio. The trust subsequently restored and donated El Cuartel, the guard's house, to the state, which has turned it into a museum.[13] The trust's operations were expanded dramatically in December 1971 when it officially accepted a $2 million gift from Irene Suski Fendon: the Casa de la Guerra-El Paseo Shopping Complex.[14]

In the City of San Diego, citizens anxious about the fate of their Victorian structures formed the Save Our Heritage Organization in 1969. Coalescing first over the imperiled Sherman-Gilbert House, they were eventually assisted by the county and found land for the historic preserve for endangered Victorians now known as "Heritage Park."[15]

By 1971, the Berkeley Architectural Heritage Committee was advocating the preservation and conservation of architecturally significant structures and sites. Members wrote articles for local newspapers, supported the 1974 city ordinance creating the Landmarks Preservation Commission, sponsored numerous tours of neighborhoods, and published an annual calendar of significant buildings.[16] The association made headlines in the fall of 1976 when it helped forestall the demolition of the Naval Architecture Building on the campus of the University of California, Berkeley. Plans to build an engineering center in its place were halted by a lawsuit that required the university to submit an environmental impact report. On March 8, 1977, Chancellor Albert Bowker announced that the building would be saved.[17]

One of the most influential organizations in northern California, the Foundation for San Francisco's Architectural Heritage, was founded by urban planner Charles Hall Page and others who believed that "San Francisco's unique cityscape was being unnecessarily destroyed by forces that did not respect the cultural and economic importance of the city's architectural heritage." Established in 1971 as "an action counterpart to the

Landmarks Board" to provide realistic alternatives to the demolition of landmarks, the privately funded corporation came into existence when the city's Redevelopment Agency was bulldozing hundreds of Victorian houses, and the Planning Commission "was adopting the Urban Design Plan which explicitly recognized the need to conserve residential and commercial buildings which give the city its unique character and liveability."[18] The group of some 1,500 members sought to educate and assist the city's citizenry through publications such as the well-received *Splendid Survivors: San Francisco's Downtown Architectural Heritage* in October 1979, a rehabilitation loan program started in 1979, and a variety of tours, lectures, and neighborhood meetings. Five years after it was founded, Heritage owned property, bought options, held historic preservation easements, and produced feasibility studies. Its staff had increased from 1 full-time person to 8 paid members and more than 150 active volunteers.[19]

Heritage's preservation advocacy and watchdog roles were evident during the lengthy Yerba Buena Center Redevelopment Project that threatened several significant properties, and the highly controversial legal battle over the preservation of the "City of Paris" building on Union Square. In *Foundation for San Francisco's Architectural Heritage v. City and County of San Francisco*, which was denied a hearing by the State Supreme Court in August 1980, the plaintiffs argued that the city could not permit the building's destruction because its planning codes encouraged the preservation of historic structures; the department store was a recognized National Register property and state landmark. Preservationists were incensed at Nieman-Marcus' plan to relocate the building's dome and rotunda into the new structure—mitigation measures that the court of appeal ruled satisfied CEQA's requirements. The impact of this decision was to underscore the judiciary's reluctance "to discover a 'penumbra' of additional protection emanating from the legislative recognition of the importance of historic places and objects or to articulate a new common law of private citizens' duties in the historic preservation field."[20]

In Sacramento, Aubrey Neasham continued his involvement in preservation causes until his death in 1982. For example, he played a pivotal role in the establishment of the Sacramento Trust for Historic Preservation in 1970 to pursue "excellence in the promotion, planning, restoration, reconstruction, and display of historic sites, buildings, and artifacts in the Sacramento area."[21] The preservation of Old Sacramento was its primary concern, and in 1973, the nonprofit Old Sacramento, Inc. emerged as an

active participant in the restoration and development of the historic downtown area. Neasham himself chaired the Old Sacramento, Inc. Committee.[22]

The problem with these proliferating local organizations was, as
Frisbee observed, that "none has exercised statewide leadership. The key
problem appears to be one of fragmentation."[23] The absence of a statewide
preservation organization, or, for that matter, an official state historical
society, was not lost on other interested parties. In 1973, for example, John
Michael, supervisor of the History Preservation Section, noted that

> Strange as it may seem, the State of California does not
> sponsor a state historical society. As part of our compre-
> hensive history plan...we are proposing that a state-spon-
> sored historical society be organized. However, at this
> point, we do not have such an organization.[24]

One early attempt to create a statewide group was led by Aubrey
Neasham, who wielded considerable influence in Sacramento. In 1973, he
and his wife, Irene, wrote to Senator Albert Rodda inquiring about the
feasibility of having the state legislature charter a private, nonprofit organization to be called "the California Trust for Historic Preservation." Already
endorsed by the American Revolution Bicentennial Committee, the proposed trust would supplement and not compete with state agencies. The
Neashams said: "Working with the State, greater effectiveness could be
reached in the preservation, integration, and enhancement of California's
cultural resources."[25]

Rodda responded affirmatively and added a handwritten postscript
asking them to "please contact this office so that we may develop the
legislation."[26] In August 1973, Rodda introduced S.B. 1458 to create the
California Trust for Historic Preservation to receive donations of significant
historic properties, to preserve and maintain these properties, and to receive
funds or other properties to carry out its preservation mandates.[27]

The bill was favorably received at first, but later that same fall
opposition began to mount. In November, Frisbee, who had initially supported the measure, asked Rodda's office for clarification. What, for example, would be the trust's emphasis? Historic preservation, he noted, had
many meanings. "To some, it refers to museums and historic house
museums while to others it means the preservation and reuse of historic and
architectural resources for continuing contemporary purposes." He informed the senator's staff that the Department of Parks and Recreation was
in the midst of developing a statewide history preservation plan that would
recommend the creation of a Department of History to administer preserva-

tion programs statewide. What, he asked, would be the relationship between these two entities? [28]

Frisbee observed that the California Trust anticipated becoming "the leader of the private sector in historic preservation matters." The difficulty, he said, was that the existing fragmentation of the preservation movement demanded that the new organization provide "a reasonable assurance of its leadership capacity on a statewide basis" before being given official approval. Frisbee was encouraged by the increasing level of preservation activity in the state and suggested that instead of creating a new body, "an appropriate" group should convene "a statewide meeting of the historic preservation community. A major objective would be to determine what is the most appropriate course to follow in establishing greater unity and coordination of activities."[29]

It was not until the summer of 1975 that another attempt was made to organize a statewide preservation advocacy group. In June, a handful of individuals gathered in San Francisco to discuss what was to become California's first statewide lobby for preservation issues. The National Trust did not encourage this budding effort until May 1976 because Frisbee apparently believed it lacked "appropriate leadership for success."[30]

Among the catalysts was Sacramento planner Roger Scharmer, who was unanimously elected chairman pro tem at the group's second meeting in August. At Heritage's Haas-Lilienthal House in San Francisco, the following statement of purpose was adopted for the still nameless group:

> To foster the protection of the historical heritage and environmental resource of structures, sites and areas of special character or of historical, architectural, archeological, and aesthetic value within both the urban and rural areas of the State; and, to promote the conservation of all heritage resources for beneficial use.[31]

The members agreed that theirs would be a preservation action organization whose goals were to provide a forum to evaluate and advocate "policies, guidelines, and legislation for historical and neighborhood preservation;" "to influence public policy" relating to preservation and "to foster the reduction of adverse environmental impact on our heritage resources by the advocation" of strong conservation legislation; and "to promote increased community awareness of the benefits of neighborhood preservation by providing information...." To accomplish these goals, the group would research issues, communicate information and concerns, and take political action at all levels.[32]

These decisions were translated into populist terms by southern California planner and historian John Merritt who invited southland preservationists to a meeting in September. Merritt, who was anxious that it not become "just another northern-based and informed activity," compared the fledgling group to "a Sierra Club for significant historic, cultural and architectural structures—a lobby for bricks and boards instead of bears and beetles." As he envisioned it, the organization would serve as a focal point for statewide preservation efforts, comment on and propose legislation, generate effective and timely political pressure, and serve as an informational clearinghouse. It was to be "a tool...aimed at Sacramento, primed with support from the fragmented, locally based preservation movement, *and* it would feed back to local groups new ammunition for their battles close to home."[33]

The time had come for the formation of a political action group to lobby for preservation concerns, an activity that the National Trust for Historic Preservation was prohibited from engaging in. From its inception, the new organization made clear that its purpose was "to fill this vacuum."[34] That they would not duplicate the National Trust's functions was emphasized: "technical aid, advisory services, and grants are best left to the Trust and the Office of Historic Preservation." This approach also reflected the professional backgrounds and interests of "the early organizers [who] were engaged in city planning and public policy and concerned about the destruction of neighborhoods by HUD and CalTrans...."[35]

Some members had great hopes for the future. When Charles C. Knill wrote to Governor Edmund G. Brown, Jr., in support of the proposed Historic Building Code, he informed the governor that "a state-wide Historic Preservation and Conservationist Organization with the objective of making available, on a massive scale, the means to preserve and conserve the architectural, cultural, and historic buildings of the State" was being organized. "We hope," he said, "to be as effective as was the Landmarks Club in preserving the California Missions at the turn of the century."[36]

Although equally optimistic about the group, Merritt was concerned about "an apparent lack of real emerging leadership or up-front willingness of some early people to follow through." Few, he said, seemed willing to "give much time or leadership...everyone is telling me they'll provide followship but can't do much more." He asked:

> Who is it that shall do the work? How will the lobby function
> without a research, drafting, button-holing, watch dog
> presence in Sacramento or with willing and ready access to

> Sacramento? It seems letters and paper will not be enough—
> there must be flesh.[37]

By December 1975, some of Merritt's fears seemed to have been allayed. He wrote to the "Sacto cabal" that the first newsletter would be sent out in January 1976. By that date, bylaws were circulating as well.[38]

In 1976, Californians for Preservation Action (CPA) began publishing a newsletter on a regular basis, elected John Merritt its first president, and held its first educational workshop in August in Santa Barbara. CPA lobbied Sacramento legislators and actively monitored and initiated preservation legislation. For example, members played an influential role in the creation of the Heritage Task Force which was authorized by the state legislature in 1981. In the meantime, in 1978, CPA created the private, nonprofit California Preservation Foundation (CPF) to raise funds "but did little to take advantage of the Foundation's tax-exempt, tax-deductible presence." CPF proved adept at raising funds and, in 1982, it received a challenge grant from the National Trust. Assisted by another grant from the State Office of Historic Preservation,

> CPF made plans to hire an executive director and set up "a 'full-service' preservation organization similar to those in other states." In 1983, CPF took over sponsorship of the annual preservation conference and began to serve local preservationists. With the emergence of CPF as "an active player in the state's preservation movement," confusion and fear grew over the possible overlapping roles of CPA and CPF.[39] After lengthy deliberations, both groups agreed in March 1984 to merge their energies and constituencies into the California Preservation Foundation, "an educational foundation promoting historic preservation." When announcing the reorganization which now included an emphasis on both education and public policy, California Preservation Foundation President James P. Stickels stated:

> CALIFORNIA PRESERVATION can develop a much broader
> support base throughout the state, through joint member-
> ship campaigns with other preservation groups, through
> association with private and public organizations, and
> through contracts with governmental units, than was
> possible with CPA.[40]

Merritt, who became the foundation's executive director, endorsed the coordinated program as a way to improve "the public policy interest and effort CPA espoused for these many years." He did so, however, with some emotion: "I want to note that I will be a bit sad to see CPA disappear as the most active force promoting preservation in the state of California."[41]

By America's Bicentennial year, preservation at the local level had undergone some significant changes. No longer was it dominated by historical societies or nativist groups. Instead, the number of city-and county-sponsored ordinances as well as heritage and landmark commissions had markedly risen. Private, nonprofit advocacy groups emerged; their vocal and visible involvement was reminiscent of the activism of the 1960s. Unlike the individual efforts of the earlier, formative decade, historic preservation was now espoused by an increasingly comprehensive coalition of constituencies.

16

Federal Preservation Programs: Slowly Expanding Horizons

Federal legislation stimulating renewed support for preservation also applied to agencies already engaged in related programs. In California, for example, the National Park Service continued its longstanding architectural and landmark surveys. Other offices suddenly found themselves with new mandates to implement, and they frequently did so with caution and some reluctance. The federal outreach was likewise exemplified by the National Trust's establishment of its first regional office.

The National Park Service

During the decade after the passage of the 1966 legislation, three of the National Park Service's landmark and preservation programs were visible in California. The California Department of Parks and Recreation viewed the Historic American Buildings Survey (HABS) program as the "best opportunity to survey and record many of the historic buildings in our State Park System." A few of the department's historic structures had been recorded during the 1930s, but little else was done except during the 1960s at Bodie and Old Sacramento. The survey could have provided the park system with a way to record and investigate historic buildings to facilitate repair, restoration, and maintenance.[1] Although HABS saw the proposal as "a commendable undertaking," their 1968 efforts were committed to studies of early twentieth century buildings in southern California that contributed to the development of modern architecture.[2]

The project that HABS Chief James C. Massey was referring to was part of a nationwide summer "series of intensive architectural surveys involving measured drawings, photographs, and written documentation of historically and architecturally significant buildings" in eleven different localities.[3] The southern California project recorded ten buildings:

The Bradbury Building, Los Angeles
Bullock's Wilshire, Los Angeles
Dodge House, Los Angeles
Theodore Irwin House, Pasadena
Lovell Beach House, Newport Beach
Los Angeles Central Library, Los Angeles
Pueblo Ribera Court, La Jolla
Richfield Building, Los Angeles
John Snowden House, Los Angeles
Horatio West Court, Santa Monica

Massey was sufficiently pleased with the results of the southern California project and evidence of local interest and support that he authorized the summer program again for 1969.[4]

The first northern California HABS team began work in the summer of 1974, recording significant structures on the San Francisco Peninsula. The work is remembered as important because it was "the first to be cosponsored by a women's organization [the Junior League of Palo Alto] and the first on which a woman [Kim Spurgeon] was the team supervisor." The project's findings were published in 1976 by Stanford University.[5]

The park service continued to survey historic sites and buildings in search of additions to its National Historic Landmarks program. In a 1971 letter regarding the National Park Service's proposed six-year schedule for review and possible revision of the thematic framework for nominations, Chief Historian Robert M. Utley asked Director Mott to suggest potential sites in California. Mott complied but cautioned that his county-by-county listing did not include every potentially eligible property in California.[6] When the thematic revisions were published in 1972, the categories had increased from twenty-one thematic periods of history and prehistory in 1959 to nine themes and forty-three subthemes. Forty-two California landmarks were included in 1972; in 1976, California could claim fifty-nine national historical landmarks.[7]

Throughout the years, the National Park Service managed to keep state park directors informed of what themes were being studied and which sites were being recommended for national landmark status. Communication between the two parties, however, was not without difficulty. For example, in 1971, when fifteen out of eighty newly designated national landmarks were identified as California sites, an irritated Mott wrote immediately to the Secretary of the Interior to inform him that many were either within the park system or had already been recognized as state historical landmarks. Mott offered the landmark advisory committee's assistance and urged the secretary to coordinate the national landmark and National Register programs with California's programs.[8]

The response from Washington indicated that other state liaison officers had similar complaints. Mott was informed that in the future, state liaison officers would receive copies of all press releases on new landmark designations and descriptions of those sites not recommended for landmark status. National Register newsletters would provide information on work in progress and the status of landmark evaluations.[9] Thereafter, copies of historic landmark studies conducted in California were forwarded to Mott for his information.[10] This practice continued after Mott's departure. For example, in 1976, Director Herbert Rhodes was informed of three new California landmarks: Edwin Powell Hubble House in San Marino for science and invention, and the Paul R. Williams House and William Grant Still House in Los Angeles for African American history.[11]

California's response to the Historic American Engineering Record (HAER) was less positive. The National Park Service established this program in 1969 to compile archival documentation on "rapidly disappearing engineering and industrial sites." In 1975, only one California structure was included in its collection: San Francisco Fire Department, Pumping Station 2.[12]

In 1974, HAER asked the Department of Parks and Recreation to co-sponsor a comprehensive inventory of sites and structures significant to California's industrial and engineering history:

> The proposed project is directly related to your State Historic Preservation Plan, since it partially fulfills the requirement for a statewide inventory of historic sites. It would also serve to explain the impact your past engineering and industrial achievements have had on the settlement and prosperity of the State.[13]

The proposal fell victim to the tug-of-war between Mott and Keeper Murtagh. Mott refused the request to divert funds because "at the present time your office is withholding approval of our comprehensive History Plan because of the manner in which your staff feels we are conducting our comprehensive statewide survey." California was, Mott insisted, "in complete compliance with the survey requirements."[14]

The HAER proposal was resurrected in the late 1970s by the Office of Historic Preservation with additional funds from Caltrans. Historian Carroll Pursell of the University of California at Santa Barbara was to review all bridges in the State Highway System and select structures and sites to be surveyed by HAER. In 1980, after three years of research, Pursell managed to complete only "a planning and literature search of historic industrial, engineering and technology sites, structures and transportation networks."[15]

The conservation of natural resources continues to be the National Park Service's greatest concern. Reorganization plans aimed at differentiating the agency's internal and external preservation responsibilities have proven to be unsuccessful. Although the service's activities have expanded, it has been a slow process hampered by lack of funds, personnel shortages, and a minimal commitment to historic preservation.[16]

Other Federal Efforts

Until the latter half of the 1970s, most federal agencies with jurisdiction over the preservation of California's vast cultural resources lacked adequate personnel and a comprehensive plan of action.

The General Services Administration, for example, was still reviewing its historic preservation plan in 1977. A draft issued to regional offices for review and comment in September 1976 had yet to be produced in final form. As of April 1977, the agency "did not have a full-time historic preservation staff in Region 9, San Francisco."[17] The situation was somewhat improved at the Treasury Department where the Bureau of Alcohol, Tobacco and Firearms had produced a handbook entitled "Environmental Protection" which discussed the bureau's responsibilities under the applicable federal legislation. The bureau contacted the Office of Historic Preservation whenever they received, for example, "applications to establish bonded wineries where the premises were near or in an area or building eligible for inclusion in the National Register."[18]

Although most federal agencies were slow to adopt in-house procedures and expand their staff to include cultural resource professionals, many quickly found themselves embroiled in mandates requiring the identification and protection of properties eligible for or already included on the National Register of Historic Places. One such instance was the eighty-seven-acre Yerba Buena Center Redevelopment Project in San Francisco whose difficulties illustrate some of the diverse dimensions and complexities of the Advisory Council's procedures.

In accordance with established guidelines, James P. Jaquet, program manager of Area C, Department of Housing and Urban Development (HUD), wrote to State Liaison Officer Mott in January 1974 requesting information on properties and artifacts of historical or archaeological significance in or near the proposed Yerba Buena Center Urban Renewal Project. He also asked for suggestions on appropriate preservation treatment.[19]

The department responded that although there were no state or National Register listings in the project area, there was at least one city landmark. This did not preclude further investigation of historical and archaeological values, however. HUD officials were cautioned that they had yet to determine which federally owned properties were potentially eligible for the Register and that their Environmental Impact Statement had to comment on whether or not the project would "contribute to the preservation and enhancement of non-federally owned districts" and properties "of historical, archeological, architectural, or cultural significance."[20]

When HUD's Draft Environmental Impact Statement was reviewed a few weeks later, several concerned voices were raised. The Department of Parks and Recreation pointed out such deficiencies as HUD's failure to identify sites of architectural and historical significance and to specify preservation and rehabilitation alternatives.[21] The draft also failed to adequately address the National Trust's earlier claim that St. Patrick's Church, the Jessie Street Substation, and other structures were significant enough to merit HUD's re-evaluation and consideration as architecturally and historically important properties.[22] Although Trust representative John Frisbee was assured that the church would be preserved "as an integral historic ornament in the Project's main concourse area," HUD's technicians declared the substation "to be 'incapable of rehabilitation.'"[23] This conclusion was challenged by the Foundation for San Francisco's Architectural Heritage whose president wrote: "if ever an architecturally significant building was feasible of recycling adaptive reuse, this [the substation] is it."[24]

The Department of the Interior warned HUD that, should both the church and substation be found eligible for the National Register, it would have to comply with the provisions of Executive Order 11593. Furthermore, because there was "high potential" for significant subsurface prehistoric and historic archaeological resources in the project area, HUD was asked to institute "a program of archeological monitoring of all earth-moving activities....If significant archeological resources are encountered during construction activities, adequate time should be allowed for their scientific study and removal."[25]

During the summer of 1974, HUD consulted with the state historic preservation officer (formerly the state liaison officer) and subsequently retained the services of Paul V. Turner, assistant professor of Architectural History at Stanford University, upon the recommendation of Kathryn Kaiser, then chair of the State Historical Landmarks Advisory Committee. Turner was to prepare a list of those properties he considered of National Register caliber.[26] In his September 1974 report, Turner concluded:

> From the beginning, it was apparent that whereas several buildings within the project area possess some architectural interest of one sort or another, only two buildings stand out as having sufficient interest or quality to justify even consideration for the National Register—these two being the Jessie St. Substation and St. Patrick's Church.[27]

HUD reacted by asking the San Francisco Redevelopment Agency to postpone action on the substation until studies and proposals for alternative action could be reviewed by all interested parties.[28] The Redevelopment Agency in turn promised HUD it would defer demolition plans as long as the studies and proposals were done expeditiously.[29] In the meantime, the substation was placed on the National Register in September as a result of the efforts of the Foundation for San Francisco's Architectural Heritage. A final Environmental Impact Statement subsequently pledged that "additional studies and proposals for preservation will be developed prior to taking any action affecting this structure."[30]

Unfortunately, these promises did not guarantee the preservation of these buildings. An alarmed Frisbee informed the Advisory Council that the Redevelopment Agency was seeking bids for the construction of the concourse bridge between Market Street and the proposed Yerba Buena Center that would demolish the substation.[31] HUD responded that because this phase of the project would take three and one-half years, there was ample time for an amicable settlement. Construction in the block where the substation was located would not begin until the second year. It was obvious, however, that HUD was not anticipating a satisfactory resolution of the problem, for the agency informed the Advisory Council of its plans to seek legal counsel to provide alternative solutions "since official approvals and funding for the acquisition and demolition of this structure were provided prior to the issuance of Executive Order 11593 and prior to the structure's inclusion on the National Register."[32]

The fate of the Jessie Street Substation continued to concern San Francisco preservationists throughout the summer of 1975. In his comments before the San Francisco Landmarks Advisory Board, Frisbee emphasized that National Register designation did not ensure the substation's survival because "HUD is not obligated to follow the Advisory Council's recommendation." At that same meeting, the board approved a study resulting from HUD's request for board review of the Yerba Buena Center project's architecturally and historically significant structures. Not only did the subcommittee recommend that St. Patrick's Church's eligibility for the Register be examined, it suggested that the Mercantile Building also met the Register criteria. The subcommittee's report reaffirmed the board's earlier statement that the Redevelopment Agency was not giving sufficient consideration to the retention and re-use of the substation. Furthermore,

> preservation today is not and cannot be directed primarily toward the museum nor the preservation of ruins and relics. Rather, preservation is finding a viable re-use for older structures.[33]

By fall 1975, the landmarks board had clearly grown disenchanted with HUD. Mrs. G. Bland Platt, president, reiterated the board's request that a determination of National Register eligibility be sought for St. Patrick's Church, the Mercantile Building, and the Senior Citizens Center. Furthermore, the board, she stated, would "'use every available means to ensure that a feasibility study is undertaken forthwith'" on the substation.[34]

Those were but a few of the problems surrounding the Yerba Buena Center Redevelopment Project. Preservationists had won a modest victory on behalf of the aforementioned structures. The new Draft Environmental Impact Statement prepared in late 1977 was deemed by Frisbee to be "far superior to the earlier 1974" statement regarding historic and architectural resources. Frisbee told HUD that the Trust was "particularly pleased by the recognition that St. Patrick's Church, the Jessie Street Substation, the Mercantile Building, 87 Third Street, and 693 Mission Street form a complex worthy of recognition." He also urged the Redevelopment Agency to pursue the rehabilitation of the Jessie hotel for residential use.[35]

The need for a Draft Environmental Impact Statement, which was necessitated by a number of major design and plan changes in the project area, led HUD to inform the state historic preservation officer that the project "does not contain significance as a potential archeological district to qualify for the National Register for Historic Places" because there are no known or strongly suspected archaeological sites in the area. HUD requested consultation on the archaeological eligibility of the project "to resolve public concern for its potential eligibility." This claim, along with HUD's request for consultation on the area's historic structures, began another protracted series of consultations, on-site inspections, reports, memoranda-of-agreement, and correspondence that continued into the 1980s.[36]

The National Trust: A Western Office

As the National Trust for Historic Preservation entered its second quarter century, it anticipated "the ever increasing awareness of historic preservation, especially in the West and among new age groups and cultural minorities." In part, this conclusion reflected sessions at the 1971 annual meeting in San Diego and Coronado where the Trust celebrated its twenty-fifth anniversary. Members heard from representatives of Native American, Black, Chinese American, Spanish-speaking, and youth groups. This westward thrust was highlighted by the opening of the Trust's first field office on July 1, 1971, in the San Francisco headquarters of the California Historical Society. The San Francisco Foundation and Mrs. John A. McCone, a member of the Board of Trustees, provided additional support for the Western Field Services Office. In less than a year, the office was moved to a more permanent location in Jackson Square, the city's first historic district.[37]

Not all Californians shared the enthusiasm that the Trust claimed westerners exhibited when they requested services or answered questions from the Trust.[38] Newly appointed Regional Services Representative John L. Frisbee III, for example, faced distrust and hostility from state government personnel who resented the fact that a sizable portion of federal preservation funds went directly to the National Trust.[39] It was therefore understandable that California's Department of Parks and Recreation wanted "the National Trust cut out of this [grant] program—they are now being treated as a '51st state,' largely through the efforts of Dr. Murtagh [keeper of the National Register]."[40] Despite these initial difficulties, Frisbee and the Trust evolved into significant contributors to California's preservation movement.[41]

Why did the Trust wait until 1971 to take an active role in preservation concerns west of the Mississippi? According to Frisbee, the Trust's eastern seaboard emphasis reflected budgetary and staff limitations as well as logistical considerations. It was, he claimed, "largely by accident of location" that the Trust had "been far more involved in historic preservation activities in the East, South and Midwest than in the West."[42]

After a year in his position, Frisbee reported that preservation in the West was not as developed as on the East Coast. Encouraged by rising popular enthusiasm for preservation, he nonetheless emphasized the need to direct western energies away from the tendency to convert every old building into a museum and toward the adaptive re-use of structures. Westerners shared with their national counterparts similar needs for funding, preservation planning, and professional and technical assistance. Several regional concerns peculiar to the West were "site and object-oriented" rather than focused on buildings and structures as in the East. These included the interpretation, development, and protection of ghost towns, archaeological sites, and places significant to a vast diversity of ethnic groups. Another western consideration during restoration, observed Frisbee, was the need to comply with seismic and other building code requirements.[43]

During his first year, Frisbee visited with some 200 organizations and individuals, traveled more than 50,000 miles to survey preservation problems and plans in eight states, and met with state liaison officers and fifteen of the Trust's sixteen advisers. He commented on issues before the San Francisco Landmarks Advisory Board with the full realization that "the National Trust by itself does not make the difference between preservation or loss of historic buildings in that city." Upon the recommendation of Trustee Robertson Collins of Jacksonville, Oregon, he promoted historic preservation in small towns.[44]

In February 1972, Frisbee spent two days in Yreka, which had a commercial center "typical of the commercial architecture of Western towns in the latter half of the 19th century." His meetings with business leaders, local politicians, and preservationists resulted in a historic district ordinance. By year's end, Miner Street had been placed on the National Register.[45] A similar visit to Eureka in May with Collins proved equally successful. These two trips encouraged Frisbee to extend his experiments to other small towns. His experiences with Yreka and Eureka, he said, demonstrated "that a two or three-day visit from a National Trust representative can generate substantial support for preservation."[46]

A successful state preservation program, stated Frisbee in his 1972 report, had "an independent state historic preservation agency," working with,but not a part of, a department of parks and recreation because "a preservation program administered by the state parks system can become diluted by the variety of functions that the department and its staff must perform."[47] The California Historical Landmarks Advisory Committee endorsed his recommendations. It expressed regret that the report's limited format did not adequately inform the public of the true extent of California's preservation activities, thereby leading to "some misunderstanding on the part of the people on the progress that California is making in this area."[48]

In the early 1970s, the Trust's historic properties program expanded beyond the operation of historic house museums. Acquisitions in
California provided the Trust with several opportunities. In addition to
preserving properties for adaptive re-use, such as at Casa Amesti, the Trust
leased properties to other organizations for restoration and interpretation.
This action was taken with its 1972 Cooper-Molera Adobe acquisition. The
adobe, the Trust's twelfth historic property and "one of California's finest
examples of two-story adobe construction," was leased to the Department of
Parks and Recreation for thirty-two years. During this period, the state
would, with Trust approval, restore and interpret the property to recreate "a
Yankee trader's home, furnished in the Mexican-American style of the period
preceding Mexican War." The structure was intended to become part of the
Monterey State Historic Park.[49]

The Trust also began to acquire exterior easements. The first was on
the Haas-Lilienthal House, built in San Francisco in 1886 and donated to
the Foundation for San Francisco's Architectural Heritage. The easement
was designed to protect the structure's exterior "from alterations or destruction and the Trust...agreed to serve as recipient of the house should the
foundation cease operation, further assuring the donors [i.e., the Lilienthal
family] of continued preservation."[50]

The Western Regional Office's interest in both Yreka and Eureka
continued throughout the 1970s. During fiscal year 1974-1975, the Trust
received $29,665 from the National Endowment for the Arts for its City
Options program. A team of staff members and consultants was sent to three
communities to assess "the planning, architectural, economic and legal
requirements to implement local preservation programs." One of the three
was Yreka.[51]

Yreka was selected because it had a historic district, created by
municipal ordinance, on the National Register and because it "demonstrated
a clear commitment to historic preservation at both public and private
levels." The town had much in common with other small- and medium-sized
cities trying to develop aesthetically and economically successful programs.
Yreka's obstacles included a district ordinance that lacked specific criteria
to evaluate proposed changes. Nor did it permit "the designation of individual landmarks or additional historic districts."[52]

In a lengthy list of recommendations, team members urged the
citizens of Yreka not to recreate a "Williamsburg of the West," where
buildings were "restored" to a specific historical period or architectural style.

Each structure should be accepted on its individual merits. "There is no reason why buildings of the 1860s, 1890s, and 1930s," concluded the report, "cannot coexist harmoniously on the same street, unified by common scale, proportions, materials, colors, street furniture, street lighting and planting." Thus,

> as a 'restored' street, Miner Street will be more interesting, more honest and probably more important in the historic preservation movement if this suggested approach is followed rather than if an attempt is made to return the street strictly to its 19th-century appearance.[53]

Historic preservation was clearly evolving away from the California State Park System's philosophy as evidenced in places such as Old Sacramento.

Progress was also being made in Eureka. By 1975, Frisbee could report that, with the Trust's intervention and assistance, the Eureka Heritage Committee was organized during 1972-1973 and in late 1973 a historic resources inventory was started. By 1975, the community had raised $9,000 for the survey, and the first phase was completed.[54]

Trustee Collins recalled the Eureka report as "an amazing, an amazing inventory" which covered every building in town. It was evaluated by preservationists such as San Franciscans Charles Hall Page and Mrs. G. Bland Platt. Although the inventory process was a lengthy one, it "did what it was supposed to in that it makes the community look at itself." Collins agreed with the decision to include "the modern, contemporary buildings, for it gives them a record that is amazing." Thus, he reflected:

> Eureka was a situation of mobilizing local energy to inventory what they had and, again, the story came back to not feel lonely, don't feel isolated. The National Trust is here to help you.[55]

The Western Regional Office made contributions elsewhere in the state. When the Sacramento city council asked interested citizens and the planning department to produce plans to preserve the city's old residential area, the Trust met with local preservationists in December 1973. The city's 1974 historic preservation plan, claimed Frisbee, "incorporated many of the ideas suggested by the National Trust staff," including recommendations for a historic resources inventory, a historic preservation revolving fund, rezoning of historic areas, and facade easements.[56]

Requests for Trust assistance increased significantly during these years. When the office was first established, Frisbee actually had to solicit inquiries. Between July and September 1971, the office responded to 53 requests; in the same period in 1974, it handled 216 requests. The size of the office staff also grew during the same period from one professional, Frisbee, and a single part-time secretary, to six people, excluding consultants.[57]

During these early years, the Trust's first regional office held numerous conferences, seminars, and preservation clinics. These included a general regional conference in northern California in Eureka in 1972, and a historic preservation clinic to identify and work on program needs in Los Angeles in 1973. The conferences and seminars provided opportunities to share information, and local groups left reinvigorated. The clinics, however, were unsuccessful because of the $250 fee per group, and because member organizations felt they had no problems or could not take the time to attend. As a result, in 1974, the Western Regional Office introduced the concept of traveling clinics with accompanying workshops for participants. Frisbee optimistically concluded at the end of his 1975 report: "The Trust is well on the way to becoming the single most effective force in historic preservation in the West."[58]

Until July 1975, the Western Regional Office was known as the West Coast Office. The title change reflected the Trust's response to increased public awareness of their heritage as the nation began preparations to celebrate the Bicentennial of the American Revolution. Pride in their collective past prompted many to participate in the preservation and conservation movements. Trust membership in 1976 rose to over 100,000, an increase of one-third over the previous year. One result was to give greater emphasis to regional service, and both the San Francisco and Chicago offices were reorganized to provide a full range of services.[59]

For Frisbee, the internal restructuring meant greater emphasis on educational programs and historic properties. His staff continued to hold preservation clinics and the office co-sponsored numerous conferences.[60] For California, one of the most important of these activities has since become the annual statewide preservation conference.

The first of these annual meetings was held in May 1976 during National Historic Preservation Week. The conference was divided into two sessions, one in the north at Filoli near Woodside (May 10-11), and the other in the south at the Mission Inn in Riverside (May 13-14). Conference organizers sought

> to bring together elected officials, appointed officials, governmental agency staffs, architects, planners, historical society representatives and members of community preservation organizations for a two day period to examine and

discuss the purposes, development and administration of state and local historic preservation programs in California.[61]

In December 1975, Lurline B. Roth gave Filoli to the Trust. The gift of 39 acres, including a 42-room Willard Polk-designed mansion and a 16 acre garden, was accompanied by a $2.5 million endowment. The non-profit Filoli Center, Inc., was organized to manage the property, and the new regional office served as the Trust's representative in the administration of the estate. Businessman Collins, who played a key role in the Trust's acquisition of Filoli, recalled that the endowment was insufficient to cover expenses such as salaries for the gardeners and upkeep of the house. Since the Trust's headquarters was too far removed and because more money was needed to maintain the property, "what has evolved at Filoli is a great example of an innovative thing that arose in the Western Regional Office and has now become a model for other property solutions in the country." In other words, said Collins, the Trust owns "the property but has contracted it back to a local group of people" who manage Filoli Center. The center's board included preservation-minded Establishment figures from neighboring communities and elsewhere in the nation who raised funds to operate the property. Collins praised the "Friends of Filoli" who run the gift shop and conduct the tours as the people who "made it all happen." Their numbers rose from a 100 to 2,000 within a few years, and profits have amounted to as much as $90,000 a year, which is given to the center for the property's maintenance. In Collins' opinion, it was this combination of enthusiastic volunteers and an influential board that made the crucial difference between success and failure. The Trust, he said, paid careful attention to what the center and its docents were doing. The lessons learned at Filoli would be replicated elsewhere.[62]

17

From the Museum into the Mainstream: Historic Preservation in 1976

By the time Californians celebrated the Bicentennial of the American Revolution in 1976, historic preservation in the state had experienced its own revolution. No longer was the preservation of the state's heritage confined to the commemoration of its past in landmark sites and museums far removed from daily life. No longer were preservation projects dominated by dedicated amateurs and park service employees without formal training in history, architecture, archaeology, or related fields. Not only had there been an evolution in preservation philosophy and participation by 1976, but new strategies and techniques had also emerged in the decades after 1940.

The groundwork for these dramatic changes was laid during the period from 1940 to 1966. The 1949 centennial celebrations of the discovery of gold and the gold rush reawakened an interest in the state's history. Led by powerful advocates such as Joseph R. Knowland, one of the last direct links to what remained of pre-World War II historic preservation, the celebrants helped to revitalize concern for California's historic sites. In the 1950s with the reappearance in state park service of former National Park Service Director Newton B. Drury and historian V. Aubrey Neasham, California's historic preservation program entered a new era of long-range planning, acquisition, and development of historic properties under the guidance of professional historians, architects, and archaeologists.

The State Division of Beaches and Parks continued to dominate California's preservation activities. With Drury and Neasham at the helm, the division developed a special organizational unit staffed by trained historians devoted solely to historic preservation matters. Although the division continued to emphasize recreational priorities, it could no longer neglect historic preservation plans and projects. When Drury and Neasham left state service at the end of the decade, the momentum toward preservation planning by trained professionals was not reversed.

In the 1960s, historic preservation became the direct beneficiary of increasingly widespread anxieties about the nation's rapidly diminishing natural resources. In California, the pervasive impact of the emerging national environmental-conservation consciousness on preservation was demonstrated in several ways. Local governments adopted ordinances creating historic and landmark commissions. Preservationists no longer came from only academic, nativist, historical, and architectural circles, but from a broader spectrum of organizations and backgrounds. The popularity of preservation was further manifested in the increasing number of state landmark applications, prompting the introduction of a Point of Historical Interest Program for local sites of significance. The state legislature also responded by calling for a statewide master plan for the preservation of California's historical resources, and for suggestions on revenue-generating usages other than museums for historic structures. This search for adaptive re-use alternatives was typical of the sixties' concern for the total human environment.

The recognition that cultural resources were an integral component of the nation's environmental resources, and that existing federal preservation programs were limited successes, prompted the passage of preservation legislation in the mid-1960s. Beginning with the National Historic Preservation Act of 1966, the federal government reaffirmed and strengthened its commitment to preservation, and encouraged state and local jurisdictions and the private sector to continue and expand their involvement. These trends were paralleled in California.

In the decade preceding the national Bicentennial, preservation in California began to feel the impact of federal and state legislation. The laws required the Division of Beaches and Parks (later the Department of Parks and Recreation) to create new mechanisms to implement the programs. Under the direction of William Penn Mott, Jr., the department reorganized its operational structure and began to hire additional personnel with expertise in such fields as architectural history and archaeology. With the assistance of local volunteers, staff members produced the requisite preservation plan and started to compile an inventory of the state's resources.

The state survey, the National Register, and other programs produced several results. They helped communities rediscover a heritage which recognized the multicultural and multiethnic contributions of California's diverse settlers. Together with a burgeoning variety of preservation tools, these new programs promoted the conservation of entire neighborhoods, as well as individual structures, for reasons beyond historic or architectural importance. Definitions of significance expanded to encompass examples of daily life, cultural continuity, and sense of place. Volunteer projects provided the experience and job skills many avocational preservationists exploited to launch careers as paid consultants and preservation professionals.

The laws also added financial incentives and building code modifications to demands for energy efficiency and raw material conservation, making it commercially viable to preserve and rehabilitate historic properties. California's archaeological resources, too, benefited from legislation encouraging preservation and conservation *in situ*, instead of salvage archaeology.

In 1976, on the threshold of this nation's third century, preservationists were still searching for more efficient and effective ways to preserve and protect the remnants of California's past. The number of people involved in historic preservation was growing and their resolve had been strengthened by renewed commitments and new strategies.

In the decade ahead, however, preservationists would continue to struggle with problems such as the lack of sufficient program funding and the absence of coordination among public preservation programs.[1] Moreover, a number of entirely new issues began to emerge as preservation and landmark preservation, in particular, became increasingly "like mom and apple pie...a revered American institution."[2] Controversies have arisen, for example, over residential revitalization, rehabilitation, and the subsequent "gentrification" of inner city neighborhoods—a process that frequently displaces low-income, elderly, and minority residents.[3]

Still other difficulties and shortcomings remain unresolved. Since Neasham's departure, the state's academic historians have not played a significant role in the preservation movement. A reason for this conspicuous absence of pro-active leadership by the historical Establishment is the lack of emphasis on California history in institutions of higher learning, particularly in the California State University where historians face heavy teaching responsibilities and receive little support for research. Some academicians have become self-taught public historians with mixed results. Meanwhile, the interests and select constituency of various statewide professional organizations have remained overly narrow.[4]

California has an outstanding diversity of historic properties, many of which have been entrusted to the state as guardian and developer in order to preserve a heritage that can be shared by long-time residents, schoolchildren, visitors, and newcomers alike. Although these properties have served their intended functions of public education, fostering patriotism, and promoting tourist revenues,[5] there are still conspicuous omissions in state holdings. For example, nothing has been done about Neasham's recommendation that the public should acquire the site and physical remains of the original Monterey Presidio. The former capital of Spanish California is not even recognized today as a state historical landmark. This, according to state park historian Joseph H. Engbeck, Jr., is "the most serious oversight in historic preservation matters in California today."[6]

Although historic preservation has become popular and profitable, structures and sites still disappear in the face of unsympathetic developers, unscrupulous pothunters, and natural disasters. A 1983 study commissioned by the National Trust for Historic Preservation for the California Heritage Task Force concluded that 40 percent of the state's pre-1940 residences had been lost to fires, demolition, or conversion to other uses. That total did not include commercial structures. In addition, of the one-half million archaeological sites in California, only 10 percent have been recorded and approximately 1,400 of these are destroyed each year.[7]

Setbacks, shortcomings, and strenuous opposition notwithstanding, the preservation and conservation of the state's historic resources have become entrenched in diverse sectors. The state, led by an Office of Historic Preservation whose existence and responsibilities have finally received statutory recognition, remains the pre-eminent leader in determining the direction of historic preservation and managing cultural resources. The State Historical Resources Commission was expanded in 1984 from seven to nine members; one of the new commissioners was to be knowledgeable in ethnic history and the other in folklife.

The economic feasibility of recycling historic properties has won new and vocal advocates. Redevelopment agencies, private developers, and public officials have joined the movement, along with individual entrepreneur-consultants who sell their knowledge of the intricacies of the various bureaucracies and the requisite paperwork, and artisans with needed skills and expertise.[8] Many have joined the increasingly activist preservation constituency which has dramatically expanded its numbers and influence.[9]

Local historical and preservation organizations continue to press their causes with frequent success. And while there still remains an absence of a truly representative statewide coalition of these interests, the perceived power of an organization such as the Heritage Action Steering Committee nonetheless often managed to convince the state legislature in the latter half of the eighties that it spoke on heritage legislation with the collective authority of a vast statewide network that included the California Preservation Foundation, the California Committee for the Promotion of History, the Conference of California Historical Societies, and the Society for California Archaeology.[10]

At the 1985 annual statewide preservation conference, participants gathered to remind themselves of what had transpired during the decade since they first met at Filoli and later at the Mission Inn. There had been enormous progress, especially when one considered that ten years before, preservationists had:

- no state-funded surveys;
- no Pasadena Heritage, Los Angeles Conservancy, Oakland Heritage, or Claremont Heritage;
- no annual conference;
- no California Preservation Foundation;
- no Historic Building Code;
- no tax-incentives that worked;
- no General Plan Historic Preservation Elements of significance;
- no CEQA protection to speak of;
- no Marks Bonds;
- few strong local ordinances and few historic districts;
- no thoughts of creating a Heritage Task Force.[11]

On the other hand, a review of the conference topics revealed that the concerns confronting preservation practitioners remained unchanged:

- how to write a National Register nomination;
- how to conduct a cultural resources survey;
- how to use CEQA effectively;
- how to respond to tax act certification standards and resolve problems resulting from the certification process;
- how to organize effectively for preservation.[12]

In the audience were many of the pioneers who had masterminded the statewide effort. Nearly everyone present knew each other, and it was evident that the preservation movement had begun to gray as well. The absence of significant numbers of new, young, or non-White middle class converts at that conference was a stark reminder of the challenges still facing preservationists.

California's historic preservationists have indeed come a long way in a short time. Their continued success, however, will depend in part on whether they can make historic preservation meaningful to a widening circle of interests and constituencies, and whether they can effectively enforce and maintain standards of excellence for increasing numbers of amateur and professional preservation entrepreneurs.

Notes

PREFACE

1. Preservation bibliographies include: Arnold Markowitz, *Historic Preservation. A Guide to Information Sources* (Detroit, Michigan: Gale Research Co., 1980); Gary L. Menges, *Historic Preservation: A Bibliography. Exchange Bibliography #79* (Monticello, Illinois: Council of Planning Librarians, May 1969); Frederick L. Rath, Jr., and Merrilyn Rogers O'Connell, *A Bibliography on Historical Organization Practices.* Volume I: *Historic Preservation* (Nashville: American Association for State and Local History, 1975); National Advisory Council on Historic Preservation, *Where to Look: A Guide to Preservation Information* (Washington, D.C.: Government Printing Office, 1982); and James N. Carder, "In the Balance: American Historic Preservation," *Choice,* April 1983, pp. 1089-1100.

2. Some of the important works on the pre-1940 years are included in the introductory chapters that follow. Examples of "how-to" handbooks include: Charles Parrot, *Access to Historic Buildings for the Disabled* (Washington, D.C.: Heritage Conservation and Recreation Service, April 1980); *Rehabilitation: Danville. A Strategy for Building Reuse and Neighborhood Conservation* (Washington, D.C.: Heritage Conservation and Recreation Service, Historic American Building Record, 1979); Arthur P. Zeigler, Jr., and Walter N. Kidney, *Historic Preservation in Small Towns: A Manual of Practice* (Nashville: American Association for State and Local History, 1980); and Advisory Council on Historic Preservation, *Remember the Neighborhoods: Conserving Neighborhoods through Historic Preservation Techniques* (Washington, D.C.: Advisory Council on Historic Preservation, n.d.). At the state level, the Office of Historic Preservation has produced a number of guides, including "Model Cultural Resources Management for California Cities and Counties" (n.d.) and "Model Archeological Ordinance" (March 1980).

Many of the cultural resource surveys funded in part by state and local governments produced local histories. For example, see: Judy Tachibana, *Gardena Historical Resources Survey, A Final Report,* (Gardena, California: City of Gardena, April 1981); Dan Peterson, *Petaluma's Architectural Heritage* (Santa Rosa, California: Architectural Associates, 1978); and Judy Wright, *Claremont: A Pictorial History* (Claremont: Claremont Historical Resource Center, 1980).

Examples of program guides are: The Nature Conservancy, *Preserving Our Natural Heritage.* Volume I: *Federal Activities* (Washington, D.C.: United States Department of the Interior and U.S. Man and the Biosphere Program, 1975); Russell V. Keune, John Frisbee III, and Terry B. Morton, *A Guide to State Programs* (Washington, D.C.: The National Trust for Historic Preservation, 1972); and Jennie B. Bull, editor, *A Guide to State Historical Preservation Programs* (Washington, D.C.: Preservation Press, 1976); and Real Estate Research Corporation, *Neighborhood Preservation: A Catalog of Local Programs* (Washington, D.C.: Office of Development and Research, Department of Housing and Urban Development, 1975).

3. Charles B. Hosmer, Jr., *Presence of the Past* (New York: G.P. Putnam's Sons, 1965), pp. 22-23. This book, together with his two-volume history, provides a comprehensive survey of the evolution of preservation in the United States. See also *Preservation Comes of Age: From Williamsburg to the National Trust, 1926-1949* (Charlottesville: The University Press of Virginia, 1981).

PART I
THE EARLY YEARS, 1875-1940

1. Alex. S. Taylor, "The Indianology of California," Fourth Series, *California Farmer,* November 28, 1862, p. 91; Robert Lee Schuyler, "Anthropological Perspectives in Historical Archaeology" (Unpublished Ph.D. Dissertation, University of California, Santa Barbara, 1975), p. 32. Taylor identified the priest involved as "the Cure of Monterey." He was most probably the resident pastor, Father S. Filoteo. See Zephyrin Englehardt, *Mission San Carlos Borromeo (Carmelo)* (Santa Barbara: Mission Santa Barbara, 1934), p. 248.

CHAPTER 1
CALIFORNIA'S PIONEER HISTORIC PRESERVATIONISTS, 1875-1925

1. Nathan Gerald Weinberg, "Historic Preservation and Tradition in California: The Restoration of the Missions and the Spanish-Colonial Revival" (Unpublished Ph.D. Dissertation, University of California, Davis, 1974), pp. 85-86. Weinberg calculated that before 1880, only four out of the twenty-one missions were intact, although in neglected condition. Two others had been destroyed by earthquakes, six had no roofs, one was removed and replaced by a parish church, another became a university chapel, and the rest were used for various religious purposes. See also pp. 108-109 for other examples of the Church's involvement in mission restoration.

2. Joseph R. Knowland, *California, A Landmark History* (Oakland, California: Tribune Press, 1941), pp. 14-15; Hosmer, *Presence of the Past,* p. 125.

3. The roof collapsed in 1852. Four remains were unearthed: Serra, Crespi, Lopez, and Lasuen. Public attention was also drawn to the mission because of its proximity to "Monterey, Queen of American Watering Places." See Weinberg, "Historic Preservation," pp. 93-94; Knowland, *Landmark History,* pp. 4-6; Hosmer, *Presence of the Past,* pp. 125-126; and Msgr. Francis J. Weber, compiler and editor, *Father of the Missions. A Documentary History of San Carlos Borromeo* (Hong Kong: Libra Press Limited, n.d.). Knowland remarked that it was only in 1936 that a new roof closer to the original design was erected.

An early visitor to the mission was author Robert Louis Stevenson, David G. Cameron's candidate for the first person to advocate the preservation of California's missions. In the November 11, 1879, issue of the Monterey *Californian,* the "Monterey Barbarian" (Stevenson's pseudonym) wrote an article ("San Carlos Day: A Barbarian at the Carmello Mission") urging that funds be raised to preserve the mission because of "sentiment, aesthetics and the historical education of generations to come" and because of its tourist value. These same reasons would be echoed many times in the years to come. A week later, the *Californian* reported that the article aroused popular interest; a week later, the rival newspaper, the *Democrat,* also spoke out in support of preservation. See David G. Cameron, "Charles Fletcher Lummis and the Landmarks Club of Southern California: Pioneering in Historic Preservation," unpublished paper presented at the Charles F. Lummis Centennial Symposium, Southwest Museum, Los Angeles, February 2, 1985, pp. 1-2.

4. Weinberg, "Historic Preservation," pp. 95-103. Also see Leonard Pitt, *The Decline of the Californios* (Berkeley and Los Angeles: University of California Press, 1966), pp. 286-293. Pitt observed that the minimizing of Mexican influences resulted in the refusal of the Spanish dons' descendants "to acknowledge their mestizo ancestry or to recognize that their grandfathers acquired Mexican, not Spanish, land grants." Furthermore, "the fact that the Franciscans buried nearly as many Indians as they converted lay beyond the mythmakers' comprehension."

5. Weinberg, "Historic Preservation," pp. 82-93, 103-107. One such artist was landscape painter Edward Deakin who began sketching and painting missions in the early 1870s. He has been credited by some with playing a major role in arousing preserve-the-mission sentiments among women's clubs near the turn of the century.

6. *Ibid.,* p. 107. Also George Wharton James, *In and Out of the Old Missions of California* (Boston: Grosset & Dunlap, 1927), pp. 383-384; and Cameron, "Charles Fletcher Lummis," pp. 2-3, 7.

7. Weinberg, "Historic Preservation," pp. 124-131. See also Knowland, *Landmark History,* pp. 21-22; Hosmer, *Presence of the Past,* pp. 126-127; and Cameron, "Charles Fletcher Lummis."

8. J.J. Warner, "Inaugural Address, January 7, 1884," *Annual Publication,* Historical Society of Southern California, 1 (1884): 7-8; also Isaac Kinley, "Inaugural Address, 1886," *Annual Publication,* Historical Society of Southern California, 1 (1886): 2-6. The society's first article on landmarks appeared in 1893. See William F. Edgar, "Historical Notes of Old Land Marks in California," *Annual Publication,* Historical Society of Southern California, 3 (1893): 22-30.

9. Knowland, *Landmark History,* p. 119.

10. *Ibid.,* pp. 106-110. Also see Hosmer, *Presence of the Past,* p. 126, and Robin Elisabeth Datel, "Historic Preservation and Neighborhood Change in Sacramento, California" (Unpublished Master's Thesis, University of Minnesota, 1978), pp. 20-22.

Datel, who worked in the California Office of Historic Preservation in the mid-1970s, observed that the Sutter's Fort effort was important because it established "a tradition of preservation projects undertaken jointly by private and public entities." She also noted, however, that when the Division of Beaches and Parks began to investigate the site in 1958, they discovered that the earlier reconstruction was inaccurate. "The Sutter's Fort Commission had mistaken the inside walls for the surrounding exterior walls, which had actually enclosed a much larger space. Returning the Fort to its original dimensions is both politically and economically unfeasible, since it is currently located in downtown Sacramento, and the surrounding land is completely built over." The methods used to restore the fort to a single era and to its original appearance blurred any distinctions between the restored and reconstructed portions. They also prevent detection of deterioration by time and the weather. The result, observed Datel, was a historical contradiction where "an old object is displayed in fresh, new-looking material." Sutter's Fort, she said, represents not only the equivalent of the state's Revolutionary War era but the perspectives of California's preservationists whose reconstruction and restoration methods and philosophy are still practiced. The Department of Parks and Recreation still espouses this approach because "they are in the business of entertaining and educating the California public, especially its children, and it is much easier for them to preach frontier virtues without the unsightly intrusion of Victorian bricks." See pp. 22-23.

11. See: Associated Veterans of the Mexican War, *History of the Celebration of the Fiftieth Anniversary of the Taking Possession of California and Raising of the American Flag by Commodore John Drake Sloat, U.S.N., July 7th, 1846. Held Under the Auspices of the Associated Veterans of the Mexican War, Assisted by the U.S. Army and Navy, the National Guard of California, the Sloat Monument Association, the California Pioneers, the Great Lodge of Free and Accepted Masons of California, Boards of Supervisors, Fraternal Societies, Public Schools, and Citizens of the State* (Oakland, California: Carruth & Carruth Printers, 1896). The Sloat Monument Association of California was comprised mainly of veterans of the Mexican War and members of the California Pioneers. Plans for the event were directed by Major Edwin A. Sherman, chair of the Committee of Arrangements. The committee raised $3,695 in Monterey and San Francisco and requested $10,000 from Congress for the monument. The procession included 150 masons representing fifty lodges, military bands, floats, and artillery, army, and naval units.

12. Knowland, *Landmark History,* pp. 89-94, 124-128.

13. This observation was made by the department's research writer and historian Joseph H. Engbeck, Jr., who has written and edited many books and monographs about the park system, interviewed Newton B. Drury who confirmed that Knowland's involvement was "genuine" and that his park work was "pure." Engbeck noted that Knowland was personally fascinated by history, and that his long and distinguished involvement in preservation even after he left public life attests to Knowland's deep feeling for preservation. Interview with author, March 23, 1987. See also Hosmer, *Preservation Comes of Age,* I:411-412. Hosmer stated that Neasham recalled Knowland's interest as "genuine." Knowland was also President of the California Historical Society (1952-1957) and Chairman of the Board of Trustees (1958-1963).

14. *Ibid.* Also, "Report of the Native Sons of the Golden West, Committee on Historic Landmarks, April 27, 1903," MS #3154, Folder 21, Joseph Knowland Papers, California Historical Society; Knowland, *Landmark History,* pp. v-vi. In the previous year, the Native Daughters of the Golden West had begun a survey of historic landmarks. Their Historic Landmarks Committee, led by Eliza D. Keith, made their report in 1902. Keith became president of the Native Daughters in June of that year. See Weinberg, "Historic Preservation," p. 141.

15. California Historic Landmarks League, "Articles of Incorporation, June 24, 1902," courtesy of Sandra Elder. Also see Laura Bridge Powers, "The California Historical Landmarks League," *Overland Monthly,* 40 (November 1902), 472-473; and "Autobiography," MS #3154, Folder 21, Joseph Knowland Papers. Hosmer identified Keith as the organizer of the league in 1902. Knowland agreed to become president a year later. Hosmer, *Presence of the Past,* p. 127.

16. Powers, "Landmarks League," p. 473.

17. Weinberg, "Historic Preservation," pp. 141-142; Knowland, *Landmark History,* pp. 60-61; Hosmer, *Presence of the Past,* p. 128. The mission was turned over to the Park Commission in 1927. In a 1908 publication, Knowland stated that the mission was given to the state after the legislature passed a law in 1905 to provide for its acquisition, preservation, and protection. Knowland later described it as the first to be turned over to the state at no cost. See Joseph R. Knowland, "The Missions of California," *Architect and Engineer of California,* XII (April 1908), Department of Parks and Recreation, Central Records Storage (hereafter abbreviated as DPR), "California Missions: Research," 536.2.

18. Deterioration was rapid, and the mission was not completely restored until after World War II. Weinberg, "Historic Preservation," pp. 142-143; Knowland, *Landmark History,* pp. 7-9; Hosmer, *Presence of the Past,* p. 128.

19. Knowland, *Landmark History,* p. 103.

20. This was in addition to $15,000 that George Marston and other local groups had previously raised to restore the "Mother Mission." *Ibid.,* pp. 1-3.

21. *Ibid.,* pp. 56-57, 24; and Weinberg, "Historic Preservation," p. 143.

22. Knowland, *Landmark History,* pp. 39-40.

23. *Ibid.,* pp. 57, 42, 22; Hosmer, *Presence of the Past,* p. 129; Weinberg, "Historic Preservation," pp. 128-129.

24. The San Diego project was not successful, and two members of the local preservation group resigned in 1910. The restoration of the mission was temporarily sidetracked after 1910 because of greater public preoccupation with events such as the 1915 fair and World War I. See Weinberg, "Historic Preservation," pp. 132-133.

25. Both Hosmer and Weinberg noted that the restoration at Pala was accomplished with mixed results. The resident priest there did not appreciate the significance of the original Indian frescoes and had the interior whitewashed. Hosmer, *Presence of the Past,* p. 126; and Weinberg, "Historic Preservation," pp. 134-135.

26. Weinberg found no other record of club activities at La Purisima. As for other projects, he claimed that the club was "instrumental in keeping the old plaza of Los Angeles from being turned into a market, and in campaigning for the retention of historic street names and place names." In the final analysis, "in its work, its publicity, and the interest it aroused, the club played an important role over two decades in sustaining an attitude which valued the Missions for their historical and architectural interest; and thus it aided in the process by which that attitude has become customary." Weinberg, "Historic Preservation," pp. 135-136, 139.

27. *Ibid.,* pp. 131-132, 136-139. See also Hosmer, *Presence of the Past,* pp. 126-127. On August 4, pilgrims at the mission purchased candles at a dollar each to carry through the buildings.

28. Knowland, *Landmark History,* pp. 175-176, 182-183; and Joseph H. Engbeck, Jr., *State Parks of California From 1864 to the Present* (Portland, Oregon: Graphic Arts Publishing Co., 1980), pp. 38-39.

29. Knowland, *Landmark History,* pp. 209-214, contains a list of plaques placed up to 1941. For a more complete listing, see Daughters of the American Revolution, *California's Seventy-Five Years: Daughters of the American Revolution, 1891-1966* (n.p., California State Society, Daughters of the American Revolution, 1966).

30. Knowland, *Landmark History,* pp. 215-231, contains a list of markers and monuments placed up to 1941.

31. Weinberg, "Historic Preservation," pp. 143-147. The Landmarks Club did not play a role in the association because Lummis believed the project should be confined to the area south of Santa Barbara. His proposal was rejected by other groups who joined the association. They included chambers of commerce, historical societies, the Automobile Club of Southern California, and the California State Automobile Association. The latter two agreed to be responsible for bell maintenance. Knowland's widespread influence was also demonstrated when he was elected one of the organization's vice-presidents.

32. See, for example, Owen C. Coy, *The Battle of San Pasqual.* A Report of the California Historical Survey Commission With Special Reference to Its Location (Sacramento: California State Printing Office, 1921).

33. Engbeck, *State Parks*, p. 39.

CHAPTER 2
EXTENDING THE FRONTIERS OF HISTORIC PRESERVATION: STATE, FEDERAL, AND LOCAL PROGRAMS, 1925-1940

1. Engbeck, *State Parks*, pp. 41-49. In 1923, league president John C. Merriam, who was now president of Washington, D.C.'s Carnegie Institute, appointed a committee on state parks to recommend a state park plan for California. Committee chair Duncan McDuffie proposed the creation of a statewide park system, a commission to act as a statewide coordinating body, and a comprehensive survey undertaken by Frederick Law Olmsted, son of the famed landscape architect who was the principal designer of New York's Central Park and a key figure in the creation of the nation's first state park, Yosemite. See also pp. 17-21.

2. *Ibid*, pp. 49-50. Because the state park commission bill was signed by the governor before his reorganization legislation, the commission "retained full executive and administrative power over the state park program." This power persuaded qualified and respected individuals to serve, and increased public confidence in the state park program. The first commissioners were: conservationist and mining law expert William E. Colby of San Francisco; conservationist and Stanford University President Ray Lyman Wilbur, who later became President Hoover's Secretary of the Interior; attorney and Los Angeles City Park Commissioner Henry W. O'Melveny; explorer, author, and amateur archaeologist Frederick Russell Burnham of Hollywood; and San Joaquin Valley agriculturalist and senator from Fresno, Wilbur F. Chandler. See also Hosmer, *Preservation Comes of Age*, I:412-413.

3. Frederick Law Olmsted, *Report of State Park Survey of California* (Sacramento: California State Printing Office, 1929).

4. Hosmer, *Preservation Comes of Age*, I:413.

5. Olmsted, *State Park Survey*, pp. 10-11. The other two historical advisers were A.L. Kroeber and Carl I. Wheat. They, along with the regional reporters, were volunteers. Aubrey Drury was Newton's brother.

6. Aubrey Drury, *Survey of Historic Sites and Landmarks in California* (San Francisco: California State Parks Council, August 15, 1928). Drury emphasized the missions "because of their unique interest, as the earliest historical landmarks in California, and because in a sense they constitute a group apart." *Ibid.*, pp. 2-6.

The variety of places included ranged from forts, monuments, ship landings and shipwrecks, buildings, mining towns, literary sites, and trees to landmarks such as Death Valley and Point Concepcion. He did not list archaeological or ethnographical sites, but did include Indian villages, pictographs, shell mounds, and caves. Drury also recommended that mountain passes, emigrant trails, ghost towns, and spots with "romantic" appeal such as locations of famous robberies and massacres be preserved as well. *Ibid.*, pp. 58-60.

7. Olmsted, *State Park Survey*, pp. 52-58. He viewed archaeological sites in much the same way. The ten sites were: Columbia, Shasta, Fort Ross, Santa Barbara County Missions, Marshall Park Extension, Pioneer Memorial and Donner Lake Parks, Mark Twain's home in Tuolumne County, Camulos Ranch in Ventura County, De La Guerra

Ranch in Santa Barbara County, and the Vallejo Home in Sonoma County. Olmsted also identified five archaeological sites: Painted Rocks in San Luis Obispo County, Santa Barbara Pictograph, Fish Traps in Riverside County, Shell Mounds in Tulare County, and the Petrified Forest in Sonoma County. See pp. 66-67.

8. *Ibid.,* p. 66.

9. Horace M. Albright, interviewed by David Tucker, January 13-14, 1974, transcript, DPR: "State Park System Interpretation and History: Reports," 511, p. 27.

10. Olmsted, *State Park Survey,* p. 17.

11. Engbeck, *State Parks,* p. 59.

12. Engbeck identified these five as: Sutter's Fort, the Sonoma Mission, the Monterey sites of Colton Hall and Custom House, and the Marshall Blacksmith Shop. *Ibid.,* p. 57. In contrast, Drury listed nine monuments: Sutter's Fort, Fort Ross, Marshall Monument and Blacksmith Shop, Junipero Serra's Landing Place, Old Monterey Theater, Mission San Francisco de Solano, Pio Pico Mansion, and San Pasqual Monument. Drury noted that the public did not understand what "state monument" meant and recommended that "'State Historic Reserve' or 'State Historic Site' would be better terms by which to refer to those historic buildings or locations preserved." See Drury, *Survey of Historic Sites,* pp. 7-9.

13. Engbeck, *State Parks,* pp. 62-63. Hosmer stated that Drury pointed out in an interview that the projects in the State Park System lacked matching monies for the required 50-50 match. One fourth of the bond money was allocated for historic properties by the Park Commission with the matching stipulation still attached. The money lasted until 1940 because of the difficulty in raising funds during the Depression. Hosmer, *Preservation Comes of Age,* I:414-415.

14. Hosmer, *Preservation Comes of Age,* I:415-417.

15. *Ibid.,* pp. 417-419. Part of Drury's difficulties were due to the publicity given to the Park Commission's 1933 agreement to set aside $15,000 for the town's acquisition. This action was taken after a San Francisco-based group, the Historic Mining Towns Preservation League, began a modest restoration program and fund-raising campaign in the same year. Additional groundwork for acquisition had been laid in 1933 when historian Hero Eugene Rensch began to research the town with funds from the Emergency Relief Administration. See also p. 415.

16. *Ibid.,* pp. 419-421. The commissioners were William Colby and Mrs. Edmund M. Brown. In April 1931, the commission committed $20,000 which was to be matched by local initiative. The commission also hired architect Irving Morrow and landscape architect Emerson Knight to report on the town's significance and preservation needs. The community's enthusiasm for preservation was exemplified by plaza property owners who accepted cash payments that represented 60 percent of their land's appraised value.

17. *Ibid.,* pp. 421-422.

18. *Ibid.,* pp. 419, 432.

19. Newton B. Drury, "California's Investment in the State Parks. An Account of the Plan of Acquisition in Building a State Park System," October 23, 1939, DPR: 511.

20. *Ibid.,* p. 1.

21. *Ibid.,* pp. 2-3.

22. *Ibid.,* p. 7.

23. *California State Parks and the W.P.A. 20 Questions Answered.* This brochure which was produced by the Division of Parks defined historic monuments as areas smaller than state parks. They are sites or buildings set aside as part of the California State Park System because they have been the scene of important events in the state's past.

24. Drury, "California's Investment," p. 8.

25. *Ibid.,* pp. 9-10.

26. See Engbeck, *State Parks,* pp. 71, 82, 87.

27. M.M. Whittaker to All Unit Supervisors, March 9, 1966, DPR: 511.

28. California State Historical Association, "Quarterly Report," March 1931, enclosed in memo from Chuck Wilson to Sandra Elder, August 12, 1981. Sandra Elder Files, Office of Historic Preservation (hereafter abbreviated as Elder: OHP).

The association was interested in the proposed California State Historical Landmarks Commission. The Quarterly Report of June 18, 1931, said the proposed $75,000 from pending legislation should be used

> toward efficient centralization rather than the creation of an additional separate body which cannot avoid duplication of function. Construction and custody of landmarks and monuments could well be provided for by a new body or undertaken by existent bodies such as the State Parks Division. But the California State Historical Association should be able to perform the historical functions of the state and should be so organized as to permit cooperation with other branches of departments which require that service.

In his June report, association director Owen Coy noted that the proposed commission would have performed "a task which is a portion of that laid out as a province of the State Historical Association, and for which the administration holds no funds to be available." The bill was not reported out of committee.

29. The extent of support was revealed by the fact that both the California State Historical Association and the State Chamber of Commerce claimed important roles in the passage of A.B. 171. See "Quarterly Report," June 18, 1931. *Ibid.* The association's interest in landmarks apparently diminished after this. Chuck Wilson of the California State Archives reported to Sandra Elder of the Office of Historic Preservation that he "looked through the folder of quarterly reports from the Association and these [i.e., the report of March and June 1931] were the only ones which had information on the landmarks program." Memo from Wilson to Elder, August 12, 1981, *ibid.* Also see California State Chamber of Commerce, "Registration History," June 16, 1945. Office of Historic Preservation Files (hereafter abbreviated as OHP): "War Services Program—Centennial Data," p. 4.

30. The issue of property owner consent became an important controversy in the mid-1960s and 1970s.

31. *Statutes of 1931*, Chapter 184, in Sandra J. Elder, comp., "Public Resources Code, Section 5020 to 5033, and Appropriate Legislation" (Office of Historic Preservation: March 1983), n.p.

32. Chamber of Commerce, "Registration History," pp. 6-7.

33. *Ibid.*, p. 4. In 1941, the committee consisted of Chairman Farquhar, Drury, Wheat, Hutchings, Wright, Robert E. Cowan, and Knowland.

34. *Ibid.* When World War II began, the Travel and Recreation Committee was renamed "War Service...to directly assist the prosecution of the war."

35. *Ibid.*, pp. 4-5.

36. See Sandra Elder, comp., "Landmarks Registered in 1932," 1982, for the 50th Anniversary Celebration of the Landmarks Program. For specific details on the landmarks, see The Department of Natural Resources and the State Park Commission in Cooperation with the California State Chamber of Commerce, *Reports* No. 1-5, 1932 (hereafter abbreviated as Chamber *Reports*), OHP: "Registered Landmarks."

37. Chamber *Reports*, No. 10, January 15, 1935.

38. Chamber *Reports*, No. 26, December 20, 1943; No. 27, April 14, 1944; and No. 28, May 1, 1947.

39. Chamber *Report* No. 41, March 14, 1952, identified landmarks No. 497-499 which were registered on December 4, 1951. Although legislation in 1949 created the Historical Landmarks Advisory Committee to approve applications, the new procedure was not implemented until 1952. See Chamber *Report* No. 42, n.d.

40. Frank McKee to Joseph Knowland, June 25, 1938, OHP: "Correspondence, Photos, etc. RE Plaques."

41. Frank McKee to J.H. Covington, September 12, 1938; George D. Nordenholt to Frank McKee, September 15, 1938. *Ibid.*

42. Frank McKee to R.K. Davies, April 24, 1939. *Ibid.*

43. R.K. Davies to Frank McKee, May 16, 1939. *Ibid.*

44. Frank McKee to R.K. Davies, May 22, 1939. *Ibid.*

45. Frank McKee to R.K. Davies, July 10, 1939. *Ibid.* McKee repeated that maps distributed by the oil companies "could be keyed in with the statewide program to promote additional travel to landmarks properly marked."

46. C.B. Garretson to Frank McKee, August 1, 1939. *Ibid.*

47. Frank McKee to C.B. Garretson, August 21, 1939. *Ibid.* The three page, single-spaced, typed letter also underscored again the educational value of the program, mentioned prominent supporters such as Knowland, agreed to a three-year program whereby the group's contribution could be divided into smaller payments, and detailed a marker maintenance plan.

48. J.E. Carpenter to J.H. Covington, October 9, 1940. OHP: "Survey and Replies: Landmarks Marked Prior to 1941." The landmarks booklet which was turned down by Covington on October 22, 1940, because of lack of funding, would become one of the most profitable best-sellers in the Department's publication program after 1960. See John H. Covington to J.E. Carpenter, October 22, 1940.

49. H.G. Prodger to J.E. Carpenter, October 22, 1941. *Ibid.*

50. See copies of letters from Joseph R. Knowland to unidentified parties in 1940. The result was a "Checklist of Historical Landmarks Registered by the State of California, As of July 1, 1940." *Ibid.*

51. Chamber of Commerce, "Registration History," p. 5. See also Chamber of Commerce, "Registered Historic Landmarks," January 29, 1944, OHP: "War Services Program—Centennial Data." This list noted that only 72 out of a total 384 registered landmarks remained unmarked as of July 1, 1941. This probably reflected the survey that Knowland and Carpenter had sent out the previous year.

52. Chamber of Commerce, "Registration History," p. 1.

53. Hosmer, *Preservation Comes of Age*, I:433. This concern for historic significance was demonstrated in 1946 when the State Chamber of Commerce provided a list of 107 "Rejected Applications for Registration of Historic Landmarks." OHP: "War Services Program—Centennial Data."

54. Engbeck, *State Parks*, pp. 64-67. Yet to be fully explored are archaeological projects sponsored by the WPA. For a brief summary of the agency's activities in one California county, see Paul G. Chace, "The History of Archaeology in Orange County," Pacific Coast Archaeological Society, Inc. *Quarterly*, 1, no. 3 (July 1965): 7-10.

55. Hosmer, *Preservation Comes of Age*, I:426-432. Joseph H. Engbeck, Jr., *La Purisima Mission State Historic Park* (Sacramento: Department of Parks and Recreation, 1979, reprint), p. 28.

56. Hosmer, *Preservation Comes of Age*, I:428, II:1019.

57. *Ibid.*, I:428-429. In his book, Knowland described the work as "the most ambitious and intelligently executed restoration yet undertaken at any of the California missions." See Knowland, *Landmark History*, p. 30.

58. Hosmer, *Preservation Comes of Age*, I:428-429, II:1019-1033. It should be noted that land was donated also by the Catholic Church and Union Oil Company. See Engbeck, *La Purisima*, p. 23.

59. Hosmer, *Preservation Comes of Age*, I:437, II:1019-1026. Also see Richard S. Whitehead, ed., *An Archaeological and Restoration Study of Mission La Purisima Concepcion.* Reports Written for the National Park Service by Fred C. Hageman and Russell C. Ewing (Santa Barbara: Santa Barbara Trust for Historic Preservation, 1980). Hageman, the

principal architect, advocated total reconstruction. Ewing, the National Park Service historian, wanted to preserve what remained.

60. Hosmer, *Preservation Comes of Age*, II:1033.

61. Hosmer implies that historian Hero Rensch had expected to be appointed project administrator. It seems that Rensch had assisted with the creation of a research staff at the Bancroft Library in 1935 with hopes of researching the landmarks. *Ibid.*, I:432-433. By this time, Rensch had co-authored two of his three-volume work, *Historic Spots in California* (1932, 1933, 1937). See Mildred Brooke Hoover, Hero Eugene Rensch, Ethel Grace Rensch, *Historic Spots in California,* revised by William N. Abeloe, 3rd ed. (Stanford: Stanford University Press, 1966), pp. v-vii.

62. Vernon A. Neasham, editor and supervisor, "California Historical Landmarks. Works Project #6461, Serial 0803-434. Off. Project #165-03-7307, Symbol #165027," Bancroft Library, Berkeley, California: OHP.

63. For a brief review of the WPA program, see Engbeck, *State Parks*, pp. 65-67.

64. Copies of the landmarks reports can be found in the Library of the Office of Historic Preservation in Sacramento, California.

65. Gary Fred Somers, "The Role of the Federal Government in Historic Preservation" (Unpublished Ph.D. Dissertation, University of Arizona, 1979), p. 14.

66. Charles R. McGimsey III, *Public Archeology* (New York: Seminar Press, 1972), p. 104.

67. National Park Service, *Historic American Building Survey. Catalog of the Measured Drawings and Photographs of the Survey in the Library of Congress, March 1, 1941* (Washington, D.C.: Government Printing Office, 1941), p. iv.

68. *Ibid.*, pp. iv-vi.

69. *Ibid.*, pp. 40-52.

70. National Park Service, *The Historic American Buildings Survey* (Washington, D.C.: Government Printing Office, 1973), n.p.

71. National Park Service, *Historic American Buildings Survey. Catalog Supplement* (Washington, D.C.: Government Printing Office, 1959), n.p.

72. Hoffman was a new arrival in the area and had joined the association in 1920. A year later, he organized the Architectural Advisory Committee to advise on plans for a new city hall and renovation of De la Guerra Plaza. Like other wealthy patrons of Santa Barbara, Hoffman also purchased and restored adobes. Among his projects was the Casa de la Guerra which faced the Plaza. By 1923, he had assumed the presidency of the association which, in 1924, was unable to convince the city to adopt a general plan. The plan, *A Major Traffic Street Plan and Boulevard and Park System,* was the work of the Olmsted brothers. The earthquake resulted in $20 million in property damage. See Weinberg, "Historic Preservation," pp. 193-208.

73. The association successfully established Old Spanish Days Fiesta as an annual event. It was not a new idea, for Santa Barbara had celebrated its Spanish heritage with costumed dancers and presentations as early as the Mission Centennial Celebration in 1886. The first fiesta in 1924 drew together the business community in search of the tourist dollar and the association in need of a suitable way to commemorate the opening of the Lobero Theater on the site of the original opera house. After a modified program in 1925, the fiesta was resumed in August 1926 with a night pageant and historical parade. *Ibid.*

74. The drafting room, for example, aided in the preparation of sketches for the Santa Barbara County Courthouse which had been approved by voters in 1926. When completed in 1929, the Spanish colonial revival style building testified to the city's commitment to its Spanish past. *Ibid.*, pp. 201-202.

75. *Ibid.*, pp. 202-203; also Knowland, *Landmark History*, p. 29.

76. The Ranchito Romula in the San Fernando Valley, for example, was restored by Mr. and Mrs. M.R. Harrington in 1930. Harrington was curator of the Southwest Museum when his wife purchased the building. See Knowland, *Landmark History*, p. 176.

77. Jean Bruce Poole, telephone conversation with author, July 12, 1983. Poole is Senior Curator of the historic park.

78. Christine Sterling, *Olvera Street. Its History and Restoration* (Los Angeles: Christine Sterling, 1947), pp. 9-14; Hosmer, *Preservation Comes of Age*, I:424.

79. Sterling, *Olvera Street*, pp. 9, 15-20; Roger Hatheway, "El Pueblo: Myths and Realities," Society of Architectural Historians, Southern California Chapter, *Review* (Fall 1981): 2; Knowland, *Landmark History*, pp. 189-190.

80. Poole, conversation with author, and Poole to author, July 20, 1987. Poole observed that six of the buildings in the Olvera, Main, and Alameda street blocks were built or used by Italians. According to Poole, El Pueblo de Los Angeles State Historical Monument became Pueblo de Los Angeles State Historic Park in 1970 when a comprehensive general plan was submitted to and approved by the Pueblo de Los Angeles State Historical Monument Commission. See: Jean Bruce Poole, "The Plaza Substation Under Governmental Ownership: 1964-1987," June 1987, p. 14; courtesy of Jean Bruce Poole. See also Chapter 4, fn. 54.

Sterling's insistence that David Alfaro Siqueros' mural, "America Tropical," be whitewashed as a condition for the renewal of the lease in the mid-1930s showed another side to her activities. The 1932 mural was controversial because it depicted a man "crucified on a double cross, which had, proudly perched on the top, the eagle of North American coins." The artist was later deported. See Richard Rowe, "On Olvera Street: One Vision Realized, Another Whitewashed," Society of California Architectural Historians, Southern California Chapter, *Review* (Fall 1981): 6-7. Historian Bill Mason noted, for example, that "in the late 1920's and early 1930's,...some Chinese were displaced, in fact, evicted. The Chinese businesses and residences east of Alameda Street were condemned and demolished between 1933 and 1935 to make way for Union Station, part of Los Angeles' ground plan for the entire civic center area....Slowly but deliberately, most if not all traces of the Chinese in El Pueblo were eliminated in the 1950's." See Bill Mason, "Como se llama el Pueblo en Chinese?", Society of Architectural Historians, Southern California Chapter, *Review* (Fall 1981): 8.

81. Hosmer, *Preservation Comes of Age*, I:424-425; Knowland, *Landmark History*, p. 95.

82. Hosmer, *Preservation Comes of Age*, I:323-324. Hosmer observed that the members quickly realized "the most challenging factor they had to deal with was the mind of the public—and actual physical preservation of the buildings could be achieved by means of delaying actions and education." See also Knowland, *Landmark History*, p. 93.

83. Hosmer, *Preservation Comes of Age*, I:324-326. Knowland, said Hosmer, "was fiercely proud of the way in which the state had taken care of its own historic sites. He did not like the intervention from the federal government in such affairs in his home country."

84. The state's share came from bond issue monies, and Monterey residents cashed in their World War I veterans' bonds. *Ibid.*, pp. 326-327.

85. *Ibid.*, pp. 326-330. Knowland and Drury selected Knight and Neasham to produce the plan and lobbied hard for their appointments. The plan described how walkways, roads, and green spaces could become integral parts of the city while maintaining areas surrounding historic structures. A foundation was also recommended to continue the needed long-term planning. The Monterey Foundation did not materialize until April 1945 and had not yet emerged as a powerful force in 1949. As for the zoning ordinance, it could advocate preservation but it lacked enforcement powers.

86. *Ibid.*, p. 330. See also Knowland, *Landmark History*, pp. 157-161.

87. Weinberg, "Historic Preservation," pp. 211-213.

88. *Ibid.*, pp. 213-219. Downie's interest in missions stemmed from his childhood. His father, a member of the Native Sons, took him on many visits to the missions. Downie lost his job during the Depression, and in the early 1930s, became building and grounds supervisor of Mission San Carlos. In that capacity, he restored the mission's roof to its 1814 appearance. Downie's restoration and reconstruction philosophy is detailed by Weinberg

who interviewed Downie in 1971. Weinberg concluded that Downie was, first and foremost, concerned "with historic appearance...and [his] solutions to practical problems were tailored so as not to violate the historical ambiance."

89. *Ibid.*, pp. 219-224.

PART II
REAWAKENING OF A PRESERVATION CONSCIOUSNESS, 1940-1966

1. Engbeck, *State Parks*, pp. 77-78.

CHAPTER 3
THE GOLD DISCOVERY AND GOLD RUSH CENTENNIALS, 1940-1950

1. J.E. Carpenter to Fred H. Bixby, January 29, 1946. OHP: "War Services Program—Centennial Data."

2. Hosmer, *Preservation Comes of Age*, I:434.

3. Engbeck, *State Parks*, pp. 77-78. Relative independence was attained when park commissioners were appointed to staggered four-year terms, instead of serving at the governor's pleasure. Warren's concern for recreation was also demonstrated by the creation of a Recreation Commission in 1947. The bill was signed on July 8, 1947, and the commission held its first meeting in October of that year. See "The Date the Commission was Created," courtesy of Sandra Elder.

4. For a copy of the resolution, see memo "to the Department of Public Works" regarding "Recommendation of the War Service Committee of the California Chamber of Commerce for the better utilization of our Historic Landmarks as travel lure for out-of-state visitors, and for the education of California citizens," June 16, 1945. OHP: "War Services Program—Centennial Data."

5. *Ibid.* Copies of the plan were to be forwarded to the governor and the Reconstruction and Re-Employment Commission.

6. *Ibid.*, "Recommendation to State Highway Department," pp. 2-3. Depending on the type of signs selected, the estimates for 500 signs ranged from $37,500 to $67,500.

7. J.E. Carpenter to Joseph R. Knowland, September 25, 1945. Carpenter told Knowland that Verne Scoggins, the governor's secretary, had suggested that "we have *you* discuss the matter with the Governor and put it up to him." *Ibid.*

8. J.E. Carpenter to Joseph R. Knowland, January 23, 1947. Carpenter informed Knowland that "through our various connections we will endeavor to handle all of these matters [relating to the project] with the exception of the write-ups and the plaques." He asked Knowland to "start the ball rolling" with regard to the Native Sons' assuming responsibility for the plaques, a possibility that he had mentioned earlier to Carpenter. See also J.E. Carpenter to San Benito County Board of Supervisors, March 27, 1947. *Ibid.*

9. G.T. McCoy to J.E. Carpenter, April 2, 1947. *Ibid.*

10. J.E. Carpenter to C.A. Henning, October 18, 1949. *Ibid.* Henning was known as "Chick." See Engbeck, *State Parks*, p. 77.

11. "Historical Landmark Plaques Placed by California Centennials Commission," April 14, 1950. OHP: "War Services Program—Centennial Data." As for the actual description of the monument and plaque, Knowland told Newton Drury, the newly appointed chief of the Division of Beaches and Parks that:

> The standard size of the tablets we had made during the centennials was 32 inches high and 34 inches wide. At the top they were rather dome shape [sic] with a bear above, and two stars on either side below the bear....In each case, during the centennial years, the individuals sponsoring the tablet always furnished the base, which saved us a large sum of money, and I think this is a good practice to continue. On two or three occasions they used a large boulder and the Centennials Commission told them that was satisfactory.

See Joseph Knowland to Newton Drury, October 5, 1951. OHP: Landmarks File. The actual design of the monuments and plaque was probably the work of Alfred Eichler. Chuck Wilson to Sandy Elder, August 12, 1981, in Elder: OHP.

12. "Outline of Organization Set-up, Historic Landmarks Program and 1948-1949 Celebration," August 3, 1945, included as enclosures in letter from J.E. Carpenter to C.A. Henning, October 18, 1949. OHP: "Historic and Other Organization Lists Prepared for 1949 Celebration."

13. J.E. Carpenter to Joseph R. Knowland, October 20, 1945, OHP: "War Services Program—Centennial Data."

14. Frederick Law Olmsted, *Report on the Columbia Historic Park Project*, August 27, 1946, DPR: "Columbia State Historic Park: Reports," 319.1-307, pp. 4-5.

15. Hosmer, *Preservation Comes of Age*, I:434-436; Aubrey Neasham, *Columbia State Historic Park: Historical Summary and Recommendations*, San Francisco, October 1, 1948, pp. 19-33, DPR: "Columbia State Historic Park: Reports," 429.1-307. Neasham was hired on a temporary basis because he was still employed by the National Park Service. His recommended master plan was completed in 1950. See: Bliss and Hurt, Trudell and Berger, *Master Plan Report for the Development of Columbia State Historic Park*, DPR: "Columbia State Historic Park: Reports," 359.1-307. The plan suggested that an additional forty structures be reconstructed and added to the forty other buildings that Neasham had specifically recommended for preservation or reconstruction. Also, *Interpretive Plan for Columbia State Historic Park*, October 28, 1963. DPR: 539.1-307; Office of the Auditor General, *Department of Parks and Recreation, Report on Columbia State Historic Park*, October 1968, DPR: 539.1-307; and *Interpretive Plan for Columbia State Historic Park*, Revised January, 1970, courtesy of John Michael. Between 1945 and 1968, $2.5 million had been spent for acquisitions and restoration at Columbia.

16. Engbeck, *State Parks*, p. 79. Engbeck claimed that Olmsted's reports were not only respected and "almost universally accepted," they were often "quoted, paraphrased, expanded,...or revised...." He concluded that Olmsted's "language and ideas tended to form the backbone of countless official reports and memorandums."

17. Frederick Law Olmsted, *General Report on Potential State Park and Recreational Areas*, to the State Park Commission, 1950, DPR: "State Park System: Research," 339.2.

18. Division of Beaches and Parks, *History, Analysis and Recommendations on the Planning for the State Park System*, March 8, 1965 and reprinted March 1967, DPR: "State Park System: Reports," 339.1, p. 17.

19. Olmsted, *General Report*, p. 3.

20. *Ibid.*, pp. 4-7. Olmsted also consulted various people, including the Park Commission and staff, legislators, and other officials and interested organizations. Beaches and Parks, *History, Analysis, Recommendations*, p. 19.

21. Olmsted, *General Report*, p. 11. Olmsted proposed a similar, statewide investigation by a committee of California archaeologists and scientists for preservation projects in their own individual disciplines and interests. He noted that "suggestions on this subject were made in the 1928 State Park Survey (p. 66 *et seq.*) but little effective action has been taken and opportunities are slipping away." *Ibid.*, p. 12.

22. Beaches and Parks, *History, Analysis, Recommendations*, pp. 19-20. The acquisition of George J. Hatfield State Park in honor of the senator also helped to placate the legislature and local officials.

23. *Statutes of 1949*, Ch. 143, in Elder, "Public Resources Code," n.p.

24. *Ibid.* The law gave the Department of Public Works the responsibility to repair those landmark monuments adjacent to state highways; county authorities were to repair markers on country roads, with city officials being responsible for streets under their jurisdiction.

25. J.E.C. to J.M., March 3, 1952, OHP: "Correspondence, Photos, Etc. RE Plaques."

26. *Ibid.*

27. J.E. Carpenter to Newton B. Drury, March 26, 1952. *Ibid.*

28. Conservation and Education Section, Department of Natural Resources, *Organization and Functions of the State Department of Natural Resources*, Sacramento, July 1960, p. 3, courtesy of Sandra Elder.

29. J.E.C. to J.M., March 3, 1952, OHP: "Correspondence, Photos, Etc. RE Plaques."

CHAPTER 4
MASTER PLANNING AND PROFESSIONALISM IN STATE PRESERVATION, 1951-1960

1. The figures are from a California State Senate Resolution given to Drury in 1966 which was appended to a memo from M.M. Whittaker to all Unit Supervisors, March 9, 1955, DPR: 511.

2. Ernest B. Camper to Newton B. Drury, October 30, 1951, OHP: "Correspondence, Photos, Etc. Re Plaques." Camper served as Drury's administrative assistant. His memo included a copy of Knowland's summary of sixteen plaque requests being considered by the Park Commission, a summary of all plaque requests including recommendations from Division Curator Carroll Hall, copies of all registered landmark descriptions included in the plaque requests, and a list of plaque bids.

3. Newton B. Drury to Joseph R. Knowland, December 13, 1951. *Ibid.*

4. Aubrey Neasham to Newton Drury, June 15, 1951, V. Aubrey Neasham Collection, Museum and History Division, City and County of Sacramento, California (hereafter abbreviated as Neasham Collection): "History Section, Daily Correspondence." As of 1983, the Neasham Collection had yet to be catalogued and consisted of forty-two archive boxes of material.

5. Engbeck stated that Drury persuaded Neasham to leave the National Park Service. See Engbeck, *State Parks*, pp. 84-85.

6. Arthur Woodward to Aubrey Neasham, June 25, 1952, Neasham Collection: "Department of Interior Correspondence."

7. Aubrey Neasham to Arthur Woodward, June 27, 1952; Aubrey Neasham to John Hussey, August 1, 1952. *Ibid.*

8. Ronald Miller to Aubrey Neasham, November 28, 1952. *Ibid.*

9. Newton Drury to Aubrey Neasham, December 12, 1952. *Ibid.*

10. Aubrey Neasham to Everett Powell, February 4, 1958, Neasham Collection: "History Section, Daily Correspondence."

11. Aubrey Neasham to Newton Drury, July 5, 1956. *Ibid.* Neasham commented that until the creation of the History Section in 1953, "help was obtained wherever possible, and included such agencies as the University of California, the Carnegie Institute, the California Historical Landmarks Advisory Committee, La Purisima Mission Advisory Committee, the Works Progress Administration, the Civilian Conservation Corps, among others." The historian's function was to expedite historical preservation and use, and to coordinate the marking of landmarks. He also consulted with various agencies regarding the preservation and interpretation of California's historical heritage.

12. Aubrey Neasham to Newton Drury, "The California Park System: Its Future Growth and Organization" (August 28, 1958); "Further Observations on the California State Park System: Its Future Growth and Organization" (October 28, 1958); and "Basic Principles of Parks, Historic Sites and Recreational Areas" (November 17, 1958). *Ibid.*

13. *Ibid.*

14. Joseph Engbeck recalled that:

> I...remember him talking about it. Drury recruited Neasham and persuaded him to come to the State Park System when Drury came back to it....So Drury

was very sympathetic to historic preservation. And respectful of Neasham's ability as a government or public historian. So when he didn't back this proposal of Neasham's, it wasn't out of any antipathy with Neasham at all. It was simply because he already knew what was feasible politically and what wasn't. And to push this proposal would have been counterproductive because it wouldn't have worked. It would have expended good will on something that wasn't going to work.

Joseph H. Engbeck, Jr., telephone interview with author, March 23, 1987. Also see Newton Drury to Aubrey Neasham, October 10, 1958. *Ibid.*

15. L.S. Hollinger to Aubrey Neasham, October 22, 1958. *Ibid.*

16. Robert Power to Aubrey Neasham, November 24, 1958. *Ibid.* Curiously, Power also promised: "If you want to get the conspirators together again my offer of Inverness still stands."

17. Engbeck, *State Parks*, p. 87.

18. Hubert O. Jenkins, "Report on the Interpretive Service of the State Parks of California," November 1, 1952, DPR: 511.

19. *Ibid.*, pp. 26-29.

20. Beaches and Parks, *History, Analysis and Recommendations*, p. 9. Jenkins' other recommendations to improve the division's interpretive efforts included better training for the full-time ranger staff in interpretive service, expansion of summer interpretive programs, and more personnel. These suggestions were received positively by park service professionals.

21. Engbeck, *State Parks*, pp. 68-70, 93-94. In 1934, newly elected Governor Frank F. Merriam, fired division chief Colonel Wing, Park Commission secretary Laura E. Gregory, north coast redwood parks superintendent Percy French and others.

22. Division of Beaches and Parks, *California State Park System. Five Year Program, July 1, 1953 to June 30, 1958.* Approved by the State Park Commission, December 19, 1952. DPR: "Project Planning and Design: Reports," 361.1, p. 5.

23. *Ibid.*, p. 6. The list of interpretive exhibit proposals mentioned four of the ten sites that Olmsted had identified in his 1929 survey: Columbia, Shasta, Fort Ross, Donner. The acquisition budget also placed a high priority on beaches. Of the total $26,750,000 for the five-year period, $20,000,000 was for beach properties. An additional $500,000 was for historic monuments such as Columbia and Shasta. Of the proposed new projects, only two were mentioned: Olvera Street was to receive $750,000; interior projects, "including River parks and Parkways, Colorado River areas, historical areas, etc." were allocated $1,500,000.

24. Newton B. Drury to Joseph R. Knowland, December 26, 1951, OHP: "Correspondence, Photos, Etc. Re Plaques."

25. *Ibid.* Also see C.D. Hall, "Present Coverage of California's History by State Historical Monuments and/or Parks (Jan. 1952)," attached to C.D. Hall to Newton B. Drury, December 19, 1951, Courtesy of Sandra J. Elder. Hall noted that "the allocation of certain units to this or that category has been arbitrarily performed." The Vallejo Home, for example, which was not built until the Early Statehood Period, "is essentially a part of the Mexican Period" and was included in that time frame. San Juan Bautista could also be placed into several categories. Of the thirty-two monuments and/or parks, twenty-four were in the northern part of the state and eight in southern California. Eighteen of California's fifty-eight counties had monuments, with Monterey's five being the most numerous. Pp. 2-3.

26. Newton B. Drury to Carroll Hall, December 26, 1951, OHP: "Correspondence, Photos, Etc. Re Plaques." Drury also noted that he was sending this letter as well as Hall's study to the Park Commission and General Warren T. Hannum, director of the Department of Natural Resources, "to indicate that we are beginning to break ground in this field."

27. Aubrey Neasham to Newton B. Drury, "Master Program of Acquisition, State Historical Areas," November 9, 1953, DPR: "Historical Preservation: General Correspondence," 348.0. Also see Beaches and Parks, *History, Analysis and Recommendations*, p. 9.

28. Neasham, "Master Program of Acquisitions," 1953.

29. Senate Interim Committee on Recreation, State Beaches and Parks, *Preliminary Report. California's State Park Program. Two Studies of Current and Selected State Park Problems* (Sacramento: Senate of the State of California, January 11, 1956), pp. 13, 39. One of the committee members was Jenkins who served as an independent consultant.

30. Division of Beaches and Parks, *California State Park System. Five Year Program, July 1, 1955 to June 30, 1960,* Approved by the California State Park Commission, November 19, 1954, DPR: 361.1. See also *California State Park System. Five Year Master Plan, July 1, 1956 to June 30, 1961,* March 1, 1956, DPR: 361.1; Engbeck, *State Parks,* pp. 87-88; and Beaches and Parks, *History, Analysis and Recommendations,* p. 32.

31. Engbeck, *State Parks,* pp. 88-90. See also *Five Year Master Plan, July 1, 1956 to June 30, 1961.*

32. Newton B. Drury to Kenneth Chorley, March 29, 1956, Neasham Collection: "History Section, Daily Correspondence." Chorley had made some remarks that Drury agreed with at Cooperstown, New York, in September 1955 in a presentation entitled "What's Wrong with Historic Preservation." The talk was to be reproduced in the division's newsletter with a foreword by Neasham. Neasham's statement was appended to Drury's letter for Chorley to review. The four principles that Drury wanted passed on to his division were:

1. 'To be valid, an historical presentation must center upon a building, object, site, or environment of *substantial* historical or cultural importance.'

2. 'The life blood of historic preservation is research.'

3. 'An historic preservation project must be clear in its purpose, its responsibilities, and its limitations.'

4. 'The value of any historic preservation project is determined by the quality of its presentation and interpretation.'

33. Aubrey Neasham to Newton Drury, "Supplemental Recommendations, Master Program of Acquisition, State Historical Areas," November 20, 1956, DPR: 348.0, p. 2.

34. Aubrey Neasham to Everett Powell, February 4, 1958, Neasham Collection: "History Section, Daily Correspondence;" and Beaches and Parks, *History, Analysis and Recommendations,* pp. 9, 29.

35. Beaches and Parks, *History, Analysis and Recommendations,* pp. 28-29. The critics included legislators, local officials, division staff and historians.

36. *Ibid.,* pp. 33-34; Engbeck, *State Parks,* pp. 91-93. Drury hoped the plan would clarify "the difference between state park responsibilities and those of...other local agencies;" and differentiate "between recreational use of man-made reservoirs...and park-style preservation of natural areas or historic sites...."

37. Lawrence Kinnaird, "Report on California's History, Routes and Sites," Sacramento: California Public Outdoor Recreation Plan Committee, 1960.

38. *Ibid.,* "Summary of Report on Historic Sites in the State of California," pp. 10-18; "Preservation of Critical Historical Areas," p. 11. It suggested that the federal government be responsible for battles during the conquest of California, military installations and federal structures, and historic sites on federal lands such as forests. The state would be responsible for historic events impacting on the entire state or events representing definite eras such as exploration and the gold rush. Local communities would be in charge of events whose impacts did not reach beyond the immediate area.

39. Beaches and Parks, *History, Analysis and Recommendations,* p. 29.

40. *Ibid.,* p. 30.

41. Sacramento *Union,* February 27, 1952; OHP: "Correspondence, Photos, Etc. Re Plaques."

42. J.E. Carpenter to Newton B. Drury, March 6, 1952. *Ibid.*

43. "Minutes," Historical Landmarks Advisory Committee (hereafter abbreviated as HLAC), March 14, 1952. OHP.

44. *Ibid.*, June 20, 1952. The three who attended were Drury, Toothaker, and Wheat. This first edition was published in 1960, and 2,500 copies were printed. See Department of Natural Resources, *California Historical Landmarks* (Sacramento: State of California, 1960).

45. "Minutes," HLAC, June 20, 1952; June 11, 1953; April 17, 1958; December 19, 1958. The larger issue of the site of Drake's disembarkation would be considered in April 1973 and later become the subject of a three-day meeting of the State Historical Resources Commission in October 1978.

46. *Ibid.*, January 23, 1953. The landmark was No. 500.

47. *Ibid.*, March 18, 1954.

48. *Ibid.*, April 17, 1958.

49. *Ibid.*, March 18, 1960. During the 1950s, it was standard practice for the Park Commission to approve landmarks and plaque them before the committee formally granted its approval at a meeting. At their April 1958 meeting in San Francisco, for example, the committee approved landmarks No. 584-639 which had already been officially registered by the Director of Natural Resources. See *ibid.*, April 17, 1958.

50. *Ibid.*, December 10, 1953.

51. *Ibid.*

52. Aubrey Neasham to C.M. Goethe, August 5, 1960, Neasham Collection: "Corporation and Office Records."

53. See "Preservation for Use. An Introduction to Western Heritage Incorporated. Sacramento, California," September 1, 1960; "Western Heritage, Inc., Develops 'Preservation for Use' Program," *History News,* XV (September 1960): 131; "Aubrey Neasham to Head Group to Preserve Heritage Sites....," *News and Views,* September 1960, p. 19. Neasham Collection: "Corporation and Office Records."

54. Aubrey Neasham to Supervisor of Development, July 31, 1958, Neasham Collection: "History Section, Daily Correspondence."

Neasham explained that in 1953, El Pueblo became a state historical monument, and the first of several agreements was signed between the state, the city, and the county to jointly manage the park. The goal of the 1958 master plan, he said, was to develop, maintain, and operate the property

> as a living memorial to the history and tradition of California life and environment, as a part of the State Park System; and to preserve and recreate the Old Pueblo of Los Angeles and the colorful life of that period; and to interpret the story of its founding, growth, and evolution into the Los Angeles of today, with the understanding that in the attainment of these objectives, cultural and economic activities in keeping with the spirit and atmosphere of the old town shall be encouraged.

While he urged the state to cooperate with the city, county, and El Pueblo de Los Angeles, Inc., he stressed that:

> it must not be forgotten, however, that this is a State Historical Monument, acquired and developed largely through State funds. The obligation on our part to maintain our leadership is not lessened by the fact that the City has been designated the agency for management.

55. Newton B. Drury to Clifford Conly, Jr., August 10, 1956. *Ibid.* The letter was written by Neasham for Drury's signature.

56. California Division of Beaches and Parks, *...Report on a Decade,* Sacramento, 1960, DPR: 339.1, pp. 11, 24.

57. *Ibid.*, p. 24.

CHAPTER 5
HISTORY PRESERVATION PROGRAMS IN THE STATE, 1960-1966

1. Engbeck, *State Parks*, pp. 99-100. At the federal level, Congress passed the Wilderness Act and legislation creating a Land and Water Conservation Fund in 1964. From fees charged at recreation areas, the conservation fund would make some $150 million available to states each year for use in park and recreation projects.

2. *Ibid.*, p. 97. See also *Statutes of 1959*, Chapter 2164, in Elder, "Public Resources Code." Section 506 of the *Public Resources Code* now reads: "Except as provided in this section, the Department of Natural Resources, acting through the Division of Beaches and Parks, succeeds to and is vested with all of the powers, duties, purposes, and responsibilities, and jurisdiction vested in the State Park Commission."

3. The Resources Agency, *The Department of Parks and Recreation* (Sacramento, California: Resources Agency, February 1962), courtesy of Sandra Elder, pp. 1-2. The other divisions in the agency were Small Craft Harbors, Recreation, and Administration. The director would be appointed by the governor.

4. Beaches and Parks, *History, Analysis and Recommendations*, pp. 37-38. The report, *Program for California's Beaches and Parks* (January 2, 1961), which was developed by division staff in consultation with the Park Commission, included "a $25 million program of historical restoration and natural history museums and exhibits." It was criticized by the aforementioned *History, Analysis and Recommendations* report because it was "not based upon a comprehensive analysis of Statewide recreational needs or Statewide analysis of natural and historical values." These were the same criticisms leveled against Neasham's plans.

5. Engbeck, *State Parks*, pp. 98-99.

6. Department of Parks and Recreation, *Accelerated Development Program Projecting to 1980 for the California State Park System*, November 1965, DPR: 339.1, pp. 1-3. By the time this report was issued, a $19 million emergency acquisition program approved by the governor and legislature in 1963 for "now or never" lands had added more than 30,553 acres and six new park units, which included Malakoff Diggins State Historic Park. There was now a total of thirty-two historic parks. See also Engbeck, *State Parks*, pp. 100-101, and Beaches and Parks, *History, Analysis and Recommendations*, p. 10. The bond act became Proposition One on the ballot.

7. Department of Parks and Recreation, *California State Park System. 1964 Legislative Requests to Study Potential State Beach, Park, Recreation, and Historical Areas*, May 1964, DPR: 339.1. See also Engbeck, *State Parks*, p. 102.

8. Engbeck, *Ibid.* DeTurk returned to his former position of chief of the Division of Beaches and Parks which had been filled by Ed Dolder. Dolder became special consultant and was later appointed chief deputy to Jones.

9. Parks and Recreation, *Accelerated Development Program*, pp. 3-4.

10. Department of Parks and Recreation and California State Park Commission, *Summaries of Feasibility Studies of Projects Not Included in the 1966 Bond Program*, January 1966, pp. 87-88, 132-133; and letters to Glenn M. Anderson, President, California State Senate, and Jesse M. Unruh, Speaker, California State Assembly, February 7, 1966, n.p. Allen Welts Collection.

11. Engbeck, *State Parks*, p. 103.

12. Division of Beaches and Parks, *A Proposal for A Historical Resources Study. Assembly Concurrent Resolution #25, by Assemblyman Paul J. Lunardi*, by Herbert L. Heinze (Sacramento: Department of Parks and Recreation, June 1962), DPR: "Historical Preservation: Reports," 348.1, p. iv.

13. *Ibid.*

14. The other individuals were: R. Coke Wood, executive secretary of the Conference of California Historical Societies; Frank M. Stanger, Harold Schutt, Stewart Mitchell, and

Walter Frame also from the Conference; Charles DeTurk, director of the Department of Parks and Recreation. The Division of Beaches and Parks was represented by James Warren, deputy chief of Technical Services; John Michael, supervisor of Interpretive Services; Jack Dyson, historian; and Sandra Elder, stenographer.

The advisory committee consisted of: Swift Berry, Placerville; William Whitney, California Historical Society, San Francisco; Margaret Cassidy, Historical Society of Southern California, Los Angeles; Walter Frame, Sacramento; Richard Harville, Eureka; Stewart Mitchell, Sacramento; Martin Ridge, San Diego; Harold Schutt, Lindsay; Frank M. Stanger, Burlingame; and Harold F. Taggart, San Mateo.

The three counties were Siskiyou, Mariposa, and San Diego. By the end of May 1962, they had completed their pilot studies. Mariposa County identified 53 individual sites and structures (27 were in Yosemite National Park), Siskiyou provided 145, and San Diego collected 195. Lassen County Historical Society offered to participate and listed 21 sites. The final total was 414 sites and structures. *Ibid.*, pp. 42-44, 48-50.

15. *Ibid.*, pp. 59-60.

16. *Ibid.*, p. 26.

17. *Ibid.*, pp. vi, 35-38. The six historical periods were identical to Aubrey Neasham's recommendations.

18. *Ibid.*, p. iii.

19. Charles A. DeTurk to Paul Mills, January 17, 1966, DPR: "California Registered Landmarks: Correspondence," 538.0. Mills was curator of the Oakland Museum.

20. "Preface to a Historical Inventory," p. 2, attachment to memo from James P. Tryner to Russell W. Porter, August 18, 1970. DPR: "History Plan-Two: General Correspondence," 348.0.

21. Hugo Fisher to Charles DeTurk, March 25, 1964, DPR: 348.1.

22. Allen W. Welts, interview with author, Sacramento, California, July 20, 1982. See also "resume," Allen W. Welts, DPR: "National Register of Historic Places: General Correspondence," 537.0. Dyson was appointed State Park Historian II in January 1964; on September 24, 1964, he was assigned to the exhibit laboratory. See Jack [Dyson] to Sandra Elder, February 14, 1987, courtesy of Sandra Elder.

23. Division of Beaches and Parks, *History Program for the Division of Beaches and Parks* (Sacramento: Division of Beaches and Parks, April 1965). See "Introduction," n.p. Courtesy of Allen Welts.

24. *Ibid.*

25. DeTurk to Mills, January 17, 1966.

26. Allen W. Welts to Elmer Aldrich, October 18, 1965, DPR: "California Registered Landmarks: Correspondence," 538.0.

27. Division of Beaches and Parks, *State Park System Program for Historical Acquisition and Restoration, 1966-86* (Sacramento: Division of Beaches and Parks, September 30, 1966).

28. *Ibid.*, n.p.

29. *Ibid.*, "Foreword," n.p.

30. Fred L. Jones to Raymond O. Mulvany, November 28, 1966, DPR: 538.0. See also Earl P. Hanson to Fred L. Jones, November 14, 1966, DPR: 538.0.

31. Beaches and Parks, *State Park System Program, 1966-86*, n.p.

32. *Ibid.* Concern for appropriate visitor comforts such as access, parking, and other facilities was also evident in the plan and consistent with the Park Commission's directive in its policy statement of 1964. See State Park Commission, "Statement of Policy," January 1, 1964, and amended in May, July, and August, 1964, p. 4. Courtesy of Sandra Elder.

33. Beaches and Parks, *State Park System Program, 1966-68*, n.p.

34. State Park Commission, "Statement of Policy," 1964, p. 4.

35. Jones to Mulvany, November 28, 1966.

36. Interpretive Services, Division of Beaches and Parks, *Interpretive Guidelines for Historical Restoration,* January 1964, DPR: 511, "Introduction," n.p.

37. "Preface to a Historical Inventory," p. 2.

38. Interpretive Services, *Interpretive Guidelines,* January 1964, "Introduction," n.p.

39. *Ibid.* The duties of the State Park Historian III were listed in the division's 1966 twenty-year plan. They included directing the division's historical interpretive program, planning statewide interpretative programs and recommending policy to the Interpretive Services supervisor, coordinating the division's interpretive program with other departmental programs, and serving as recording secretary for the California Historical Landmarks Advisory Committee. See Beaches and Parks, *State Park System Program, 1966-86,* section on "Staffing," n.p.

40. Division of Beaches and Parks, *Plan for Progress. Field Reorganization* (Sacramento: Division of Beaches and Parks, February 1964). The plan's objective was to create a more decentralized approach to the management of the park system's resources. The Task Force stressed that the mechanics of any program would be handled at the regional level and policy and program development would be the responsibility of the headquarters staff. See pp. 3, 43-44, 64-66. There were also thirty unstaffed units and twenty-seven units administered by local governments.

The idea of regional historians was not a new concept and had been suggested as early as 1957 for the six districts in the park system. The reorganization plan did not materialize. In February 1966 when a guide to the department was issued, it reiterated the continued existence of six district headquarters which were "assisted in the historical and conservation fields by division staff headquartered in Sacramento." See Management Analysis Section, compilers, "Division of Beaches and Parks," in "A Guide to the Organization and Functions of the State of California, Resources Agency, Department of Parks and Recreation," February 1966, n.p.

41. Earl P. Hanson to Charles A. DeTurk, March 24, 1965, DPR: 538.0. The personnel should include a research historian, architectural historian, construction expert, archaeologist, and stenographer.

42. Robert F. Uhte to Elmer Aldrich, September 2, 1965, DPR: 538.0. Each structure would be evaluated on a point system, with those falling below seventy points not given a priority rating.

43. See "Historic Preservation Guidelines" in *ibid.,* pp. 1-3, 5-6. Uhte described ten architectural styles: Spanish Colonial (Mission Period), Mexican Colonial (Hacienda Period), Military (Mission and Gold Rush periods), California Western (Gold Rush and Transition periods), Pioneer Industrial (Gold Rush and Transition periods), Greek Revival (Gold Rush and Transition periods), Victorian (Transition Period), Gothic Revival (Transition Period), Romanesque Renaissance (Transition Period), and California Rustic (Contemporary Period). See pp. 6-7.

44. See Robert F. Uhte, "Historic Preservation Guidelines. Department of Parks and Recreation, Division of Beaches and Parks," June 27, 1966, DPR: 348.1. Also see Uhte to Archie Newsom, August 9, 1965, DPR: "Statewide Interpretation: General Correspondence," 520. Properties were generally acquired as gifts or upon recommendations from a legislator, parks commissioner, private individual or group, or division personnel. If the division staff concurred on the property's importance, they recommended its acquisition to the Park Commission. If approved, funds would be requested from the legislature for both structure and land. Should monies be available, research would be compiled for restoration which was then phased in over several years.

45. Uhte, "Historic Preservation Guidelines," p. 3.

46. Earl P. Hanson to Richard G. Titus, September 30, 1966. DPR: 538.0. The other staff members were one naturalist, one exhibit supervisor, three clerical, and five exhibit specialists or technicians. In the field, there were two naturalists, one historian, several historic guides, and thirty-four summer seasonal naturalists.

47. As of June 1959, the HLAC had met a total of 18 times. One of the committee's early concerns was the question of their role as designated under the terms of Assembly Concurrent Resolution No. 25. After expressing a desire for more information at several meetings in 1961, committee members finally heard a progress report in March 1962, and at their July meeting passed a resolution endorsing the Historical Resources Study proposed by the Historical Interim Study Advisory Committee. See: "Minutes," HLAC, July 7, 1961; December 15, 1961; March 9, 1962; July 27, 1962.

48. "Minutes," HLAC, September 15, 1961, and December 15, 1961. Dyson replaced Neasham in September 1960 as the committee's staff historian. Ridge was professor of History at San Diego State College.

49. "Statement of Policy for State Historical Landmark Registration," "Minutes," HLAC, December 15, 1961.

50. See Elder: OHP for a list of these landmarks. Also, Sandra Elder, interview with author, Redondo Beach, California, November 2, 1984.

51. "Minutes," HLAC, July 7, 1961, and September 15, 1961. By the time the committee met again in September, the Temple Israel Cemetery application had been approved by the director.

52. Charles A. DeTurk to Ray Varley, March 27, 1963. See Reuel Colt Gridley landmark file, OHP. DeTurk further explained that Gridley's contribution of $275,000 for the Sanitary Fund, an early equivalent of the Red Cross, during the Civil War by the sale of auctioned flour had already been recognized by appropriate markers. Furthermore, most of Gridley's efforts had occurred in Nevada, not California. Also, because other famous individuals were buried in the same cemetery and had yet to be honored, DeTurk was "doubtful whether revision of opinion might be expected."

53. Alan Short to Glenn Kennedy, December 2, 1964. *Ibid.*

54. Glenn A. Kennedy to Charles DeTurk, December 11, 1964. *Ibid.*

55. Charles A. DeTurk to Hugo Fisher, December 21, 1964. *Ibid.*

56. Charles DeTurk to Glenn Kennedy, January 18, 1965. *Ibid.* DeTurk's letter contained his regrets over "the impasse which had developed and the lapse of time involved...."

57. "Minutes," HLAC, March 19, 1965.

58. See Reuel Colt Gridley landmark file, OHP.

59. Hanson to Titus, September 30, 1966.

60. "Minutes," HLAC, December 2, 1960. Michael suggested that bronze plaques be put only at important sites, with smaller metal signs on other properties. The committee objected because some "felt this would stimulate hard feelings in local areas...."

61. *Ibid.*, December 15, 1961.

62. *Ibid.*, March 9, 1962.

63. John Michael to James P. Tryner, July 30, 1965, DPR: 538.0. Michael questioned procedures that required property owners to send authorization for landmark registration to the Park Commission and that landmark applications had to be approved by the commission. "It has always seemed strange to me," he said, "that these requests for registration which are handled by the Governor's duly appointed representative, the California Historical Landmarks Advisory Committee, should be part of the State Park Commission's responsibility."

64. "Minutes," HLAC, September 11, 1964.

65. James R. Mills to Martin Ridge, March 23, 1965, DPR: "California Points of Historical Interest: Correspondence," 539.0.

66. Martin Ridge to John [Michael], April 19, 1965. *Ibid.*

67. See A.B. 2166. *Ibid.*

68. "Minutes," HLAC, December 28, 1965.

69. Rough draft of a letter from Fred L. Jones to Chairman, County Board of Supervisors, January 12, 1966, attached to a letter from Richard F. McCarthy to Fred L. Jones, January 12, 1966, DPR: 539.0.

70. John H. Michael to Richard F. McCarthy, January 11, 1966. *Ibid.*

71. "Minutes," HLAC, March 18, 1966. The design was also sent to the San Francisco Art Commission for their opinion.

72. Allen W. Welts to Rudolph J. Israel, April 19, 1966, DPR: 539.0.

73. Richard F. McCarthy to Ileana Welch, January 6, 1967. *Ibid.*

74. John H. Michael to Mr. Chairman, August 26, 1968. *Ibid.* The list of counties responding to his letter was attached to the August 26 correspondence.

75. Earl P. Hanson to Fred L. Jones, August 19, 1965, DPR: 538.0.

76. State Archeological, Historical, and Paleontological Task Force, *The Status of California's Heritage: A Report to the Governor and Legislature of California*, by W.R. Green, *et al.* (Sacramento: State Archeological, Historical, and Paleontological Task Force, September 1, 1973), p. 6. Hereafter abbreviated as AHP Task Force.

77. *Ibid.*, p. 7.

78. California Heritage Preservation Commission, *The Preservation, Organization and Display of California's Historic Documents.* Report to the California State Legislature (Sacramento: California Heritage Preservation Commission, May 25, 1973), p. 3. The commission included legislators appointed by the Speaker of the Assembly and the President pro Tempore of the Senate, knowledgeable private citizens, and representatives of the State Library, Department of Parks and Recreation, the State Archives, the University of California, and the State University and College system.

79. AHP Task Force, p. 6.

CHAPTER 6
PRESERVATION OF THE STATE'S ARCHAEOLOGICAL RESOURCES: A SMALL BEGINNING

1. AHP Task Force, pp. iv, 1-2. The loss of archaeological resources was due to natural causes as well as mining, dredging, urban growth, road and reservoir construction, industrial and recreation developments, agriculture, logging, military activities, off-road vehicles, and other factors.

2. Francis A. Riddell, "The State Administered Archeological Program in California," unpublished paper, c. 1965, p. 1.

3. Clement W. Meighan, "The Preservation of Archaeological Remains in California" (Los Angeles: University of California, June 1960), DPR: "Historical Preservation: Reports," 348.1, pp. 1-2.

4. *Ibid.*, pp. 1, 40. Riddell, who was the state archaeologist for the Division of Beaches and Parks, sent out a questionnaire in the early sixties asking about the status of all known archaeological sites. The returns showed that 390 sites in seventeen counties had been heavily damaged or destroyed. In descending order, the reasons were: land leveling, urban development, reservoir construction, vandalism, highway or road construction, miscellaneous construction, farming, use as fill or other construction material, and railroad construction. See Riddell, "The State Archeological Program," pp. 1-2.

5. Meighan, "Preservation of Archaeological Remains," pp. 1-2. Meighan proposed several solutions: a regional approach to archaeological site conservation instead of attempts to preserve individual sites; "a major campaign of survey and excavation" which would include expansion of existing National Park and state park surveys; and a public education campaign to foster appreciation for archaeological remains. See pp. 39-42.

6. J. Bradley O'Connell, Thomas J. Owen, and Mary Warner, *Historic Preservation in California. A Legal Handbook* (Stanford, California: Stanford Environmental Law Society, 1982), p. 120.

7. These include two common practices: "Avoidance of resources and their preserva-tion in situ is the preferred course of action today. Inquiring about the existence of cultural resources in a project or planning area is one part of cultural resource surveys today." Somers, "Federal Government," pp. 13-14. Also see O'Connell, *et al., Historic Preservation,* p. 121.

8. McGimsey, *Public Archeology,* p. 104.

9. *Ibid.,* pp. 104-105; National Park Service brochure, *Interagency Archeological Program,* 1976. The committee of four was sponsored by the American Council of Learned Societies, the Society for American Archaeology, and the American Anthropological Association.

10. McGimsey, *Public Archeology,* pp. 105, 247-249. The law established procedures for coordinating archaeological investigations and salvage operations when dams were being planned and built by federal agencies. It also specified the responsibilities of all agencies involved in planning and construction and "established the procedure whereby archaeo-logical and historical salvage would be performed in advance of construction activities." Somers, "Federal Government," p. 15. Also see O'Connell, *et al., Historic Preservation,* p. 122.

11. Thomas F. King and Margaret M. Lyneis, "Preservation: A Developing Focus of American Archaeology," *American Anthropologist,* 80 (December 1978): 874.

12. David A. Frederickson and Albert Mohr, "Appraisal of the Archeological Resources of New Melones Reservoir, Calaveras and Tuolumne Counties, California, May 1949." Prepared for the Pacific Coast Division, River Basin Surveys, Smithsonian Institution. Pp. 1, 5.

13. Somers, "Federal Government," pp. 46-49.

14. *Ibid.,* pp. 40-41.

15. *Ibid.,* pp. 32-33, 35, 41.

16. *Ibid.,* p. 41.

17. King and Lyneis, "Preservation," p. 877.

18. AHP Task Force, pp. 10-13.

19. *Public Resources Code,* ch. 1.7, secs. 5097.1 and 5097.5. See Janice Balme, comp., *A Handbook of Federal and State Legislation Affecting Historic Preservation in California,* Vol. II: *State Legislation* (Sacramento: Office of Historic Preservation, 1982), n.p.

20. *Public Resources Code,* ch. 1.7, sec. 5097.2. *Ibid.*

21. *Ibid.,* sec. 5097.3.

22. *Ibid.,* sec. 5097.4; O'Connell, *et al., Historic Preservation,* pp. 128-129.

23. California *Administrative Code,* Title 14, sec. 4307. AHP Task Force, p. 10.

24. California *Administrative Code,* Title 14, sec. 4309. *Ibid.*

25. *Ibid.* Also see Balme, Vol. II: *State Legislation;* and O'Connell, *et al., Historic Preservation,* p. 129.

26. Senate Concurrent Resolution No. 43 in AHP Task Force, p. 10.

27. *Ibid.,* pp. 12-13.

28. McGimsey, *Public Archeology,* p. 109.

29. Alan P. Garfinkel, *An Historical Perspective on the Value of the California Department of Transportation Archaeology Program* (Sacramento: California Department of Transporta-tion, August 1982), pp. 1-2. See also Riddell, "State Archeological Program," pp. 2-4. The committee included the engineer of design and representatives from the Bridge Department and the Bureau of Public Roads. A Department of Parks and Recreation representative presented the case for excavation and salvage.

30. Riddell, *ibid.,* pp. 2-3; also see Garfinkel, *An Historical Perspective,* p. 2.

31. *Ibid.*

32. Garfinkel, *An Historical Perspective*, pp. 3, 19-20.

33. *Ibid.*, pp. 20-21.

34. *Ibid.*, pp. 3, 16. For example, David Frederickson carried out in 1960 "one of the earliest archaeological investigations contracted by Caltrans." This became the foundation of his later doctoral dissertation, "The Early Cultures of the North Coast Ranges, California," University of California, Davis, 1973. See also pp. 30-31, 42.

35. Robert Lee Schuyler, "Anthropological Perspectives in Historical Archaeology" (Unpublished Ph.D. Dissertation, University of California, Santa Barbara, 1975), pp. 108-115.

36. *Ibid.* Examples of cooperative ventures include studies of the Hugo Reid Adobe in Los Angeles under the direction of William J. Wallace of the University of Southern California, and the Vallejo Adobe in Petaluma which was directed by Adan Treganza of San Francisco State College and graduate students from the University of California, Berkeley.

37. *Ibid.*, pp. 115, 118-119. See R.K. Beardsley, "The Monterey Custom House Flagpole: Archaeological Findings," *California Historical Society Quarterly* 25 (1946):204-218. At Fort Humboldt, the Central California Archaeological Foundation under contract to the division explored the entire area, and by determining the site of the flag pole was able to locate the approximate position of the fort's various buildings.

38. Schuyler, "Anthropological Perspectives," pp. 116-117. In the division's files are: William W. Campbell, *Sutter's Fort: Preliminary Report of a Stratigraphic Study,* 1958; C.L. Gebhardt, *Sutter's Fort: A Study in Historical Archaeology with Emphasis on Stratigraphy,* 1958; and William H. Olsen, *Preliminary Reports on the 1959 Archaeological Investigations at Sutter's Fort,* 1959.

39. Schuyler, "Anthropological Perspectives," pp. 122-127.

40. Aubrey Neasham to J.C. Harrington, June 3, 1954, V. Aubrey Neasham Collection: "History Section, Daily Correspondence."

41. Resume, DPR: "National Register of Historic Places: Correspondence," 537.0. Also see Francis A. Riddell, interview with author, Sacramento, California, July 27, 1982, and March 30, 1983.

42. Schuyler, "Anthropological Perspectives," pp. 161-167. Excavated sites included the Indian village at Mission San Juan Bautista (1961), Vallejo's Casa Grande (1960, 1962), Petaluma Adobe (1961, 1962), Los Encinos State Historic Monument (1962), and Fort Humboldt (1966).

One of the most controversial projects was the $43,000 contract given to the Department of Anthropology at the University of California, Davis, for the Old Sacramento salvage effort. Not only was the project itself of great local concern because of the proposed freeway, but many of the archaeologists involved did not stay with the study long enough to produce reports and analyses in a timely fashion. Excavation focused on the 761 brick structures built to replace the 100 buildings lost in the fire of 1852. Retired park historian Neasham was the historical consultant. Also see: Garfinkel, *An Historical Perspective*, Table 1, Item No. 27, n.p.

43. Riddell, "State Archeological Program," pp. 4-5, and "Resume."

44. AHP Task Force, p. 19. These excavations included projects at "Oroville, San Luis, Whalerock, Castaic, Pyramid, Hardluck, Perris, Delta Peripheral Canal, Los Banos, Little Panoche," and "the canal alignment at Buena Vista Lake."

45. *Ibid.*, pp. 19-20.

46. Riddell, "State Archeological Program," pp. 4-5. See also Francis A. Riddell, "State Service Archeology," paper delivered at the Southwest Anthropological Association Conference, Davis, California, April 8, 1966, p. 1.

47. Fred L. Jones to Charles A. DeTurk, October 14, 1965, DPR: "Statewide Interpretation: General Correspondence," 520. The legislation was S.B. 246.

48. Fred L. Jones to Hubert S. Hunter, October 20, 1965, DPR: 520.

49. *Ibid.*

50. Office of Architecture and Construction, Department of General Services, "Notes of Conference," January 20, 1966, DPR: 520.

51. AHP Task Force, pp. 14-15.

52. Heizer had been Riddell's graduate adviser at Berkeley. Riddell completed his B.A. in 1948 and M.A. in 1954 in Anthropology.

53. AHP Task Force, pp. 14-15.

54. "Regional Archaeological Program," 1980. Unpublished draft report, OHP.

55. Meighan, "The Preservation of Archaeological Remains," p. 2.

56. Garfinkel, *An Historical Perspective*, p. 2.

57. Ernestine S. Elster to Heritage Task Force, January 11, 1983.

58. Thomas F. King, "Archeology and Historic Preservation: A Case for Convergence," reprinted from *Social Archeology: Beyond Subsistence and Dating* (New York: Academic Press, 1978), p. 432.

59. *Ibid.*

CHAPTER 7
PRIVATE SECTOR AND LOCAL PRESERVATION:
NEW FACES, NEW METHODS

1. See, for example, "Minutes," HLAC, July 27, 1962, and December 16, 1966. Richard McCarthy (1959-1967) who served as committee chairman was president of the Native Sons. Committee members Henrietta Toothaker (1952-1959) and Eileen Dismuke (1960-1967) were presidents of the Native Daughters. See *A Handbook of Basic Reference Materials for the State Historical Resources Commission*, compiled by Sandra J. Elder (Sacramento: Office of Historic Preservation, June 1982).

2. *Albert Shumate, San Francisco Historian and Catholic Layman*, interview by Ruth Teiser and Catherine Harroun, 1978, (Berkeley: Regional Oral History Office, Bancroft Library, 1981), p. 199. Hereafter abbreviated as Shumate Interview.

3. *Ibid.*, p. 200.

4. The society's interest in state landmarks in the 1930s was mentioned throughout *Historic Spots in California* by Mildred Brooke Hoover, Hero Eugene Rensch, and Ethel Grace Rensch (Stanford, California: Stanford University Press, 1948), revised by Ruth Teiser.

See Shumate Interview, pp. 144-145, 164-166. One of the plaque dedications that Shumate described was the 1957 dedication of the Krug winery. The California Historical Society, then headed by Knowland with Shumate chairing the arrangements committee, sponsored the official state landmark plaque. Shumate attributed his selection as trustee to the successful event. Shumate later chaired the society's landmarks committee. His lengthy tenure as trustee is unique and, as he noted, cannot be repeated by anyone else due to a change in bylaws.

5. Shumate Interview, pp. 165, 173-174. Shumate stated that in Spring 1970, "the trustees went on record as saying that for the next three years they would go into deficit financing, and that after three years they felt that there would be such statewide publicity and acceptance that the membership would be increased and that the prestige of the society would be increased, and that thus the society would be financially better and be a real state historical society." Shumate was adamantly opposed to the deficit budgets because he felt it "unwise spending more money than we're taking in." He lamented: "We were a small society from the rebirth of the society in the 1920s to 1970, but we were slowly growing, owed no money, had acquired a fine piece of property with three buildings, and a truly great library. Now we are a larger society but in debt and our buildings have greatly deteriorated from lack of upkeep."

6. *Ibid.*, pp. 202-203. Shumate had succeeded Harding as president of the California Historical Society.

7. Richard S. Moore to Knox Mellon, July 17, 1980. OHP.

8. Shumate Interview, pp. 202-203.

9. *Ibid.*, pp. 200-201. Shumate, who became a member in 1966, commented: "At one time, I understand, many years ago they were a little bit Anglo-Saxon oriented, and the Mexican-Spanish, while eligible, were not welcomed as members. That is not true now, because a great number of the Pioneers are now in the Pioneers from their Spanish California background." Another change was that the society more readily accepted members without requiring detailed credentials. Shumate noted that the society numbered some one thousand members.

10. *Ibid.*, p. 151. Kenneth M. Castro, comp., *E Clampus Vitus Plaques* (N.p.: E Clampus Vitus, 1981), p. 1. According to Shumate, the idea to revive the Clampers was not a spur-of-the-moment decision but "had been brewing, so to speak in his [Wheat's] head long before that." Shumate Interview, pp. 151-152. In fact, Shumate noted that Wheat was actually mistaken when he claimed there was no Clamper activity between 1900 and 1930. In his research, he had discovered evidence of Clamper activity between 1900 and 1918. See pp. 255-256. See also Hoover, *et al., Historic Spots*, p. 165, which noted: "The society, under the title of E. Clampus Vitus Redivivus, has recently been reorganized by a few members of the California Historical Society who are interested in preserving the lore of '49 and the '50s."

11. Telephone conversation with author, October 14, 1983. Arbuckle was also one of fifteen Clamp Proctors who comprise the Grand Council or executive committee of the organization.

12. Castro, *E Clampus Vitus*, p. 77.

13. H.L. Heinze to Archie Stevenot, April 9, 1962, DPR: "E Clampus Vitus: General Correspondence," 535.0.

14. Archie Stevenot to H.L. Heinze, June 4, 1962, DPR: 535.0. The meeting was held in Murphys, May 26, 1962. To this day, the plaques are still recorded. Conversation with Sandra J. Elder, March 16, 1983, Sacramento, California.

15. Shumate Interview, pp. 151, 154; and Castro, *E Clampus Vitus*, p. 7.

16. AHP Task Force, p. 6. The report observed that there was very little coordination between local historical societies and that they shared little research and information.

17. *Ibid.* It was the task force, in particular, that had mixed feelings about the success of the conference. See also Shumate Interview, pp. 192, 195-197. Shumate noted that materials the conference provided to its members were later adopted by the American Association for State and Local History. He also indicated that some historians were apparently unhappy with the conference, in part, because they felt that it should have been housed in Sacramento under state supervision and not at the University of the Pacific where it is still located. Shumate served as conference president from 1967-1969.

18. Eileen Dismuke to Adriana Gianturco, October 23, 1977, Eileen Dismuke Files. See also Eileen Dismuke interview with author, Santa Barbara, California, August 11, 1982.

19. Ralph N. Kleps to Senator John J. Hollister, November 5, 1958, Dismuke Files.

20. Dismuke to Gianturco, 1977.

21. Ralph Buffon to A.A. Erhart, November 18, 1958, Dismuke Files.

22. Ralph Buffon to Eileen Dismuke, December 9, 1958, Dismuke Files. He enclosed a copy of the association's resolution requesting the legislature to eliminate all references to Highway 101 as the Cabrillo Highway.

23. Eileen Dismuke to Charles Storke, December 29, 1958, Dismuke Files.

24. Dismuke to Gianturco, 1977. The Schrade bill was introduced in 1957 but "pigeon-holed" until 1959. It had limited its applicability to entrances and exits to mission communities along the highway, but this was later expanded "through the cooperation of the Governor's Office through personal consultations we had with him." Dismuke recalled that:

twenty-two of the original bells placed in the 1959 program were bells that had been salvaged by the Automobile Club of Southern California from those bypassed during the freeway construction in the late '30s and early '40s, and it was those bells which were placed at the entrances on the highway to California Mission communities. The new bells, funded by the Committee for El Camino Real, and raised through donations from such organizations as the Native Daughters of the Golden West and other history and civic oriented organizations, were placed at the intervening areas between mission communities.

25. *Ibid.* The state program did not please the committee or Dismuke. Instead of using the metal alloy that the committee had selected, aluminum was chosen along with a new manufacturer. The mold for the bells was also changed. Unlike the bells funded by the committee, the new ones were not cast in the mold of the original 1906 bells. To make matters worse, originally the bells, standards, and signs had been olive green. The state had decided to paint the bells copper and keep the standards green. As late as 1977, these problems were unresolved.

26. Grady Gammage, Jr., Philip N. Jones, and Stephen L. Jones, *Historic Preservation in California. A Legal Handbook* (Stanford, California: Stanford Environmental Law Society, 1975), p. 52.

27. *Ibid.* The statute stated:

The legislative body [of the city] may provide for places, buildings, structures, works of art, and other objects, having a special character or special historical or aesthetic interest or value, special conditions or regulations for their protection, enhancement, perpetuation or use, which may include appropriate and reasonable control of the use or appearance of neighboring property within public view, or both.

See California *Government Code,* sec. 37361. Section 25373 applies to counties and uses the same wording.

28. Gammage, *et al., Historic Preservation,* p. 53. Also see pp. 54-60 for a detailed discussion on legal challenges to historic zoning. Additional information can be found in O'Connell *et al., Historic Preservation,* pp. 31-39; and Charles Mehlert, "The Origin and Use of Aesthetic and Historic Zoning," June 1960, unpublished report, DPR: 511.

29. Allen Welts to Superintendent, District 3, December 2, 1966, DPR: 538.0. The review board's power was confined to "a review of exterior design and construction."

30. Harry W. Brelsford to Architectural Board of Review, November 13, 1953. Courtesy of Mary Louise Days. Brelsford was referring to the *City of New Orleans v. Dan Levy* decision which reaffirmed two earlier opinions. In 1941, the Louisiana Supreme Court had ruled that the New Orleans ordinance applied to alterations that were not visible from the street and that it also applied to all structural exteriors (*City of New Orleans v. Impastato,* 1941). In that same year, the court also ruled that the ordinance applied to all buildings in the district, including those that were not historically significant (*City of New Orleans v. Pergamente,* 1941). The Levy case upheld these two rulings and restated the view that "commercial advantages derived warranted the imposing of restrictions under the police power" of the government to enact laws to protect the health, morals, safety, and welfare of its citizens. See Mehlert, "Aesthetic and Historic Zoning," pp. 8-11; and Gammage *et al., Historic Preservation,* p. 56.

31. The Levy decision reaffirmed the opinion that "this particular architectural control was a proper exercise of the police power." Furthermore, the preservation of the Vieux Carre benefited not only the inhabitants of the city because of its sentimental value, but its commercial importance was equally beneficial. See Brelsford to Architectural Board of Review, November 13, 1953.

32. *Ibid.*

33. "Preservation Legislation Important to Santa Barbara and California," n.d. Courtesy of Mary Louise Days.

34. "Resolution No. 4125. Resolution of the City of Santa Barbara Creating the Santa Barbara Advisory Landmark Committee, May 10, 1960." Courtesy of Mary Louise Days.

35. "Preservation Legislation Important to Santa Barbara and California."

36. *Ibid.*

37. Gammage, *et al., Historic Preservation,* p. 72. Proposition 11 required a state constitutional amendment because the constitution required "uniform taxation of property on the basis of the fair market value."

38. John Pope, "Historic Preservation in Los Angeles-A Critique of the Cultural Heritage Board" (Unpublished student paper, June 1, 1977), p. 3, and "Appendix B," p. 1.

39. By this time, the A.I.A. had begun a preservation program at the national level "to meet the menace of destruction and mutilation faced everywhere by our historic buildings" with the cooperation of the National Park Service, the National Trust for Historic Preservation, and the Society of Architectural Historians. Their collective goal was to record and protect buildings through public education "in advance of menace." See description of meeting of May 15, 1958, in Los Angeles, California, in William Woollett Files.

40. Those present at the meeting included Ed Ainsworth of the Los Angeles *Times*; Gustave Arlt, dean of the Graduate Division at UCLA and president of the Historical Society of Southern California; Milton Brievogel, County Planning Department; Averill M. Chapman, Los Angeles City Board of Education; William H. Claire, Community Redevelopment Agency; D.J. Frierman, president, Society of Architectural Historians; Arthur Gallion, dean of the School of Architecture at the University of Southern California (USC); Theodore S. Peck, Jr., art historian from USC; Ray S. Marvin, president of the City Planning Commission; Glen Price, historian from the Division of Beaches and Parks; Rufus Von Kleinschmidt, chancellor, USC; J.S. Putnam, vice president of Security First National Bank; and six local architects. *Ibid.*

41. See William Woollett, "Remarks" before the City Council of Los Angeles, January 15, 1962.

42. Kenneth Ross to William Woollett, November 13, 1961. William Woollett Files.

According to architect Raymond Girvigian, he engineered the successful adoption of Woollett's ordinance:

> After months of intensive effort, he [Woollett] became ill and I continued on with this task alone as acting Chairman of the [Historical Buildings] Committee, eventually co-authoring the ordinance and assisting its passage through City Hall. Not only was it a local turning point in the preservation movement in those days, but it also focused national attention on Los Angeles. For the first time, a major urban entity in this country had adopted a preservation ordinance that covered the entire city, rather than on a limited, district basis.

Girvigian also noted:

> On the first day of business in August of 1961, with Chairman Woollett presiding, I submitted the first six landmarks to the newly formed Cultural Heritage Board, all of which were threatened in some way. But the one in most danger was the Leonis Adobe in the Calabasas district of the city, whose site was already in the process of being demolished for a supermarket parking lot. Within hours the stop work order had been hand carried through the various agencies of City Hall and the demolition stopped, the site was saved. The non-profit foundation which I co-founded with others, eventually restored the landmark, which is now opened as a living museum. This was to be my first technical restoration experience.

See "A Personal and Professional VITA of Raymond Girvigian, F.A.I.A.," January 1982, p. 2; and interview with author, September 8, 1982, Sacramento, California.

43. "L.A. Landmark Board Proposed by Yorty," Los Angeles *Times*, December 8, 1961. William Woollett Files.

44. Woollett, "Remarks" before the City Council, 1962.

45. Woollett, "That the Past Shall Live" (paper presented to the Fourth Annual Southern California Symposium of the Conference of California Historical Societies, Santa Ana, California, February 10, 1962). The criteria stated that a cultural or historical monument was one which reflected "the broad cultural, political, economic, or social history of the nation, state or community;" was "identified with historic personages or with important events in the main currents of national, state, or local history;" or embodied "the distinguishing characteristics of an architectural-type specimen, inherently valuable for a study of a period style or method of construction, or a notable work of a master builder, designer or architect whose individual genius influenced his age." See Pope, "Historic Preservation," "Appendix B," p. 2.

46. Pope, "Historic Preservation," p. 4 and "Appendix B," p. 2. When the Department of Building and Safety, which issued building or demolition permits, received four copies of the board's designation, it "red flagged" the address of the monument on its books so that when a permit request was received, it would know that an additional step was required.

47. *Ibid.*, p. 5.

48. *Ibid.*, pp. 5-6. Also see "Historic-Cultural Monuments as Designated by the Cultural Heritage Board, City of Los Angeles," October 1980. The board failed with a residence in Boyle Heights which was vandalized and demolished after plans to relocate it collapsed. See also Ileana Welch, interview with author, Los Angeles, California, April 19, 1982; and "Cultural Heritage Board," 4-82, courtesy of Ileana Welch.

49. Pope, "Historic Preservation," pp. 3-4. By 1980, the board had designated a total of 229 cultural and historical monuments. See Peggy Rinard, "Heritage Board Guards Legacy," Los Angeles *Times*, February 17, 1980.

50. *Ibid.*, pp. 9-10. Pope noted that several California court decisions, especially *Bohannon v. City of San Diego* (1973), ruled that historic preservation was constitutionally permissible "if it is intended to contribute to the general and economic welfare of the city." Santa Barbara's initial ordinance was similarly vague. In 1977, the city's municipal code was changed to include this objective. See also Gammage *et al., Historic Preservation.*, pp. 57-60.

51. Ileana Welch, interview with author, April 19, 1982.

52. Woollett, "Remarks" before the City Council, 1962.

53. Woollett, "That the Past Shall Live." Also see William Woollett, "Los Angeles Landmarks" (Remarks to the National Trust for Historic Preservation, ca. July-August, 1966). The board would provide information and guidance regarding historic preservation concerns, promote appreciation for historic and cultural events, and encourage businesses and private individuals to purchase and restore properties. He also hoped the board, through its support of educational programs which emphasized the importance of historic architecture, would assume many of the time-consuming duties and out-of-pocket expenses of his A.I.A. preservation committee. The ordinance permitted the board to provide various city departments with lists of historic buildings and participate in public functions and publicity campaigns.

54. Pope, "Historic Preservation," pp. 56-62. In 1977, for example, the board's total budget for salaries, printing, mailing, and project costs was a mere $26,800. Pope noted that Los Angeles had the smallest preservation board budget when compared to that of Chicago, Indianapolis, Louisville, New Orleans, New York, and Portland. Again, Los Angeles ranked last in dollars allocated to historic preservation per million dollars in comparison to San Francisco, San Diego, Santa Barbara, Pasadena and Sacramento.

Although the grant application process was complicated and burdensome, other cities had successfully secured support. Los Angeles had attempted only one grant application thus far. Pope concluded that this fact demonstrated that "this and past Boards have not been sufficiently committed to the need for such funds. Only by seeking outside sources of funding can the Board overcome the underbudgeting and its resulting problems."

55. *Ibid.*, pp. 63-64. In 1968, the board with the assistance of Home Savings was able to print and distribute 50,000 booklets dealing with historic preservation; as of 1977, no similar project enlisting private support had been undertaken.

56. It should be emphasized that the landmark commission, or in this specific instance the Cultural Heritage Board, differs from a historic district review board in several ways. A landmark commission can designate landmarks anywhere in the city, but the historic district review board is limited to a specific area in the city or county. The landmark commission also deals with the historic or architectural merits of individual structures and sites, whereas the district review board regulates both historic and nonconforming structures within the district. See Gammage *et al.*, *Historic Preservation*, p. 63.

After July 1, 1980, the board had to obtain the approval of the city council before a property could be declared a Historic-Cultural Monument. As advisers to the Cultural Affairs Commission, the board needed its approval to suspend permits. See "Cultural Affairs Board," 4-82, courtesy of Ileana Welch.

57. Gammage, *et al.*, *Historic Preservation*, pp. 64-65, 115. Landmark commissions could legally be given power to prohibit demolition of structures. The commission's limitations are only those imposed on it by the city council "based on the sense of community and legal opinion of the city attorney....The limitations placed on local commissions are the result of either political considerations or the erroneous belief that stronger ordinances cannot be legally justified." See also Ileana Welch, interview with author, April 19, 1982.

58. Beaches and Parks, *A Proposal for A Historical Resources Study*, p. 33.

59. Allen Welts to Superintendent, District 3, December 2, 1966, DPR: 538.0.

60. Ileana Welch, interview with author, April 19, 1982; William Woollett, interview with author, Santa Barbara, California, August 10, 1982.

61. Ileana Welch, interview with author, April 19, 1982.

62. See "Cultural Affairs Board," 4-82, and Los Angeles Administrative Code, "Cultural Heritage Board," per Ordinance 153,893, Operative on July 1, 1980. Both courtesy of Ileana Welch. By 1980, the board had become advisers to the Cultural Affairs Commission and required its approval to suspend permits.

63. Ileana Welch, interview with author, April 19, 1982.

64. See "Ordinance No. 152,422," approved May 15, 1979, courtesy of Ileana Welch.

65. Larry Gordon, "Gingerbread or Stucco? City's First Historic Preservation Zone is Put to the Test," Los Angeles *Times*, June 23, 1985.

66. For an excellent description of the Old Sacramento project, see Robin Elisabeth Datel, "Historic Preservation and Neighborhood Change in Sacramento, California" (Unpublished Master's Thesis, University of Minnesota, 1978), pp. 23-44. Datel concluded that one reason for the absence of an active advocacy group was the city's emphasis on other issues such as agriculture, business, and government. In addition, "members of the design professions... were not especially attracted to Sacramento." There was also, perhaps, "an inferiority complex derived from being in the shadow of San Francisco."

67. *Ibid.*, pp. 48-51. Datel observed that "arguments in favor of Old Sacramento centered on cultural memory and economic gain." See p. 60.

68. Carroll D. Hall, *Old Sacramento. A Report on Its Significance to the City, State and Nation, with Recommendations for the Preservation and Use of Its Principal Historical Structures and Sites* (Sacramento: Division of Beaches and Parks, 1958), Part I, p. 9. Hall recommended that Sutter's Embarcadero fronting the river be added to the project area.

69. *Ibid.*, pp. 10-11, 15-16. The estimates excluded State Office Building No. 1 which would be acquired only when it was no longer needed for office space.

70. Datel, "Historic Preservation," pp. 51-55. In the end, the freeway was built between Second and Third Streets, a better alternative than the riverfront plan which would have cut the commercial district off from the river.

71. *Ibid.*, p. 52. The landmark commission's request for an 18-month time period for permit delay was rejected in favor of a mere 90 days, although the council extended the period many times. A month before the council acted on the ordinance, the city's Redevelopment Agency finally volunteered to be responsible for encouraging the private sector to participate in the preservation of Old Sacramento.

72. This concept was reflected in the title of Aubrey Neasham's publication for the Sacramento Historical Landmarks Commission and the city's Redevelopment Agency in 1965: *Old Sacramento. A Reference Point in Time.* The monograph justified Old Sacramento's commemoration of the early gold rush years to 1880, to the exclusion of other dimensions. In 1965, Neasham was the commission's historical consultant.

73. Datel, "Historic Preservation," pp. 58-60.

74. The consulting firm of Candeub, Fleissig and Associates completed their report in 1964. It was titled *Old Sacramento Historic Area and Riverfront Park* and was quoted in *Old Sacramento State Historic Park Study. Requested by House Resolution No. 91, Statutes of 1964* (Sacramento: Division of Beaches and Parks, March 1965), pp. 7-8.

75. In 1964, the division updated the 1958 Hall study. See *Progress Report on Planning for the Historic Restoration of Old Sacramento. Requested by Assembly Concurrent Resolution No. 53, Chapter 117, Statutes of 1963* (Sacramento: Division of Beaches and Parks, May 4, 1964), pp. 3-4.

76. *Old Sacramento State Historic Park Study,* March 1965, pp. 1-4.

77. *Ibid.*, p. 5.

78. Datel, "Historic Preservation," p. 61.

79. *Ibid.*, pp. 63-66; also *Old Sacramento State Historic Park Study,* March 1965, p. 7.

80. Neasham, *Old Sacramento,* p. 19.

81. Datel, "Historic Preservation," pp. 64-65. Tax increment funding refers to freezing the tax base of a project when renewal programs begin. Until the project is completed, revenues are frozen at this level. Improvements generate tax increments which are then used by the renewal agency to reinvest in the area and "to secure the sale of tax allocation bonds to help pay for the project."

82. *Ibid.*, pp. 56-57.

83. *Ibid.*, pp. 92-93. The criteria used for the inventory have since vanished. The compilation also omitted addresses west of 10th Street. Datel speculated that this "reflects the unwillingness on the part of the Planning Department to identify significant structures located in the territory of the Redevelopment Agency, who later would have to tear the structures down." Seventy-nine of the buildings had been demolished by 1972.

84. One of these publications was produced by the Sacramento Branch of the American Association of University Women, *Vanishing Victorians* (1973). It demonstrated that the city had a significant architectural heritage to protect. For an account of the AAUW project, see Paula Boghosian, "Saving Historic Homes: Research, Identification and Publicity," *California Historian,* 20 (March 1974): 24, 28. Another catalyst was the abortive campaign to save the Alhambra Theater which had been a local landmark since 1927. The fight to prevent its replacement by a Safeway supermarket in 1972-1973 forced disparate groups to discuss preservation and adaptive re-use issues. See Datel, "Historic Preservation," pp. 160-166. The memory of the Alhambra Theater lingers on. On February 26, 1983, for example, the Sacramento *Bee* ran an article by Katherine Knight in which the adaptive re-use question was raised again: "It was probably the lack of a productive use that cost Sacramento its most impressive movie theater—the Alhambra, an Art Deco masterpiece (complete with foundations)...." Former city councilman John Roberts and others "believe the shock of losing the Alhambra may have been what opened Sacramento's eyes to the need for preserving its historic structures." See Knight, "New Life for Old Theaters," Sacramento *Bee*, February 26, 1983. That Roberts was probably correct was underscored by the fact that by the end of 1973, both the city

council and planning commission took steps to prepare a comprehensive preservation program for the city. An interim demolition ordinance was prepared and in March 1974, the council appointed the Historical Structures Advisory Committee to develop the plan. The committee's four arguments supporting preservation were included in the ordinance: cultural memory, environmental diversity, economic gain, and neighborhood stability. See "Sacramento Old City. A Preservation Program," revised, n.a., n.p., August 1976, pp. 1-3; and Datel, "Historic Preservation," pp. 167-192 for details on the ordinance.

85. Roger Olmsted and T.H. Watkins, *Here Today. San Francisco's Architectural Heritage* (San Francisco: Junior League of San Francisco, Inc., 1968), p. viii.

86. *Ibid.*, pp. viii-ix.

87. *Ibid.*, p. xi.

88. Ralph A. Meade to Allen W. Welts, April 24, 1970, DPR: "National Register of Historic Places: General Correspondence," 537.0.

89. Shumate Interview, p. 212.

90. Mary M. Friman to Sandra J. Elder, September 21, 1982, OHP: Elder.

CHAPTER 8
THE FEDERAL PRESENCE IN CALIFORNIA: AN ERA OF LIMITED CONCERNS

1. *With Heritage So Rich*, A Report of a Special Committee on Historic Preservation, under the auspices of the United States Conference of Mayors with a grant from the Ford Foundation, Albert Rains, Chairman (New York: Random House, 1966), p. 204.

2. National Park Service, *The National Survey of Historic Sites and Buildings* (Washington, D.C.: Government Printing Office, 1959), n.p.

3. *Ibid.*

4. National Park Service, *Your National Parks. A Brief History* (Washington, D.C.: Government Printing Office, n.d.). Courtesy of Thomas Mulhern.

5. National Park Service, *National Survey*, 1959, n.p.

6. National Park Service, *A National Program for the Conservation of Historic Sites and Buildings* (Washington, D.C.: Government Printing Office, n.d.). Includes a list of sites declared eligible through December 31, 1963. N.p.

7. National Park Service, *Sites Eligible for the Registry of National Landmarks. A Program to Promote the Conservation of Sites of Historical and Scientific Significance* (Washington, D.C.: Government Printing Office, n.d.). Sites declared eligible through January 31, 1965 included: Big and Little Petroglyph Canyons, Inyo County; First Pacific Coast Salmon Cannery, Sacramento County; Gunther Island Site 67, Eureka; Lake Merritt Wild Duck Refuge in downtown Oakland; Lower Klamath National Wildlife Refuge, Siskiyou County; Frank Norris Cabin, Santa Clara County; and San Francisco Cable Cars.

8. The National Monuments program was established by the Antiquities Act of 1906. See National Park Service, *Your National Parks*, n.p.; National Park Service, *Index. National Park System and Related Areas as of June 30, 1979* (n.p., n.d.), courtesy of Thomas Mulhern; and Chapter 6.

9. John A. Hussey to author, February 11, 1983.

10. See, for example, the following: *Ruins Stabilization*, Volume 23, of the *National Park Service Administrative Manual* (Washington, D.C.: National Park Service, 1949); *Handbook for Ruins Stabilization, Part 2: Field Methods*, (Washington, D.C.: National Park Service, 1962); and *Historic and Prehistoric Structures Handbook* (Washington, D.C.: National Park Service, 1963).

11. National Park Service, *National Survey*, 1959, n.p.

12. Horace M. Albright, interview with author, Los Angeles, California, February 16, 1983.

13. Among the many existing publications on the National Trust are: Hosmer, *Preservation Comes of Age*, especially Chapter 10, pp. 809-865; David E. Finley, *History of the National Trust for Historic Preservation, 1947-1963* (Washington, D.C.: National Trust for Historic Preservation, 1965); and Elizabeth D. Mulloy, *The History of the National Trust for Historic Preservation, 1963-1973* (Washington, D.C.: The Preservation Press, 1976).

14. National Trust for Historic Preservation, *Goals and Programs. A Summary of the Study Committee to the Board of Trustees of the National Trust for Historic Preservation*, Chaired by Robertson E. Collins (Washington, D.C.: The National Trust for Historic Preservation, September 1973), p. 8. Rath served as executive director between 1950 and 1956.

15. National Trust for Historic Preservation, *Members and Member Organizations of the National Trust for Historic Preservation* (Washington, D.C.: The National Trust for Historic Preservation, January 1956), pp. 7, 11.

16. Aubrey Neasham, "Criteria for Evaluating Historic Sites and Buildings," *News and Views*, 13 (September 1, 1956): 8-9. Also see National Trust for Historic Preservation, "Criteria for Evaluating Historic Sites and Buildings," A Report by the Committee on Standards and Surveys (Washington, D.C.: National Trust for Historic Preservation, May 1956).

17. National Trust, *Goals and Programs*, p. 9. Also see National Trust for Historic Preservation, *Annual Report*, 1960, p. 11; and 1962, p. 1.

18. *With Heritage So Rich*, p. 207.

19. *Ibid.*, pp. 207-208.

20. Somers, "Federal Government," p. 16. Also see *With Heritage So Rich*, pp. ix-x.

21. *With Heritage So Rich*, p. 208.

CHAPTER 9
LEGISLATIVE FOUNDATIONS: CORNERSTONES FOR A NEW ERA

1. *With Heritage So Rich*, A Report of a Special Committee on Historic Preservation, under the auspices of the United States Conference of Mayors with a grant from the Ford Foundation, Albert Rains, Chairman (New York: Random House, 1966).

2. O'Connell, *et al.*, *Historic Preservation*, pp. 11-12.

3. Public Law 89-665, 80 Stat. 915 (1966).

4. *Ibid.*, sec. 101. For a recent update of the National Historic Preservation Act, see: Barry Mackintosh, *The National Historic Preservation Act and the National Park Service. A History* (Washington, D.C.: National Park Service, 1986); and *The Secretary of the Interior's 20th Anniversary Report on the National Historic Preservation Act* (Washington, D.C.: Government Printing Office, 1986).

5. Louis S. Wall, interview with author, Riverside, California, September 26 and 28, 1982. Wall was chief of the Western Division of Project Review of the Advisory Council on Historic Preservation at the time of the interview. He has since retired from that post.

The Advisory Council was composed of seventeen members, including the secretaries of the Interior, Housing and Urban Development, Commerce, and Treasury; the administrator of the General Services Administration; the attorney general; the chairman of the National Trust, and ten presidential appointees from outside the federal government. Their duties included advising the president and Congress on historic preservation matters, recommending ways to coordinate preservation activities among private and public sectors, encouraging preservation projects and education, and recommending studies pertaining to historic preservation. See *ibid.*, Title II.

6. Public Law 89-665, 80 Stat. 917 (1966), Sec.106.

7. Somers, "Federal Government," pp. 16-17.

8. The Trust's Annual Report "noted in passing that the Trust not only had a major role in framing the Historic Preservation Act, but it has also provided the key personnel to

implement the Park Service responsibilities under the Act." National Trust for Historic Preservation, *Annual Report*, 1966-1967, p. 3.

9. It was the 1966 law that created the Federal Highway Administration. Somers, "Federal Government," p. 48. For an evaluation of the FHA's efforts, see Somers, pp. 46-50.

10. *Department of Transportation Act of 1966*, 49 U.S.C. sec. 1653 4 (f).

11. Somers, "Federal Government," p. 49. The decision was known as *Overton Park* (1971). Section 4(f) was amended by the Federal Highway Aid Act of 1968 but was not notably altered.

12. Public Law 91-190, 83 Stat. 852 (1970), sec. 101 (b).

13. *Ibid.*, sec. 2; and Somers, "Federal Government," p. 18.

14. P.L. 91-190, 83 Stat. 852 (1970), sec. 102 (c). Also, O'Connell, *et al., Historic Preservation*, p. 81.

15. Executive Order 11593, May 13, 1971, *Federal Register*, Vol. 36, No. 95, May 15, 1971, as reprinted in Janice Balme, comp., *A Handbook of Federal and State Legislation Affecting Preservation in California*. Volume I: *Federal Legislation* (Sacramento: OHP, 1982), n.p. See also, King, "Archeology and Historic Preservation," p. 433.

16. O'Connell, *et al., Historic Preservation*, pp. 81-82.

17. *Archaeological and Historic Preservation Act of 1974*. "Statement of Program Approach." *Federal Register*, Vol. 44, No. 59, March 26, 1979, p. 18118. Also see P.L. 93-291, 88 Stat. 174-176. The act is also known as the Moss-Bennett Amendment to the Reservoir Salvage Act.

18. O'Connell, *et al., Historic Preservation*, p. 126.

19. *Ibid.* Thomas King, once a supporter of the law, saw it in 1978 as another salvage statute, "reflecting a traditional archeological approach to the increasingly widespread federally assisted destruction of cultural resources." King, "Archeology and Historic Preservation," p. 433.

20. *Archeological and Historical Preservation Act of 1974*, p. 18118.

21. Interagency Archeological Services Division, "A Status Report to the Archeological Community," March 1976, p. 1. IAS described themselves as "a prominent member of the Office of Archeology and Historic Preservation."

22. Advisory Council on Historic Preservation, "Issues in Archeology," *Report*, V (March-April-May 1977), Part II: "Report Prepared for the Meeting of the Chairman's Task Force on Archeology" (January 24, 1977), p. 74.

23. Mackintosh, *The National Historic Preservation Act*, pp. 14-19. In 1981, HCRS's five historic preservation units were put under the supervision of Jerry Rogers: National Register, State Plans and Grants, Interagency Archeological Services, National Architectural and Engineering Record, and Technical Preservation Services. Also see Somers, "Historic Preservation," pp. 53-55. HCRS's responsibilities also included the National Landmarks program and the Office of Archeology and Historic Preservation. The latter office handled the National Register of Historic Places, the Grants-in-Aid Program, Interagency Archeological Services, Technical Preservation Services, the Historic American Building Survey, the Historic American Engineering Record, and the Historic Site Survey.

24. Quoted in National Trust for Historic Preservation, *Annual Report, 1966-1967*, pp. 1, 4.

25. *Urban Mass Transportation Assistance Act of 1970*, 49 U.S.C. sec. 1610.

26. P.L. 92-362, 86 Stat. 503, sec. 203; and P.L. 93-383 (August 22, 1974), in Balme, Vol. I, *Federal Legislation*. See also Gammage, *et al., Historic Preservation*, p. 25.

27. Title II, *National Historic Preservation Fund of the Land and Water Conservation Fund of 1976*, P.L. 94-422, 90 Stat. 1319 (1976). Also see Somers, "Historic Preservation," p. 20.

28. P.L. 94-422, 90 Stat. 1320-1322 (1976). Also see Somers, "Historic Preservation," pp. 20-21.

29. O'Connell, *et al., Historic Preservation*, pp. 56-59. See Chapter 5, pp. 56-78 for a concise summary of various recent tax incentives. Also see Public Law 94-455, 90 Stat. 1916-19, Tax Reform Act of 1976; and National Register of Historic Places, "Historic Preservation and the Tax Reform Act of 1976," October 26, 1976. With the exception of the section on charitable contributions, all preservation-related items were scheduled to last until 1981.

30. See O'Connell, *et al., Historic Preservation*, pp. 60-69, for specifics. Also, National Trust for Historic Preservation, "Summary of Preservation Tax Incentives in the Economic Recovery Tax Act of 1981," from "Preservation Alert," August 17, 1981, in Balme, Vol. I, *Federal Legislation; and National Historic Preservation Act Amendments of 1980*, P.L. 96-515, 94 Stat. 2989-90.

31. Advisory Council on Historic Preservation, *Report to the President and the Congress of the United States, 1981* (Washington, D.C.: U.S. Government Printing Office, 1982), pp. 26, 28.

32. See Gregory Gordon, "Turnabout Trend. Middle-Class Whites Return To Cities," *Sacramento Bee*, November 20, 1977; Vernon E. Jordan, Jr., "Pushing Out the Urban Poor. Revitalization is Devitalization," *Los Angeles Times*, January 17, 1979; and David Blum, "My Turn: The Evils of Gentrification," *Newsweek*, January 3, 1983, p. 7. Also see O'Connell, *et al., Historic Preservation*, pp. 7-9, and Chapter 7, "Historic Preservation and Urban Revitalization," pp. 108-119. O'Connell and his co-authors point out that although most studies agree that "crucial" shifts have occurred in "race, age, family size, and type of tenancy" in the revitalized neighborhoods, these "are considered incidental to changes in socio-economic status." They agreed that "the social significance of 'revitalization,' however, is entirely dependent upon whether the transformations result from the replacement of poor residents with more affluent residents or from improvements in the existing residents' standards of living." They further concluded that existing data showed that the usual result of "revitalization" was the displacement of the poor. The controversy has also reflected differing definitions of displacement. For example, in a 1979 study, the Advisory Council on Historic Preservation found little evidence of displacement in two of the four cities it had studied "because it classified the removal of transients and vagrants as displacement of 'undesirable uses rather than of people.' The study involved no inquiry about how long the affected individuals (i.e., the 'transients') had lived in the neighborhoods." See pp. 115, 118.

33. *California Environmental Quality Act of 1970* as quoted in California *Public Resources Code*, secs. 21064, 21002.1 (West 1977); see also O'Connell, *et al., Historic Preservation*, pp. 98-105 for a discussion of CEQA's intent and application.

34. California *Public Resources Code*, sec. 21001 (b) (West 1977).

35. *Ibid.*, sec. 21060.5.

36. O'Connell, *et al., Historic Preservation*, pp. 75-78. See also California *Government Code*, secs. 50280-50290 (West Supp. 1981).

37. Bion M. Gregory to Senator James Mills, July 25, 1977, Raymond Girvigian Files. Also see O'Connell, *et al., Historic Preservation*, pp. 73, 76-77. The cancellation penalty of 12.5 percent "of the full value of the property at the time of cancellation" was added in 1978. See sec. 50286.

38. Gregory to Mills, July 25, 1977. Mills introduced legislation to make the necessary changes in the 1972 statutes. See also: California Heritage Task Force, *A Report to the Legislature and People of California* (Sacramento: August 1984), pp. 56-57. The Task Force's report stated: "Since its passage in 1972 fewer than six property owners in California have taken advantage of its provisions." In 1985, the legislature passed A.B. 2104 which simplified some of the existing requirements and shortened the contract period to ten years. See Heritage Action Steering Committee, "Current Status of 1985 Legislation," July 4, 1985, p. 2; and Hisashi B. Sugaya to Members of the Board, California Preservation Foundation, "Legislative Committee Report," November 1985.

39. O'Connell, *et al., Historic Preservation*, pp. 77-78.

40. Engbeck, *State Parks*, pp. 118-119. The campaign for Proposition One was led by *Sunset Magazine* publisher Bill Lane. Other effective campaigners included Department Director William Penn Mott, Jr., and Governor Ronald Reagan. Also see Chapter 1.6, "State Beach, Park, Recreational, and Historical Facilities Bond Act of 1964," and Chapter 1.67, "State Beach, Park, Recreational and Historical Facilities Bond Act of 1974," of the *Public Resources Code* in Department of Parks and Recreation, *Policies, Rules, Regulations, and Orders of the California State Park and Recreation Commission and the Department of Parks and Recreation*, December 1978, pp. 134-157.

41. Chapter 1.67, *ibid.*, sec. 5096.72, p. 145.

42. *Ibid.*, sec. 5096.85, pp. 149-150.

43. *Ibid.*, sec. 5096.97, p. 156. Section 5096.90 identified "deficiencies in history" as one of three priority needs to be considered when projects were reviewed. The other two were deficiencies in preserving scenery and landscape and providing recreation. Pp. 153-154.

44. Chapter 1.6, *ibid.*, sec. 5096.28, pp. 144-145.

45. Additions to the Public Resources Code that changed the responsibilities of the State Historic Landmarks Advisory Committee are discussed in Chapter 12.

46. See Gammage, *et al.*, *Historic Preservation*, pp. 91-95; and O'Connell, *et al.*, *Historic Preservation*, p. 135.

47. Roger Scharmer, "Historic Preservation-A Planning Opportunity," unpublished paper submitted for presentation at "Confer—In '74," n.d. The A.I.P's national policy stated:

> HISTORIC PRESERVATION ELEMENT. To preserve our historical and cultural past, state planning enabling legislation should require that each state and local general plan have an historical preservation element. This element should set inventories and priorities of historical and cultural significance to be preserved through planning for the future. This should reflect the concept of equal opportunity and preserve the unique pasts of all groups.

See Scharmer, p. 2. At the time he wrote the article, Scharmer was Community Development Specialist, California Department of Housing and Community Development.

48. S.B. 2309, California *Statutes of 1974*, ch. 1267; California *Government Code*, sec. 65303 (j), DPR: 530.0.

49. State of California, Office of Planning and Research, *Historic Preservation Element Guidelines* (Sacramento: Office of Planning and Research, September 1976). Historic preservation elements were adopted by Santa Clara County in 1973 and still earlier, Monterey County in 1968. See Gammage, *et al.*, *Historic Preservation*, pp. 92-93.

50. Roger Scharmer to Kathryn Kaiser, April 19, 1974. DPR: 530. Although Scharmer was unable to attend the committee meeting, his request for support was granted, and the committee transmitted their decision directly to Senator Behr. See John H. Michael to Peter H. Behr, May 19, 1974. *Ibid.*

51. Roger Scharmer to author, November 16, 1982. Scharmer was recognized by the Sacramento Valley A.I.P. Section with its 1974 Section Award for Legislation. See Janet M. Ruggiero to Roger Scharmer, April 9, 1975, courtesy of Roger Scharmer.

52. California *Health and Safety Code*, secs. 37601 and 37620, cited in Balme, Vol. II: *State Legislation*, n.p.

53. "Historical Preface," p. 8-3; and "Explanatory Note," p. 8-2, Title 24, "Building Standards," Part 8, "State Historical Building Code," California *Administrative Code, California Administrative Register* 79, No. 34-B, August 25, 1979, Sacramento: Department of General Services, Office of Administrative Hearings. See also O'Connell, *et al.*, *Historic Preservation*, pp. 146-147. Details on efforts to obtain passage of the code by the State Legislature are discussed in a later chapter.

54. California Heritage Task Force, 1984, p. 46.

55. See Senate Bill No. 2321 in Sandra J. Elder to Past and Present Members and Staff, State Historical Resources Commission, October 26, 1984. Also see California Preservation Foundation, "Status Report. California Heritage Task Force Recommendations. April 1986," n.p.

56. See Executive Order B-64-80 and Senate Bill No. 1652, OHP. Additions were made to Sections 5024 and 5024.5 of the Public Resources Code. The state historic preservation officer was also to maintain a master list of all inventoried resources that were determined to be significant; the list would be updated annually after July 1984 and each agency would also be required to include a statement of its preservation activities during the year. To assist the agencies, State Historic Preservation Officer Knox Mellon and staff developed a "Model Historic Preservation Policy" for distribution to state agency heads. See Knox Mellon to Wilson C. Riles, n.d.

57. Chapter 1.75, "Native American Historical, Cultural and Sacred Sites" of the *Public Resources Code* in Department of Parks and Recreation, *Policies*, secs. 5097.91-5097.97, pp. 178-180. Also see Dwight A. Dutschke, "Public Interest or Science? A Review of Public Archeology in California," *Contract Abstracts and CRM Archeology*, Vol. 3, No. 1 (1982), p. 28. See also Assembly Bill No. 4239, OHP. The law also gave the commission authority to: recommend significant sites for state acquisition, recommend procedures to the legislature to encourage private preservation of important sites and access to the sites by Native Americans, forward recommendations regarding the State Indian Museum to the director of the Department of Parks and Recreation, bring legal action "to prevent severe and irreparable damage to, or assure appropriate access for Native Americans" to cultural and religious sites, to "assist Native Americans in obtaining appropriate access to sacred places" located on public lands, and to "assist state agencies in any negotiations with agencies of the federal government for the protection of Native American sacred places that are located on federal lands."

CHAPTER 10
CALIFORNIA IMPLEMENTS THE HISTORIC PRESERVATION ACT OF 1966: THE CREATION OF A STATE MECHANISM, 1966-1970

1. Engbeck, *State Parks*, pp. 103-104; William Penn Mott, Jr., "Biographical Information," DPR: 537.7. Also see Earl P. Hanson to William Penn Mott, Jr., May 24, 1967, DPR: 537.0. Mott worked for seven years with the National Park Service, beginning in 1933. After World War II, he revitalized Oakland's park program as superintendent of parks. In 1962, he was appointed general manager of the East Bay Regional Park district where he reorganized and expanded the park system through his flair for attracting private contributions and volunteers.

2. Engbeck, *State Parks*, pp. 104-105. Also see Department of Parks and Recreation, *Organization Plan for the Department of Parks and Recreation*, November 1, 1967. The same legislation also authorized the department director "to organize the department in the manner he deems necessary, subject to the approval of the Governor." *Organization Plan*, November 1, 1967, p. 1.

3. Hanson to Mott, May 24, 1967. Also see Beaches and Parks, *State Park System Program, 1966-86*. Hanson's letter to Mott was in response to a letter from George B. Hartzog, Jr., director of the National Park Service, to Mott on April 10, 1967, DPR: 537.0. Hartzog told Mott: "We shall deeply appreciate your helping us to devise a system for the conduct of this program that is administratively sound and as simple as possible." Hanson told Mott that as of May, the department had not received any guidelines or directions for grant applications from the Secretary of the Interior despite several requests.

4. William Penn Mott, Jr. to Paul Mills, July 3, 1967, DPR: "Historical Landmarks: General Correspondence," 530.0. Mills was curator of the Oakland Art Museum.

5. William Penn Mott, Jr. to Ernest Allen Connally, October 6, 1967, DPR: 537.0. Mott said that the $50,000 request represented half of the department's estimated needs to

complete the survey. For a brief summary of the National Park Service's internal organization and a description of key personnel, see Mackintosh, *The National Historic Preservation Act*, pp. 1-12.

6. Department of Parks and Recreation, *Partial Inventory. Historic Sites and Buildings in California*, October 1967, DPR: "Historical Landmarks: Research," 531. The "preface" is dated August 9, 1967, and is described as a "rough draft." N.p.

7. *Ibid.*, "Preface."

8. Norma [T. Hawkins] of the Conference of California Historical Societies to Allen [Welts], September 2, 1967, DPR: 520.

9. "Preface," in *Partial Inventory*, n.p. The inventory submitted to Connally consisted of 161 sites that Welts described on National Register inventory forms provided by the National Park Service. Each site included such details as its common and historic name, ownership, inventory and survey status, location map, photograph, physical description, and a historical summary.

10. "National Historic Preservation Act Conference, Asilomar, March 17, 18, and 19, 1968," DPR: 537.0. Departmental invitees included Mott, Ray Hunter, James Tryner, James Warren, Russell Porter, John Michael, Robert Uhte, and Elmer Aldrich. The organizations represented there were: the American Institute of Planners, American Institute of Architects, Society for California Archeology, Los Angeles Cultural Heritage Board, San Diego Colonial Dames, Santa Barbara Trust for Historical Preservation, Sacramento Historical Preservation Society, and the Monterey History and Art Association. The list also included representatives from the State Archives, State Library, universities and colleges, the State Historical Landmarks Advisory Committee, and the State Legislature.

11. James E. Warren to William Penn Mott, Jr., April 8, 1968, DPR: 538.0. The concerns that Warren (chief, Planning and Development Division) raised were then brought to the attention of Deputy Director Ray Hunter by Russell Porter (manager, Grants Administration and Local Services Branch) who had actually written Warren's letter to Mott. Porter told Hunter he wanted to see a permanent task force established under Hunter's direction because of "a growing problem—the site survey, planning, and registry of historic sites associated with the Historic Preservation Act." Porter had been finding it difficult to respond to inquiries from local jurisdictions who wanted to know how sites in their areas could become part of the National Register. The problem, said Porter, was that the department was not yet sufficiently organized to implement the nomination process. Warren was Porter's supervisor. Russell Porter to Ray Hunter, April 25, 1968, DPR: 538.0.

12. William Penn Mott, Jr. to Director's Staff, May 2, 1968, DPR: 537.0. Mott told his staff that the Resource Management and Protection Division was to handle the survey and that the grants section of the Planning and Development Division would coordinate all funding efforts. Much of this would be confirmed at a meeting later that month. Finally, the director informed them that, until the National Park Service approved California's master plan, they could not expect any federal funding.

13. Russell W. Porter to James Warren, May 16, 1968, DPR: 538.0. The group agreed that all county supervisors would be asked to complete a historic site survey of their county and appoint an official contact who would work with the department. Porter and Allen Welts were to draft the letter to the boards of supervisors. The meeting on May 15 was attended by Hunter, Warren, Michael, Welts, and Porter.

14. *Ibid.*

15. George Hartzog to William Penn Mott, Jr., ca. January 1969, DPR: 537.0. He asked Mott to submit a five year projected program of costs for surveys and plans and for preservation projects such as rehabilitation, restoration, and landscaping. Allocations were as follows: fiscal 1967: $2 million; fiscal 1968, 1969, 1970: $10 million each.

16. William Penn Mott to George Hartzog, February 14, 1969, DPR: 537.0.

17. Incomplete memo to Herbert Rhodes, June 24, 1975, DPR: "California History Plan (hereafter abbreviated as CHP): General Correspondence," 348.0.

18. James Warren to William Penn Mott, Jr., May 12, 1971, DPR: 537.0. The number of inquiries rose gradually between 1968 and 1971. In addition to telephone calls which were not recorded, Warren noted that written inquiries totaled two in 1968, nine in 1969, two in 1970, and one in early 1971.

19. James Warren to William Penn Mott, Jr., October 30, 1969, DPR: 537.1. Warren anticipated the state would receive notification of their grant by the end of November 1969.

20. Frederick A. Meyer to William Penn Mott, Jr., November 6, 1969, and William C. Dillinger to William Penn Mott, Jr., November 5, 1969; DPR: 537.0.

21. James Warren to William Penn Mott, Jr., December 17, 1969; DPR: 530. As Warren envisioned it, the California History Plan would encompass ten steps: a review of all previous plans; the classification of history by eras ("racial, national, geographical, social, religious, cultural and political aspects"); the appointment of a committee or expert for each classification to develop that portion of the plan; a list of criteria for each classification; the selection of priority events and examples for each category; an inventory of what remained of each classification; an evaluation of the status and deficiencies of each category with a priority list of what needed to be included in the state's program; a determination of areas of responsibilities for governmental and private sectors; the development of a five- and twenty-year plan "for the preservation and interpretation of California history in the State Park System;" and the submission of the plan to the Historical Landmarks Advisory Committee, which would be responsible to the director's office.

As for the National Register program, not only would the Resource Management and Protection Division develop the criteria, it would also negotiate with counties and regions to establish local committees to develop surveys and nominate properties to the National Register, recommend National Register nominations to the Historical Landmarks Advisory Committee, and forward "the survey list for the Register as an input inventory of the Historical Plan portion of the California Outdoor Recreation Resources Plan."

It should also be noted that by this time, James Tryner had returned to his post as division chief.

22. *Ibid.*

23. William C. Dillinger to Director Mott, December 31, 1969, DPR: 530.

24. Russell W. Porter to William Penn Mott, Jr., January 28, 1970, DPR: 537.0. The membership of the Historical Landmarks Advisory Committee had not yet been expanded, nor had criteria been determined.

25. See William Penn Mott, Jr. to Division Chiefs and Supervisory Personnel, February 9, 1970 and April 20, 1970; DPR: 537.0. The April memo that was actually sent was a revision of the February memo. The latter was drafted by Porter for Mott's signature.

26. John Michael to Sandra Elder, *c.* spring 1986.

27. Mott to Division Chiefs, April 20, 1970. The establishment of the in-house committee did not wait for Mott's official approval. It began to meet early in 1970 and by mid-March had convened for the third time. Unfortunately, the committee's minutes are not complete; the few copies that exist are filed in different folders. See "Memo to Files," In-House Advisory Committee on History Meeting, March 18, 1970, DPR: 537.0.

28. Russell W. Porter to Leland Lutz, James Tryner, William Dillinger, F.C. Butcher, Gordon Kisbaugh, Elmer Aldrich, John Caffrey; August 12, 1970, DPR: 537.0.

29. William Penn Mott to all Division Chiefs, August 7, 1969. DPR: CHP, 348.0.

30. James P. Tryner to William Penn Mott, Jr., March 13, 1970, DPR: 348.0. Tryner, chief of the Resource Management and Protection Division, noted that the federal requirements were used by Welts as he expanded his chronology.

31. Allen W. Welts to All Section Heads, November 13, 1969, DPR: 520.

32. Frederick A. Meyer to Allen Welts, November 21, 1969, DPR: 520. Meyer was now supervisor, Environmental Resources Section. Hussey's categories were as follows:

Aboriginal Life (no dates)
Era of Early European Exploration (1540-1769)
Era of European Settlement and Pastoral Life (1769-1846)
Era of Early Development of California as an American Province (1846-1869)
Era of Technological Advance and Social Ferment (1869-1915)
Emergence to National Leadership (1915-present)

See also John H. Michael to James P. Tryner, December 10, 1969, DPR: 538.0.

33. Allen W. Welts to W. Turrentine Jackson, February 3, 1970, DPR: 520. Jackson wrote to Welts a week later: "I have examined the outline with care and I think the breakdown, or large classification, of the material under its headings is logical. It also appears to me that you have included every topic that anyone could hope to have covered...." February 10, 1970, DPR: 520.

34. James P. Tryner to William Penn Mott, Jr., March 13, 1970, DPR: 530. Appended was the draft chronology dated the same day. Each of the items in the following outline included a specific section on cause, effect, and cultural manifestations:

I.	Before 10,500 B.C:	Early Man; Pleistocene Man (Theme)
II.	10,500-7,000 B.C.:	Big Game Hunters
III.	7,000-5,000 B.C.:	The San Dieguito Complex and Others
IV.	5,000-2,000 B.C.:	The Early Period; Modern Indigenous Man (Theme)
V.	2,000 B.C.-A.D. 250:	The Middle Period
VI.	A.D. 250-1540:	The Late Period
VII.	16th Century (1540-1600):	Europeans Reach Alta California
VIII.	17th Century (1600-1700):	New Spain's Interest in Alta California
IX.	18th Century (1700-1800):	Spanish Occupation of Alta California and Its Effect on the Aboriginal People
X.	19th Century (1800-1900):	A Time of Upheaval and Transposition
XI.	20th Century (1900-):	California's Rise to National Prominence (Theme)

35. James P. Tryner to William Penn Mott, Jr., February 22, 1973, DPR: 538.0. Tryner noted that the Welts proposal had "received wide review and endorsement from eminent historians outside the Department."

36. Department of Parks and Recreation, *Preliminary California History Plan* (Sacramento: Department of Parks and Recreation, September 1, 1970), pp. 8-12. Sub-era classifications could also be included. The Indian era, for example, was broken down into Paleo-Indian Sub-era (15,000-2,000 years ago) and Recent Indian Sub-era (2,000 years ago to 1848). The plan included a breakdown of the architectural category and suggestions for additional themes such as the Gold Rush and the Chinese in California. See p. 8.

37. Russell W. Porter to William Penn Mott, Jr., January 28, 1970, DPR: 537.0.

38. William Penn Mott to Honorable John D. Murphy, Chairman, Alameda County Board of Supervisors, February 27, 1970, DPR: 530. Each letter was sent to a specified individual. Mott downplayed the required details, saying that, at this time, all the state needed was "a simple inventory...with a brief description of their historical or architectural and archeological values." Also see Mott to Division Chiefs and Supervisory Personnel, February 9, 1970, DPR: 537.

39. "Progress Report. National Register of Historical Places," June 24, 1970, DPR: 537.0. It is unclear what progress, if any, the other two counties had made.

40. *Ibid.* Also see, "Status of the California Effort on the National Historic Preservation Program—Register, Survey, Plan, Project Applications," June 24, 1970, DPR: 537.0. During June, Welts continued to encourage the counties through telephone calls and letters and urged them to "proceed with all possible dispatch." See Allen W. Welts to Lincoln E. Covington, June 8, 1970, DPR: 537.0.

41. William Penn Mott, Jr., to Mark Lawton, September 24, 1971, DPR: 537.0.

42. "Progress Report. National Register," June 24, 1970.

43. "Preface to a Historical Inventory," appended to James P. Tryner to Russell W. Porter, August 18, 1970, DPR: "California History Plan-Two (hereafter abbreviated as CHP-II): General Correspondence," 348.0.

44. Department of Parks and Recreation, *The California History Plan.* Volume Two, *Inventory of Historic Features* (Sacramento: Department of Parks and Recreation, August 1973). The inventory included all submissions gathered by September 1, 1972.

45. See Parks and Recreation, *Preliminary California History Plan,* p. 15. The sources listed were those projects proposed by the California History Plan Committee, National Register nominations, state landmarks, previous studies and programs of the Department of Parks and Recreation, the archaeological site survey under the jurisdiction of the University of California at Berkeley and Los Angeles, and the county inventories being submitted to the department.

46. See "Minutes," History Committee meeting, June 30, 1970, DPR: "California History Plan-One (hereafter abbreviated as CHP-I): Reports," 348.1; and Russell Porter to William Penn Mott, Jr., July 6, 1970, DPR: CHP-I: "General Correspondence," 348.0. Porter attended a meeting of the state liaison officers from Hawaii, California, and Nevada with Park Service representatives including Keeper Murtagh on June 29, 1970. It was agreed that the preliminary "plan for a plan" could be submitted by September 1, 1970 to Washington, D.C., and still meet the minimum qualifications for participation in the National Register program.

47. Ernest Allen Connally to State Liaison Officers, July 17, 1970, DPR: 537.0.

48. James E. Warren to William Penn Mott, Jr., June 24, 1970, DPR: CHP-I, 348.0.

49. William Penn Mott, Jr., to James E. Warren, July 6, 1970, DPR: CHP-I, 348.0. According to Mott, Murtagh showed great interest in citizen-supported projects such as Allensworth and encouraged Mott to make it part of his interpretive program. It was not, however, included in the preliminary plan as a proposed project. Murtagh also expressed interest in the department's treks and trails activities for their historic significance and as part of a potential youth hostel system. These were not incorporated into the plan. Murtagh's support for living museum efforts such as La Purisima, San Diego Old Town, and Columbia apparently coincided with Mott's priorities, for these were included in the plan's list of funding projects needed to meet thematic deficiencies in the park system. See Parks and Recreation, *Preliminary California History Plan,* pp. 22-25.

50. The plan reluctantly included this suggestion, noting that budgets projected that far in advance were bound to change. The plan did include projects for the requested fiscal years but with estimated costs and no details. Parks and Recreation, *Preliminary California History Plan,* p. 22.

51. Mott to Warren, July 6, 1970.

52. Parks and Recreation, *Preliminary California History Plan,* p. 9. As for the work schedule, Mott reminded Warren that the rough draft was due by September 1 and that the timetable would have to be revised if the necessary reviews were to be accomplished. The plan was submitted on schedule. Mott to Warren, July 6, 1970.

53. Parks and Recreation, *Preliminary California History Plan,* p. 1.

54. *Ibid.,* pp. 16, 18, 22.

55. William Penn Mott, Jr. to Ernest Allen Connally, December 15, 1970, DPR: 537.0. Also, Ernest Allen Connally to William Penn Mott, Jr., December 31, 1970, DPR: CHP-I, 348.0.

The plan identified the following persons as members of the California History Plan Committee:

William N. Davis, Jr., Ph.D., Chief, State Archives
Elliot Evens, Ph.D., Curator, Society of California Pioneers
William H. Hutchinson, Professor of History, Chico State College
Joseph A. McGowan, Ph.D., Chairman, History Department, Sacramento

State College
Clement Meighan, Ph.D., Professor of Anthropology, University of
California at Los Angeles
Doyce B. Nunis, Jr., Ph.D., Professor of History, University of Southern
California
Allan R. Ottley, Chief, California Section, California State Library
Rev. Francis J. Weber, Archivist, Archdiocese of Los Angeles and
Professor of History, Queen of Angel's Seminary

See Parks and Recreation, *Preliminary California History Plan*, p. 3. Professors Hutchinson, McGowan, and Nunis had been involved in the earlier Welts inventory.

56. Incomplete memo to Herbert Rhodes, June 24, 1975.

57. John H. Michael to Robert G. Bates, May 10, 1968, DPR: 538.0. Bates was chief of Information and Interpretation. Michael wrote that local historical societies provided his section with donations and located historical objects for his program. Michael thought that Mott had reservations over how he ran the landmarks program, and he told his supervisor that to his knowledge, the committee was pleased with the progress of the program. He said: "If the Director has misgivings I would like to know where we are ineffectual." The clerical staff member that Michael was referring to was Sandra J. Elder who spent 15 percent of her time on committee activities.

58. James P. Tryner to William Penn Mott, Jr., December 5, 1968, DPR: 538.0.

59. Robert G. Bates to William Penn Mott, Jr., December 13, 1968, DPR: 538.0. Bates' memo bears Michael's initials.

60. William Penn Mott, Jr. to Jim Tryner, January 6, 1969; DPR: 538.0.

61. "Minutes," HLAC, March 14, 1970.

62. Russell W. Porter to William J. Murtagh, May 17, 1968, DPR: 538.0.

63. A.B. No. 1213, DPR: 538.0. Also see Elder, "Public Resources Code," n.p.

64. "Minutes," HLAC, July 22, 1970.

65. William Penn Mott, Jr. to William J. Murtagh, August 28, 1970, DPR: 530.

66. William Murtagh to William Penn Mott, Jr., September 1, 1970, DPR: 530.

67. "Minutes," HLAC, May 25, 1967. The committee recommended that a landmark application be sent. One had been mailed in 1955 in response to a similar request but the committee did not hear from the city.

68. "Minutes," HLAC, November 20, 1968.

69. William Penn Mott, Jr. to all members of the State Legislature, November 9, 1967, DPR: 530. See also David A. Tucker to Rev. Allison L. Burbank, September 28, 1970, DPR: 538, regarding Senate Resolution No. 106 requesting landmark designation for St. John's Episcopal Church in Wilmington.

70. "Statement of Policy for State Historical Landmark Registration and Point of Historical Interest Registration," adopted July 22, 1970, in "Minutes," HLAC, July 22, 1970. At the recommendation of committee member Kathryn Kaiser, the application form was also revised. See "Minutes," HLAC, March 14, 1970.

71. John H. Michael to Lousiana Clayton Dart, March 4, 1969, DPR: 538.0.

72. "Statement of Policy for State Historical Landmark Registration," July 22, 1970, p. 6.

73. "Minutes," HLAC, August 7, 1968. As with his first letter in 1966, Michael received "less than overwhelming" responses. Out of fifty-eight counties, only twenty-three responses were recorded. There was no indication what these consisted of. John Michael to County Supervisors, August 26, 1968, DPR: 539.0.

74. Allen W. Welts to California Historical Landmarks Advisory Committee, July 15, 1968, DPR: 539.

75. R. Coke Wood to Allen Welts, August 26, 1968, DPR: 539.

76. "Statement of Policy for State Historical Landmark Registration," July 22, 1970, p. 6.

CHAPTER 11
CALIFORNIA'S HISTORIC PRESERVATION PROGRAM:
COMPLETION OF STATE PLANS AND INVENTORIES, 1971-1975

1. Department of Parks and Recreation, "Organization Chart, August 7, 1972," courtesy of Sandra Elder. Also see David Tucker to Janet Skinner, November 17, 1972, DPR: 538.0. According to the "Minutes," HLAC, June 21, 1972:

> "...with so much emphasis on history [in the Interpretive Services Section], changes were needed. Therefore the functions of the Historical Landmarks Advisory Committee are being moved to the Design and Development Division, Grants and Statewide Studies Branch, History Preservation Section with John Michael as section supervisor and David Tucker and Sandra [Elder] as part of his staff. This is the unit that handles the Federally funded history program and therefore the Landmarks Committee should logically be associated with this branch."

John Knight, head of the Operations Division, recalled that another reason behind the reorganization was that there were "rumblings from field personnel who resented being told by headquarters what their displays and interpretive programs should consist of." They wanted to be in charge of their own programs in the field, and thus it was logical that the Operations Division receive the historic interpretation unit for field activities. John H. Knight, telephone conversation with author, April 15, 1983, Sacramento, California.

2. James M. Doyle to Janet Zeiser, October 18, 1974, DPR: 530. See also, DPR, "Organization Chart, August 7, 1972."

3. William Penn Mott, Jr. to Kathryn Kaiser, January 9, 1974, DPR: CHP-I, 348.0.

4. "National Register and Landmarks Section," ca. 1972, Elder: OHP.

5. *Ibid.* In the beginning, Michael was assisted by Harold Bradshaw, assistant Parks and Recreation Specialist; Richard Hastings, archaeologist; and David A. Tucker, staff historian. By the time Michael departed, his staff had changed with the exception of Sandra J. Elder who served as secretary to the unit's supervisor and to the advisory committee during the entire decade. On the eve of his departure, Michael had the following full-time professionals on his staff: Aaron Gallup, architectural historian; Eugene Itogawa, historian; William E. Padgett and Barry W. Jones, both Parks and Recreation specialists.

6. John H. Knight, telephone conversation with author, April 15, 1983, Sacramento, California. Michael was replaced for a month by Gallup. Also see John Michael to Sandra Elder, ca. spring 1986.

7. Doyle began work in the section in 1973 as assistant supervisor. The staff under his supervision consisted of: Elder, Gallup, Itogawa, Padgett, and William Seidel, archaeologist. See Department of Parks and Recreation, *The California Historic Preservation Plan.* Volume Three: *Annual Program* (Sacramento: Department of Parks and Recreation, June 1975), pp. 38-39; hereafter abbreviated as CHP-Three. Also see: "Experience-James M. Doyle," n.d.

8. Ronald L. Rawlings to Norman Hongola, August 19, 1971, DPR: CHP-I, 348.0. Staffing concerns had been resolved by the time work began in August. See William Dillinger to Messrs. Tryner and Warren, April 9, 1971, DPR: 538.0. The department's In-house History Committee had been making preparations for this concentration of effort and resources.

9. William Penn Mott, Jr. to various county commissions and other groups, August 25, 1971, DPR: CHP-I, 348.0.

10. Russell W. Porter to William Penn Mott, Jr. and James E. Warren, May 4, 1972, DPR: CHP-I, 348.0. See CHP-Three, June 1, 1972.

11. Porter to Mott and Warren, May 4, 1972. Bisbee's sudden retirement "shocked" Porter. Michael recalled that Bisbee "retired the day I took over....Bisbee and I had no problems (we had been friends for many years); he was 'sick' of the system." Michael to Elder, ca. Spring 1986.

12. Department of Parks and Recreation, *The California History Plan.* Volume One: *Comprehensive Preservation Program* (Sacramento: Department of Parks and Recreation, December 1973), title page and p. vii; hereafter abbreviated as CHP-One.

13. William Penn Mott, Jr. to James E. Warren, September 29, 1971, DPR: CHP-I, 348.0. Mott's staff sought input to the history plan from ethnic groups such as the Chinese Historical Society. See Harold D. Bradshaw to Mark Lai, November 12, 1971, DPR: 537.0. Bradshaw wrote several chapters in Volume One and was responsible for all of Volume Three.

14. Bruce Kennedy to Leland Lutz, July 5, 1972, DPR: CHP-I, 348.0. Kennedy, an economist, was concerned that the plan gave the impression that the preservation of history "is almost entirely a matter of salvaging and restoring old buildings," and that there was little attention paid to other physical objects and museums or the need for the education and training of personnel. Lutz was chief of the Administrative Services Division.

15. CHP-One, p. 73.

16. In a memo to Mott, Chief James P. Tryner of the Resource Management and Protection Division promised a draft of the directives "shortly." Appended to the memo was a copy of Welts' "Man in California-A Topical Chronology" (1970). Although it had been rejected in favor of the "era" system, Tryner informed Mott that: "From the standpoint of archeological and historical resources, the Welts' chronology seems to highlight the 'flow of history', and may be a springboard from which we can launch an effective implementation of the concept." See Tryner to Mott, February 22, 1973, DPR: 538.0. The "flow of history" is discussed in Chapter 13.

17. "Minutes," HLAC, April 26, 1973. Mott's opinion of the committee was clear: they were strictly advisory. He was more concerned with obtaining the approval of the Park and Recreation Commission. "If they approve the concept, it will represent the policy for the Department in connection with its interpretation of history." William Penn Mott, Jr. to Jeannette P. Rosson, May 23, 1973, DPR: 538.0.

18. CHP-One, p. v. The seven chapters were:
    I.   Major Preservation Problems and Recommendations
    II. Summary of California History
    III. The History of History Preservation in California
    IV. History Preservation Philosophy
    V.   Preservation Planning's Relationship to Other State Planning
    VI. Historical Survey and Planning
    VII. Project Selection Process

19. Russell W. Porter to William Penn Mott, Jr., April 18, 1973, DPR: CHP-I, 348.0. The chapter on preservation philosophy was to treat "the social, economic, and environmental aspects of California's heritage" along with its "relationship to education and leisure" and contain "a statement on the intrinsic values for preservation." Also see James Earp to Ross T. Henry, April 13, 1973, DPR: CHP-I, 348.0.

20. William Penn Mott, Jr. to N. B. Livermore, March 21, 1973, DPR: CHP-I, 348.0.

21. CHP-One, pp. 1-9. The categories and recommendations were:
    General Recommendations (12 recommendations)
    Recommendations for Federal Action (3 recommendations)
    Recommendations for Action at the State Level (5 recommendations)
    Recommendations for Action by Local Agencies (4 recommendations)
    Recommendations for Action by the Private Sector (2 recommendations)
    Findings, Priorities, and Project Recommendations for the State
        Department of Parks and Recreation (6 recommendations)
The task force mentioned in Recommendation No. 1 was the Archaeological, Paleontological, and Historical Resources Task Force created in 1971 by S.B. 215. See Chapter 13 for a discussion of S.B. 215.

Recommendation No. 1 also included authorization and funding for the Department of Parks and Recreation "to assume an expanded statewide role in identifying historic features; in planning for preservation, restoration, and reconstruction of historic features of statewide significance; in interpreting at the historic units within the State Park System the culture of California; and in providing local governmental agencies with technical assistance in the preservation and interpretation of history."

22. N. B. Livermore, Jr. to William Penn Mott, Jr., March 30, 1973, DPR: CHP-I, 348.0. Livermore also said: "I must observe that the Plan is most ambitious and does not include a schedule indicating stages of implementation and related costs to State Government. If this Plan is accepted and reviewed by the Federal Government as a concept of what the State feels would be a desirable program, rather than what would be a practically achievable program, then it appears to be alright. If it is the latter, however, I feel that I would have to indicate that it is not practically achievable, at least in the near term."

23. William Penn Mott, Jr. to Norman B. Livermore, Jr., June 18, 1973, DPR: CHP-I, 348.0.

24. Kathryn Kaiser to William Penn Mott, Jr., July 2, 1973, DPR: CHP-I, 348.0. Kaiser also told Mott that the administrator would need a professional staff with expertise in fields such as anthropology, architecture, architectural history, history, and planning. She was also critical of the lack of proposed state legislation to implement the recommendations and to serve as models for local communities.

25. Kathryn H. Kaiser to William Penn Mott, Jr., July 23, 1973, DPR: CHP-I, 348.0.

26. Kathryn H. Kaiser to Members, California Historical Landmarks Advisory Committee, August 17, 1973, DPR: CHP-I, 348.0. In her letter, Kaiser advised the committee to endorse the new wording at their meeting in September rather than approve it by telephone or letter. She reasoned that the printer could wait that long. Unfortunately, she was mistaken. Porter informed Mott on August 31, 1973, that he felt he could not wait for the committee's formal approval and had ordered the department's Publication Section to make the change in wording and proceed with the printing. "I did this on the basis that both John Michael and I felt that the other committee members would agree with this wording. Our judgement has been borne out in that five out of the seven committee members have responded affirmatively. Two members did not respond at all." Russell W. Porter to William Penn Mott, Jr., August 31, 1973, DPR: CHP-I, 348.0.

27. Members, Historical Landmarks Advisory Committee to William Penn Mott Jr., January 3, 1974, DPR: CHP-I, 348.0. Also see "Minutes," HLAC, January 3, 1974.

28. William Penn Mott, Jr. to Kathryn H. Kaiser, January 9, 1974, DPR: CHP-I, 348.0. Mott noted that office would mean: "(1) a separate commission and staff; (2) a department with an advisory commission; (3) a separate unit of government attached to the Governor's Office, the Lt. Governor's Office, or a single department; or (4) a unit within any operating department."

29. Kathryn H. Kaiser to William Penn Mott, Jr., January 25, 1974, DPR: CHP-I, 348.0. Kaiser told Mott she wanted to see the legislature recognize the committee's expanded responsibilities and jurisdiction.

30. William Penn Mott, Jr. to Kathryn H. Kaiser, February 6, 1974, DPR: "California Historical Landmarks Advisory Committee," 023.

31. CHP-One, p. 6.

32. *Ibid.*, p. 4. Computerization is becoming a reality. The Office of Historic Preservation and its archaeologist, William Seidel, began to computerize archaeological and historical site inventories in 1980. In 1984, the California Heritage Task Force recommended that "there should be a well-designed, statewide Heritage Resources Data Management System, developed and supported as a public/private partnership." In March 1984, the California Heritage Data Management Advisory Committee was established. It was "born of the assumption that greater economy and efficiency in the management and use of information pertaining to California's cultural heritage might be realized through increased coordina-

tion among the various entities collecting and using such data." The committee of fifteen quickly came to consensus on goals and objectives which include coordinating and producing "a comprehensive and integrated statewide Heritage Resource Data Management System," and advising "the California Office of Historic Preservation on pertinent aspects of Historic, Socio-cultural, and Archeological Inventory Systems." See: California Heritage Task Force, *A Report to the Legislature and the People of California* (Sacramento: August 1984), pp. 36-37; and *Annual Report From the California Heritage Data Management Advisory Committee, 1984.* Prepared for the Office of Historic Preservation, March 10, 1985, pp. 1-8; also L. Mark Raab and Santa Barbara County Heritage Planning Group, *Comprehensive Heritage Resource Management Plan: Santa Barbara County Element. Draft 1.* Submitted to California OHP, October 1985, courtesy of William C. Seidel.

33. CHP-One, p. 8. The second recommendation mentioned was No. 1 under the category of recommendations specifically for the Department of Parks and Recreation. Also see N. B. Livermore, Jr. to W. P. Mott, Jr., March 30, 1973; Mott to Livermore, June 18, 1973. DPR: CHP-I, 348.0.

34. "Minutes," History Committee Meeting, June 30, 1970, DPR: CHP-I, 348.0.

35. See, for example, Meighan's comments on "The California History Plan," August 7, 1970, DPR: CHP-I, 348.0.

36. William J. Murtagh to Herb Rhodes, May 22, 1975, DPR: CHP-I, 348.0. In March 1975, newly elected Governor Edmund G. Brown, Jr., appointed Rhodes to replace Mott as Director of the Department of Parks and Recreation.

37. *Ibid.*

38. *Ibid.*

39. *Ibid.* Mott had hoped that Volume One would make the state eligible for federal funds for ten years. William Penn Mott, Jr. to Norman B. Livermore, June 18, 1973, DPR: CHP-I, 348.0. Instead, California's eligibility to receive grants was continued through June 30, 1975. This date had been extended to March 31, 1976, in anticipation of revision of both Volumes One and Two, and the receipt of an interim submission. Murtagh to Rhodes, May 22, 1975, DPR: CHP-I, 348.0.

40. CHP-Three, "Annual Preservation Program for Fiscal Year 1977," July 1976, pp. 5, 17. The discussion during 1975 regarding Volume One was carried on by new faces in California. In December 1975, for example, Knox Mellon, historic preservation coordinator, wrote to State Park Historian Robert W. Reese to inform him that his office (i.e., the Office of Historic Preservation) had discovered "numerous inaccuracies and other problems associated with the listing" of themes and deficiencies in Volume One and now considered that list "inoperative." He told Reese the National Register had recently approved his office's revised list of themes: aboriginal, architecture, arts/leisure, economic/industrial, exploration/settlement, government, military, religion, and social/education. Mellon to Reese, December 11, 1975, DPR: CHP-I, 348.0. These same themes were used to organize California's historic sites in the 1976 edition of Volume Two. See Department of Parks and Recreation, *The California History Plan.* Volume Two, *California Inventory of Historic Resources* (Sacramento: Department of Parks and Recreation, March 1976); hereafter abbreviated as CHP-Two, 1976.

41. Department of Parks and Recreation, *The California History Plan.* Volume Two: *Inventory of Historic Features* (Sacramento: Department of Parks and Recreation, August 1973), hereafter abbreviated as CHP-Two, 1973. Pp. 1-3. The Historic Eras were: Indian Era (Early-15,000 B.C. to 1 A.D., and Recent-1 A.D. to 1848 A.D.); Hispanic Era (Spanish occupation-1542 to 1822, and Mexican occupation-1822 to 1848); and American Era (1848 to 1900, and After 1900).

42. *Ibid.*, p. 3.

43. CHP-One, p. 77. Also, William Penn Mott, Jr. to William Murtagh, February 15, 1974, DPR: CHP-II, 348.0. Mott's letter described the state's procedure in great detail and

insisted that the state maintained "at all times...complete control over all phases of the inventory from the initial contact and workshop to the filing and computerization of the information."

44. CHP-One, p. 78.

45. William Penn Mott, Jr. to George F. Emery, February 1, 1974, CHP-I, 348.0.

46. William Murtagh to William Penn Mott, Jr., March 29, 1974, DPR: CHP-II, 348.0. The keeper stated that state leadership was crucial because "each potential listing must be measured against the comprehensive survey effort before being accepted as part of the inventory. No local individual, no matter how well advised can properly evaluate potential additions to an inventory without comprehensive knowledge of the statewide survey. It therefore follows that [the] survey must be a centralized State function [so] that comparative professional evaluations may be properly made." Murtagh also said that California's deficiencies were due to the lack of assurance "that (1) all aspects of California history are receiving coverage and (2) there will be any input from specific localities, counties, and regions as a comprehensive coverage of the State."

47. William J. Murtagh to William Penn Mott, Jr., May 14, 1974, DPR: CHP-II, 348.0. See also Mott to Murtagh, April 18, 1974.

48. William J. Murtagh to Herbert Rhodes, June 13, 1975, DPR: CHP-I, 348.0.

49. Murtagh to Rhodes, May 22, 1975. Murtagh's suggestion that both the cover and title page be given an edition number was not accepted.

50. CHP-One, p. 77.

51. John H. Michael to Russell W. Porter, August 1, 1973; draft letter from William Penn Mott, Jr. to general public, n.d., CHP-II, 348.0. Mott requested that some of the letters be written on his personal stationery. By this date, survey inventory forms had also been revised to make it easier for local groups to use. Staff Historian Tucker was hopeful that the reorganized and revised forms would "be easily comprehended by local volunteer groups." See David A. Tucker to John H. Michael, December 29, 1972, CHP-II, 348.0; and "Press Release," October 19, 1973, DPR: CHP-II, 348.0. For a copy of the schedule, see Michael to Porter, August 1, 1973.

52. James M. Doyle to John H. Michael, November 2, 1973, OHP. Doyle reported that attendance at the meetings averaged thirty persons, who took materials back to their respective organizations.

53. Aaron A. Gallup to Trisha Whittaker, June 10, 1974, DPR: CHP-II, 348.0; William E. Padgett to Russell W. Porter, May 31, 1974, OHP.

54. William E. Padgett to James M. Doyle, June 17, 1975, OHP. In March 1974, the number of sites in the state inventory was 24,930. See CHP-Three, "Annual Program," June 1975, p. 12. Until June 1975, Volume Three was entitled, "Annual Preservation Program."

55. Lowell Smith to William Penn Mott, September 1, 1973, DPR: CHP-II, 348.0. Mott to Smith, October l, 1973, DPR: CHP-II, 348.0. The creation of an officially recognized state historical society was brought to fruition in 1979 when the California Historical Society was so designated by the state legislature.

56. CHP-Two, 1976, p. ix.

57. Knox Mellon to Herbert Rhodes, November 26, 1975, DPR: CHP-II, 348.0.

58. William E. Padgett to Robert B. Rettig, December 15, 1975, DPR: CHP-II, 348.0.

59. Earlier submissions to the National Park Service consisted of work plans which were requests for funding for the forthcoming fiscal year. In April 1971, for example, Mott submitted a request for a planning grant of $40,000 and for funds to acquire Allensworth and preserve buildings in Old Sacramento and Old Town San Diego. The total requested was $363,854. See Department of Parks and Recreation, "Annual Work Program Under the National Historic Preservation Act, Public Law 89-665, 89th Congress, S. 3035, October 15, 1966," April 30, 1971, DPR: "Historical Preservation: California History Plan Three (hereafter abbreviated as CHP-III): Reports," 348.1. California subsequently received its requested $40,000 planning grant and an additional $18,500 (FY 1970-1971), and $30,535

(FY 1971-1972) to preserve the B.F. Hastings Building in Sacramento. CHP-Three, 1973, p. 10.

60. CHP-Three, 1972, pp. 1-3. By the end of 1971, California had received $240,292 under the terms of the federal preservation legislation. These matching funds were or would be allocated for the first preliminary plan, work on the comprehensive plan, and for four development projects on state-owned properties.

61. *Ibid.*, p. 5. These priorities were:

- Review and stabilize all sites and structures within the State Park System;
- Acquire all private lands within historic units and from contiguous areas needed for successful protection and development;
- Acquire the most significant State historic resources before destruction by urban and industrial development;
- Transfer local or national sites to appropriate local or federal agencies.

62. *Ibid.* To meet these needs and matching fund requirements, the state planned a $250 million bond issue in June 1974. Of that total, $15 million would be specifically allocated for historic preservation with an additional $90 million "for local recreation and related history preservation." As for the 1972-1973 fiscal year, the department asked for $80,000 for survey and planning, $790,000 for two acquisitions, and $1.5 million for nine development projects. See pp. 6-9.

63. *Ibid.*, p. 1.

64. William J. Murtagh to William Penn Mott, Jr., February 7, 1975, DPR: CHP-III, 348.0.

65. William J. Murtagh to William Penn Mott, Jr., December 6, 1972, DPR: CHP-III, 348.0. These comments did not preclude the National Park Service from granting monies to California. In September 1972, the department was notified that they would receive $40,000 for survey and planning and $127,197 for departmental and local planning. See Harold D. Bradshaw to John H. Michael, October 3 and November 6, 1972, OHP.

66. Barry Jones to John H. Michael, September 1, 1973, OHP. In 1973, California received $207,777 in grant funds. Of this, $80,000 was for survey and planning; $63,888 for four state projects; and $63,889 for three local projects. See James M. Doyle to John H. Michael, December 5, 1973, OHP. The state had requested $2,218,302 for twenty-four state park projects and ten local projects. The list had been prioritized; the first ten were state park requests. CHP-Three, 1973, pp. 34-40.

67. CHP-Three, 1973, p. 15. The policy included the position that the state should acquire what was of state significance and local agencies should do the same for locally important projects. Those archaeological sites that were acquired and developed should include the following categories:

- Evidence of early man in California
- Sites or objects that depict a way of life of early man
- Sites that are important to present-day Indian populations
- Sites at which contact took place between Indians and explorers or early settlers

68. *Ibid.*, pp. 14-16. The plan also indicated the numbers of National Register, landmark, and points of historical interest applications processed as well as how many environmental impact reports were reviewed. See pp. 21-22.

69. The state requested $11,067,956 for eighteen locally owned projects, twenty-seven state projects, and seventeen private projects. The matching funds for many of these projects would come from the 1974 bond act. See CHP-Three, 1974, pp. 28-42. In October 1974, the state was given $800,000. The History Preservation Section prepared applications for $93,000 in survey planning and $707,000 for acquisition and development. See Barry Jones to James M. Doyle, November 8, 1974, OHP.

70. The recommendations were the first four: the creation of an Office of History, creation of a historic data pool, development and operation of regional historic museums, and implementation of an archaeological inventory survey; and No. 11 which called for modifications of the Uniform Building Code. CHP-Three, 1974, pp. 10-11.

71. The appendix included a copy of sample forms used in the process which called for subjective decisions made by professional historians and archaeologists via a filtering process based on analyses of theme deficiency and level of significance, integrity and endangerment ratings, and a bonus rating for resource values. Although the process was developed for the State Park System, it could be adapted by local governments for their use. *Ibid.*, pp. 45-53.

72. *Ibid.*, pp. 13-14.

73. William Penn Mott, Jr. to Samuel J. Cullers, August 7, 1972, DPR: CHP-I, 348.0.

74. Murtagh to Mott, February 7, 1975. The following recommendations made by Murtagh were accepted: a map, certification of the governor's review of the plan, resumes for the staff and review board.

75. William E. Padgett to James M. Doyle, February 10, 1975, OHP. This was an increase of 243 percent. The 1975 plan included a request for $92,500 for planning and survey projects. See CHP-Three, 1975, pp. 23-35.

76. CHP-Three, 1975, p. 15.

77. *Ibid.*

78. Herbert Rhodes to William J. Murtagh, May 23, 1975, DPR: CHP-III, 348.0.

79. Russell W. Porter to Herbert Rhodes, October 3, 1975, *ibid.*; William Penn Mott, Jr. to Kathryn H. Kaiser, August 7, 1974, DPR: 537.0.

Mott had requested in 1974 that "the [Historical Landmarks Advisory] Committee develop a set of criteria for the distribution of funds for the local level as well as the state. The criteria should relate to the history plan and should be developed with the thought that federal as well as other funds may be available, such as our bond funds or special appropriations." He recommended that the committee hold public hearings to determine "to what extent the public wishes the state to establish standards and criteria for both the private sector and public sector to use in the preservation of historic structures and sites." He reminded Chairperson Kaiser that departmental priorities were: preservation first, restoration second, and reconstruction third. The hearings would also provide insight into how far state and local agencies could go in preserving and protecting the state's cultural heritage and who would accept responsibility for the work, and stimulate public awareness and interest in the preservation of the state's cultural heritage. See Mott to Kaiser, August 7, 1974, *ibid.*

80. James E. Warren to William Penn Mott, May 12, 1971; Mott to Warren, June 2, 1971; and Mott to Kaiser, August 7, 1974, DPR: 537.0.

81. Mott to Warren, June 2, 1971, *ibid.*; and Ronald D. Rawlings to Norman Hongola, September 13, 1971, DPR: 348. The task force consisted of three men: Michael (Division of Information and Interpretive Services), Rawlings (Division of Planning and Development), and Francis Riddell (Division of Resource Management and Protection). Their recommendations included consideration for endangerment, significance, and public use. These were incorporated into the criteria established by the federal government and adopted by the Historical Resources Commission in 1975. The four priority categories were: Sponsorship and Stewardship, Public Benefit, Preservation and Interpretive Benefits, and Quality and Condition of the Site. See Russell W. Porter to Herbert Rhodes, October 3, 1975, DPR: 348; and "Minutes," State Historical Resources Commission, March 6, 1975.

82. CHP-Three, 1975, pp. 16-17, 35. A total of $92,500 was requested for survey and planning activities. The 1977 annual plan stated that between 1976-February 1977, ten local surveys had been funded on a 50-50 match. The program involved an agreement between the local community agency and the state which allowed for:

hiring a professional consultant to direct the survey effort and ensure the quality and accuracy of the resulting inventory, determination of UTM coordinates for computerization, and recording of all surveyed sites on topographic maps for use on the State planning level. These contracts also often involve nomination of a percentage of properties to the National Register, official adoption of the inventory and its incorporation into local plans.

See CHP-Three, 1977, n.p. For a listing of local surveys, see Office of Historic Preservation, *Survey of Surveys. A Summary of California's Cultural Resource Surveys* (Sacramento: Office of Historic Preservation, May 1981).

CHAPTER 12
STATEWIDE PRESERVATION PROGRAMS
ADMINISTERED BY THE HISTORY PRESERVATION SECTION, 1972-1976

1. See "Suggested Revised Program: National Register Unit," ca. 1978, OHP. OHP staff apparently conducted a survey of Register programs in other states and concluded that "California is the only State which bases its program entirely on random acceptance of applications from the public. 10 programs in the country are entirely staff-initiated; 23 others are based on joint staff initiation and public suggestions ranked according to staff priorities; 16 are based on joint staff initiation and public input."

2. David A. Tucker to John H. Michael, February 6, 1973, OHP.

3. CHP-Three, 1974, p. 19; CHP-Three, 1976, pp. 39-41.

4. William Penn Mott, Jr. to William J. Murtagh, May 18, 1973, DPR: 537.0.

5. William Murtagh to William Penn Mott, Jr., July 13, 1973. *Ibid.* Murtagh declined Mott's invitation to chat with the committee because he had no plans to be in California in the near future.

6. William Penn Mott, Jr. to Russell W. Porter, July 24, 1973. *Ibid.* Porter agreed with Mott but advised him to wait until the state inventory was completed before taking action:

> My feeling on this matter now is that it might be best to wait for one year until a major part of our current statewide inventory has been completed. In that period of time, we may very clearly see how a California 'latitude of interpretation' may be applied to local, state and national register sites and in so doing be able to apply more stringent criteria to local sites and state sites based upon quality and quantity of the type of resources that have been inventoried.

Mott apparently agreed with this recommendation, noting "OK" with his initials beside this comment. Porter also promised not to drop the matter. See Porter to Mott, August 20, 1973. *Ibid.*

7. R. Bruce Payne to William Penn Mott, Jr., August 26, 1974, and Mott to Payne, September 19, 1974. *Ibid.* Payne feared that National Register selections could be influenced by political maneuvering rather than historical and/or architectural merit as properly intended."

Mott's letter to Payne referred to Murtagh's "recent" decision to allow states to "set up their own criteria for placing sites and buildings on the National Register providing those criteria did not conflict with the national criteria." This was apparently done by his staff according to an undated policy statement entitled "National Register of Historic Places. Criteria of Evaluation: Interpretation and Policy," courtesy of Sandra J. Elder, Office of Historic Preservation. The staff would prepare commentary-evaluation sheets for four areas of significance: events, persons, architecture, and potential yield of historic or prehistoric information. Only those rated moderate, relatively strong, or strong would be considered eligible for nomination. "Local" significance would be equated with "county" significance, thus limiting California's contributions to the Register "to properties deemed to be the most significant in any given category or sub-category on the county-wide inventory of districts, sites, buildings, structures, and objects." It was recognized that limitations on the number of sites nominated were necessary to avoid "diluting" the Register program.

8. John Michael to Tom King, February 5, 1974, and February 28, 1974. *Ibid.*

9. Barry Keene to William Penn Mott, Jr., February 14, 1975; Mott to Keene, February 25, 1975. *Ibid.* It is clear from Mott's letter that there was more involved. Mott mentioned Caltrans and the Federal Highway Administration, and said his staff was trying "to move as fast as we can" in the Eureka Freeway project that was being stopped while structures were being evaluated for eligibility on the National Register. Mott commended the citizens of Eureka "for their interest in historic preservation such as the renewal of their downtown commercial area and a proposal to safeguard many historically and architecturally valuable buildings by relocating them." He noted that "these programs can be incorporated into the Federal procedures." Keene, who represented the Eureka area, expressed concern that municipalities be "given ample warning of and the opportunity to participate in such" programs.

10. David M. Kinchen, "Property Rights, Preservation Debated," Los Angeles *Times*, June 27, 1976. *Ibid.* The review board rejected the La Jolla application, and the Volcano request was withdrawn by the applicant.

11. Knox Mellon to Robert B. Rettig, March 2, 1976. *Ibid.* Owners were also to be notified when their properties were officially listed on the Register.

12. Knox Mellon to Clare Berryhill, March 29, 1976. *Ibid.* Mellon informed Berryhill that if property owner consent was deleted from the bill, his office would agree that once an application was received, they would notify the appropriate governmental jurisdiction and seek their input. Letters would be mailed no later than 30 days before the meeting of the state review board. S.B. 1514 died in Assembly committee on August 9, 1976. See also William E. Padgett to Susan Mead, August 11, 1976, DPR: 530.

13. Cultural Heritage Board, City of Los Angeles, to State, County & Federal Affairs Committee of the City Council, City of Los Angeles, October 19, 1977. DPR: 530.0. This action was taken after the State Historical Resources Commission recommended the nomination of the Pasadena Athletic Club to the Register in July 1977 despite strenuous objections from the City of Pasadena. See Knox Mellon to Herbert Rhodes, July 21, 1977, OHP.

14. "Minutes," State Historical Resources Commission (hereafter abbreviated as SHRC), July 12-13, 1979, OHP. A.B. 772 gave local jurisdictions forty-five days in which to transmit written comments to the commission. See California *Statutes of 1979*, ch. 624, in Elder, *Public Resources Code*, March 1983, n.p.

15. P.L. 96-515, 94 Stat. 2989-2990 (1980).

16. CHP-Three, 1973, p. 21; CHP-Three, 1975, p. 19.

17. William Penn Mott, Jr. to Robert Moretti, February 21, 1973, DPR: 538.0. See pp. 2-3 of the chronology enclosed in the letter to Moretti.

18. "Minutes," HLAC, August 17, 1972, and October 27, 1972, DPR: 023. In August, the Landmarks Advisory Committee's comments indicated that they were not in agreement with the words "concentration camp." Warren Furutani who represented both the JACL and the Manzanar Committee told the Landmarks Advisory Committee: "You are not willing to change your mind nor are we willing to change our opinion about the wording." In October, the Landmarks Committee again tried unsuccessfully to agree on terminology for a plaque. At both meetings, John Michael was instructed to come up with a solution agreeable to all parties.

19. Mott to Moretti, February 21, 1973. The meeting Mott referred to when the phrase "concentration camp" was approved occurred in Mott's office in November 1972 with Frank Iwama of the JACL, committee chair Kathryn Kaiser, Mott, Michael, and historian David Tucker in attendance.

20. Sue Kunitomi Embrey, "Manzanar Committee. Chronology of Events," May 1973, in Manzanar Landmark File, OHP.

21. John H. Michael to Sue Embrey, undated rough draft, ca. February or March, 1973. *Ibid.*

22. John H. Michael to Glen A. Settle, September 12, 1972. *Ibid.* Eight or nine people were in attendance.

23. Embrey, "Chronology of Events," p. 2. See also John Michael to Sandra Elder, ca. spring 1986.

24. *Ibid.*

25. Mott to Moretti, February 21, 1973.

26. *Ibid.* Mott also proposed that the sentence could read: "May the injustices and humiliations suffered in this concentration camp never emerge again."

27. Embrey, "Chronology of Events," pp. 2-3.

28. John H. Michael to Amy Grossman, October 26, 1973; Manzanar Landmark File, OHP. Michael also wrote:

> The plaque wording commemorating the Manzanar Relocation Center was a result of deliberations of several organizations and individuals for over a year. Representatives of Americans of Japanese ancestry who were incarcerated in the various camps, the Japanese-American Citizens League, members of the California Historical Landmarks Advisory Committee, historians, members of the Legislature and other interested persons took part in the decision to incorporate 'concentration camp' in the wording. Their feeling is that the term is correct as defined in standard dictionaries; that is, 'an enclosed camp for the confinement of prisoners of war, political prisoners, aliens, etc..' The plaque wording also states the term 'relocation center' and cites the principal causes for these camps to have been established.

29. William Penn Mott to Shonin Yamashita, December 28, 1973. *Ibid.*

30. In May 1976, the State Historical Resources Commission rejected the proposed plaque wording which referred to Tule Lake as a "concentration camp." According to Commission Chair Clement Meighan, their reasons included: public confusion over the meaning of "concentration camp;" plaques should record history instead of editorializing on it; the wording would increase instead of reduce tension and prejudice; and the JACL should put up its own monuments which could express whatever sentiments they wanted. See "Minutes," SHRC, May 6, 1976; and C. Meighan to Herbert Rhodes, 6 May 1976, in Tule Lake Landmark File, OHP.

In March 1977, State Historic Preservation Officer Herbert Rhodes reversed the commission's decision to ensure "that this generation as well as future generations be reminded of the incarceration, and that we should guard against it ever happening again." He inserted the word "American" into the proposed JACL plaque wording, which now read:

> Tule Lake was one of ten American Concentration Camps established during WWII to incarcerate 110,000 persons of Japanese ancestry, of whom the majority were American citizens behind barbed wire and guard towers without charge, trial or establishment of guilt.
>
> These camps are reminders of how racism, economic and political exploitation, and expediency can undermine the constitutional guarantees of United States citizens and aliens alike. May the injustices and humiliation suffered here never recur.

Rhodes was hopeful "that the plaque would in some way contribute to the spirit of guarding against these types of camps happening again in this country." See "Tule Lake State Historical Landmark," press release, March 16, 1977, in Tule Lake Landmark File, OHP.

31. Mott to Yamashita, December 28, 1973. Manzanar Landmark File, OHP.

32. David Ushio to William S. Briner, March 28, 1973. *Ibid.*

33. William S. Briner to Frank La Haye Metal Works, Inc., March 20, 1973. *Ibid.*

34. See A.C.R. 99, June 12, 1972. *Ibid.* A.C.R. 99 was entered into the Assembly *Journal* as H.R. No. 135 on November 28, 1972. Because it was estimated that the cost of the studies

would total $10,000, James Tryner, chief of the Resource Management and Protection Division, and Robert Uhte, chief of the Design and Construction Division, recommended that no action be taken without funding. Tryner and Uhte to Robert H. Meyer, chief deputy director, May 18, 1973. *Ibid.* It is John Michael's recollection that "in the beginning, the JACL merely wanted a plaque at the site and a 'Roadside Rest' where the story could be told. They didn't want a full scale restoration/interpretation. That was Mott's idea." Michael to Elder, ca. Spring 1986.

35. William Penn Mott, Jr. to Frank Ogawa and to Masamori Kojima, April 3, 1974. *Ibid.*

36. William Penn Mott, Jr. to Russell W. Porter, April 16, 1974. *Ibid.*

37. See: "The Manzanar Relocation Center-A Cultural Resources Study," N.d.; and Russell Cahill to Floyd Mori, April 10, 1978. *Ibid.* The department conducted three workshops in October and November 1978 (Lone Pine, Independence, and Little Tokyo in Los Angeles) in an effort to obtain the advice and counsel of internees and other interested parties in "planning for possible development of a state historical park at Manzanar." See press release, "Workshops on Manzanar Scheduled," October 13, 1978, OHP; and "Manzanar Committee releases views on 'camp' park proposal," *Rafu Shimpo,* November 6, 1978.

38. "Minutes," HLAC, April 26, 1973.

39. *Ibid.,* September 6, 1973. When Mott asked his staff to consider the possibility that Drake landed at Bolinas Lagoon as advocated in *Drake's California Landing* by Aubrey Neasham and Bill Pritchard, he was told: "We would hope that research can be continued in sufficient time to make a final determination before the 1976 Centennial [*sic*] celebration." James P. Tryner to William Penn Mott, Jr., February 8, 1974. Furthermore, after discussing the Bolinas possibility, his staff concluded that

> it is an interesting concept but very theoretical at this point. The proponents for the Drake's Bay landing and inner-San Francisco Bay landing have presented tremendous amounts of evidence to support their contention. However, this theory seems to be based on a piece of tar and what might be discovered under the Bolinas Lagoon Reservoir. I believe the report deals mostly in conjecture at this point,...

Russell W. Porter to Mott, February 15, 1974. DPR: 520.

40. "Minutes," SHRC, October 21-23, 1978. Two commissioners were absent: archaeologist Ernestine Elster and Native American Joy Sundberg.

41. CHP-Three, 1973, p. 22.

42. *Ibid.,* 1974, p. 20.

43. *Ibid.,* 1975, p. 19.

44. *Ibid.,* 1976, p. 8. By March 1, 1976, there were 498 historic resources in the program.

45. Kathryn Kaiser to Knox Mellon, January 25, 1976, DPR: "California Points of Historical Interest: General Correspondence," 539.0. She asked that commission practice "to accept almost every Point submitted as long as it has the signature of the Chairman of the County Board of Supervisors" be agendized for the next commission meeting in March. She presented a written report to the commission at their May meeting. See "Minutes," SHRC, May 6, 1976, "Attachment C."

46. In addition to certification of local significance by the county board of supervisors, approval from the appropriate local historical society or heritage commission was also requested. See "Statement of Policy for State Historical Landmark Registration and Point of Historical Interest Program," revised May 1, 1975 [*sic?*], OHP. This policy statement was still in use in 1982. See Sandra J. Elder, comp., *A Handbook of Basic Reference Materials for the State Historical Resources Commission* (Sacramento: Office of Historic Preservation, June 1982).

These additions were suggested to the commission in a letter from Knox Mellon, executive secretary to the commission, February 20, 1976, OHP. Mellon also suggested that the commission may "want to do away with the program in its entirety and to retain only the National Register and State Historical Landmark programs."

47. See "Excerpts from State Historical Resources Commission Meeting of May 6, 1976," OHP; Kelsey to Nadine I. Hata, September 22, 1976. A similar opinion was expressed by Pauline Pace, chairman, Historical Heritage Commission, Santa Clara County to State Historical Resources Commission, April 21, 1976, OHP.

48. "Minutes," SHRC, January 6, 1978.

49. *Ibid.*, May 10, 1978. Knox Mellon to Gerald A. Smith, July 14, 1978, DPR: 539.0.

50. See Barbara A. Henderson to State Historical Resources Commission, October 18, 1978, DPR: 539.0. Henderson, who chaired the County of Los Angeles Historical Landmarks Committee, requested the commission to reconsider the National Register requirement because "most organizations, such as local historical societies, are unable to meet the technical requirements." That the National Register submission has not been enforced was confirmed by Aaron Gallup, conversation with author, May 12, 1983, San Francisco; and Sandra Elder, telephone conversation with author, February 3, 1992.

51. David A. Tucker to John H. Michael, October 13, 1972, OHP.

52. David A. Tucker to John H. Michael, December 29, 1972. *Ibid.* Also see Chapter 14.

53. CHP-Three, 1973, p. 22.

54. David A. Tucker to John H. Michael, May 2, 1973, OHP.

55. Aaron A. Gallup to John H. Michael, June 8, 1973, Aaron Gallup Files. In May, thirty-five environmental impact statements were reviewed.

56. Aaron A. Gallup to John H. Michael, August 8, 1973, and August 31, 1973. *Ibid.*

57. Aaron A. Gallup to John H. Michael, November 1, 1973, and December 3, 1973. *Ibid.* During November, 125 reviews were conducted. Although this represented a decline, there was an actual increase in Section 106 reviews which represented "a considerable expenditure of staff time."

58. CHP-Three, 1974, p. 20.

59. Aaron A. Gallup to John H. Michael, March 4, 1974, and April 1, 1974, Aaron Gallup Files.

60. Aaron A. Gallup to John H. Michael, May 7, 1974. *Ibid.*

61. William E. Padgett to James M. Doyle, July 3, 1974, OHP. The six staff members were: Supervisor James M. Doyle, State Park Historian II Aaron A. Gallup, State Park Archeologist William C. Seidel, Historian I Eugene Itogawa, William Padgett, and Senior Stenographer Sandra J. Elder. See CHP-Three, 1975, pp. 38-39.

62. William E. Padgett to James M. Doyle, August 5, 1974, OHP.

63. William E. Padgett to James M. Doyle, December 4, 1974. *Ibid.* The request that agencies and consultants do their own research before contacting the state was based on the fact that of the 228 projects reviewed in November, 92 "were as a result of direct letters to the State Historic Preservation Officer requesting information in the preparation of environmental statements or reports." Staff also agreed to limit letters on federally assisted subdivision projects to those "over 10 acres except in critical areas of concern."

64. See Aaron A. Gallup to Russell W. Porter, February 10, 1975, OHP. Also see CHP-Three, 1975, p. 4, which states:

> As of April, 1975, California had 72 active cases of projects before the National Advisory Council on Historic Preservation involving conflicts between the projects and present or potential National Register sites. This number of cases represents almost twice as many as any other state in the country. Most of these cases have been detected through the environmental review process. Once potential effect is determined, the National Advisory Council and the State Historic Preservation Officer seek alternatives to the proposed project or at least ways to mitigate the damaging effects of the project on the site. This critical review and consultation activity has taken great amounts of staff time.

The report also recommended streamlining the process to allow staff "to concentrate on

conflicts of a critical nature and to shift efforts toward early computerization of data...."
Furthermore, attempts would be made "to further clarify and formalize review and
consultation procedures with federal agencies." See p. 18.

65. CHP-Three, 1976, p. 9.

66. These included EIRs (2,600), Section 106 (130), determinations of eligibility (525),
local public works grants (3,700), and A-95 reviews, including "significant state and local
projects with no federal involvement or NEPA documents" (4,800). See CHP-Three, 1977,
n.p.

67. William E. Padgett to James M. Doyle, February 10, 1975, OHP.

68. CHP-Three, 1976, p. 9. The report concluded: "Consequently, environmental
documents prepared by HUD Block grant recipients are being reviewed."

69. John H. Michael to Thomas F. King, February 27, 1973, DPR: 537.0.

70. John H. Michael to Kathryn H. Kaiser and Committee Members, February 20, 1974,
DPR: 023. Before their February 15 workshop, Mott had advised Chairperson Kaiser: "I
would suggest that you develop ideas to strengthen the present Committee and to indicate
in a new title its broader responsibility." Mott to Kaiser, February 6, 1974, DPR: 023.

71. "Minutes," HLAC, September 6, 1973, and January 3, 1974; and Michael to Kaiser,
February 20, 1974. The names suggested included Commission of California's Historical
and Cultural Heritage, and History and Cultural Heritage Commission.

72. Russell W. Porter to William Penn Mott, Jr., February 20, 1974, DPR: 023. One staff
response came from Francis A. Riddell, then supervisor of the department's Cultural
Resources Section, who felt the new commission would have little value unless supported
by a professional staff of experts. He believed the proposal did not address those crucial
issues raised by the Historical, Archaeological, and Paleontological Task Force. Riddell
observed: "Although a full-blown Heritage Department is presently out of reach as regards
financing, it would be well to implement the HAP Task Force recommendations as fully as
possible—and make improvements over time." Riddell to James Tryner, March 4, 1974,
DPR: 023. Riddell had a vested interest in the task force; he served as its executive director.
Appended to Riddell's memo to Mott was a note from James P. Tryner, Chief of the
Resource Management and Protection Division, dated March 4, 1974: "Mr. Riddell's
comments are brief, after an initial review, but are well taken and I concur in them."

73. Karl Schnetz to John Michael, May 13, 1974; Robert H. Meyer to Eugene A. Chappie,
May 19, 1974. *Ibid.*

74. When first introduced on April 29, 1974, the bill proposed that the commission chair
serve as state historic preservation officer. This was opposed by the department as being
unrealistic because commission members were all volunteers. See "Bill Analysis," Resources Agency, May 21, 1974; A.B. 4146, as Amended in Assembly, June 20, 1974. *Ibid.*

75. "Bill Analysis," May 21, 1974.

76. Russell W. Porter to William Penn Mott, Jr., July 29, 1974, DPR: 537.0.

77. See William Penn Mott, Jr. to Kathryn H. Kaiser, August 7, 1974, DPR: 537; and
"Minutes," HLAC, September 5, 1974.

78. *Public Resources Code*, sec. 5020.4 (West Supp., 1981). Also see *California Statutes
of 1974*, ch. 1156.

79. *Public Resources Code*, sec. 5020.5 (West Supp., 1981). Also see *California Statutes
of 1975*, ch. 859; Elder, "Public Resources Code," n.p.; N.B. Livermore, Jr., to Ronald
Reagan, February 28, 1974, DPR: "Historical, Archaeological and Paleontological Task
Force," 027; and State of California, Legislative Analyst, *California's Heritage (Pursuant to
ACR 274, 1974 Session)*, Sacramento, March 1975, pp. 1, 11-13. The five agencies were: the
State Archives, the California Heritage Preservation Commission, the Historical Landmarks
Advisory Committee, the Cultural Resources Section and the Department of Parks and
Recreation, and the proposed State Historical Resources Commission. The legislative
analyst also recommended

in order to reduce the isolation of the State Historical Resources Commission from the operations of the Department of Parks and Recreation and especially the State Park and Recreation Commission, the Governor should appoint the chairman or vice-chairman of the Historical Resources Commission to the Park and Recreation Commission. This will permit better communication between the two commissions and facilitate understanding of problems where both commissions have an interest.

Arnett's bill also included the legislative analyst's recommendation that the definition of historical units in the park system be expanded to include archaeological sites.

80. "Minutes," HLAC, July 6, 1973. Mott was requested to send copies of the resolution to the governor, president of the senate, and the speaker of the assembly. See John H. Michael to William Penn Mott, Jr., July 15, 1975, DPR: 023. The resolution was brief:

> WHEREAS the State Capitol has served as the seat of California government for almost 100 years; and
>
> WHEREAS the State Capitol is an outstanding example of the Classic Revival style of architecture; and
>
> WHEREAS the State Capitol is the symbol of government in California;
>
> NOW, THEREFORE, BE IT RESOLVED that the California Historical Landmarks Advisory Committee reaffirms its position to preserve and restore the State Capitol to be used as the seat of government and as one of the State of California's most important landmarks;...

81. For a brief summary of the project, see John Berthelsen, "A Capitol Tug-of-war," in a special supplement, "The Restored Capitol," Sacramento *Bee*, January 3, 1982. For an idea of the restoration proposal, see "Restoration and Development of the Capitol for the Joint Committee on Rules, California State Legislature," Sacramento, February 1975. Girvigian helped to spearhead the drive to save and preserve the capitol as chair of the California A.I.A. Historic Resources Committee in 1972-1973; in 1974, he began to research and develop the capitol restoration program, "eventually proposing and guiding the development of its public museum program and its art and antique furnishing projects as well." See "A Personal and Professional Vita of Raymond Girvigian, F.A.I.A.," January 1982, p. 5.

82. "Minutes," HLAC, July 6, 1973. See also John H. Michael to William Penn Mott, Jr., July 13, 1973, DPR: 023, for a copy of the resolution which was subsequently forwarded to Secretary for Resources, N.B. Livermore, Jr.

83. "Minutes," HLAC, November 8, 1973; Raymond Girvigian to John Michael, November 15, 1973, Raymond Girvigian File, OHP.

84. "Minutes," HLAC, March 4, 1974.

85. William Penn Mott, Jr. to John H. Michael, April 8, 1974, DPR: 023.

86. Restoration and Building Codes Meeting, May 14, 1974; Raymond Girvigian, "Proposed State Historical Building Code," April 4, 1975, in "Appendix," DPR: 023.

87. *California Statutes of 1975*, ch. 906; also see O'Connell, *et al, Historic Preservation*, pp. 146-147.

88. National Trust for Historic Preservation, "California: Building Codes and Preservation," February 1978, p. 4; O'Connell, *et al., Historic Preservation*, p. 147. See also State Historic Building Codes Advisory Board, *California State Historic Building Code*, n.d.; and *California Statutes of 1984*, ch. 1314.

89. *California Statutes of 1976*, ch. 192.

90. "Minutes," HLAC, September 23, 1971; Glen A. Settle to William Penn Mott, Jr., October 4, 1971, DPR: 023.

91. William Penn Mott, Jr. to Glen A. Settle, December 22, 1971. *Ibid.*

92. John H. Michael to William Penn Mott, Jr., October 26, 1972. *Ibid.* R. Coke Wood to John Michael, October 31, 1972. *Ibid.*

93. Department of Parks and Recreation, *California Historical Landmarks* (Sacramento: Department of Parks and Recreation, 1975). See also William Penn Mott, Jr. to Kathryn H. Kaiser, March 15, 1974, DPR: 023.

94. In their 1984 report, the California Heritage Task Force submitted specific recommendations designed to clarify and strengthen the State Historical Resources Commission. In contrast to the 1974 legislation, S.B. 1252, which was approved by the governor on September 10, 1984, increased the size of the commission from seven to nine members who had to demonstrate expertise in prehistoric archaeology, historic archaeology, architectural history, ethnic history, and folklife, as well as history and architecture. Two of the nine were required to be public members or experts in fields the governor determined to be necessary for the commission to function; all were to serve four-year terms. The commission's relationship to the Office of Historic Preservation and the state historic preservation officer was defined. Additional responsibilities included: development and adoption of criteria for rehabilitation of historic structures; establishment of policies for and annual updates of the statewide historical resources plan which then considered architecture, history, archaeology, and folklife; preparation of recommendations to the department based on the statewide plan and prioritizing of historical resource projects; development of criteria and procedures for a California Register of Historical Resources; development of criteria and procedures for selection of federally funded preservation projects; and preparation of a budget to fulfill mandated commission duties. Public consultation was required for many of these responsibilities. See: California Heritage Task Force, *Report*, pp. 32-34; and *California Statutes of 1984*, ch. 1289.

95. Engbeck, *State Parks*, p. 122. Rhodes was appointed in March.

96. Herbert Rhodes to Edmund G. Brown, Jr., May 8, 1975, DPR: "National Conference of State Historic Preservation Officers," 024. Rhodes requested that Brown appoint him to the position as soon as possible and enclosed a draft letter for his consideration. Also see Brown to Stanley K. Hathaway, ca. May 22, 1975.

97. William E. Padgett to James M. Doyle, May 12, 1975, OHP.

98. David A. Tucker to Claire T. Dedrick, February 8, 1975, DPR: 024.

99. Claire Dedrick to David A. Tucker, March 6, 1975. *Ibid.*

100. Mrs. Leland S. Lewis to Claire T. Dedrick, February 1, 1975. *Ibid.*

101. Claire Dedrick to Mrs. Leland S. Lewis, March 17, 1975. *Ibid.*

102. Clement Meighan to Herbert Rhodes, May 3, 1975, Clement Meighan Files, OHP; and Russell W. Porter to Herbert Rhodes, May 6, 1975. *Ibid.* Also see "Minutes," HLAC, May 1, 1975, OHP.

103. William Penn Mott, Jr., interview with author, December 16, 1982, Oakland, California.

104. Knox Mellon to Herbert Rhodes, March 31, 1976, OHP. James M. Doyle was reassigned on October 17, 1975. Mellon to Duane Frink, November 7, 1975, OHP.

105. Robert Berner, Urban Conservation Officer, Heritage, to Claire T. Dedrick, May 26, 1976, DPR: 530. Berner sent copies to Charles Hall Page, Californians for Preservation Action, and John Frisbee of the National Trust. Knox Mellon was sent a "blind copy."

106. Milton Marks to Claire Dedrick, June 3, 1976; Dedrick to Marks, June 25, 1976, *ibid.* Dedrick stated that by remaining with the department, the Office of Historic Preservation would be able to enjoy "excellent support facilities, as well as close working coordination with other professional preservationists within the State Park System."

107. Knox Mellon to Robert Berner, June 7, 1976. *Ibid.* Earlier, Mellon had written to Rhodes: "This time they at least sent me a carbon. The facts as usual are distorted. It's the same Charles Page, Heritage group. I think I would just ignore them." Mellon to Rhodes, May 28, 1976. Rhodes did not take Mellon's advice; instead, he requested that Mellon write to Berner and stated: "I want to review it before it goes out." N.d.

108. Knox Mellon to Herbert Rhodes, September 10, 1976. *Ibid.*

109. Knox Mellon to Herbert Rhodes, July 6, 1977. *Ibid.*

110. Russell W. Cahill to Edmund G. Brown, Jr., September 7, 1977, OHP; Edmund G. Brown, Jr. to Cecil B. Andrus, September 21, 1977, OHP; and Engbeck, *State Parks*, p. 123.

111. California Heritage Task Force, *Report*, pp. 31-32; California Preservation Foundation, "Status Report. California Heritage Task Force Recommendations, April 1986," p. 1; California *Statutes of 1984*, ch. 1289. The state historic preservation officer (SHPO), a gubernatorial appointee, serves as the executive secretary to the commission and head of the Office of Historic Preservation. The SHPO is responsible for the preservation and enhancement of California's historical resources.

The functions of the Office of Historic Preservation include serving as staff to the commission and SHPO; recommending properties for the National Register, Historical Landmark, and Point of Historical Interest to the commission and SHPO; administering a variety of state and federal preservation programs; providing public education, information and technical assistance; promoting the preservation and enhancement of historical resources to local, state, and national agencies and organizations; cooperating with cultural and ethnic commissions; and reviewing and commenting on the impact of publicly funded projects by governmental bodies on historical resources.

CHAPTER 13
A DECADE OF EXPANSION IN OTHER STATE PRESERVATION PROGRAMS

1. Department of Parks and Recreation, *California State Park System Plan* (Sacramento: Department of Parks and Recreation, 1968), p. 6. Historical units were defined as "areas limited in size which preserve objects of historical interest, and places commemorating important persons or historic events." In 1968, the acreage had a market value exceeding $800 million.

In 1968, there were also fifty state parks, fifteen scenic or scientific reserves, twenty-eight state recreation areas, seventy-one state beaches, and nine unclassified areas.

2. *Ibid.* Also see Engbeck, *State Parks*, p. 107. The groundwork for the plan was laid in 1967 with the publication of a three-volume work. See Department of Parks and Recreation, *Policy Statements for Planning and Development of Park Units Within the California State Park System* (3 vols., Sacramento: Department of Parks and Recreation, 1967), DPR: "State Park System Plan: Reports," 339.1.

3. See Hanson to Mott, October 25, 1967, DPR: 339.0. Also, Parks and Recreation, *State Park System Plan*, 1968, pp. 50-55, 68-70. The twenty-year acquisition plan totaled $150 million, with two-thirds to be used for combined preservation and recreation projects. See pp. 50, 54.

4. The functions have not changed over the years. In 1982, they were described as "Missions:" Cultural Heritage, Natural Heritage, and Recreation. See Department of Parks and Recreation, *Mission 1990. 1982 Update of the State Park System* (Sacramento: Department of Parks and Recreation, June 1982), pp. 5, 9, 12. The system's cultural heritage mission in 1982 was described as follows:

> The State Park System, in concert with other agencies, preserves and interprets outstanding examples of California's colorful past for public enjoyment, education, and inspiration. The system should provide an adequate number and a balance of areas and facilities that best represent the periods of human experience in California.

To accomplish this, the department

1. Acquires significant sites, structures, and artifacts that best represent the themes of each era of California history.
2. Maintains, restores, and reconstructs significant historic sites, structures, and artifacts in the system to protect their historical integrity.
3. Develops interpretive programs that present significant aspects of each era and theme in the state's history.

4. Provides and permits developments and activities that enhance the public's understanding and enjoyment of historic units.

As of July 1981, the State Park System had expanded to 1,045,050 acres in 277 units of which 37 were historical units.

5. Department of Parks and Recreation, *State Park System Plan*, 1968, pp. 1-3, 42-47. Also, CHP-One, pp. 10, 80. The only difference in categories was that the 1973 plan consolidated "architecture and dwellings" and "agriculture" into the larger "domestic" category. Both plans stressed that acquisitions had to be of statewide significance. The 1968 plan identified "now-or-never" priority historical acquisition projects; Columbia State Historic Park was at the top of the list.

6. William Penn Mott, Jr., interview with author, December 16, 1982, Oakland, California. Also, Engbeck, *State Parks*, pp. 104-105.

7. Department of Parks and Recreation, *State Park System Plan*, 1968, p. 5; and Department of Parks and Recreation, *Organization Plan for the Department of Parks and Recreation*, November 1, 1967, pp. 3-4.

8. John Knight, telephone conversation with author, May 4, 1983.

9. See "Benefits of Park and Recreation Areas," December 3, 1968, DPR: 339. The six-page, typewritten report concluded:

> it can be demonstrated that the California State Park System not only is an economic asset to the State, but it insures an environmental quality which in no small part contributes to the fact that California is now the number one State in the Union. Continuing the development of the State Park System and the acquisition of lands for future development is good business. The small percentage of the State's General Fund which goes toward the support of the State Park System is paid back to the State many times, both in new dollars spent by visitors coming to the State and in revenues received from concessions, fees and charges, as well as the intrinsic values which can be attributed directly to the quality of the State parks which give California its unique environmental quality.

10. James E. Warren to James E. Fisher, May 14, 1969, DPR: 339.

11. The plan reproduced the era chart from the 1970 plan, provided a narrative description of the eras and cultural values, and identified deficiencies in the park system for future interpretation or expansion. See Department of Parks and Recreation, *California Coastline Preservation and Recreation Plan* (Sacramento: Department of Parks and Recreation, August 1971; reprinted November 1972), pp. 77-90, 106-108.

12. Department of Parks and Recreation, *Resource Management Directives for the California Department of Parks and Recreation* (Sacramento: Department of Parks and Recreation, January 1974), p. 27. Also see *Resource Management Directives for the California Department of Parks and Recreation*, revised edition, May 1979, 1832.3 (60). The 1979 edition contains a significant change in wording regarding preservation and restoration of historic structures or features in the park system. They would be preserved and/or restored "unless they are *not historically important* within the primary period for the unit...," (italics mine), 1832.3 (64-b). The 1974 version stated: "...unless they are *of less than primary importance* within the period...," (italics mine), p. 28.

As for the designation of historic units as "monuments" or "parks," the 1974 directives explained:

> Originally, all units of the State Park System were either State Parks or State Historical Monuments. Following the establishment of unit classification by the Legislature in 1961, the Historical Units were designated by name either as State Historical Monuments or State Historic Parks. In May 1970 the generic term "Monument" was dropped (except for Hearst San Simeon SHM), and all such historical units were then designated as State Historic Parks.

See p. 8.

Other plans were not as inclusionary. In 1974, Russell W. Porter, chief of the Grants and Statewide Studies Division, had to request that the proposed *Coastal Land Environment* publication include sections on cultural resources because "historical, architectural and archeological resources are significant aspects of the coastal environment...." Porter to James P. Tryner, chief, Resource Management and Protection Division, July 16, 1974, DPR: 530.

13. Mott, interview with author, December 16, 1982.

14. Robert G. Bates to James P. Tryner, October 18, 1968, DPR: 520.

15. James P. Tryner to Robert G. Bates, November 7, 1968, DPR: 538.0.

16. The project ran into difficulty very early. In the spring of 1969, Mott was informed that little progress had been made on the project to date. Information Officer William Dillinger, who stressed the importance of the project, committed his section to completing the study. "We feel that all ethnic groups should be incorporated in all our interpretations wherever appropriate. I think we realize that all races have made material contributions to California's heritage and should be recognized." It was estimated that Michael's section could complete the study in "three man weeks" in comparison to Tryner's estimated "four man months." See William Dillinger to William Penn Mott, Jr., February 17, 1969, DPR: 538.0. The initials "JHM" at the bottom of Dillinger's letter indicate that it was probably written by Michael.

Supervisor Allen W. Welts, Historical Resources Section, disapproved of the Interpretive Services Section's research efforts which he characterized as "indicative of a desire to serve or of more than a common capacity for work" or "it might indicate excessive involvement in tasks outside the perimeter of work normally assumed to be the responsibility of the Interpretive Services Section." Considering the shortage of trained personnel, he expressed "surprise that Interpretive Services has the personnel and time to do, not only the work expected of them, but our work as well." Furthermore, he noted:

> In all fairness, we must confess that this situation is not common to Interpretive Services alone. Repeatedly, over the years, historical research has been done by people trained in a variety of disciplines other than history. As a result, historical and archeological resources have been inadvertently encroached upon, damaged or ruined. The historical and archeological resources of this state are not so expansive or expendable as to permit their careless manipulation. Yet we find interpreters, landscape planners, state park planners, park developers, operations personnel and even administrative personnel assessing historical and archeological sites and deciding what must be done with them.

He insisted: "categorically this type of service is the responsibility of the Resource Management and Protection Division." See Welts to James P. Tryner, March 14, 1969, DPR: 520.

17. Grant Proposal, Department of Parks and Recreation, "California Ethnic Minority Historic Resources Survey," May 25, 1976, OHP; Knox Mellon to Jerry Rogers, March 20, 1978, OHP. Survey coordinators were: Eleanor Ramsey (Afro-American); Nancy Wey (Chinese American); Isami Waugh (Japanese American); Lee Dixon (Native American); and Jose Pitti (Spanish-surname). The final report was finally published in December 1988. See Department of Parks and Recreation, *Five Views. An Ethnic Sites Survey for California.*

18. William Penn Mott, Jr. to J.M. Souza, April 26, 1967, DPR: 538.0; Robert F. Uhte to Elmer Aldrich, September 2, 1965, DPR: 538.0; Robert F. Uhte, "Historic Preservation Guidelines," Department of Parks and Recreation. Division of Beaches and Parks, June 27, 1966, DPR: 348.0; Uhte to All Regional Supervisors, January 26, 1967, DPR: 348.0; Uhte to James P. Tryner, June 2, 1969, DPR: 348.0. Uhte was encouraged that Tryner planned to make available an historian to do restoration research. In the past, the department had contracted with architects to do the necessary architectural-historical research, and when historical studies were produced, Uhte considered them "as somewhat of a bonus."

19. Mott to Souza, April 26, 1967.

20. Department of Parks and Recreation, "Historical Structures Task Force Report," March 1, 1969, DPR: "Historical Structures Task Force Report," 027.1. Other task force members included John Michael, Allen Welts, and Earl Carlson (Planning and Development Division). The absence of master plans was underscored by historian Welts a week later. See Allen W. Welts to James P. Tryner, March 14, 1969, DPR: 520.

21. Engbeck, *State Parks*, pp. 108, 110-111.

22. N.B. Livermore, Jr., to Ronald Reagan, May 22, 1969, DPR: "Colonel Allensworth State Historic Park: General Correspondence," 319.0-341.

23. William Penn Mott, Jr. to All Division Chiefs, March 27, 1970, DPR: 319.0-341; Department of Parks and Recreation, *Colonel Allensworth State Historic Park. General Development Plan and Resource Management Plan* (Sacramento: Department of Parks and Recreation, April 1976), revised preliminary, DPR: "Colonel Allensworth State Historic Park: Unit Background," 089-341. This preliminary plan, "as far as I know, was never approved." See Beth C. Walls to Donald T. Hata, Jr., February 11, 1983. Also see William Penn Mott, Jr. to Ronald Reagan, April 7, 1969, DPR: 089-341.

24. Mott to Division Chiefs, March 27, 1970. Also see Department of Parks and Recreation, "Progress Record-Allensworth," n.d.; James E. Warren to Mott, May 20, 1969; and Mott to Warren, May 29, 1969 in DPR: 089-341.

25. Department of Parks and Recreation, *Allensworth Feasibility Study. Requested by Senate Bill No. 557, Senate Concurrent Resolution No. 66, Statutes of 1970* (Sacramento: Department of Parks and Recreation, November 1971), DPR: 089-341, pp. x, 11-13. The educational and cultural center would include a museum, library, research and student study center, and administrative and seminar facilities.

26. Parks and Recreation, *Allensworth. General Development Plan*, April 1976, pp. 3-4, 12.

27. Not only had the legislature voted to establish a state park at Columbia in 1945, they directed the Division of Beaches and Parks in 1955 to research and prepare a master plan for the park's "restorational development." They also authorized a museum. See *Public Resources Code*, secs. 5040-5041 (West Supp. 1981); *Statutes of 1955*, ch. 71. The *Public Resources Code*, sec. 5042, also discusses the Columbia State Historic Park Association which had been in existence since 1947; its role was to advise the Park Commission (and after 1959, the department) regarding the master plan and any other policies for the preservation, restoration, and management of the park.

28. [Allen W. Welts], Department of Parks and Recreation, "Columbia State Historic Park. Identification of Building Sites - Summary of Type, Location and Recommended Use of Buildings in That Historic Park," n.d.[ca.1964], DPR: "Columbia State Historic Park: Reports," 359.1-307, pp. 1-2. Welts was concerned about construction of: a parking lot on or near the site where gold was discovered in Columbia, an out-of-period Columbia House Restaurant, and the Eagle Cottage and the Columbia Gazette, which were both off their original sites. In 1963, he prepared an interpretive plan for the park. By that time, the total number of proposed structural reconstructions had reached 385; 16 restorations had been completed. See Department of Parks and Recreation, *Interpretive Plan for Columbia State Historic Park* (Sacramento: Department of Parks and Recreation, Revised January 1970), in John Michael Files, p. 8.

29. Office of the Auditor General, State of California, *Department of Parks and Recreation. Report on Columbia State Historic Park*, October 1968, DPR: "Columbia State Historic Park: Reports," 519.1-307, pp. 2-6. By 1986, $2.5 million had already been spent for acquisition and restoration projects with an anticipated $3.8 million still needed to complete the effort. The auditor general's office predicted that based on the past rate of accomplishment, it would take another two decades before the planned development could be completed. They recommended that the department give priority to accelerating the process to complete the park unit in a reasonable time. See pp. i, 2.

30. Parks and Recreation, *Interpretive Plan for Columbia*, 1970, pp. iii, iv, 14. According to the plan, it was Frederick Law Olmsted in his early reports who urged "the concept of a living historic community" which would retain or recreate the community's original features and "retain certain later period and modern features and conveniences, suitably concealed, as would allow people of the 20th Century to live and work comfortably in the old surroundings." See p. 1.

To maintain the park's integrity in the face of aggressive land development in surrounding areas, the 1970 plan recommended acquiring properties within the boundaries proposed in 1948 by Aubrey Neasham. Protective zoning rather than outright acquisition, which Mott supported, was suggested as a way to create an adequate buffer zone and overcome funding shortages. See pp. 11-12; and William Penn Mott, Jr. to James P. Tryner, March 20, 1970, DPR: "Columbia State Historic Park: Reports," 429.1-307.

31. David A. Tucker to John H. Michael, August 3, 1970, DPR: "Columbia State Historic Park: General Correspondence," 429.0-307. In 1971, writing as a member of the California Historical Landmarks Advisory Committee, Clement W. Meighan observed the following after a committee meeting at Columbia in January. He described the town as a "result of a series of compromises and half-way measures without a consistent and clear policy governing its development." The compromises that prevented Columbia "from attaining its potential" included:

- the "compromise between state and private ownership" which resulted in assigning capital investment, losses and subsidies to the state while profits belonged to the concessionaires. Meighan recommended adoption of the suggestion in the 1946 Olmsted report that a non-profit public corporation be created whereby anyone making a profit from Columbia had to be shareholders in the corporation.

- the "compromise between historical integrity and financial considerations" which resulted in restoration, stabilization, or construction without adequate prior historical and archaeological research. Another problem was "the compromise between making a buck for the concessionaires and hewing to a correct atmosphere which may not bring in quite as much revenue." Meighan recommended authentic period items such as the old square nails at the Monterey Customs House be made available to visitors, a bookstore where appropriate books and replicated newspapers and posters could be purchased, and greater availability of art works from the period.

- the "compromise between the goal of a 'live' town and the goal of a museum" which he personally felt did not come "off too well." He suggested that the museum be moved out of the center of town because "there was no museum at all in Columbia when it was a living town." He felt that the pharmacy was "a museum set-piece in the middle of a live town, jarring as a Disneyland set in the middle of any real town."

Finally, he suggested that the state "get the cars out....control the signs a little better...[and that] landscaping...be improved." See Clement W. Meighan to Wm. Penn Mott, 16 January 1971, Meighan Files.

32. See Parks and Recreation, *Interpretive Plan for Columbia*, 1970, p. iv; and James P. Tryner to John H. Knight, September 25, 1975. *Ibid.* Tryner saw chickens roosting on a wagon that needed repair. Also: the wig on the schoolteacher was battered and not appropriate for the costume, the recording at the school house was not understandable, signs were confusing or misleading, and there were "cars, cars everywhere."

33. Engbeck, *State Parks*, p. 113; William Penn Mott, Jr., "California State Parks Foundation, Board of Trustees Meeting," May 5, 1970, DPR: "Foundations: California State Park Foundation," 026.

34. William Penn Mott, Jr. to William Randolph Hearst, Jr., May 25, 1972, DPR: 026.

35. Engbeck, *State Parks*, p. 113; Mott, "Board of Trustees Meeting," pp. 8-9. Robert Howard was named Executive Secretary.

36. Norman B. Livermore to American Motors Conservation Awards, November 3, 1971, DPR: 026.

37. Herbert Rhodes to Joseph M. Long, August 27, 1975. *Ibid.* Long chaired the Board of Trustees from its inception through 1975. Mott became president of the foundation after he left state service in 1975.

Foundation projects were undertaken with input from departmental staff and concern for master plans for acquisition and the protection of historic areas. In 1974, for example, Mott asked his staff for ideas for possible foundation projects. Of eighteen ideas forwarded to the foundation for consideration, four were preservation-related: restoration of Romillard Mansion in Hillsdale, acquisition of "the original site of the Sonoma Mission," acquisition of Buenavista Winery, and conversion of buildings at Bodie State Park into interpretive facilities. See William Penn Mott, Jr. to Robert Howard, January 10, 1975. *Ibid.*

The foundation continues to assist the department. Upon departmental request, as of November 1983, the foundation had undertaken forty-nine projects, donated $55 million in artifacts, money, and 20,000 acres of new park land. See Judy Tachibana, "Parks Department Has Its Santa. Foundation Donates Land, Money For Improvements," Sacramento *Bee*, November 21, 1983.

38. California *Statutes of 1971*, ch. 827.

39. Clyde Kuhn, "The SCA Planning and Development Model Proposal," unpublished paper submitted to the annual meeting of the Society for California Archaeology, 15 March 1978, pp. 6-7; and Garfinkel, *An Historical Perspective*, pp. 6-8. The California Archaeology Survey was to have been assisted by the California Archaeology Board which would administer the agency's activities, "including archaeological site survey, evaluation of archaeological and paleontological resources, development of preservation plans for such resources, and contracting with other agencies for execution of these plans. The sum of $80,000 was to be appropriated for the purposes of the act."

40. California *Statutes of 1971*, ch. 827.

41. Dutschke, "Public Interest or Science?" p. 28. Resources Secretary Livermore noted in 1974: "This is the first instance where the California Indian has participated in deliberations which involved matters protecting his heritage and that of other Californians. The input of Indian members on the task force was significant, and the experience gained by those members was most valuable." See N.B. Livermore, Jr. to Ronald Reagan, February 28, 1974, DPR: "Historical, Archaeological and Paleontological Task force," 027.

42. Garfinkel, *An Historical Perspective*, p. 8. The five archaeologists were: Robert Heizer, D.L. True, Jerald Johnson, Michael Moratto, and Riddell. Other members represented California Indians, Caltrans, the California Farm Bureau Federation, University of California, California Historical Society, California state colleges, California Academy of Sciences, California Division of Mines and Geology, the Department of Parks and Recreation, Department of Education, State Lands Division, U.S. Bureau of Outdoor Recreation, and the Society for California Archaeology. See also AHP Task Force, p. i. S.B. 215 did not specify how large the task force was to be but identified the following categories of individuals to be appointed: "representatives of public agencies, representatives of the scientific and scholastic community, one native California Indian resident from northern, central, and southern California respectively, and public members with backgrounds in California archaeological, paleontological, and historical resources study and preservation." See California *Statutes of 1971*, ch. 827.

43. "Minutes," Historical, Archeological, and Paleontological Task Force (hereafter abbreviated as HAP), September 28, 1972, DPR: 027.

44. "Minutes," HAP, October 26, 1972. Moratto agreed to submit another draft to the task force at their November meeting. See Michael J. Moratto, "Suggested Operational Parameters for for a California Heritage Agency (Second Draft)," November 1972, DPR: 027.

45. See William Penn Mott, Jr. to James P. Tryner, November 6 and 13, 1972, DPR: 027. Mott requested to speak with Riddell who he felt had inaccurately informed the task force that the department would not request "that its park system units be exceptions to the work

of the Heritage Department." Mott claimed that he had never discussed the matter with Riddell and that he was uncertain if "we want to release to the Heritage Council, if it is ultimately established, this kind of responsibility." His reservation was based on previously unsatisfactory "relationships with other servicing organizations at the State level, and I have the feeling that we ought to be doing our own work rather than letting someone else try to do it for us." Mott to Tryner, November 6, 1972.

46. William Penn Mott, Jr. to Norman B. Livermore, Jr., November 27, 1972. *Ibid.* The recommendation was again reiterated by Michael J. Moratto, "The Status of California Archaeology: A Report to the Governor and Legislature of California for the State Archaeological Task Force," January 1, 1973, pp. V-3 to V-6, DPR: 027.

47. "Proposed California Heritage Legislation," p. 8 in AHP Task Force. Also, AHP Task Force, p. 24.

48. Robert J. Stoddard to Norman Livermore, September 5, 1973, DPR: 348.0.

49. "Minutes," HAP, April 5, 1973, DPR: 027. John Michael attended a task force meeting and reviewed the state history plan with them. Historical Landmarks Advisory Committee Chair Kathryn Kaiser distributed copies of the task force report to the committee. She, too, complained that it left out history. See John H. Michael to California Historical Landmarks Committee, August 17, 1973; and Kaiser to Members, California Historical Landmarks Advisory Committee, August 17, 1973, DPR: CHP-I, 348.0.

50. John L. Frisbee III, to Francis A. Riddell, August 10, 1973, DPR: 027. Frisbee felt the proposed legislation did not even discuss the problems encountered at state and local levels by various historical societies, preservation groups, and commissions: "At the state and local levels in California, historical societies, historic preservation organizations, and county and city landmarks commissions and boards are working together to retain living historical and architectural environments. This act has barely touched the surface of their problems and needs. As heritage legislation, it needs to be far more comprehensive."

As proposed, the Heritage Board would consist of thirteen members who had to include:

> The Governor or his designee, The Director of the Department, One person of California Indian ancestry qualified in the field of Indian heritage, One person of Spanish or Mexican ancestry qualified in the field of California's Spanish-Mexican heritage, One person of Oriental ancestry qualified in the field of California's Oriental heritage, One professional architectural historian, One professional historian, One professional archaeologist, One professional paleontologist, One representative of the Federal Government, One representative of private enterprise in the State.

See "Proposed California Heritage Legislation," attached to AHP Task Force, pp. 16-17.

51. Frisbee to Riddell, August 10, 1973. *Ibid.*

52. William Penn Mott, Jr. to N.B. Livermore, Jr., October 31, 1973; and John H. Michael to Members, California Historical Landmarks Advisory Committee, August 17, 1973, DPR: CHP-I, 348.0.

53. Mott to Livermore, October 31, 1973. Mott's other concern was the agency's "separateness" which could "place it out of touch with all other planning agencies." His department was trying to coordinate statewide efforts with departmental activities, and "the task force recommendation," he wrote, "seems to me a step in the opposite direction."

54. Livermore to Reagan, February 28, 1974.

55. Robert F. Heizer to Norman B. Livermore, February 20, 1974, Michael J. Moratto Files. Concern for site records maintenance is discussed in Chapter 14.

56. Legislative Analyst, *ACR 274*, pp. 9-12. Another of the proposed department's functions would have been to establish criteria and standards for individuals and institutions "engaged in the field investigation, preservation, or interpretation of heritage sites or remains." The licensing issue continues to be hotly debated, particularly among archaeologists. See "Proposed California Heritage Legislation" in AHP Task Force, p. 14.

57. William Penn Mott, Jr. to Norman Livermore, October 31, 1973, DPR: 348.0.

58. "Minutes," HAP, March 1, 1973, DPR: 027.

59. Francis A. Riddell to Walter Frame, May 29, 1973. *Ibid.* Riddell said: "we have yet to discover any particular concern by historians in the preservation of California's heritage by the opportunity provided by the creation of this Task Force."

60. Francis A. Riddell to N.B. Livermore, Jr., June 4, 1973. *Ibid.* Frye had resigned, said Riddell, "because of the workload imposed upon him by his regular duties." Riddell nominated Carl S. Dentzel, director of the Southwest Museum, to replace Frye. It is unclear as to whether or not Dentzel was formally appointed inasmuch as the September 1973 report fails to mention him.

61. AHP Task Force, pp. 23-24.

62. "Minutes," HAP Task Force, November 16, 1973; DPR: 027.

63. Frank E. Sylvester to Director, Bureau of Outdoor Recreation, U.S. Department of the Interior, February 19, 1974. *Ibid.*

64. George W. Webber to Arthur D. Pheland, Sr., April 15, 1975. *Ibid.* Also, Michael J. Moratto to Herbert Rhodes, June 8, 1975; and Rhodes to Moratto, June 18, 1975, DPR: 022.

65. California *Statutes of 1976*, ch. 1332. Also see Dutschke, "Public Interest or Science" p. 28. Chapter 1.75 of the Public Resources Code was changed from "Archaeological, Paleontological, and Historical Resources" to "Native American Historical, Cultural, and Sacred Sites."

66. Caltrans' archaeology program is discussed in Chapter 14.

67. Aaron A. Gallup to John H. Michael, May 7, 1974, Aaron Gallup Files; Department of Transportation, *Policy & Procedure on Paleontological, Archaeological, and Historical Resources*, July 22, 1974, No. P74-46, pp. 1-2, courtesy of Duane Frink. This policy statement did not change when new guidelines were issued in 1982. See Department of Transportation, *Policy & Procedure. Archaeological, Historical, and Cultural Resources*, November 24, 1982, No. P74-46, Revised, courtesy of Duane Frink.

68. Knox Mellon to "interested parties," November 20, 1975, OHP: Reading File.

69. Aaron A. Gallup to John H. Michael, March 4, 1974, Aaron Gallup Files.

70. Aaron A. Gallup to Knox Mellon, January 19, 1976. *Ibid.*

71. *Ibid.* Gallup stated that of the 300, at least 50 were significant enough to warrant review and evaluation in accordance with National Register criteria.

72. Knox Mellon to Duane Frink, November 7, 1975, OHP: Reading File.

73. See Herbert Rhodes to James R. Gordon, January 14, 1976 and Herbert Rhodes to Omar L. Homme, May 10, 1976. *Ibid.* Gordon was chief of Environmental Planning, Caltrans; Homme was California Division administrator, Federal Highway Administration. Rhodes told Gordon that Eureka was particularly significant because it had "miraculously escaped the 'progress,' which has destroyed the character of so many of our California cities and has retained one of the finest, most complete collections of Victorian era architecture in the State...."

74. Legislative Analyst, *ACR 274*, pp. 1-5. The report identified the department's duties as: acquiring outstanding examples of landscape for preservation; acquiring, restoring, maintaining, planning, designing, reconstructing, and interpreting structures and properties which depict the state's history; serving as the official state archaeologist; providing limited research as required by the department; preparing a state history plan and allocating federal funds.

75. *Ibid.*, pp. 8-9.

76. *Ibid.*, p. 13.

77. "Minutes," SHRC, May 1, 1975, OHP.

78. Kathryn H. Kaiser to A. Alan Post, May 16, 1975, DPR: 530.0.

79. Dixon Arnett to Kathryn H. Kaiser, May 27, 1975. *Ibid.* Arnett's bill also proposed that the commission's staff would consist of the History Preservation Section and that the

commission assume full responsibility for both state and federal preservation programs. See State Resources Agency, "Bill Analysis," May 21, 1974, DPR: 530. Not only was the department opposed to the legislation for reasons stated earlier, it also believed the commission would be unable to accomplish their duties because of limited staff.

80. California *Statutes of 1975*, ch. 859. Also see F.C. Butcher to Knox Mellon, November 10, 1981, DPR; "Historical Resources Commission: General Correspondence," 022.0.

81. James M. Doyle to Katherine H. Rich, October 10, 1975, OHP: Reading File.

82. Allen W. Welts to Bernita Stage, November 8, 1968, DPR: 520. Welts was not totally discouraging. He suggested that if San Jose State College was amenable to the department's concerns and could "work with us in an equable manner, we would be pleased to discuss the program further. We might actually be able to find a little money with which to defray expenses." Welts was able to find several institutions willing to provide students to assist in research projects. See, for example, Gary L. Shumway to Allen W. Welts, January 4, 1971, DPR: 520. Shumway was willing to provide students from his oral history class to assist Welts "on historical projects common to the need of our history program in Southern California." Welts to Shumway, February 2, 1971.

The idea of assigning students to do research was resurrected in 1974 when "five volunteer state service interns from two local universities worked in the History Preservation Section on a variety of important projects. This was the first year that this valuable source of labor was used." See CHP-Three, 1975, p. 10. In 1977, the number had increased to "an average of 10" such volunteers from nearby universities who worked sixteen hours a week. See CHP-Three, 1978, n.p.

83. William Penn Mott, Jr. to Kenneth H. Cardwell, August 25, 1969, DPR: 348.0.

84. AHP Task Force, pp. 14-15.

85. One early preservation course was offered by historian Ephraim K. Smith at California State University, Fresno, beginning in the fall of 1974. The publicity flyer described it as "one of the few undergraduate courses in historic preservation in the United States. As a basic introductory course, it is open to anyone interested in historic preservation as well as to those students who are considering future studies and careers in the field of historic site preservation and administration." See "Preserving the Past: Historic Site Preservation and Administration in the United States Since 1790. A New Course," Fall 1974, Department of History, California State University, Fresno.

In 1975, Cypress College expressed an interest in offering an undergraduate course in historic preservation. Historic Preservation Coordinator Mellon commented: "It is our belief, based in part on actual experience, that the response to historic preservation classes will be indeed promising, and that institutions offering such are fulfilling a genuine public service." Knox Mellon to Thomas V. Reeve III, December 22, 1975, DPR: 530.

Elsewhere, cultural resource management courses were being offered in the Anthropology departments. For example, Rob Edwards, research associate and lecturer at the University of California, Santa Clara, invited Aaron Gallup to speak to his class in 1975 and enclosed a course outline dating from Spring 1973. See Edwards to Gallup, January 10, 1975, DPR: 530.

86. Peter Mellini and Edgar W. Morse to James Michael Doyle, July 18, 1975, DPR: 348.0; and "Historic Preservation at Sonoma State," n.d. Students could take a major in any field because the program was designed to be a "minor" of twenty units. Also see Peter Mellini, "Historic Preservation Minor Program," n.d. (received by OHP, March 23, 1978).

87. See Robert Kelley to Entering Class, Graduate Program in Public Historical Studies, July 13, 1976; University of California, Santa Barbara, *The Graduate Program in Historical Studies*, September 1976.

88. Ray Brandes to Colleague, August 2, 1977. This program was part of the university's extension offerings. Brandes noted that a master's program in American history with an option in historic preservation would be established soon.

89. Leon G. Campbell to Knox Mellon, November 13, 1979, DPR: 348.0. The Western American Studies Program had been in existence since 1972.

90. Ephraim K. Smith to Knox Mellon, September 28, 1979. *Ibid.*

91. In spring 1980, Dominguez Hills initiated a concentration in Cultural Resources Management in the Bachelor of Arts program in Anthropology, and in spring 1982, a Master of Arts in Public History and Historic Preservation was added. In fall 1980, Sonoma State began a Master's program in Cultural Resources Management. Hayward offered an option in Public History under the History Master's program in fall 1983. William Dermody to Nadine Hata, August 25, 1983. Dermody also stated that San Diego State University was planning to offer a Master's degree in Public History in the near future.

General information materials began to appear by the mid-1970s. For example, A.I.A. Institute Scholar Marsha Glenn produced *Historic Preservation: A Handbook for Architecture Students* (Washington, D.C.: American Institute of Architects, 1974); and Matthias E. Kayhoe of the University of Virginia's School of Architecture published a report on "Preservation Education," July 1976; both courtesy of Dan Petersen.

Historians were equally productive in the 1980s. See Committee on Public History, Organization of American Historians: "Historic Preservation. A Guide for Departments of History," (1982); "Educating Historians for Business. A Guide for Departments of History," (1983); and "Teaching Public History to Undergraduates. A Guide for Departments of History," (1984).

For a recent update on the status of preservation-related degrees and curricula, see California Preservation Foundation, *Preservation Degrees in California.* A report prepared by the California Preservation Foundation (Oakland, California: 1989).

92. David A. Frederickson, "Preservation Education! The Cultural Resources Perspective," paper prepared for panel on "Preservation in the College Curriculum," 1984 California Historic Preservation Conference, Sacramento, April 28, 1984.

93. Ronald Tobey, "Preservation Education: The Historic Resources Perspective," remarks prepared for panel on "Preservation in the College Curriculum," 1984 California Historic Preservation Conference, Sacramento, April 28, 1984.

The need to provide students with a theoretical framework as well as practical skills to survive in reality was addressed by Marie McLean, "A Preservation Studies Curriculum With An Annotated Bibliography," June 1980. McLean's study was partially funded through the Office of Historic Preservation.

For a geographer's perspective, see R.M. Newcomb, "A Business and A Charity: Conservation in Transition," Norma Wilkinson Memorial Lecture, 1982, *Geographical Papers* No. 83, University of Reading, Department of Geography, courtesy of R.M. Newcomb.

94. Anne C. Roark, "Colleges Take Scolding from Carnegie Panel," Los Angeles *Times,* November 2, 1986. The Carnegie Foundation for the Advancement of Teaching issued a report on the American undergraduate college and concluded that it is "a 'troubled institution'" in need of reform. According to the *Times,* the report concluded:

> 'Driven by careerism and overshadowed by graduate and professional education, many of the nation's colleges and universities are more success-ful in credentialing than in providing a quality education for their students. It is not that the failure of the undergraduate college is so large, but that the expectations are so small.'

95. See California Heritage Task Force, *Report,* pp. 84-87. One early effort by a teacher was that of Cynthia Mathews, "Teachers' Handbook for Historic Enrichment. Curriculum, Resources, Activities," Santa Cruz County: The Historic Enrichment Project, Spring 1978.

96. As part of the Task Force's study, Allan L. Petersen, dean of Program Evaluation and Approval in the Chancellor's Office of the California Community Colleges, sent out a survey to the state's 106 colleges in July 1983. Of the sixty-two respondents, fifty-four reported no preservation-related programs or courses. Of the eight who reported affirmatively, seven had courses only peripherally related to preservation. These included architectural history,

California history, and survey courses in construction technology. Gavilan College was not one of the eight. See Nadine Hata to Museums, Archives, and Education Committee, California Heritage Task Force, 18 September 1983; and Gavilan College, "Construction Technology & Rehabilitation," n.d.

Tom Reeve of Cypress College reported on his survey sheet that he had little success in implementing his preservation program because of lack of students to meet the high enrollment figures now required. Of forty enrolled students, only twenty completed the program.

CHAPTER 14
ARCHAEOLOGICAL PRESERVATION: NEW POLICIES AND NEW DIRECTIONS

1. King and Lyneis, "Preservation," p. 874.

2. *Ibid.*, p. 877.

3. National Park Service, *Archeological and Historic Data Recovery Program,* Fiscal Year 1976, pp. 7-8.

4. King and Lyneis, "Preservation," p. 877.

5. Comptroller General of the United States, *Are Agencies Doing Enough or Too Much for Archeological Preservation? Guidance Needed.* A Report to the Chairman, Committee on Interior and Insular Affairs, House of Representatives (Washington, D.C.: United States General Accounting Office, April 22, 1981), pp. 37-38.

6. King and Lyneis, "Preservation," pp. 877-79.

7. Gammage, *et al.*, *Historic Preservation,* pp. 90-91; O'Connell, *et al.*, *Historic Preservation,* pp. 130-131; and T. F. King, "Mitigation of Mammoths in California and Other Bizarre Stories," *The Missouri Archaeologist,* 35 (January-June 1973): 32-35.

8. King, "Mitigation of Mammoths," p. 33.

9. King and Lyneis, "Preservation," pp. 883-84. The Society for California Archaeology also drafted emergency guidelines for agencies involved in EIRs on how to include archaeology in EIRs and EISs. See Society for California Archaeology, "Memorandum. Recommendations for Preparation of Environmental Impact Reports Pertaining to California Archaeological Resources," n.d. This was later updated to include a comprehensive set of procedures. See Thomas F. King, Michael J. Moratto, and N. Nelson Leonard III, compilers, "Recommended Procedures for Archaeological Impact Evaluation." Report on a study by the Society for California Archaeology in cooperation with the Archaeological Survey, University of California, Los Angeles, n.d.

10. McGimsey, *Public Archeology,* pp. 133, 230-234; AHP Task Force, p. 12. Also see Marin County Ordinance No. 1589.

11. Thomas F. King, interview with author, September 26, 1982, Riverside, California. The Inyo ordinance was passed on August 7, 1967, and the Marin Ordinance on June 20.

12. King and Lyneis, "Preservation," p. 885.

13. King interview with author, 1982. Also see King and Lyneis, "Preservation," p. 885; and Chapter 12 of this work.

14. *Ibid.* The controversy also had a direct impact on King himself because it destroyed his consultant market: "nobody would hire a consultant who goes around and sues his clients." What King was referring to, in part, was the cultural resource study that began in 1978. Directed by David A. Frederickson, the project area encompassed 5,900 of the total 17,000 acres on the National Register, including sixty-five already identified prehistoric and twenty-three historic sites. The Corps of Engineers also agreed with King's assessment of the importance of: "the great breadth of cultural resources being examined, ranging from the usual archeological and historical materials, to ethnobotanical sites and processes, linguistic study of the local Native American language, and the careful documentation of the Corps' project itself." See U.S. Army Corps of Engineers, *Fiscal Year 1978. Cultural*

Resources Investigations for Civil Works Activities (Washington, D.C.: Office of the Chief of Engineers, April 1979), pp. 6, 839-840; also Will Morgan, *The Effect of Federal Water Projects on Cultural Resources: Implementation of the Historic Preservation Act of 1966 by the Army Corps of Engineers, Bureau of Reclamation, and TVA* (Washington, D.C.: Environmental Policy Institute, September 1977), p. 26.

15. Comptroller General of the United States, *Uncertainties Over Federal Requirements for Archeological Preservation at New Melones Dam in California*, Report to the Chairman, Committee on Interior and Insular Affairs, House of Representatives of the United States (Washington, D.C.: General Accounting Office, December 21, 1979), pp. 14-15, 17.

One of the important sites that disappeared under the waters of the dam was Melones, "the largest nineteenth and early twentieth century development in the project area...." One of the historical archaeologists who investigated the Mother Lode gold rush town was Julia G. Costello, former member and chair of the State Historical Resources Commission who synthesized "the documentary, ethnographic, and archaeological work conducted on the townsite of Melones" for the Bureau of Reclamation in January 1983. See Julia G. Costello, *Melones. A Story of A Stanislaus River Town*, Sacramento: Bureau of Reclamation, U.S. Department of the Interior, January 1983, pp. 3-4.

16. Comptroller General, *Uncertainties Over New Melones*, pp. 3, 15, 21-24. From 1968 through mid-1975, the National Park Service was responsible for the studies and had produced seven separate surveys for $152,000. Beginning in October 1975, the Corps of Engineers took over direct responsibility for the studies. By November 1979, the corps claimed that the total contract costs for this phase was $1.9 million.

17. Their one victory was the state Water Control Board's Decision 1422 of 1973 which "declared the Stanislaus canyon 'a unique asset to the state and the nation' that should not be destroyed until there was an actual need for storing water. The need was to be proven with signed contracts between water-using agencies and the U.S. Bureau of Reclamation which would run the dam." After several favorable court decisions, a change in governors marked the end of the board's litigation battles, and in March 1983, the board succumbed and announced that the dam would be filled. See *ibid.*, pp. 8-10. The Friends of the River tried unsuccessfully for nearly a decade to save that stretch of the Stanislaus River. Also see Thorne Gray, "Watery End to Battle Against New Melones," Sacramento *Bee*, March 14, 1983.

18. Comptroller General, *Uncertainties Over New Melones*, pp. 13-14. The estimated cost for the dam was $346 million. Did, for example, the 1 percent limit under the 1974 legislation apply to all costs incurred or obligated by the corps, thus leaving only $900,000 out of $3.46 million for the remainder of the cultural resource program? Or was the Department of the Interior's position valid: that it applied only to the work done under the 1978 contract, thus leaving some $1.5 million for future mitigation work. Note that the latter figure was derived from the difference between $3.46 million and the work covered by the 1978 contract. To complicate matters and confuse accountability, the cultural resource program was transferred away from the corps to the Heritage Conservation and Recreation Department in 1979.

19. Michael Moratto, interview with author, March 15, 1983, Sonora, California. For a list of his reports and a review of his efforts, see *ibid.*, pp. 17, 20-21, 28. Science Applications had a staff that reached 60 with costs exceeding $1.4 million by March 1979. They tested forty-nine prehistoric Native American sites, reviewed seventy-eight historic sites, and recovered over 150,000 artifacts.

20. Comptroller General, *Guidance Needed*, 1981, p. 6.

21. *Ibid.*, cover of report.

22. Mary E. Brant to Knox Mellon, April 28, 1977, OHP.

23. Herbert Rhodes to Soil Conservation Service, July 21, 1976, DPR: 537.0.

24. C.E. Stearns to Knox Mellon, April 29, 1977, OHP.

25. Somers, "Federal Government," p. 35.

26. Michael J. Moratto, *The Status of California Archaeology*, Special Report No. 3, Society for California Archaeology, May 1973, pp. 7-8.

27. Donald S. Miller to William Padgett, November 25, 1975, OHP. He included copies of the Forest Service's management manuals which referred to the agency's policies for consultation with the state historic preservation officer.

28. Somers, "Federal Government," pp. 32-35. The new law declared that public lands would "'be managed in a manner that will protect the quality of scientific, scenic, historic, ecological, environmental, air and atmospheric, water resources, and archeological values.'"

29. Ed Hastey to Knox Mellon, April 14, 1977, OHP.

30. Somers, "Federal Government," p. 35.

31. Moratto interview with author, 1983.

32. King, "Mitigation of Mammoths," p. 33.

33. The phrase "creative anarchy" was Tom King's. See *ibid.*, and McGimsey, *Public Archeology*, p. 131.

34. AHP Task Force, p. 1.

35. Clark W. Brott, "The Society for California Archaeology: Founding Purposes and Future Directions," in *A Symposium. The Society for California Archaeology: Founding Purposes and Future Directions*, The Annual Meeting of the Society for California Archaeology, April 3, 1980 (hereafter abbreviated as *Symposium: SCA Founding*), p. 1. Also see King interview with author, 1982; Moratto interview with author, 1983.

36. Brott, *ibid.*, p. 1.

37. A few months earlier, a meeting was convened at Petaluma which was convened by the Northwestern California Archaeological Society. Tom King, who had just returned from a tour of duty with the Navy and had just embarked on his studies and professional work, recalled that almost every archaeologist in the state with the exception of Berkeley's Heizer attended to discuss how to handle the state's archaeological records. King interview with author, 1982.

38. Dave Frederickson, "The Society for California Archaeology: A Report from the Acting President 1966-1967," in *Symposium: SCA Founding*, p. 2. State archaeologist Francis Riddell, who was also at the meeting, supported the decision. He, too, called for the immediate establishment of a statewide committee to "concern itself with the multitudinous problems facing California archeology." See Francis Riddell, "State Service Archeology," paper delivered at the Southwest Anthropological Association Conference, Davis, California, April 8, 1966, pp. 5-6.

39. The others were: Clark Brott, private museums; Joe Chartkoff, University of California, Los Angeles; George Coles, community colleges; Al Elsasser, University of California, Berkeley; Dave Frederickson, University of California, Davis; George Kritzman, avocational groups; Francis Riddell, state government; Paul Schumacher, federal government; Albert Spaulding, University of California, Santa Barbara; and Adan Treganza and his assistant Rob Edwards, state colleges. The committee was chaired by Frederickson who credited Brott with the idea of "a congress of California archaeologists." See Frederickson, *Symposium: SCA Founding*, pp. 2-3.

The committee proposed to accomplish their goal by establishing a code of ethics, holding annual meetings to discuss problems, publishing a newsletter, and coordinating member research and activities through the state archaeological program. See Paul Chace, "Cradle, Credo, and Cross," *Symposium: SCA Founding*, p. 7.

Also see King interview with author, 1982. King would later become president of SCA while still a graduate student.

40. Paul Chace, "Cradle, Credo, and Cross," unpublished paper, June 1975, which was later summarized in *Symposium: SCA Founding*, pp. 3-8. In 1978, Chace was chair of SCA's Constitution Committee. The Articles of Incorporation were signed in October 1967 and filed in October 1968.

41. Garfinkel, *An Historical Perspective*, pp. 4-5.

42. *Ibid.*, pp. 5-8. Also see "History of the Regional Office Program," OHP, ca. 1980; Kuhn, "SCA Planning and Development Model," p. 8; Chester King to District Archaeologists, August 7, 1973. King, who was SCA president, attached a draft "Proposal: SCA District Archaeological Clearinghouses;" and Paul G. Chace, "Text of White Paper on SCA Clearinghouses, Their Creation, Current Status, and Recommendations for the Future," SCA *Newsletter*, 12 (August 1978): 21-22.

According to Garfinkel, just after the department's departure from the Caltrans program, SCA conducted two 16-hour courses at Caltrans' request. The sessions were "to train...engineers who normally walk highway alignments in the planning stage of projects, to recognize and report on archaeological sites." The courses were discontinued because "some professional archaeologists were uncomfortable with...engineers conducting archaeological surveys and site recording."

43. "History of the Regional Office Program," OHP. Until they began receiving funding in 1976, the regional offices charged a small fee for their services. They controlled access to site records and were required to send copies of new records to Sacramento whose "records were to be the master records and available to be reviewed at no cost by qualified individuals." In fiscal 1977-78, $48,000 was budgeted for the regional offices; in 1980, $95,000 was divided among the regional officers. By 1980, their contracts required: "(1) updating regional records and maps in their region, (2) assigning new site numbers, (3) sending copies of new site records to the Office of Historic Preservation (OHP), (4) maintaining archaeological reports and (5) developing bibliographies of reports, (6) developing referral lists of professional archeologists, (7) reviewing up to four National Register nominations, (8) encoding all new sites of OHP computations, (9) developing files on all incomplete site records, and (10) attending at least two meetings called by OHP."

Also see Chace, *ibid.*; William E. Padgett to The Regional Officers, Statewide Site Surveys, January 31, 1977, OHP; and W.C. Seidel, "Cultural Resource Management in the State of California," *Proceedings of the Third National Conference, Task Force on Recreation Use and Resource Management*, Portland, Oregon, May 12-15, 1980, pp. 170-172.

44. Frederickson, *Symposium: SCA Founding*, p. 5.

45. Seidel, "Cultural Resource Management," p. 171. Also see a recent draft handbook: Office of Historic Preservation, *California Archeological Inventory. Handbook for Completing An Archeological Site Record (DPR 422 A-I-Rev. 5/86)*, Review-Draft, June 1986, courtesy of William C. Seidel.

46. These objectives are discussed in Chapter 13 of this work. They included the governor's veto of A.B. 1788 and the failure of the State Archaeological, Historical, and Paleontological Task Force's attempt to create a separate heritage department. The work on the task force was actually done by its vice chairman, Michael Moratto, who was then president of SCA. See Moratto interview with author, 1983; and Kuhn, "SCA Planning and Development Model," pp. 7-8, 16-18.

47. Kuhn, *ibid.*, p. 4; and Russell L. Kaldenberg, "The Future of the Society for California Archaeology - An Examination of the Kuhn Model," unpublished paper presented to the SCA meeting in Bakersfield, California, April 9-11, 1981. Courtesy of Paul Chace. According to Kaldenberg, SCA president in 1981-1982, Kuhn was paid $750 by the society for his efforts.

48. See papers presented at the Annual Meeting of the Society for California Archaeology, Redding, California, April 3, 1980, collected in *Symposium: SCA Founding*. In 1981, Kaldenberg proposed that the Kuhn model be re-examined and altered "to fit the needs of California archaeology today." At the SCA meeting, he announced plans to publish the model in a future newsletter. Kaldenberg, *ibid.*, pp. 1, 3.

49. AHP Task Force, p. 14.

50. One of his first responsibilities was "to set up contracts for all the Districts and appropriate local institutions in order for them to perform archeological surveys for Caltrans. This objective was realized for most Districts by September 1973." Garfinkel, *An*

Historical Perspective, p. 9.

51. *Ibid.* By 1982, Caltrans had thirty archaeologists on its staff. Some of the in-house work was actually forced on the agency by hiring freezes or contract cancellations in 1975-1976.

52. Louis S. Wall to author, February 22, 1983.

53. As with other units in the department, the names of this section changed frequently. In 1967, for example, Riddell headed the Archaeology Section under the Resource Management and Protection Division; in 1972, it was called the Cultural Resources Section. In 1976, it became the Cultural Archeological and Historical Services Unit under the Cultural Heritage Section in the Resource Preservation and Interpretation Division. See "Resume," Francis A. Riddell; and Department of Parks and Recreation, *Organization. Department of Parks and Recreation, July 1976*, pp. 21-28.

54. Department of Parks and Recreation, "A History of Archeological Work in the State Park System as Reflected in the Cultural Heritage Section Library," November 1979, courtesy of Francis A. Riddell.

55. Francis A. Riddell, "Historic Archaeology in the California State Park System," ca. 1975, unpublished paper, pp. 3-4.

56. Tom King to John H. Michael, January 23, 1974, DPR: 537.7.

57. John H. Michael to Tom King, February 5, 1974, DPR: 537.0.

58. Thomas F. King to John H. Michael, April 1, 1974, DPR: 537.0. Some of King's letters were sharply critical. In this one, for example, he told Michael that his insistence on property owner notification "reflects your continued unwillingness to acquaint yourself with archaeological reality."

59. Clement Meighan, "Suggested Policy on Archaeological Districts," April 30, 1975, Clement Meighan File, OHP.

60. "Minutes," SHRC, July 10, 1975. See appended "Policy Statement. Archeological District Submissions for the National Register of Historic Places," July 10, 1975. Meighan produced additional guidelines that were sent to applicants who requested materials for archaeological nominations. "Guidelines for Nominations of California Archaeological Sites to the National Register of Historic Places," July 1977. Also C. Meighan to James M. Doyle, 23 September 1975. See Clement Meighan File, OHP.

61. Clement Meighan, "Hints on National Site Nomination. Registration of Archeological Sites as Historical Monuments," *SCA Newsletter*, 8 (6), 1974, p. 3, Meighan File, OHP.

62. John M. Fritz to Herbert Rhodes, September 10, 1975; Rhodes to Fritz, September 23, 1975; DPR: 537.0. Fritz was president-elect, Society for California Archaeology.

63. Francis A. Riddell to Deborah L. Spence, March 12, 1976, DPR: 537.0.

64. Clement Meighan to author, 2 July 1982.

65. Thomas F. King, "Preservation and Rescue. Challenges and Controversies in the Protection of Archaeological Resources," *Journal of Field Archaeology*, 6 (1979): 225.

66. *Ibid.*, pp. 225-226. Examples such as Tahquitz Canyon Dam have been discussed earlier in this chapter.

67. *Ibid.*, p. 226. Also see Dutschke, "Public Interest or Science?" p. 28. One issue continues to smolder: the question of reinterment of Native American remains.

68. Seidel, "Cultural Resource Management," p. 170.

69. Comptroller General, *Guidance Needed*, 1981, p. i; Dutschke, "Public Interest or Science?" p. 29.

70. See "Minutes," Organizational Meeting, Heritage Preservation Task Force, Los Angeles, California, October 16, 1982, p. 3; and Senate Concurrent Resolution No. 4, 1981 (Resolution chapter 75). At that organizational meeting, Task Force Chairman Roger Holt

reviewed the legislative history of SCR 4, which originally had included archeology, but was amended to exclude it at the urging of Senator Ray Johnson in order to gain his necessary support for passage. However, the archeological appointment to the Task Force was retained. It was generally agreed that a subcommittee chaired by Paul Chace (the archeologist on the Task Force) might be appropriate. The overriding concern was that the issue of archeology might overshadow the rest of the work of the Task Force. Generally, those present felt the Task Force also has a moral commitment to Assemblyman [*sic*] Johnson because of the legislative history.

CHAPTER 15
PRESERVATION-RELATED EFFORTS ELSEWHERE IN CALIFORNIA:
A RISING TIDE OF ACCEPTANCE

1. Office of Historic Preservation, "Historic Preservation Elements in California" (Sacramento: ca. 1980), pp. iii, iv. The Office of Historic Preservation cautioned that this survey, which was sent out by the Office of Planning and Research, was probably incomplete because there was no way to ensure an accurate or complete response to the questionnaire.

By 1969, several local governments passed historic district ordinances that recognized the importance of historic zoning as a preservation weapon. These included the cities of Fremont, San Diego, Sacramento, Santa Barbara, San Gabriel, Monterey, Nevada City, and Folsom. See William Penn Mott, Jr. to Richard W. Hale, Jr., December 17, 1969, in DPR: 348.0.

For additional specifics, see Gammage, *et al.*, *Historic Preservation*, pp. 57-58 and 92-93. On pp. 112-121, they provide brief summaries of preservation ordinances enacted by: Claremont (1970), Del Norte County (1973), Fremont (n.d., 1974), Inyo County (n.d.), Livermore (1973, 1974), Los Angeles City (1962), Los Gatos (n.d.), Marin County (n.d.), Mendocino County (n.d.), Nevada City (n.d.), Nevada County (n.d.), Ojai (1974), Pasadena (1969), Riverside City (1968), Sacramento City (1970, 1972), San Diego City (1971), San Francisco City (n.d., 1972), San Leandro (n.d.), Santa Barbara (n.d., 1960, 1966), Santa Clara County (n.d.), Santa Rosa (1972), South Pasadena (1971), Stockton (1971), Ventura City (n.d.), Ventura County (n.d.), Yreka (1972).

2. See Office of Historic Preservation, "Historic Preservation Elements," p. 10; City of Santa Cruz, Planning Department, *Historic Preservation Plan*, 1974, p. 45; City of Santa Cruz, Ordinance No. 75-25, Chapter 24.29, November 27, 1975; Historic Preservation Commission of the City of Santa Cruz, *Policy Statement and Administrative Guidelines. Revolving Fund for Historic Preservation. Report and Recommendations*, April 1976, p. 1.

3. Office of Historic Preservation, "Historic Preservation Elements," pp. iii-iv. By 1980, the Office of Historic Preservation had also produced guidelines for "the preparation of local ordinances that provide for cultural resources, including historical, architectural, and cultural landscape features." Archaeological resources were excluded because of their "sensitive nature" which required "a different approach." See Office of Historic Preservation, "Model Cultural Resource Management Ordinance for California Cities and Counties," n.d.

4. National Trust for Historic Preservation, *Directory of Landmark and Historic District Commissions* (Washington, D.C.: The Preservation Press, October 1976), pp. 10-13.

5. Sandra Elder, "Heritage and Landmark Commissions," March 1977, Elder: OHP.

6. City of San Buenaventura, Historic Preservation Commission, *Be a Part of Ventura's History. Designating Landmarks in San Buenaventura*, n.d.

7. National Trust, *Directory of Commissions*, p. 58.

8. City of San Diego, "Ordinance No. 9322," December 7, 1965. Also see Marco Thorne to California Historical Landmarks Advisory Committee, June 26, 1968, DPR: "California Registered Landmarks: General Correspondence," 538.0. National Trust, *Directory of Commissions*, pp. 58-59. With the city council's approval, another 180 days could be granted.

9. See City of San Jose, "Ordinance No. 17927," November 25, 1975; and National

Trust, *Director of Commissions*, p. 59. By 1976, San Jose had designated thirty landmarks. The commission also advised the director of planning on proposed construction, alterations, demolition, or removal of landmarks.

10. Ralph A. Mead to Allen W. Welts, April 24, 1970, DPR: "National Register of Historic Places: General Correspondence," 537.0; National Trust, *Directory of Commissions*, p. 59; and Gammage, *et. al.*, *Historic Preservation*, pp. 123-126. Also see Chapter 7. The board also had access to graphic services from the Department of City Planning of which it was a part, to title services from various city and county agencies, and to archaeological expertise if needed. The 180-day moratorium could be extended an additional 180 days by the board of supervisors.

11. Mead to Welts, April 24, 1970.

12. Frisbee was the director of the Trust's Western Regional Office. See John L. Frisbee III, *Preservation in the West. The 1971-1972 Report of the Western Regional Field Office of the National Trust for Historic Preservation.* n.d., p. 16.

13. El Cuartel was acquired in 1964. Santa Barbara Trust for Historic Preservation, *El Presidio de Santa Barbara State Historic Park*, n.d.; Walter A. Tompkins, "El Paseo Complex Put in Public Trust," Santa Barbara *News-Press*, December 5, 1971. The park brochure stated: "it is hoped that the entire Presidio quadrangle will be authentically restored and reconstructed as it was in the 1790's." The presidio is the focal point of the historic district created in 1960.

Although acknowledging that acquisition and development of the presidio were of primary importance, some of the founders of the trust also envisioned a larger role for their organization. Trust President William F. Luton and Vice President Pearl Chase, for example, wrote:

> While the interest of the Santa Barbara Trust for Historic Preservation is primarily concerned with the acquisition and development of the old Royal Presidio in Santa Barbara, it is, under its charter, able to act throughout Santa Barbara County. As a member of the National Trust for Historic Preservation and the California Conference of Historical Societies, the Santa Barbara Trust is interested in all feasible means of increasing knowledge of and interest in historic sites and monuments throughout California.

Luton and Chase to California State Parks and Recreation Commission, January 9, 1968, DPR: 348.0.

14. The gift was the largest single donation in the city's history. The property's transfer agreement specifically stated: "that the present and future architecture shall conform to the Hispanic styles as defined in the 'Historical Structures' chapter of the city's Municipal Code,..." thereby assuring El Paseo's historic, cultural and aesthetic integrity. See Tompkins, *ibid.*

15. Carol Lindemulder to William J. Murtagh, September 11, 1969, DPR: 537.0. See also Save Our Heritage Organization, *Preservation is Working for San Diego*, n.d.

16. Berkeley Architectural Heritage Association, *Newsletter*, September 1974.

17. Ann Gibbons, "Bowker Decides to Save Naval Arch.," *Daily Californian*, March 9, 1977.

18. "Heritage: 10 Years of Service to San Francisco," Heritage *Newsletter*, IX (Fall 1981): 6-7; unpublished two-page summary of the organization's activities, 1981. Courtesy of the Foundation for San Francisco's Architectural Heritage.

19. By 1981, the loan program had assisted more than twenty low-income homeowners. Rehabilitation loans were offered at 6 percent for exterior rehabilitation of vintage residences, Heritage received a $200,000 grant from the city's Office of Community Development to subsidize the loans through Crocker Bank at below market rates. See "Preservation Loan Program Rehabs Vintage Homes," Heritage *Newsletter*, IX (Winter 1981): 5. The organization also accepts historic preservation easements and holds significant properties such as the Haas-Lilienthal House in trust. The Victorian was acquired in May

1973. See The Foundation for San Francisco's Architectural Heritage, *Heritage*, n.d.; and "San Francisco's Heritage Provides Inspiration," *Newsletter*, Californians For Preservation Action, I (July 1976): 3-4.

Heritage's evolution into "the most developed preservation group in California," said Californians for Preservation Action in 1976, was due to: the commitment and expertise of its young and energetic nine founders; the rallying point provided by taking on the San Francisco Redevelopment Agency that was destroying hundreds of Victorians in the Western Addition; the use of the Western Addition Victorian project as a vehicle to promote "the broad and ambitious concept of conserving the architectural heritage of the city as a whole;" development and implementation of viable alternatives to save structures which gave the organization credibility; a sustained and successful membership drive; excellent communication through a newsletter that emphasizes conservation concerns of interest to a large constituency; visibility and a tangible presence made possible through ownership and operation of the Haas-Lilienthal House; an effective conservation program run by a paid staff director as of March 1975, whose title as urban conservation officer reflected Heritage's purpose; talented and dedicated staff and volunteers; cooperation with other like-minded groups; and compilation of an inventory of architectural resources.

Another useful publication is: Jay Turnbull, ed., *Directory 77: The Foundation for San Francisco's Architectural Heritage. Rehabilitation Advice and Useful Sources for Owners of Vintage Buildings*, 2nd ed. (San Francisco: Foundation for San Francisco's Architectural Heritage, May 1977).

20. O'Connell, *et al.*, *Historic Preservation*, pp. 104-106. Although the court of appeal ruled against the plaintiffs, "the opinion is nonetheless notable among CEQA historic preservation decisions for the relative detail in which the court examined the intricacies of the project approval process and the competing considerations regarding the disposition of the site." Also see "City of Paris Fight Ends," Heritage *Newsletter*, VIII (October 1980): 1-2. For details on the Yerba Buena controversy, see Chapter 16.

21. From a two-page, typewritten, undated description of the Sacramento Trust, written for a February 5, 1970, dinner meeting in Sacramento at which time the trust was made public for the first time. See V. Aubrey Neasham Collection: "Sacramento Trust for Historic Preservation."

22. Old Sacramento, Inc. Committee, to Sacramento Trust for Historic Preservation, February 20, 1973. *Ibid.*

23. Frisbee, *Preservation in the West*, p. 16.

24. John H. Michael to William W. Jorgenson, May 30, 1973, DPR: 538.0. In 1979 the California Historical Society was named the state's official historical society. No funding was provided to support this honor. See California, *Government Code*, sec. 429.5 in Balme, Vol. II: *State Legislation*, n.p.

25. V. Aubrey Neasham and Irene S. Neasham to Albert Rodda, July 5, 1973, Neasham Collection.

26. Albert Rodda to V. Aubrey Neasham, July 9, 1973. *Ibid.*

27. Senate Bill No. 1458, August 27, 1973. *Ibid.*

28. John L. Frisbee III, to Millard Mangum, November 15, 1973.

29. *Ibid.*

30. Robert Berner to Roger P. Sharmer [*sic*], July 10, 1975; Scharmer to Those interested in a California Preservation Action Organization, July 31, 1975, Aaron Gallup Files. The meeting was held on June 28, 1975. Berner was Heritage's urban conservation officer. Also see John Merritt to author, March 1987.

31. "Organization Meeting #2," August 9, 1975, Notes by Mardi Gualtieri, *ibid.*

32. Roger Scharmer to All Those Interested in California Preservation Action Organization, September 12, 1975. *Ibid.* At the second meeting, it was agreed that all persons present would write their legislators requesting support of the proposed Historic Building Code.

33. John Merritt to Fellow Preservationist, August 30, 1975. *Ibid.* Also, Merritt to

author, March 1987.

34. "Notes on Meeting held Saturday, September 13, 1975, Pasadena;" and "Preservation Conference Attendance List-September 13, 1975, Pasadena Central Library," Aaron Gallup Files. There were twenty-six in attendance at the meeting at which $26 was collected. The meeting did not produce unanimity on the organization's purpose. Some believed that political action was of primary importance, whereas others stressed service to local groups. Some expressed concern that hard pressure political action would alienate allies and supporters. There was unanimity, however, on the position "that the organization should be statewide even if it was later to prove more efficient to regionalize or halve the structure." Questions were also raised about time to be spent on education and terminology, and "a 'non-elitist' terminology was accepted."

35. "Functions and Duties," n.d. *Ibid.* Also, Merritt to author, March 1987.

36. Charles C. Knill to Governor Edmund G. Brown, Jr., September 16, 1975. Aaron Gallup Files.

37. John [Merritt] to Judith [Waldhorn], November 3, [1975]. *Ibid.* Also, Merritt to author, March 1987.

38. John Merritt to Bill, Pam, Aaron, Roger, Mary & the rest of the Sacto cabal, December 15, 1975. *Ibid.*

39. See *Newsletter,* Californians for Preservation Action, Volume I, Number 4, October 1976, pp. 6, 8; and untitled draft of CPF's statement of mission, objectives, finance, organizational planning, and history, 9/10/84, p. 11. Identified as CPF trustees in the 1978 Articles of Incorporation were: Stephen L. Taber, Judith Lynch Waldhorn, and Harold K. Major. Waldhorn and Major were both elected to CPA's first board in June 1976.

40. From a two-page, typewritten description of California Preservation Foundation, n.d., no formal title. Also see Mark Ryser, President, Californians for Preservation Action, to CPA Member, n.d.; and James P. Stickels to Preservationist, March 9, 1984.

41. John F. Merritt to The Members of Californians for Preservation Action and of the California Preservation Foundation, March 13, 1984.

CHAPTER 16
FEDERAL PRESERVATION PROGRAMS: SLOWLY EXPANDING HORIZONS

1. Ernest Allen Connally to William Penn Mott, Jr., July 26, 1968; Robert F. Uhte to Russell Porter, September 12, 1968, and William Penn Mott, Jr. to Ernest Allen Connally, September 17, 1968, DPR: 530. It was hoped that matching funds could be obtained for the project to focus on park structures lacking architectural drawings or historical documentation. These included Bidwell Mansion, Weaverville Joss House, Will Rogers structures, and buildings in Monterey and San Juan Bautista. The department was also hoping to secure help from the state universities and colleges.

2. James C. Massey to William Penn Mott, Jr., October 3, 1968. *Ibid.*

3. Connally to Mott, July 26, 1968. *Ibid.* The southern California project was aimed at surveying early twentieth century architectural landmarks between Santa Barbara, Los Angeles, and San Diego. Measured drawings, photographs, historic, and architectural analyses and location maps were to be prepared. See Historic American Buildings Survey, "1968 Roster of Summer Field Projects and Personnel." *Ibid.*, p. 5. Among those involved were David Gebhard of the University of California at Santa Barbara, architect Raymond Girvigian, and architectural historian Esther McCoy. The HABS field office was in the School of Architecture and Fine Arts at the University of Southern California.

4. James C. Massey to David Gebhard, October 3, 1968; Ernest Allen Connally to William Penn Mott, Jr., n.d., ca. March 1969. *Ibid.* Massey shared a few concerns with Gebhard about the 1968 project which were apparently resolved. To continue the project, he said, "It would be necessary, however, to arrange a firmer and more systematic program of local support. It would also be advisable to have a group of regular architectural students

working on National Park Service appointments, although these could be supplemented by other help. In the future also should be a significant exhibit and publication of these studies; possibly a traveling exhibit would be effective. A new expanded and revised HABS catalog for California will also be needed in the coming years."

5. Board of Advisors, National Trust for Historic Preservation, *Preservation in the States. Annual Report 1974-75* (Washington, D.C.: National Trust for Historic Preservation, October 1975), n.p. According to Kathryn Kaiser Gualtieri, who was then book project director for the Junior League of Palo Alto, the project was led by architect Kim Spurgeon of Kansas State University. Telephone conversation with author, May 20, 1983, Sacramento, California. The book was authored by Dorothy Regnery, *An Enduring Heritage: Historic Buildings of the San Francisco Peninsula* (Stanford: Stanford University Press, 1976). In 1974, HABS was also working on a two-year project in San Diego.

6. Robert M. Utley to William Penn Mott, Jr., May 19, 1971; William Penn Mott, Jr. to Robert M. Utley, September 7, 1971. DPR: 537.0.

7. National Park Service, *The National Survey of Historic Sites and Buildings* (Washington, D.C.: National Park Service, 1959), n.p.; and *Part One of the National Park System Plan. History* (Washington, D.C.: National Park Service, 1972), pp. vii-viii. The revisions were aimed at defining "a National Park System that is balanced and complete in its representation of the Nation's historical heritage;" and identifying "the 'gaps' that presently exist in this representation." The themes were: The Original Inhabitants; European Exploration and Settlement; Development of the English Colonies, 1700-1775; Political and Military Affairs; Westward Expansion, 1763-1898; America at Work; The Contemplative Society; Society and Social Conscience.

That the themes are more exclusionary than inclusionary was pointed out to the chair of the Historic Landmarks Program in 1979:

> A perusal of the designated National Historic Landmarks for California reveals glaring omissions of sites which are significant to the state's many ethnic groups. Not only have Asian and Pacific Americans been ignored, but the contributions of California's Black, Indian, Hispanic and "white" groups have not been recognized....
>
> ...Too often, only those landmarks which reflect our "glorious past" are designated national sites while others which reveal the dark underbelly of our heritage are confined to the historical dustbin. If we are not to repeat our mistakes, we cannot forget them. If we are truly a culturally pluralistic nation, we must acknowledge the debt we owe to all who have built our nation and state. The recognition of architectural monuments must be only one part of the national heritage we preserve for posterity. And the National Historic Landmarks program must reflect the varied contributions of all our peoples...for it is this diversity which is our strength.

See Don Hata, Jr. and Nadine Hata to William Lebovich, 19 November 1979.

See National Park Service, *National Historic Landmarks. A Preservation Program of the National Park Service* (Washington, D.C.: National Park Service, 1976), pp. 13-19. The National Survey is still incomplete and the search continues for significant landmarks. Thematic topics are also being explored and expanded, and publications have appeared on completed thematic research. For example, see Robert G. Ferris, series editor, *The National Survey of Historic Sites and Buildings.* Volume XI: *Prospector, Cowhand and Sodbuster. Historical Places Associated with the Mining, Ranching, and Farming Frontiers in the Trans-Mississippi West* (Washington, D.C.: Government Printing Office, 1967).

8. William Penn Mott, Jr. to Walter J. Hickel, May 18, 1970, DPR: 537.0.

9. Roy E. Appleman to William Penn Mott, Jr., June 22, 1970. *Ibid.*

10. See, for example, correspondence from Robert M. Utley to William Penn Mott, Jr., April 10, 1972; and Mott to Utley, May 12, 1972. *Ibid.* The material sent to Mott was divided into two categories: sites recognized as landmarks and sites considered for designation but not recognized.

11. Cornelius W. Heine to Herbert Rhodes, September 9, 1976, DPR: 530.

12. National Park Service, *Historic American Engineering Record Catalog, 1976*, compiled by Donald E. Sackheim (Washington, D.C.: Government Printing Office, 1976), pp. vi, 2-3.

13. A.R. Mortensen to William Penn Mott, Jr., March 29, 1974, DPR: 537.0. Mortensen was director of the Office of Archeology and Historic Preservation in the National Park Service.

14. William Penn Mott, Jr. to A.R. Mortensen, April 17, 1974. *Ibid.*

15. Office of Historic Preservation, *A Survey of Surveys. A Summary of California's Cultural Resource Surveys* (Sacramento: Office of Historic Preservation, May 1981), p. 44. Also Donald S. Napoli, telephone conversation with author, May 19, 1983.

16. For a detailed discussion of the reorganization efforts, see Somers, "Federal Government," pp. 27-30.

17. Mary E. Brant to Knox Mellon, April 28, 1977, OHP. Brant was Region 9's regional historic preservation liaison (RHPL). She told Mellon that:

> The historic preservation program is coordinated by the RHPL, who draws upon the capabilities of agency architects, engineers, designers, realty specialists, and buildings managers. All but the most rudimentary archaeological studies must still be contracted for, as must some services of architectural historians.

Brant was "optimistic" about the General Service Administration's historic preservation program in her region "primarily because of the increased consciousness and active interest of our own personnel and our improved working relationship with the staffs of the State Historic Preservation Officers and the Advisory Council."

18. Department of the Treasury, Bureau of Alcohol, Tobacco and Firearms, *Handbook. Environmental Protection*, January 6, 1976, n.p., OHP. See Mary G. Toki to Knox Mellon, 26 April 1977. The bureau reported receiving several such applications in the past year, with none having an adverse impact.

19. James P. Jaquet to William Penn Mott, Jr., January 10, 1974, DPR: "Executive Order 11593: General Correspondence," Yerba Buena Center Project, 537.50-38.

20. Russell W. Porter to James P. Jaquet, February 25, 1974, *ibid.*

21. Russell W. Porter to James P. Tryner, May 10, 1974. *Ibid.*

22. John L. Frisbee III, to James P. Jaquet, February 12, 1974. *Ibid.* Although other structures were also mentioned, these two buildings became the focal point of preservationist-led opposition to the HUD project.

23. James P. Jaquet to John L. Frisbee III, March 1, 1974. *Ibid.*

24. Charles Hall Page to James H. Price, April 18, 1974, May 2 and May 17, 1974. *Ibid.* Page stated: The substation was designed by "Willis Polk, one of the two or three most influential and important architects of California architecture during the first part of this century." He claimed that "perhaps its lack of more universal acclaim is due to the fact that it was not visible from the street until a number of the surrounding buildings were cleared for parking lots."

25. Webster Otis to James P. Jaquet, May 15, 1974, OHP. Webster said that communication with several experts, including Michael J. Moratto and James Heid of the Adan E. Treganza Anthropology Museum at California State University, San Francisco, and John Frisbee of the National Trust "strongly indicate" that both structures would qualify for the Register. The last quote on archaeological resources would plague the project for years.

The Department of the Interior's warning was based also on correspondence received several months before from James Heid of the Treganza Anthropology Museum. Heid stated that the archaeology section of the Environmental Impact Report which had been submitted to the city and county of San Francisco was "misleading and incomplete" because no archaeological excavation had ever been done in the area. No doubt, he said, because of the nature of the proposed construction, "they will reach the depth of very early cultures." While construction was being halted by litigation, Heid recommended "a research project that would decide if archaeology is feasible." He said: "I feel that a planned professional and scientific excavation could find important and major archaeological data." See Heid to Keith Anderson, December 13, 1973, DPR: 537.50-38.

26. James P. Jaquet to William Penn Mott, Jr., June 17, 1974; Jaquet to Mott, August 28, 1974. *Ibid.*

27. Paul V. Turner, "Report on the Architectural Significance of Existing Structures in the Yerba Buena Center Area, San Francisco," 10 September 1974, p. 1. *Ibid.*

28. James P. Jaquet to Robert L. Rumsey, October 11, 1974. *Ibid.*

29. Arthur F. Evans to James P. Jaquet, November 20, 1974. *Ibid.*

30. Charles Hall Page to Arthur Evans, April 29, 1975. *Ibid.* The PG&E Substation was placed on the National Register on September 6, 1974.

31. John D. McDermott to Robert H. Baida, January 10, 1975. *Ibid.*

32. Robert H. Baida to John H. McDermott, April 3, 1975. *Ibid.*

33. "Minutes," San Francisco City Landmarks Advisory Board, June 18, 1975; Mrs. Bland Platt and James Ream to Members of the San Francisco City Landmarks Preservation Advisory Board, Re "Request by HUD/SFRA for Landmarks Board Review of the Turner Report and other applicable buildings in the Yerba Buena Center area," June 18, 1975; and Mrs. Bland Platt to Arthur F. Evans, September 3, 1975. *Ibid.*

The subcommittee was created at the board's December 4, 1974, meeting when the existing architectural review committee was augmented with other experts as well as the two board officers. The board's decision to accept the subcommittee's seven-page report was not unanimous. Dr. Albert Shumate abstained. The "Minutes" state that he said that "anything which would hold up Yerba Buena would not be in the city's best interest. Whether a building is or is not magnificent is really not the issue; the overriding issue must be what happens to Yerba Buena. If the board were to take any action which is wrong for the City as a whole, he felt the Board would be very parochial."

The subcommittee also recommended an adaptive re-use feasibility study that could have been completed by mid-1975 if HUD had acted on the request from the Foundation for San Francisco's Architectural Heritage to undertake the project. Heritage had a grant of $7,500 from the National Trust in the spring of 1975 but had yet to receive an answer from the Redevelopment Agency. Also see Charles Hall Page to Arthur Evans, April 29, 1975, and July 8, 1975. *Ibid.*

34. Platt to Evans, September 3, 1975. *Ibid.* The Redevelopment Agency informed Mott that they would oppose the inclusion of the Mercantile Center Building on the Register. The rehabilitation of the building continues to be as "infeasible now" as it was in 1967-1968 when studied by "experienced entrepreneurs and their highly qualified professional consultants." Furthermore, Turner "did not consider the property" in 1974 to possess "sufficient architectural character to merit listing on the National Register." See Arthur F. Evans to William Penn Mott, Jr., October 1, 1975. *Ibid.*

35. The new report was necessitated by a number of major design and plan changes. See John L. Frisbee III, to George B. Adams, March 14, 1978. *Ibid.*

36. Tad Masaoka to Knox Mellon, January 31, 1978; and Mellon to Masaoka, February 14, 1978. A formal report was published in August 1979 by Roger R. Olmsted, Nancy L. Olmsted, Allen Pastron, and Jack Prichett, *The Yerba Buena Center. Report on Historical Cultural Resources. Prepared for the San Francisco Redevelopment Agency. Ibid.*

37. National Trust for Historic Preservation, *Annual Report, 1971-1972,* pp. 3, 5, 11-12. Other examples that the Trust pointed to were the acquisition of the Cooper-Molera Adobe, which is across the street from Casa Amesti, and Cliveden, built in 1763-1767 in Germantown, Pennsylvania, a gift from the Chew family. The Trust planned that its West Coast Office would enable them to "increasingly...fulfill [their] obligations to all Americans." See p. 5. Pamela McGuire became Frisbee's secretary and the Trust's second West Coast staff member.

38. *Ibid.,* p. 3. The Trust was "determined to be a vital force for preservation in the West."

39. This continues to be a source of friction between all states and the Trust. Although the actual amount varies, the apportionment formula allocates some 80 percent of the total

preservation fund for state use, 5 percent to the Secretary of the Interior's discretionary fund, and 15 percent for administrative expenses to the National Park Service and the National Trust. Kimberly D. Allen to George Miller, July 28, 1977, OHP. The amount received by the Trust, for example, from the federal government via the park service was $2.7 million in fiscal 1974-1975, and $2.5 million in 1975-1976. Note that in 1974-1975, the states divided $17.6 million; of that, the largest amounts of $800,000 each went to California, Massachusetts, New York, and Pennsylvania. See National Trust for Historic Preservation, *Annual Report, 1974-1975*, pp. 4, 33; *Annual Report, 1975-1976*, p. 6.

40. "Minutes," History Committee Meeting, June 30, 1970, DPR: 348.0. In an undated departmental press release ca. spring 1970, the department noted that "while Congress had authorized $32 million over a four-year period for planning and project grants, only about $3 million had been appropriated, and much of this has benefited the National Trust for Historic Preservation." DPR: 537.

41. See, for example, the earlier discussion in this same chapter in the section on "Other Federal Efforts" regarding the Yerba Buena Center Redevelopment project which witnessed Frisbee's very active participation.

42. Frisbee, *Preservation in the West*, p. 1.

43. *Ibid.*, pp. 3-5, 20-25. Of the sixty-two organizations that Frisbee surveyed, forty-nine indicated that historic house museums and history museums were most important. Although adaptive re-use is considered in urban areas such as Los Angeles, Monterey, and San Francisco, in other locales and particularly in small towns, the museum alternative is most frequently the only alternative considered when a building is facing demolition.

44. *Ibid.*, "Introduction," and pp. 2, 30. Also see Robertson E. Collins, interview with author, June 12, 1982, Jacksonville, Oregon; and John L. Frisbee III, interview with author, April 8, 1983, Washington, D.C.

45. Frisbee, *Preservation in the West*, pp. 30-31. It was formally placed on the Register on December 11, 1972; John H. Michael to Mayor, City of Yreka, December 21, 1972, OHP. It became a registered landmark in 1976.

46. Frisbee, *Preservation in the West*, pp. 31-32, 36.

47. *Ibid.*, p. 40. Frisbee stated that a successful program also required "qualified staff with the sole responsibility of managing the state preservation agency." He further cited the need for state agencies and private organizations to provide more technical information, for stronger preservation legislation and utilization of legal devices such as district and landmark ordinances, easements, transfer of development rights and deed restrictions. See pp. 41-42 for additional suggestions and recommendations.

48. "Minutes," HLAC, September 6, 1973.

49. National Trust for Historic Preservation, *Annual Report, 1972-1973*, n.p. The adobe was built in 1829 by Juan Bautista Rogers Cooper and given to the Trust by Frances M. Molera.

50. *Ibid.*

51. National Trust, *Annual Report, 1974-1975*, p. 16. The other cities were Port Townsend, Washington, and Honokaa, Hawaii. In the same year, the West Coast Office was also awarded a contract from the Bureau of Land Management to "develop prototype stabilization and restoration plans for Eagle and Fort Egbert, Alaska."

52. National Trust for Historic Preservation, Western Regional Office, *Miner Street Historic District, Yreka, Calif.: A Plan for Preservation* (Washington, D.C.: Preservation Press, 1976), p. 1.

53. *Ibid.*, p. 2.

54. John L. Frisbee III, *Three-Year Report, July 1972-June 1975. Western Regional Office, National Trust for Historic Preservation* (Washington, D.C.: Preservation Press, 1975), p. 7.

55. Collins reiterated that the Trust was able to deliver experts to assist local preservationists. See Collins interview with author, 1982.

56. Frisbee, *Three-Year Report*, 1975, p. 8. The December meeting was with Frisbee and the office's planner and included members of the Sacramento Historic Structures Advisory Committee. The regional planner met again with the advisory committee and the planning staff in early 1974 and later provided both groups with information to assist in their planning. Frisbee anticipated that when the plans moved to the implementation stage, the Trust would be called in for assistance again.

57. *Ibid.*, pp. 1-2.

58. *Ibid.*, pp. 11-14, 18. The trust held clinics in Salt Lake City (1972) and in Hawaii and New Mexico (1974). In Los Angeles, the Trust met with members of the Colonial Dames, Los Angeles Cultural Heritage Foundation, the Pasadena Cultural Heritage Committee, South Pasadena Cultural Heritage Board, Historical Society of the Centinela Valley, and Santa Barbara Trust for Historic Preservation. The panel of experts included an architect, attorney, public relations specialist, historian, and museologist.

59. See Frisbee, *Three-Year Report*, 1975, "Contents," n.p.; *Annual Report, 1974-1975*, pp. 3-4, p. 45; and *Annual Report, 1975-1976*, pp. 6-7, 16, 36. Corporate Associates rose during the same year from fifteen in June 1975 to sixty-four by June 1976. Visitations to Casa Amesti rose from 341 in fiscal year 1975 to 2,267 in fiscal year 1976, an increase of 564.8 percent.

The emphasis on regionalization reflected a recommendation in the Trust's in-house study conducted by board chair Gordon Gray. The report recommended that regional offices should continue to provide technical services as well as "develop a capability of responding to requests for information about other National Trust programs. These offices should be considered full-fledged regional offices of the National Trust and their managers should have the title of Regional Director." Regional offices were designed to provide "a nearby source of basic historic preservation assistance." National Trust, *Goals and Programs*, p. 20.

60. National Trust, *Annual Report, 1975-1976*, p. 18.

61. Conference brochure, *Southern California Historic Preservation Conference*, May 13-14, 1976, Mission Inn, Riverside, California; sponsored by the National Trust for Historic Preservation, Department of Parks and Recreation, State Historical Resources Commission; co-sponsored by the California State Office of Planning and Research, Californians for Preservation Action, and the Riverside Cultural Heritage Board.

62. See Collins interview with author, 1982, and *Annual Report, 1975-1976*, pp. 18, 29.

CHAPTER 17
FROM THE MUSEUM INTO THE MAINSTREAM:
HISTORIC PRESERVATION IN 1976

1. Advisory Council on Historic Preservation, *The National Historic Preservation Program Today*. Report to Henry M. Jackson, Chairman, Committee on Interior and Insular Affairs, U.S. Senate (Washington, D.C.: Government Printing Office, 1976), pp. 1, 59. California's Office of Historic Preservation agreed with the council's findings that these two issues were continuous problems. See Knox Mellon to Truett Latimer, March 23, 1976, in DPR: 024: "National Conference of State Historic Preservation Officers."

2. Sam Hall Kaplan, "Preservation: Major Redevelopment Resource. Old Buildings Getting New Lease on Life," Los Angeles *Times*, May 12, 1985.

3. See, for example, Laura Meyers, "West Adams Bows to Charms of the Past," Los Angeles *Times*, November 3, 1985; Sandy Banks, "The 'Battle' of West Adams. White Restorationists Buying Homes in Largely Black L.A. Neighborhood and Hostility to Them Has Risen," Los Angeles *Times*, December 1, 1985; Sam Hall Kaplan, "Street Fair Celebrates Miracle Mile. Historic District Displays Signs of Gentrification," Los Angeles *Times*, October 28, 1984.

4. See Kenneth N. Owens, professor of history at California State University, Sacramento, "Preserving and Managing California's Historical Resources," typescript, n.d., ca. 1986, pp. 22-23. Owens observed that unlike archaeologists, the state's historians stood

on the sidelines as the field of cultural resources management began to expand in the 1970s. Not only did the archaeologists organize to push and protect their interests, they had a history of professional contract activity dating to the 1930s, and "they had training in dealing with the sites and objects of material culture; they had devised a site-specific methodology appropriate to NHPA, NEPA, and CEQA requirements; their discipline was experienced in serving government on salvage archaeology projects." See p. 14. The "history without historians" in cultural resources management work began to change in 1981 when the California Committee for the Promotion of History became affiliated with the National Committee for the Promotion of History and reconstituted itself in 1981. Membership was broadened and the group's focus was expanded beyond obtaining jobs "to create a historians' movement for promoting history's role in the public sector." See pp. 17-18.

5. For a detailed discussion of the importance of historic resources to the state's tourist industry, see Paula Huntley and Hisashi B. Sugaya, *Heritage and Tourism in California*, Prepared for and sponsored by the California Heritage Task Force, March 1984. For example, in 1982, more than 17 million people visited state historic parks and parks with historic interest; of all the parks in the state park system, Old Town San Diego was the most popular. In 1983, 4,057,312 visitors went to San Diego; 853,266 visited Hearst San Simeon. The San Simeon figure was unusually low because Highway 1 was temporarily closed. See pp. 20-21.

6. Telephone conversation between author and Engbeck, March 23, 1987.

7. J. Laurence Mintier, "California's Historical and Cultural Resources. A Background Report Prepared for the California Heritage Task Force and the National Trust for Historic Preservation," December 1983, pp. 1-2. Mintier stated that the state has 1.1 million buildings constructed before 1940 and some 150,000 date from the nineteenth century. He estimated that 1,353,000 residences, or 1 out of every 7, were located in a pre-1940 structure. In 1980, one out of every eight Californians lived in a pre-1940 building. Mintier also observed that there is a shortage of comprehensive and easily accessible information on the state's historical and cultural resources. Mintier's bibliography on pp. 20-24 should also prove useful.

Recent demolitions in Los Angeles include the First Methodist Church, Tiny Naylor's drive-in, the Richfield Building, and houses by Greene & Greene, Irving Gill, Richard Schindler, and Richard Neutra. See Kaplan, "Preservation," May 12, 1985.

Destruction of historical properties by earthquake is a perpetual concern in California. The impact of the Mexico City quake of 1985 resulted in an article by Sam Hall Kaplan, "Quake Jolts Preservationists. They Fear Owners May Destroy Landmarks," Los Angeles *Times*, November 3, 1985.

Unprincipled scavengers run the gamut from those who plunder Native American sites to individuals who strip historic buildings of interior furnishings. See Alan Maltun, "Pasadena Moves to Protect Heritage. Emergency Law Prevents Further 'Rape' of Blacker House," Los Angeles *Times*, June 6, 1985.

8. The Los Angeles *Times* began to print articles underscoring the ever-widening acceptance of recycling historic properties. See, for example: Cliff Dektar, "L.A. Finds Use for Old Buildings," January 15, 1984; Sam Hall Kaplan, "Discarding the Notion of the 'Throwaway City,'" January 25, 1985; Kaplan, "The Wiltern Returns in Confidence," April 28, 1985; Evelyn de Wolfe, "Former Broadway Flagship Gets New Life. $25-Million Rehabilitation Planned for New Uses of Landmark Department Store," February 10, 1985. The Broadway project later received full-page coverage in an advertisement which announced: "The Broadway Centre. A historic rehabilitation of a classic downtown building...completely retrofitted and returned to the glamour and classic style of a bygone era...coupled with state-of-the-art services, modern facilities, and new interiors." Los Angeles *Times*, December 18, 1985.

Although there are few detailed studies on the economic impact of rehabilitation projects in California, Mintier estimated that in 1983, the estimated $50 million in certified rehabilitation work would generate some $155,890,000 in total spending in the state's economy. Mintier, "California's Historical and Cultural Resources," pp. 14-16.

Other articles reinforce the public's perception that preservation makes good economic sense. See: Peter Weaver, "Mind Your Money. Renovate a Landmark for Tax Break," Los Angeles *Times*, September 18, 1983; Betsy Bauer, "Taking the Past and Building the Future. Big Tax Credits Draw Investors to Historic Projects," *U.S. News and World Reports*, 101 (November 3, 1986): 58-60.

9. Sam Hall Kaplan observed: "In Los Angeles and Pasadena, the preservationist community has grown from a handful of concerned citizens just five years ago, to an estimated core of about 5,000 persons. Their influence extends way beyond their numbers and the boundaries of the cities. Working through such groups as the Los Angeles Conservancy, Hollywood Heritage and Pasadena Heritage, preservationists have raised the collective public consciousness to the value of protecting remnants of the region's past to enrich its future." "Preservation," Los Angeles *Times*, May 12, 1985.

The Los Angeles Conservancy, for example, was formed in June 1978. In the face of the threatened demolition of city landmarks, 150 people paid $25 to attend the first public meeting to hear founding president Margaret Bach explain that the Conservancy's goals of "awareness, assistance and action" were the "means toward making preservation part of the regular urban process rather than a series of reactive screams each time a landmark looks to be imperiled." See Art Seidenbaum, "Standing Up for Old L.A.," Los Angeles *Times*, June 23, 1978; and Ray Hebert, "Group to Preserve Landmarks Formed," Los Angeles *Times*, June 6, 1978.

10. The Heritage Action Steering Committee was formed in 1984 to "work for the advancement of heritage legislation in California." Bill Sugaya, Bill Burkhart, Jim Williams, and John Parker to Heritage Supporter, April 30, 1985.

Mintier provided impressive statistics on the status of preservation organizations and activities as of 1983. These included:

- 32 State Historic Parks, with an additional 36 of historical interest;
- 878 Native American sites recorded in the California Indian Sites Protection and Inventory Program by the Native American Heritage Commission (December 1982);
- 500 members in Californians for Preservation Action;
- 400 individual and 50 organization members in the California Preservation Foundation;
- 644 members (including 32 museums, 62 libraries, 257 local historical societies) in the California Conference of Historical Societies;
- 55,000 cubic feet of historical State documents in the California State Archives;
- 300 local historical societies with combined membership over 100,000;
- more than 100 cities and counties have completed systematic historical resource surveys, 35,000 buildings are included;
- 57 local landmark commissions;
- 362 museums are cited in the 1982 *Official Museum Directory* for the U.S. and Canada; of which two-thirds are devoted to the preservation of history or have historical or archaeological holdings;
- more than 40 formal oral history programs.

See Mintier, "California's Historical and Cultural Resources," pp. 8-9.

11. John F. Merritt, "California Preservation Foundation. Ten Years After," *California Preservation*, X (April 1985): 2.

12. A review of the brochures and handouts for the ten preservation conferences shows that in 1976, there was no single unifying theme. In 1977, the conference asked, "It Took So Long to Build: How Can They Throw It Away?" In 1978, the topic was "Preservation of the Total Environment: Building the Preservation/Conservation Constituency." A year later, the conference asked: "Can Historic Preservation Survive in the 1980s?" In 1980, the topic was: "Historic Preservation: A Legislative, Administrative and Technological Process." In 1981, it was "Strengthening the Local Preservation Process;" in 1982, "Reinvesting in America;" in 1983, "Preservation is Working for America;" and in 1984, "Preservation-Long Term Capitol Gain." And in 1985, the focus was on effective community preservation techniques.

Bibliography

The historical range and diversity of this study preclude a comprehensive listing of materials on the evolution of historic preservationism in California. Although such a listing would prove valuable, because none exists, it would be excessively long for it would need to include technical manuals, regional and local surveys and histories, as well as untold numbers of individual articles on specific sites and issues. The following list includes only those items that were vital to the topics treated in this work, and those that were essential to an understanding of the subject.

Many of the documents and materials cited in the text came from either the Central Records Storage Section of the Department of Parks and Recreation (abbreviated in the Notes as DPR) or from the uncatalogued files of the State Office of Historic Preservation (abbreviated in the Notes as OHP). Other sources of information were found in private collections. With the exception of those departmental studies of substantial size and substantive contents, none of the documents, letters, memos, or other materials is individually identified. Those listed in the "documents" category show the same abbreviations as above: DPR and the record group; and OHP.

During the research, nearly a hundred knowledgeable participants and observers were interviewed, and some provided additional insights to the author through detailed letters. Although everyone who was contacted had informative comments and explanations to share, only those who are quoted in this study are identified.

Archival and Manuscript Collections

California. Department of Parks and Recreation. Central Records Storage. Sacramento.
- 021. State Historical Buildings Code Advisory Board.
- 022. Historical Resources Commission.
- 023. California Historical Landmarks Advisory Committee.
- 024. National Conference of State Historic Preservation Officers.
- 026. Foundations.
  - Folder 1. General Correspondence.
  - Folder 2. California State Park Foundation.
  - Folder 3. California State Park Foundation: Minutes of Meeting.
  - Folder 4. California State Park Foundation: Bylaws.
- 027. Historical, Archaeological, and Paleontological Task Force.
- 027. Historical and Interpretive Programs Task Force.
- 027.1. Historical Structures Task Force Report.

089-341. Colonel Allensworth State Historic Park: Unit Background.

319.0-341. Colonel Allensworth State Historic Park: General Correspondence.

319.1-307. Columbia State Historic Park: Reports.

339. State Park System Plan.
339.0. General Correspondence.
339.1. Reports.
339.2. Research.

348. Historical Preservation.
348.0. General Correspondence.
348.1. Reports.

348. California History Plan.
348.0. General Correspondence.
348.1. Reports.

348. California History Plan. One.
348.0. General Correspondence.
348.1. Reports.

348. California History Plan. Two.
348.0. General Correspondence.
348.1 Reports.

348. California History Plan. Three.
348.0. General Correspondence.
348.1. Reports.

359.1-307. Columbia State Historic Park. Research.

361. Project Planning and Design: Reports.

429.0-307. Columbia State Historic Park: General Correspondence.
429.1-307. Reports.

51. State Park System Interpretation and History.
511. Reports.
512. Research Material.

519.1-307. Columbia State Historic Park: Reports.

52. Statewide Interpretation and History.
520. General Correspondence.
521. Reports.

53. Historical Landmarks.
530. Correspondence.
531. Reports.
535.0. E Clampus Vitus: General Correspondence.
536.2. California Missions: Research.
537.0. National Register of Historic Places: General Correspondence.
537.50-38. Executive Order 11593: Yerba Buena Center Project.
538.0. California Registered Landmarks: General Correspondence.
539.1. California Registered Landmarks: Reports.
539.0. California Points of Historical Interest: General Correspondence.

California. Department of Parks and Recreation. Office of Historic Preservation. Sacramento.

Correspondence. Miscellaneous.

Minutes, Historical Landmarks Advisory Committee and Historical Resources Commission, 1952-1983.

State Landmark Program: Folders.
State Registered Landmarks.
Survey and Replies: Landmarks Marked Prior to 1941.

Correspondence, Photos, etc. RE Plaques.
Historic and Other Organization Lists Prepared for 1949 Celebration.
War Services Program-Centennial Data.
State Landmark Program: Individual Files.
    No. 801: Reuel Colt Gridley Monument.
    No. 850: Manzanar Relocation Center.
WPA Projects on California Historical Landmarks: Reports.
Dismuke, Eileen. Papers. Eileen Dismuke Personal Files. Santa Barbara, California.
Elder, Sandra. Papers. Sandra Elder Personal Files. Office of Historic Preservation, Sacramento, California.
Gallup, Aaron. Papers. Aaron Gallup Personal Files. Sacramento, California.
Girvigian, Raymond. Papers. Raymond Girvigian Personal Files. Pasadena, California.
Knowland, Joseph R. Papers. MS 3154, Folders 21-25. California Historical Society, San Francisco, California.
Neasham, V. Aubrey. Papers. Neasham Collection. Museum and History Division, City and County of Sacramento, California.
Woollett, William. Papers. William Woollett Personal Files. Santa Barbara, California.

Documents

Advisory Council on Historic Preservation. *The National Historic Preservation Program Today.* Report to Henry M. Jackson, Chairman, Committee on Interior and Insular Affairs, U.S. Senate. Washington, D.C.: Government Printing Office, 1976.

_____. "Issues in Archeology." *Report* V (March-April-May 1977).

_____. *Report to the President and Congress of the United States, 1981.* Washington, D.C.: Government Printing Office, 1982.

California. Department of Natural Resources. *California Historical Landmarks.* Sacramento: Department of Natural Resources, 1960.

_____. Conservation and Education Section. *Organization and Functions of the State Department of Natural Resources.* Sacramento: Department of Natural Resources, July 1960. Courtesy of Sandra Elder.

_____. Department of Natural Resources and the State Park Commission in Cooperation with the California State Chamber of Commerce. *Reports* No. 1-67. Sacramento: Department of Natural Resources, 1932-1962. In OHP.

California. Department of Parks and Recreation. Division of Beaches and Parks. *California State Park System. 1964 Legislative Requests to Study Potential State Beach, Park, Recreation, and Historical Areas.* Sacramento: Division of Beaches and Parks, 1964.

_____. *History, Analysis and Recommendations on the Planning for the State Park System.* Sacramento: Division of Beaches and Parks, March 8, 1965. Reprinted March 1967. In DPR: 339.1.

_____. *History Program for the Division of Beaches and Parks.* Sacramento: Division of Beaches and Parks, 1965. Revised April 1966. Courtesy of Allen Welts.

_____. *Old Sacramento State Historic Park Study. Requested by House Resolution No. 91, Statutes of 1964.* Sacramento: Division of Beaches and Parks, March 1965.

_____. *Plan for Progress. Field Reorganization.* Sacramento: Division of Beaches and Parks, February 1964. Courtesy of Sandra Elder.

_____. *Progress Report on Planning for the Historic Restoration of Old Sacramento. Requested by Assembly Concurrent Resolution No. 53, Chapter 117, Statutes of 1963.* Sacramento: Division of Beaches and Parks, May 4, 1964.

_____. *A Proposal for a Historical Resources Study. Assembly Concurrent Resolution #25, by Assemblyman Paul J. Lunardi.* By Herbert L. Heinze. Sacramento: Division of Beaches and Parks, June 1962. DPR: Historical Preservation: Reports, 348.1.

_____. ...*Report on a Decade.* Sacramento: Division of Beaches and Parks, 1960. DPR: 339.1.

_____. *State Park System Program for Historical Acquisition and Restoration, 1966-86.* Sacramento: Division of Beaches and Parks, September 30, 1966.

_____. Interpretive Services. *Interpretive Guidelines for Historical Restoration.* Sacramento: Division of Beaches and Parks, January 1964. DPR: 511.

_____. Management Analysis Section, compilers. *A Guide to the Organization and Functions of the State of California, Resources Agency, Department of Parks and Recreation.* Sacramento: Division of Beaches and Parks, February 1966.

California. Department of Parks and Recreation. *Accelerated Development Program Projecting to 1980 for the California State Park System.* Sacramento: Department of Parks and Recreation, November 1965. DPR: 339.1.

_____. *California Coastline Preservation and Recreation Plan.* Sacramento: Department of Parks and Recreation, August 1971. Reprinted November 1972.

_____. "California Ethnic Minority Historic Resources Survey. A Grant Proposal." May 15, 1976.

_____. *California Historical Landmarks.* Sacramento: Department of Parks and Recreation, 1975.

_____. *The California History Plan.* Volume One: *Comprehensive Preservation Plan.* Sacramento: Department of Parks and Recreation, December 1973.

_____. *The California History Plan.* Volume Two: *Inventory of Historic Features.* Sacramento: Department of Parks and Recreation, August 1973.

_____. *The California History Plan.* Volume Two: *California Inventory of Historic Resources.* Sacramento: Department of Parks and Recreation, March 1976.

_____. *The California History Plan.* Volume Three: *Annual Preservation Program.* Sacramento: Department of Parks and Recreation, 1972-1977.

_____. "California State Park System: Goals and Policies. Working Draft." Sacramento: Department of Parks and Recreation, November 1977.

_____. *California State Park System Plan.* Sacramento: Department of Parks and Recreation, June 1968.

_____. "A Guide to the Organization and Functions of the State of California-Resources Agency, Department of Parks and Recreation." Sacramento: Department of Parks and Recreation, February 1966.

_____. "A History of Archeological Work in the State Park System as Reflected in the Cultural Heritage Section Library." Sacramento: Department of Parks and Recreation, November 1979.

_____. *Interpretive Plan for Columbia State Historic Park.* Sacramento, January 1970, Revised. Courtesy of John Michael.

_____. *Mission 1990. 1982 Update of the State Park System Plan.* Sacramento: Department of Parks and Recreation, June 1982.

_____. *Organization. Department of Parks and Recreation, July 1976.* Sacramento: Department of Parks and Recreation, July 1976.

_____. "Organization Chart, August 7, 1972." Sacramento: Department of Parks and Recreation, August 7, 1972. Courtesy of Sandra Elder.

_____. *Organization Plan for the Department of Parks and Recreation.* Sacramento: Department of Parks and Recreation, November 1, 1967.

_____. *Partial Inventory. Historic Sites and Buildings in California.* Sacramento: Department of Parks and Recreation, October 1967. DPR: 531.

_____. *Policies, Rules, Regulations, and Orders of the California State Park and Recreation Commission and the Department of Parks and Recreation.* Sacramento: Department of Parks and Recreation, December 1978.

_____. *Preliminary California History Plan.* Sacramento: Department of Parks and Recreation, September 1, 1970.

_____. *Resource Management Directives for the California Department of Parks and Recreation.* Sacramento: Department of Parks and Recreation, 1974. Revised 1979.

_____. Department of Parks and Recreation and California State Park Commission. *Summaries of Feasibility Studies of Projects Not Included in 1966 Bond Program.* Sacramento: Department of Parks and Recreation, January 1966. Courtesy of Allen Welts.

California. Department of Parks and Recreation. Office of Historic Preservation. *Five Views. An Ethnic Sites Survey for California.* Sacramento: Office of Historic Preservation, December 1988.

_____. "Historic Preservation Elements in California." Sacramento: Office of Historic Preservation, n.d.

_____. "Model Archeological Ordinance." Sacramento: Office of Historic Preservation, March 1980.

_____. "Model Cultural Resources Management Ordinance for California Cities and Counties." Sacramento: Office of Historic Preservation, n.d.

_____. *Survey of Surveys. A Summary of California's Cultural Resource Surveys.* Sacramento: Office of Historic Preservation, January 1978. Third revision May 1981.

California. Department of Transportation. *Policy & Procedure on Paleontological, Archaeological, and Historical Resources.* P74-46. Sacramento: Department of Transportation, July 22, 1974. Revised November 24, 1982, retitled as *Policy & Procedure. Archaelogical, Historical, and Cultural Resources.* Courtesy of Duane Frink.

California. Legislative Analyst. *California's Heritage (Pursuant to ACR 274, 1974 Session).* Sacramento: Legislative Analyst, March 1975.

California. Office of Planning and Research. *Historic Preservation Element Guidelines.* Sacramento: Office of Planning and Research, September 1976.

California. Resources Agency. *The Department of Parks and Recreation.* Sacramento: Resources Agency, February 1962. Courtesy of Sandra Elder.

California. State Archeological, Historical, and Paleontological Task Force. *The Status of California's Heritage.* A Report to the Governor and Legislature of California. By W.R. Green, *et al.* Sacramento: State Archeological, Historical, and Paleontological Task Force, September 1, 1973.

California. State Legislature. Senate Interim Committee on Recreation, State Beaches and Parks. *Preliminary Report. California's State Park Program. Two Studies of Current and Selected State Park Problems.* Sacramento: State Senate, January 11, 1956.

California. State Park Commission. "Statement of Policy," January 1, 1964; amended in May, July, and August 1964. Courtesy of Sandra Elder.

California Heritage Preservation Commission. *The Preservation, Organization, and Display of California's Historic Documents.* Report to the Legislature. Sacramento: California Heritage Preservation Commission, May 25, 1973.

California Heritage Task Force. *A Report to the Legislature and People of California.* Sacramento: August 1984.

California Historic Landmarks League. "Articles of Incorporation, June 24, 1902." Courtesy of Sandra Elder.

California State Historical Association. "Quarterly Reports." March and June 1931. Courtesy of Sandra Elder.

Elder, Sandra J., compiler. *A Handbook of Basic Reference Materials for the State Historical Resources Commission.* Sacramento: Office of Historic Preservation, June 1982.

Federickson, David A., and Mohr, Albert. "Appraisal of the Archaeological Resources of New Melones Reservoir, Calaveras and Tuolumne Counties, California, May 1949." Prepared for the Pacific Coast Division, River Basin Surveys, Smithsonian Institution. N.p.

Frisbee, John L. III. *Preservation in the West. The 1971-1972 Report of the Western Regional Field Office of the National Trust for Historic Preservation.* N.p.

_____. *Three Year Report. July 1972-June 1975. Western Regional Office, National Trust for Historic Preservation.* Washington, D.C.: Preservation Press, 1975.

Hall, Carroll D. *Old Sacramento. A Report on Its Significance to the City, State and Nation, with Recommendations for the Preservation and Use of Its Principal Historical Structures and Sites.* Sacramento: Department of Beaches and Parks, 1968.

Jenkins, Hubert O. "Report on the Interpretive Service of the State Parks of California to the Division of Beaches and Parks," November 1, 1952. In DPR: 511.

King, Thomas F.; Moratto, Michael J.; and Leonard, N. Nelson III, compilers. "Recommended Procedures for Archaeological Impact Evaluation." Report on a study by the Society for California Archaeology, in cooperation with the Archaeological Survey, University of California, Los Angeles. N.d. Typescript.

Kinnaird, Lawrence. "Report on California's History, Routes and Sites." Sacramento: California Public Outdoor Recreation Plan Committee, 1960.

Mehlert, Charles. "The Origin and Use of Aesthetic and Historic Planning." June 1930. In DPR: 511.

Mellon, Knox. Report on the History Preservation Section, Department of Parks and Recreation [untitled], March 31, 1976.

Moratto, Michael J. "The Status of California Archaeology: A Report to the Governor and Legislature of California for the State Archaeological Task Force," January 1, 1973. In DPR: 027.

National Trust for Historic Preservation. *Annual Report.* Washington, D.C.: National Trust for Historic Preservation, 1957, 1960, 1962, 1963-1964, 1966-1967, 1971-1972, 1972-1973, 1974-1975, 1975-1976.

_____. "California: Building Codes and Preservation," February 1978.

_____. *Criteria for Evaluating Historic Sites and Buildings.* A Report by the Committee on Standards and Surveys. Washington, D.C.: National Trust for Historic Preservation, 1956.

_____. *Directory of Landmark and Historic District Commissions.* Washington, D.C.: The Preservation Press, October 1976.

_____. *Goals and Programs.* A Summary of the Study Committee to the Board of Trustees, the National Trust for Historic Preservation. Chaired by Robertson E. Collins. Washington, D.C.: National Trust for Historic Preservation, September 1973.

_____. *Historic Preservation Tomorrow. Principles & Guidelines for Historic Preservation in the United States.* Colonial Williamsburg: National Trust for Historic Preservation, 1967. Revised.

_____. *Members and Member Organizations of the National Trust for Historic Preservation.* Washington, D.C.: National Trust for Historic Preservation, January 1956.

_____. Board of Advisors. *Preservation in the United States. Annual Report 1974-75.* Washington, D.C.: National Trust for Historic Preservation, October 1975.

_____. Western Regional Office. *Miner Street Historic District, Yreka, California: A Plan for Preservation.* Washington, D.C.: Preservation Press, 1976.

Neasham, Aubrey. "Master Program of Acquisition, State Historical Areas," November 9, 1953. In DPR: Historical Preservation: General Correspondence, 348.0.

_____. "Supplemental Recommendations, Master Program of Acquisition, State Historical Areas," November 20, 1956. In DPR: 348.0.

Neasham, Vernon A., editor and supervisor. "California Historical Landmarks. Works Project #6461, Serial 0803-434. Off. Project #165-03-7307, Symbol #165027." Berkeley, California: Bancroft Library, n.d. In OHP.

Olmsted, Frederick Law. *General Report on Potential State Park and Recreational Areas.* Sacramento: State Park Commission, 1950. DPR: 339.2.

_____. *Report of the State Park Survey of California.* Prepared for the California State Park Commission. Sacramento: California State Printing Office, 1929.

"Preservation Legislation Important to Santa Barbara and California." N.d., n.p. Courtesy of Mary Louise Days.

"Restoration and Development of the Capitol for the Joint Committee on Rules, California State Legislature." Sacramento: February 1975.

"Sacramento Old City. A Preservation Program." N.p., n.d., Revised August 1976.

San Diego, City of. "Ordinance No. 9322. An Ordinance Amending Article 6, Chapter II of the San Diego Municipal Code by Adding Thereto Section 26.02, Establishing a Historical Site Board." December 7, 1965.

San Jose, City of. "Ordinance No. 17927. An Ordinance of the City of San Jose Amending Article VIII of the San Jose Municipal Code by adding a new chapter, Chapter 14, thereto to provide for the preservation of structures and sites of historical, architectural, cultural, or aesthetic interest or value." November 25, 1975.

Santa Barbara, City of. "Resolution No. 4125. Resolution of the City of Santa Barbara Creating the Santa Barbara Advisory Landmark Committee." May 10, 1960. Courtesy of Mary Louise Days.

_____. "Resolution of City Council Establishing Committees having Various Powers and Duties. Resolution No. 79-093." September 4, 1979. Courtesy of Mary Louise Days.

Santa Cruz, City of. Historic Preservation Commission. *Policy Statement and Administrative Guidelines. Revolving Fund for Historic Preservation. Report and Recommendations.* Submitted to the City Council of Santa Cruz. April 1976.

_____. Planning Department. *Historic Preservation Plan.* 1974.

Society for California Archaeology. "Memorandum and Recommendations for Preparation of Environmental Impact Reports Pertaining to California Archaeological Resources." N.d.

U.S. Army Corps of Engineers. *Fiscal Year 1978. Cultural Resource Investigations for Civil Works Activities.* Washington, D.C.: Office of the Chief of Engineers, April 1979.

U.S. Comptroller General. *Are Agencies Doing Enough or Too Much for Archeological Preservation? Guidance Needed.* Report to the Chairman, Committee on Interior and Insular Affairs, House of Representatives of the United States. Washington, D.C.: U.S. General Accounting Office, April 22, 1981.

_____. *Uncertainties Over Federal Requirements for Archeological Preservation at New Melones Dam in California.* Report to the Chairman, Committee on Interior and Insular Affairs, House of Representatives of the United States. Washington, D.C.: U.S. General Accounting Office, December 21, 1979.

U.S. Department of the Interior. National Park Service. *Archeological and Historic Data Recovery Program.* Fiscal Year 1976.

_____. *Index. National Park System and Related Areas as of June 30, 1979.* Courtesy of Thomas Mulhern.

_____. "Manual for State Historic Preservation Review Boards (Draft)." Washington, D.C.: National Park Service, 1981.

_____. *National Historic Landmarks. A Preservation Program of the National Park Service.* Washington, D.C.: National Park Service, 1976.

_____. *A National Program for the Conservation of Historic Sites and Buildings. The Registered National Historic Landmark Program.* Sites declared eligible through December 31, 1963. Washington, D.C.: National Park Service, n.d.

_____. *The National Survey of Historic Sites and Buildings.* Washington, D.C.: National Park Service, 1959. Revised.

_____. *Part One of the National Park System Plan. History.* Washington, D.C.: National Park Service, 1972.

_____. *Sites Eligible for the Registry of National Landmarks. A Program to Promote the Conservation of Sites of Historical and Scientific Significance.* Sites eligible through January 31, 1965. Washington, D.C.: National Park Service, n.d.

_____. Interagency Archeological Services Division. "A Status Report to the Archeological Community," March 1976.

U.S. Department of the Treasury. Bureau of Alcohol, Tobacco and Firearms. *Environmental Protection.* January 1976.

With Heritage So Rich. A Report of the Special Committee on Historic Preservation under the auspices of the United States Conference of Mayors with a grant from the Ford Foundation. Albert Rains, Chairman. New York: Random House, 1966.

Federal and State Legislation

An Act to Amend the National Historic Preservation Act of 1966. Public Law 96-515. 94 *Stat.* 2987, *et seq.* (1980).

Archeological and Historical Preservation Act of 1974. "Statement of Program Approach." *Federal Register.* Vol. 44, No. 59 (March 26, 1979): 18117-18119.

Balme, Janice, compiler. *A Handbook of Federal and State Legislation Affecting Historic Preservation in California.* Vol. I: *Federal Legislation.* Vol. II: *State Legislation.* Sacramento: Office of Historic Preservation, 1982.

California. *Administrative Code.* Title 24. "Building Standards." Part 8. "State Historical Building Code." *California Administrative Register* 79, No. 34-B, August 25, 1979. Sacramento: Department of General Services, Ch. 9, Office of Administrative Hearings.

California. *Government Code.* Sec. 429.5: "Historical Society."

_____. Secs. 50280-50290: "Historical Property Contracts" (*West Supp. 1981*).

_____. Sec. 65303 (j): "Elements Permitted as Part of General Plan" (*West Supp. 1980*).

California. *Public Resources Code.* Secs. 5020-5022: Historical Resources Commission; Registered Historical Landmarks, Points of Historical Interest (*West Supp. 1981*).

_____. Secs. 5024.-5024.5: Executive Order B-64-80 (*West Supp. 1981*).

_____. Secs. 5040-5042: Columbia Historic State Park.

_____. Secs. 21000-21165: *California Environmental Quality Act (CEQA).*

California. *Statutes of 1955,* Ch. 71.

_____. *Statutes of 1971,* Ch. 827.

_____. *Statutes of 1974,* Ch. 1165 and Ch. 1627.

_____. *Statutes of 1975,* Ch. 906.

_____. *Statutes of 1976,* Ch. 1332.

Department of Transportation Act of 1966. 49 *U.S. Code,* sec. 1653 f.

Elder, Sandra J., compiler. "Public Resources Code, Section 5020 to 5033, and Appropriate Legislation." Sacramento: Office of Historic Preservation, March 1983.

Land and Water Conservation Act of 1976. Public Law 94-422. Title II. *National Historic Preservation Fund*. 90 *Stat*. 1319, *et seq*.

National Environmental Policy Act. Public Law 91-190. 83 *Stat*. 852, *et seq*. (1970).

National Historic Preservation Act of 1966. Public Law 89-665. 80 *Stat*. 915, *et seq*.

Tax Reform Act of 1976. Public Law 94-455, 90 *Stat*. 1519, *et seq*.

U.S. Department of the Interior. National Park Service. Western Regional Office. "National Historic Preservation: Legislation, Executive Order 11593, Procedures-Advisory Council on Historic Preservation," November 1975. Revised October 1982.

Unpublished Secondary Sources

California Preservation Foundation. "Status Report. California Heritage Task Force Recommendations. April 1986."

Cameron, David G. "Charles Fletcher Lummis and the Landmarks Club of Southern California: Pioneering in Historic Preservation." Paper presented at the Charles F. Lummis Centennial Symposium, Los Angeles, California, February 2, 1985.

Cimarelli, Peter Alfred. "California's Outstanding Points of Historical Interest." Unpublished Master's Thesis, California State University, Sacramento, 1970.

Datel, Robin Elisabeth. "Historic Preservation and Neighborhood Change in Sacramento, California." Unpublished Master's Thesis, University of Minnesota, 1978.

"The Date the Recreation Commission was Created," ca. 1969. Typewritten. Courtesy of Sandra Elder.

Elder, Sandra, compiler. "Landmarks Registered in 1939," 1982. Typewritten.

Foundation for San Francisco's Architectural Heritage. "Summary of Activities, 1981." Typewritten.

Frederickson, David A. "Preservation Education. The Cultural Resources Perspective." Paper prepared for panel on "Preservation in the College Curriculum," 1984 California Historic Preservation Conference, Sacramento, California, April 28, 1984.

Huntley, Paula, and Sugaya, Hisashi B. *Heritage and Tourism in California*. Prepared for and sponsored by the California Heritage Task Force, March 1984.

Kaldenberg, Russell L. "The Future of the Society for California Archaeology- An Examination of the Kuhn Model." Paper presented at the Annual Meeting of the Society for California Archaeology, Bakersfield, California, April 9-11, 1981. Courtesy of Paul Chace.

Kuhn, Clyde. "The SCA Planning and Development Model Proposal." Submitted to the Society for California Archaeology, 15 March 1978.

Mathews, Cynthia. "Teacher's Handbook for Historic Enrichment. Curriculum, Resources, Activities." Santa Cruz County: The Historic Enrichment Project, Spring 1978.

McLean, Marie. "A Preservation Studies Curriculum with an Annotated Bibliography," June 1980.

Meighan, Clement W. "The Preservation of Archaeological Remains in California." Los Angeles: University of California, June 1980. DPR: Historical Preservation: Reports, 348.1.

Mintier, J. Lawrence. "California's Historical and Cultural Resources. A Background Report Prepared for the California Heritage Task Force and the National Trust for Historic Preservation." December 1983.

Owens, Kenneth N. "Preserving and Managing California's Historical Resources," ca. 1986. Typewritten.

Pope, John. "Historic Preservation in Los Angeles—A Critique of the Cultural Heritage Board." Prepared for Law 312, UCLA School of Law, June 2, 1977.

Riddell, Francis A. "Historic Archeology in the California State Park System," ca. 1975.

_____. "The State Administered Archeological Program in California," ca. 1965.

_____. "State Service Archeology." Paper presented at the Southwest Anthropological Association Conference, Davis, California, April 8, 1966.

Scharmer, Roger P. "Historic Preservation—A Planning Opportunity." Submitted for presentation at "Confer—In '74." N.d.; n.p.

Schuyler, Robert Lee. "Anthropological Perspectives in Historical Archaeology." Unpublished Ph.D. dissertation, University of California, Santa Barbara, 1975.

Somers, Gary Fred. "The Role of the Federal Government in Historic Preservation." Unpublished Ph.D. dissertation, University of Arizona, 1979.

Tobey, Ronald. "Preservation Education. The Historic Resources Perspective." Remarks prepared for a panel on "Preservation in the College Curriculum," 1984 California Historic Preservation Conference, Sacramento, California, April 28, 1984.

Weinberg, Nathan Gerald. "Historic Preservation and Tradition in California: The Restoration of the Missions and the Spanish-Colonial Revival." Unpublished Ph.D. dissertation, University of California, Davis, 1974.

Williamson, Frederick C. "Challenges to the Preservation of Minority Communities." Paper presented at the 4th Annual Conference on Historic Preservation and the Minority Community, Atlanta, Georgia, October 14, 1982.

_____. "Federalism and Preservation." Remarks made at the Annual Meeting of Preservation Action, Washington, D.C., May 9-10, 1982.

Woollett, William. "Los Angeles Landmarks." Remarks to the National Trust for Historic Preservation, ca. July-August 1966.

_____. "Remarks" before the City Council of Los Angeles, January 15, 1962.

_____. "That the Past Shall Live." Paper presented at the Fourth Annual Southern California Symposium of the Conference of California Historical Societies, Santa Ana, California, February 10, 1962.

Books and Monographs

Advisory Council on Historic Preservation. *Where to Look: A Guide to Historic Preservation.* Washington, D.C.: Government Printing Office, 1982.

_____. *Remember the Neighborhoods: Conserving Neighborhoods Through Historic Preservation Techniques.* Washington, D.C.: Advisory Council for Historic Preservation, 1981.

American Association of University Women, Sacramento Branch, *Vanishing Victorians: A Guide to the Historic Homes of Sacramento.* N.p.: AAUW, 1973.

Associated Veterans of the Mexican War. *History of the Celebration of the Fiftieth Anniversary of the Taking Possession of California and Raising of the American Flag by Commodore John Drake Sloat, U.S.N., July 7th, 1846. Held Under the Auspices of the Associated Veterans of the Mexican War, Assisted by the U.S. Army and Navy, the National Guard of California, the Sloat Monument Association, the California Pioneers, the Grand Lodge of Free and Accepted Masons of California, Boards of Supervisors, Fraternal Societies, Public Schools and the Citizens of the State.* Oakland, California: Carruth & Carruth Printers, 1896.

Bull, Jennie B., editor. *A Guide to State Historic Preservation Programs.* Washington, D.C.: Preservation Press, 1976.

California Preservation Foundation. *Preservation Degrees in California.* A report prepared by the California Preservation Foundation—August, 1989. Oakland.

Castro, Kenneth M., compiler. *E Clampus Vitus Plaques. A compilation of historical plaques dedicated by the several chapters of the Ancient and Honorable Order of E Clampus Vitus during the first fifty years of the revived organization, 1930-1980.* N.p.: E Clampus Vitus, 1981.

Costello, Julia G. *Melones. A Story of A Stanislaus River Town.* Sacramento: Bureau of Restoration, U.S. Department of the Interior, January 1983.

Coy, Owen C. *The Battle of San Pasqual.* A Report of the California Historical Survey Commission with Special Reference to Its Location. Sacramento: California State Printing Office, 1921.

Daughters of the American Revolution. *California's Seventy-Five Years: Daughters of the American Revolution, 1891-1966.* N.p.: California State Society, Daughters of the American Revolution, 1966.

Drury, Aubrey. *Survey of Historic Sites and Landmarks in California.* San Francisco: California State Parks Council, August 25, 1928.

Engbeck, Joseph H., Jr. *La Purisima Mission State Historic Park.* Sacramento: Department of Parks and Recreation, 1979. Reprint.

_____. *State Parks of California From 1864 to the Present.* Portland, Oregon: Graphic Arts Publishing Co., 1980.

Englehardt, Zephryn. *Mission San Carlos Borromeo (Carmelo).* Santa Barbara, California: Mission Santa Barbara, 1934.

Ferris, Robert G., series editor. *The National Survey of Historic Sites and Buildings.* Vol. XI: *Prospector, Cowhand, and Sodbuster. Historic Places Associated with the Mining, Ranching, and Farming Frontiers in the Trans- Mississippi West.* Washington, D.C.: Government Printing Office, 1967.

Finley, David E. *The History of the National Trust for Historic Preservation, 1947-1963.* Washington, D.C.: The National Trust for Historic Preservation, 1965.

The Foundation for San Francisco's Architectural Heritage. *Splendid Survivors. San Francisco's Downtown Architectural Heritage.* San Francisco: The Foundation for San Francisco's Architectural Heritage, 1979.

Gammage, Grady, Jr.; Jones, Philip N.; and Jones, Stephen L. *Historic Preservation in California. A Legal Handbook.* Stanford: Stanford Environmental Law Society, 1975.

Garfinkel, Alan P. *An Historical Perspective on the Value of the California Department of Transportation Archaeology Program.* Sacramento: California Department of Transportation, August 1982.

Hoover, Mildred Brooke; Rensch, Hero Eugene; and Rensch, Ethel Grace. Revised by Ruth Teiser. *Historic Spots in California.* Stanford: Stanford University Press, 1948.

Hosmer, Charles B., Jr. *Presence of the Past. A History of the Preservation Movement in the United States Before Williamsburg.* New York: G.P. Putnam's Sons, 1965.

_____. *Preservation Comes of Age. From Williamsburg to the National Trust, 1926-1949.* 2 vols. Charlottesville, Virginia: University Press of Virginia for the Preservation Press of the National Trust for Historic Preservation in the United States, 1981.

James, George Wharton. *In and Out of Old Missions of California. An Historical and Pictorial Account of the Franciscan Missions.* New York: Grosset & Dunlap, 1927.

Keune, Russell V.; Frisbee, John III; and Morton, Terry B. *A Guide to State Programs.* Washington, D.C.: National Trust for Historic Preservation, 1972.

Knowland, Joseph R. *California, A Landmark History. Story of the Preservation and Making of Early Day Shrines.* Oakland, California: Tribune Press, 1941.

Los Angeles, City of. Cultural Heritage Board. *Historic-Cultural Monuments, as Designated by the Cultural Heritage Board, City of Los Angeles.* Los Angeles: City Printing Division, 1980.

Mackintosh, Barry. *The National Historic Preservation Act and the National Park Service. A History.* Washington, D.C.: National Park Service, 1986.

Markowitz, Arnold. *Historic Preservation: A Guide to Information Sources.* Detroit, Michigan: Gale Research Co., 1980.

McGimsey, Charles R. III. *Public Archeology.* New York and London: Seminar Press, 1972.

Menges, Gary L. *Historic Preservation: A Bibliography.* Exchange Bibliography #79. Monticello, Illinois: Council of Planning Librarians, May 1969.

Moratto, Michael J. *The Status of California Archaeology.* Special Report No. 3. Society for California Archaeology, May 1973.

Morgan, Will. *The Effect of Federal Water Projects on Cultural Resources: Implementation of the Historic Preservation Act of 1966 by the Army Corps of Engineers, Bureau of Reclamation, and TVA.* Washington, D.C.: Environmental Policy Institute, September 1977.

Mulloy, Elizabeth D. *The History of the National Trust for Historic Preservation, 1963-1973.* Washington, D.C.: Preservation Press, 1977.

Nature Conservancy. *Preserving Our Natural Heritage.* Vol. I: *Federal Activities.* Washington, D.C.: U.S. Department of the Interior, and U.S. Man and Biosphere Program, 1975.

Neasham, V. Aubrey. *Old Sacramento. A Reference Point in Time.* Sacramento: Sacramento Historic Landmarks Commission and the Redevelopment Agency of the City of Sacramento, August 21, 1965.

O'Connell, J. Bradley; Owen, Thomas J.; and Warner, Mary. *Historic Preservation in California. A Legal Handbook.* Stanford: Stanford Environmental Law Society, 1982.

Olmsted, Roger, and Watkins, T.H. *Here Today. San Francisco's Architectural Heritage.* The Historic Sites Project of the Junior League of San Francisco, Inc. San Francisco: Junior League of San Francisco, Inc., 1968.

Parrott, Charles. *Access to Historic Buildings for the Disabled.* Washington, D.C.: Heritage Conservation and Recreation Service, April 1980.

Peterson, Dan. *Petaluma's Architectural Heritage.* Santa Rosa, California: Architectural Associates, 1978.

Pitt, Leonard. *The Decline of the Californios.* Berkeley and Los Angeles: University of California Press, 1966.

Rath, Frederick L.; and O'Connell, Merrilyn Rogers. *A Bibliography on Historical Organizational Practices.* Vol. I: *Historic Preservation.* Nashville: American Association for State and Local History, 1975.

Real Estate Research Corporation. *Neighborhood Preservation: A Catalog of Local Programs.* Washington, D.C.: Office of Policy Development and Research, Department of Housing and Urban Development, 1975.

Regnery, Dorothy. *An Enduring Heritage: Historic Buildings of the San Francisco Peninsula.* Stanford: Stanford University Press, 1976.

Rehabilitation: Danville. A Strategy for Building Reuse and Neighborhood Conservation. Washington, D.C.: Heritage Conservation and Recreation Service, Historic American Building Record, 1979.

Sterling, Christine. *Olvera Street. Its History and Restoration.* Los Angeles: Christine Sterling, 1947.

Tachibana, Judy. *Gardena Historical Resources Survey. Final Report.* Gardena, California: City of Gardena, April 1981.

Turnbull, Jay, ed. *Directory 77: The Foundation for San Francisco's Architectural Heritage.* San Francisco: The Foundation for San Francisco's Architectural Heritage, May 1977. Second edition.

U.S. Department of the Interior. National Park Service. *Handbook for Ruins Stabilization.* Part 2: *Field Methods.* Washington, D.C.: National Park Service, May 3, 1962.

_____. *Historic American Buildings Survey. Catalog of the Measured Drawings and Photographs of the Survey in the Library of Congress, March 1, 1941.* Washington, D.C.: Government Printing Office, 1941.

_____. *Historic Buildings Survey. Catalog Supplement.* Washington, D.C.: Government Printing Office, 1959.

_____. *Historic American Engineering Record Catalog, 1976,* by Donald E. Sackheim, compiler. Washington, D.C.: Government Printing Office, 1976.

_____. *Historic and Prehistoric Structures Handbook.* Washington, D.C.: National Park Service, May 17, 1963.

_____. *National Park Service Administrative Manual.* Vol. 23: *Ruins Stabilization.* Washington, D.C.: National Park Service, 1949.

Weber, Francis J. *Father of the Missions. A Documentary History of San Carlos Borromeo.* Hong Kong: Libra Press Limited, n.d.

Whitehead, Richard S., ed. *An Archaeological and Restoration Study of Mission La Purisima Concepcion.* Reports Written for the National Park Service by Fred C. Hageman and Russell C. Ewing. Santa Barbara, California: Santa Barbara Trust for Historic Preservation, 1980.

Wright, Judy. *Claremont: A Pictorial History.* Claremont: Claremont Historical Resource Center, 1980.

Zeigler, Arthur P. and Kidney, Walter N. *Historic Preservation in Small Towns: A Manual of Practice.* Nashville: American Association for State and Local History, 1980.

Articles

Banks, Sandy. "The 'Battle' of West Adams. White Restorationists Buying Homes in Largely Black L.A. Neighborhood and Hostility to Them Has Risen." Los Angeles *Times*, December 1, 1985.

Bauer, Betsy. "Taking the Past and Building the Future. Big Tax Credits Draw Investors to Historic Projects." *U.S. News and World Reports* 101 (November 3, 1986): 58-60.

Berkeley Architectural Heritage Association. *Newsletter.* September 1974.

Berthelsen, John. "A Capitol Tug-of-War." Special section on "The Restored Capitol." Sacramento *Bee*, January 3, 1982.

Blum, David. "My Turn: The Evils of Gentrification." *Newsweek*, January 3, 1983, p. 7.

Boghosian, Paula. "Saving Historic Homes: Research, Identification and Publicity," *California Historian* 20 (March 1974): 24, 28.

Brott, Clark. "The Society for California Archaeology: Founding Purposes and Future Directions." *A Symposium. The Society for California Archaeology: Founding Purposes and Future Directions.* Annual Meeting of the Society for California Archaeology, April 3, 1980.

Carder, James N. "In the Balance: American Historic Preservation." *Choice*, April 1983, pp. 1089-1100.

Chace, Paul. "Cradle, Credo and Cross." *A Symposium. The Society for California Archaeology: Founding Purposes and Future Directions.* Annual Meeting of the Society for California Archaeology, April 3, 1980. Paper was originally written in June 1975.

_____. "The History of Archaeology in Orange County." Pacific Coast Archaeological Society, Inc. *Quarterly* I, no. 3 (July 1965); 3-23.

_____. "A White Paper on SCA District Clearinghouses: Their Creation, Current Status, and Recommendations for the Future." SCA *Newsletter* 12 (August 1978): 21-22.

"City of Paris Fight Ends." Heritage *Newsletter* VIII (October 1980): 1-2.

Dutschke, Dwight A. "Public Interest or Science? A Review of Public Archeology in California." *Contract Abstracts and CRM Archeology* 3, no. 1 (1982): 26-29.

Edgar, William F. "Historical Notes of Old Land Marks in California." Historical Society of Southern California, *Annual Publication* 3 (1893): 22-30.

Frederickson, Dave. "The Society for California Archaeology: A Report from the Acting President, 1966-1967." *A Symposium. The Society for California Archaeology: Founding Purposes and Future Directions.* Annual Meeting of the Society for California Archaeology, April 3, 1980.

Gibbons, Ann. "Bowker Decides to Save Naval Arch." *Daily Californian*, March 9, 1977.

Gordon, Gregory. "Turnabout Trend. Middle-Class Whites Return to Cities." Sacramento *Bee*, November 20, 1977.

Gordon, Larry. "Gingerbread or Stucco? City's First Historic Preservation Zone Is Put to the Test." Los Angeles *Times*, June 23, 1985.

Gray, Thorne. "Watery End to Battle Against New Melones." Sacramento *Bee*, March 14, 1983.

Hatheway, Roger. "El Pueblo: Myths and Realities." Society of Architectural Historians, Southern California Chapter. *Review*, Fall 1981, pp. 1-5.

"Heritage: 10 Years of Service to San Francisco." Heritage *Newsletter* IX (Fall 1981): 6-7.

Jordan, Vernon E., Jr. "Pushing Out the Urban Poor. Revitalization Is Devitalization." Los Angeles *Times*, January 17, 1979.

Kaplan, Sam Hall. "Discarding the Notion of the 'Throwaway City.'" Los Angeles *Times*, January 25, 1985.

_____. "Preservation: Major Redevelopment Resource. Old Buildings Getting New Lease on Life." Los Angeles *Times*, May 12, 1985.

_____. "Quake Jolts Preservationists. They Fear Owners May Destroy Landmarks." Los Angeles *Times*, November 3, 1985.

_____. "Street Fair Celebrates Miracle Mile. Historic District Displays Signs of Gentrification." Los Angeles *Times*, October 28, 1984.

_____. "The Wiltern Returns in Confidence." Los Angeles *Times*, April 28, 1985.

King, Thomas F. "Archeology and Historic Preservation: A Case for Convergence." Reprinted from *Social Archeology: Beyond Subsistence and Dating.* New York: Academic Press, 1978, pp. 431-437.

_____. "Mitigation of Mammoths in California and Other Bizarre Stories." *The Missouri Archaeologist* 35 (January-June 1973): 32-35.

_____. "Preservation and Rescue. Challenges and Controversies in the Protection of Archaeological Resources." *Journal of Field Archaeology* 6 (1979): 225-228.

_____, and Lyneis, Margaret M. "Preservation: A Developing Focus of American Archaeology." *American Anthropologist* 80 (December 1978): 873- 893.

Kinley, Isaac. "Inaugural Address, 1886." *Annual Publication*, Historical Society of Southern California 1 (1886): 2-6.

Knight, Katherine. "New Life for Old Theaters." Sacramento *Bee*, February 26, 1983.

Knowland, Joseph R. "The Missions of California." *Architect and Engineer of California* 12, no. 3 (April 1908): n.p. In DPR: 536.2.

Maltun, Alan. "Pasadena Moves to Protect Heritage. Emergency Law Prevents Further 'Rape' of Blacker House." Los Angeles *Times*, June 6, 1985.

Mason, Bill. "Como se llama el Pueblo en Chinese?" Society of Architectural Historians, Southern California Chapter. *Review*, Fall 1981, p. 8.

Meighan, Clement. "Hints on National Site Nomination. Registration of Archaeological Sites as Historical Monuments." SCA *Newsletter* 8, no. 6 (1974): 3, 5, 7.

Merritt, John F. "California Preservation Foundation. Ten Years After." *California Preservation* X (April 1985): 2.

Meyers, Laura. "West Adams Bows to Charms of the Past." Los Angeles *Times*, November 3, 1985.

Neasham, Aubrey. "Criteria for Evaluating Historic Sites and Buildings." *News and Views* 13 (September 1, 1956): 8-9.

"Preservation Loan Program Rehabs Vintage Homes." Heritage *Newsletter* IX (Winter 1981): 5.

Powers, Laura Bride. "The California Historical Landmark League." *Overland Monthly* 40 (November 1902): 472-473.

Rinard, Peggy. "Cultural Heritage Board Guards Legacy." Los Angeles *Times*, February 17, 1980.

Roark, Anne C. "Colleges Take Scolding from Carnegie Panel." Los Angeles *Times*, November 2, 1986.

Rowe, Richard. "On Olvera Street: One Vision Realized, Another Whitewashed." Society of California Architectural Historians, Southern California Chapter. *Review*, Fall 1981, pp. 6-7.

"San Francisco's Heritage Provides Inspiration." Californians for Preservation Action *Newsletter* I (July 1976): 3.

Seidel, W.C. "Cultural Resource Management in the State of California." *Proceedings of the Third Annual Conference, Task Force on Recreation Use and Resource Management,* Portland, Oregon, May 12-15, 1980, pp. 170-172.

Tachibana, Judy. "Parks Department Has Its Santa. Foundation Donates Land, Money for Improvements." Sacramento *Bee*, November 21, 1983.

Taylor, Alex S. "The Indianology of California." Fourth Series. *California Farmer*, November 28, 1862, p. 91.

Tompkins, Walter A. "El Paseo Complex Put in Public Trust." Santa Barbara *News-Press*, December 5, 1971.

Warner, J.J. "Inaugural Address, January 7, 1884." Historical Society of Southern California, *Annual Publication* I (1884): 7-13.

Weaver, Peter. "Mind Your Money. Renovate a Landmark for Tax Break." Los Angeles *Times*, September 18, 1983.

de Wolfe, Evelyn. "Former Broadway Flagship Gets New Life. $25-Million Rehabilitation Planned for New Uses of Landmark Department Store." Los Angeles *Times*, February 10, 1985.

Brochures and Pamphlets

California. State Division of Beaches and Parks. *California State Parks and WPA. 20 Questions Answered.* Souvenir brochure, 1940. Courtesy of Sandra Elder.

California. State Historic Advisory Board. *California State Historic Building Code.* N.d.

California State College, Sonoma. *Historic Preservation at Sonoma State.* N.d.

The Foundation for San Francisco's Architectural Heritage. *Heritage.* N.d.

Gavilan College. *Construction Technology & Rehabilitation.* N.d.

Northern California Historic Preservation Conference. Filoli, Woodside, California, May 10-11, 1976.

San Buenaventura, City of. Historic Preservation Commission. *Be a Part of Ventura's History. Designating Landmarks in San Buenaventura.* N.d.

Santa Barbara Trust for Historic Preservation. *El Presidio de Santa Barbara Historic Park.* N.d.

Save Our Heritage Organization. *Preservation Is Working for San Diego.* N.d.

University of California, Santa Barbara. *The Graduate Program in Public Historical Studies,* September 1976.

U.S. Department of the Interior. National Park Service. *The Historic American Building Survey.* Washington, D.C.: Government Printing Office, 1973.

_____. *Interagency Archeological Program*, 1976.

_____. *Your National Parks. A Brief History.* N.d.

Correspondence and Interviews

Albright, Horace M. Interview by David Tucker, January 13-14, 1974. Transcript in DPR: 511.

_____. Interview with author. Los Angeles, California, February 16, 1983.

Arbuckle, James. Telephone conversation with author. October 14, 1983.

Brandes, Ray. Letter to Colleague, August 7, 1977.

Brelsford, Harry W. Letter to Architectural Board of Review. Santa Barbara, California, November 13, 1953. Courtesy of Mary Louise Days.

Collins, Robertson. Interview with author. Jacksonville, Oregon, June 12, 1982.

Dermody, William. Letter to author, August 25, 1983.

Doyle, James. Interview with author. Sacramento, California, March 22, 1982.

Elder, Sandra J. Interview with author. December 2, 10, 1981, April 1, 1982. Conversation with author. March 16, 1983. Sacramento, California.

Engbeck, Joseph H., Jr. Telephone conversation with author. March 23, 1987.

Frisbee, John L. III. Interview with author. Washington, D.C., April 8, 1983.

Gualtieri, Kathryn Kaiser. Telephone conversation with author. Sacramento, California, May 20, 1983.

Hussey, John A. Letter to author, February 11, 1983.

Kelley, Robert. Letter to Entering Class, the Graduate Program in Public Historical Studies, University of California, Santa Barbara, July 13, 1976.

King, Thomas F. Interview with author. Riverside, California, September 26, 1982.

Knight, John. Interview with author. March 29, 1983. Telephone conversation with author. Sacramento, California, April 15, 1983.

Michael, John. Interview with author. Sacramento, California. July 27, 1982.

Moratto, Michael J. Interview with author. Sonora, California, March 25, 1983.

Mott, William Penn, Jr. Interview with author. Oakland, California, December 16, 1982.

Poole, Jean Bruce. Telephone conversation with author. July 12, 1983.

Riddell, Francis A. Interview with author. Sacramento, California, July 27, 1982, March 30, 1983.

Shumate, Albert. *San Francisco Physician, Historian, and Catholic Layman.* Interview by Ruth Teiser and Catherine Harroun, 1978. Berkeley, California: Bancroft Library, Regional Oral History Office, 1981.

_____. Interview with author. San Francisco, California, July 22, 1982.

Wall, Louis. Interview with author. Riverside, California, September 26, 28, 1982.

_____. Letter to author, February 22, 1983.

Welch, Ileana. Interview with author. Los Angeles, California, April 19, 1982.

Welts, Allen. Interview with author. Sacramento, California, July 20, 1982.

Woollett, William. Interview with author. Santa Barbara, California, August 10, 1982.

Index

General plan
    archaeological element, 195
    historic preservation element, 123-24, 227-28
General Services Administration, 214, 240
General Vallejo Memorial Association, 14
Gentrification, 120-21, 253
Girvigian, Raymond, 94, 142, 144, 179-81, 283n.42, 311n.81, 331n.3
Gledhill, W. Edwin, 92-3
Gold Discovery and Gold Rush Centennials, 29, 31-9, 251
Governor's Mansion (Sacramento), 191
Grant, Madison, 11
Grants Administration and Local Assistance Branch, 130, 131
Grants and Statewide Studies Division, 147, 166, 183
Grants-in-aid, 127, 129-31, 147, 156, 162-63, 167, 179, 222, 302n.59, 304n.79,
    304n.82, 334n.39
Grass Valley, 227
Gualtieri, Kathryn Kaiser, 185. *See also* Kaiser, Kathryn

Haas-Lilienthal House (San Francisco), 246
HABS. *See* Historic American Buildings Survey
Half Moon Bay, 227
Hall, Carroll, 45
Hanson, Earl P., 63-4, 65-6, 71, 128, 187
Harding, George, 87
Harrell, Alfred, 29
Harriman, Gertrude, 69
Hartzog, George, 130, 292n.3
Hastings, Richard, 298n.5
Hata, Don and Nadine, 332n.7
Hearst, William Randolph, 6, 194
    Foundation, 26
Hearst San Simeon State Historical Monument, 63, 337n.5
Heid, James, 333n.25
Heinze, Herbert L., 57, 62, 88, 191
Heizer, Robert F., 83, 198, 318n.42
Henderson, Barbara A., 309n.50
Henning, A.E., 33
Heritage Action Steering Committee, 255
Heritage Conservation and Recreation Service, 116-17, 289n.23
Heritage Task Force. *See* State Heritage Task Force
Highway 101, 89-90
Highway salvage archaeology, 78-9, 114-15, 218-19
Hill, Lawrence, 17
Historic American Buildings Survey, 22-3, 84, 94, 105, 138, 237-38, 331n.3
Historic American Engineering Record, 239-40
Historic districts, 91, 227-28, 282n.27
Historic preservation coordinator, 184
Historic preservation element, 123, 127-28, 291n.47
Historic preservation in 1983, 338n.10
Historic preservation ordinances. *See* general plans; landmark commission and
    ordinances; zoning ordinances
Historic Preservation Overlay Zones, 97-8
Historic preservation philosophy, Preliminary History Plan, 139, 299n.19
Historic Sites Act (1935), 22, 74, 75, 105, 114
Historic sites survey, 129-31, 133, 136-38

deficiencies, 156
Inyo County, archaeological ordinance, 211
In-House History Committee, 133
Ishii, Amy, 170
Itogawa, Eugene, 298n.5, 298n.7, 309n.61

Jackson, Helen Hunt, 3
Jackson, W. Turrentine, 135
JACL. *See* Japanese American Citizens League
Japanese American Citizens League, Manzanar Relocation Center State Historical
    Landmark, 169-72
Jaquet, James P., 240-41
Jenkins, Hubert O., 44
Jessie Street Substation (San Francisco), 241, 242-43, 333n.25
John Muir National Historic Site, 106
Johnson, Jerald, 318n.42
Johnson, Lyndon B., 55
Johnson, Orvel, 64
Jones, Barry W., 298n.5
Jones, Fred, 56-7, 61, 62, 71, 81-2
Junior League of San Francisco, 101-02

Kagiwada, George, 171
Kaiser, Kathryn, 151-53, 170, 174, 197, 204, 242, 300n.24, 300n.26. *See also*
    Gualtieri, Kathryn
Kasch, Charles, 29
Keane, Augustin, 87, 102
Keene, Barry, 167
Keeper of the National Register. *See* Murtagh, William J.
Kelsey, Harry, 174
Kelso, Tessa L., 4
Kemble, John H., 173
King, Thomas, 84, 211, 212, 216, 217, 222, 289n.19, 323n.14, 325n.37
Kinnaird, Lawrence, 49
Knight, Emerson, 26
Knight, Goodwin, 47
Knight, John, 148, 189, 298n.1
Knill, Charles C., 234
Knott's Berry Farm, 194
Knowland, Joseph Russell, 5, 6, 7, 12, 14, 18, 20, 21, 25, 27, 29, 31, 33, 34, 38,
    45, 46, 50, 52, 54, 55, 85, 86, 182, 251, 259n.13
Knowland, William F., 55
Kojima, Masamori, 172
Kritzman, George, 325n.39
Kuhn, Clyde, 220

La Jolla, 168
La Purisima. *See* Mission La Purisima Concepcion
Land and Water Conservation Fund Act (1976), 118-19
Landmark commissions and ordinances, 90-101, 227-30, 285nn.56-57
Landmarks Club of Southern California, 4, 7-8, 234, 260n.26
Lassen County Historical Society, 273n.14
Legislative analyst, 198-99, 203-04
Leonis Adobe (Calabasas), 95, 283n.42
Lewis, Mrs. Leland S., 183